RULING BEFORE THE LAW

How do legal systems actually operate outside of Western European or North American liberal democracies? To understand law and legal institutions globally we must go beyond asking if countries comply with idealized, yet under-theorized, rule of law principles to determine how they work in practice. Examining legal regimes across different areas of criminal and civil law in both urban and rural China and Indonesia during distinct periods from 1949 to the present, William Hurst offers a new way of understanding how cases are adjudicated (and with what implications) across authoritarian, developing, postcolonial, and newly democratizing settings. This is the first systematic comparative study of the world's largest Communist and majority-Muslim nations and the most comprehensive scholarly work in many years on the micro-level workings of either the Chinese or Indonesian legal system at the grassroots, based on a decade of research and extensive fieldwork in multiple Indonesian and Chinese provinces.

WILLIAM HURST is Associate Professor of Political Science at Northwestern University, Illinois. For this book, he completed more than two years of field research across rural and urban settings of multiple provinces in both Indonesia and China. His first book, *The Chinese Worker after Socialism* (Cambridge, 2009), explored the economic, social, and political causes and ramifications of more than 35 million job losses in China's state-owned enterprises, and was based on two years of fieldwork and over 350 interviews in nine Chinese cities.

CAMBRIDGE STUDIES IN LAW AND SOCIETY

Founded in 1997, Cambridge Studies in Law and Society is a hub for leading scholarship in socio-legal studies. Located at the intersection of law, the humanities, and the social sciences, it publishes empirically innovative and theoretically sophisticated work on law's manifestations in everyday life: from discourses to practices, and from institutions to cultures. The series editors have longstanding expertise in the interdisciplinary study of law, and welcome contributions that place legal phenomena in national, comparative, or international perspective. Series authors come from a range of disciplines, including anthropology, history, law, literature, political science, and sociology.

A list of books in the series can be found at the back of this book.

RULING BEFORE THE LAW
The Politics of Legal Regimes in China and Indonesia

William Hurst
Northwestern University, Illinois

CAMBRIDGE
UNIVERSITY PRESS

CAMBRIDGE
UNIVERSITY PRESS

University Printing House, Cambridge CB2 8BS, United Kingdom

One Liberty Plaza, 20th Floor, New York, NY 10006, USA

477 Williamstown Road, Port Melbourne, VIC 3207, Australia

314–321, 3rd Floor, Plot 3, Splendor Forum, Jasola District Centre, New Delhi – 110025, India

79 Anson Road, #06-04/06, Singapore 079906

Cambridge University Press is part of the University of Cambridge.

It furthers the University's mission by disseminating knowledge in the pursuit of education, learning, and research at the highest international levels of excellence.

www.cambridge.org
Information on this title: www.cambridge.org/9781108427203
DOI: 10.1017/9781108551502

First published 2018

Printed in the United Kingdom by Clays, St Ives plc

A catalogue record for this publication is available from the British Library.

ISBN 978-1-108-42720-3 Hardback

CONTENTS

FIGURES

TABLES

PREFACE

On the frieze of the portico above the main entrance to Harvard Law School's Langdell Hall is an imposing inscription: "Non sub Homine, Sed sub Deo et Lege." Such lofty rhetoric embodies a classic ideal of the Rule of Law (though some might prefer to leave God out of it). But what about when this is not the ideal (or only faint lip-service is paid to it) – as in illiberal, revolutionary, democratizing, or most post-colonial contexts, or indeed even at many times and in many places among the long-established avowedly liberal democracies where a rule of law is most frequently and stridently trumpeted? Should we classify all possible deviations from the imagined inerrant archetype simply as "non–rule of law"? Or are they in some way lesser, partial, or diminished subtypes of the rule of law? How many such subtypes are valid, and which ones are closer to or further from the rule of law? What are the political, economic, and social stakes and risks of being in one subtype or another? And how might a country "progress" or "evolve" into a "better" one?

Such debates and intellectual machinations become moot if we examine legal, political, and social realities from a less rigidly teleological and normative perspective. Indeed, the diversity of legal regimes this book explores in Indonesia and China over the past seventy years tells us much more about law and politics, both in those countries and in general, than would trying to fit their complex realities into the Procrustean bed of a standard rule of law template. Both countries absolutely have had functioning law and legal systems, even at the height of what might appear to be periods of lawless social upheaval, hopeless corruption, or ruthless authoritarianism – which a rule of law framework would occlude rather than illuminate. Legal regimes – defined by how open or contested the polity is, as well as by how much empowered actors from outside the formal legal system intervene in the adjudication of specific cases – let us parse the contours of law and politics in a wide variety of contexts and offer to shed additional light back onto legal systems previously classified as one or another rule of law subtype. The empirical research presented in the following chapters also aspires to be among the most comprehensive to date on the ground-level functioning of Chinese and Indonesian legal institutions, especially (though not exclusively) courts of the first instance and their work in both criminal law and civil dispute resolution, from roughly 1949 to the present.

I began to work on this project almost as soon as I started to wrap up revisions to my previous book, when I was a newly appointed postdoctoral fellow at Oxford in fall 2005. As I was employed in the Institute for Chinese Studies, I started with the China portion of the research, supported by a grant from the British Academy and Economic and Social Research Council to spend part of spring 2006 based at the Sichuan Academy of Social Sciences in Chengdu. I followed this with research based in Beijing in summer and early fall 2006, and then another round of research in Jiangxi, Guangdong, and Shandong in spring 2007, supported with funding attached to my position from the Higher Education Funding Council for England (HEFCE). Colleagues at Beijing University, the Jiangxi Province Academy of Social Sciences, Shandong University, and Qinghua University facilitated my research during those trips, and also in subsequent rounds of fieldwork I undertook in 2008, 2009, and 2011.

After I relocated to the University of Texas at Austin, I began the Indonesia research with greater focus, beginning with library work in Singapore (based at the Institute for Southeast Asian Studies, ISEAS, at the National University of Singapore) and preliminary research in Jakarta and Yogyakarta in summer 2008, supported by a Summer Research Assignment grant from the UT-Austin College of Liberal Arts. I followed this with the China research in 2008, 2009, and 2011 mentioned earlier, which was supported by internal grants from UT-Austin's Program in British Studies and Center for East Asian Studies, as well as its Department of Government. In Austin, colleagues were very helpful with advice and suggestions, including Catherine Boone, Daniel Brinks, Clement Henry, Gary Jacobsohn, David Leal, Roger Louis, Tse-min Lin, Patricia MacLachlan, H.W. Perry, Bartholomew Sparrow, and Peter Trubowitz.

The largest body of Indonesia research was completed during the 2009–10 academic year, when I was a Fulbright researcher and visiting lecturer in the faculties of social and political sciences and law at Airlangga University in Surabaya. UT-Austin's College of Liberal Arts also generously supplemented my Fulbright (CIES) grant for that year with a College Research Fellowship. Besides Surabaya and other parts of East Java, I also returned to Manado, where I had been an Indonesian language student at the 2004 Consortium for the Teaching of Indonesian and Malay (COTIM) program (then hosted by Sam Ratulangi University), to conduct research in North Sulawesi.

In 2011 and 2012, I was fortunate to be based at the University of Toronto, where I was able to do a great deal of secondary source and document-based research in the excellent collections of Robarts Library. I also benefited a great deal from the advice of many colleagues there, including Joshua Barker, Jacques Bertrand, Alana Boland, Ran Hirschl, Tania Li, Lucan Way, and Joseph Wong.

Soon after I moved to Northwestern, I completed critical final rounds of research in fall 2013 and fall 2014 that were made possible by a grant from Northwestern's Equality, Development, and Globalization Studies (EDGS) program, funded by the Rajawali Foundation in Indonesia. In September and October 2013, the History Department of Shanghai Jiaotong University gave me access to invaluable archival materials colleagues there had collected. From September through November 2014, I returned to both East Java and North Sulawesi to complete important follow-up rounds of research with assistance from colleagues at both Airlangga and Sam Ratulangi Universities.

I then benefitted greatly from a book workshop, also funded by EDGS and held at Northwestern in May 2015, attended by Karen Alter, Jordan Gans-Morse, Tom Ginsburg, Alan Lepp, Andrew Mertha, Ethan Michelson, and Jeffrey Winters. Yuchen Liu, at the time a first-year Northwestern political science graduate student, assisted with taking notes on the day's discussion, in addition to participating. I learned more than I could have hoped from my colleagues, who gave selflessly of their time and energy to engage carefully with my work. But I unfortunately can only be confident that I have failed to make full use of their myriad excellent and incisive suggestions and advice; and I thus remain fully responsible for the shortcomings remaining in the book.

The manuscript was completed and revisions started while I was appointed as a fellow of Harvard University's Radcliffe Institute for Advanced Study during the 2015–16 academic year. Radcliffe really is the paradise it is acclaimed to be. Judy Vischniac, director of the fellowship program, played an especially important role in making my time there as wonderful as it was, as did Radcliffe Dean Lizabeth Cohen, Sharon Bromberg-Lim, all of Radcliffe's other administrative and coordinating staff, and most of all my fellow fellows, who are too numerous to be thanked by name here but collectively were the most exceptional group of warm, kind, friendly, and brilliant people I have ever encountered anywhere.

Though it did not directly reproduce material from the book, some broad arguments and general points discussed in the following chapters were previewed in my article, "Chinese Law and Governance: Moving beyond Responsive Authoritarianism and the Rule of Law," published in the *Journal of Chinese Governance*, Volume 1, Issue 3 (Hurst 2016); available online at www.tandfonline.com/doi/full/10.1080/23812346.2016.1212549.

At Cambridge, I began working with Lucy Rhymer on this project some time ago and she has remained both exceedingly patient and extremely helpful at every turn throughout the process. When it was determined that my work was suitable for inclusion in the Law and Society series, Finola O'Sullivan assumed primary responsibility for the project and has guided it through the final stages both expertly and generously. I am grateful to both editors, and to the series editors (especially Sally Engle Merry), for looking favorably upon my work and for helping me improve and refine it.

Beyond these formal channels, others also played important roles in helping me think about the research, structure the book, and revise the text. Thomas Bernstein, Sida Liu, Adnan Naseemullah, Dorothy Solinger, and Christian Sorace all read and commented on critical parts of the manuscript at critical points. Michael Buehler, Rachel Stern, and Benjamin van Rooij also offered important critiques and suggestions on the manuscript as a whole, and more pointedly on specific parts of it. Donald Clarke offered extensive comments and advice on a draft of the full manuscript. Finally, I received timely, incisive, and much appreciated suggestions from the participants in the American Bar Foundation's Chicago Area Legal History Workshop, where I presented part of the book in November 2016. The help of all these friends and colleagues, along with the sage guidance of two anonymous reviewers, helped take the book from rough draft to its present form. As with the book workshop participants, I must apologize and take responsibility for not meeting all of their hopes or expectations.

Research cannot proceed in the absence of libraries. Specifically, I could not have completed this project without a great deal of help and support from librarians at the University of Oxford, the University of Texas at Austin, the National University of Singapore (including at ISEAS), Airlangga University, the University of Toronto, Harvard University, and Northwestern University. Besides these, I also must thank Gao Qi and all of the librarians and staff of the Universities Service Centre (USC) at the Chinese University of Hong Kong, many of whom have been working there since the first time I visited as a graduate student eighteen years ago. That the USC remains the gold standard in the world for research libraries focused on contemporary China is testament to their tireless efforts and admirable dedication.

Beyond those already mentioned, friends, colleagues, and mentors in China and Indonesia, too numerous for me to name all of them here, helped me in a wide variety of ways in the field. Indeed, without their assistance and counsel, I would never have been able to make much headway at all. In China, I must especially thank Cao Shuji, Chen Qi, Gao Ping, Guan Kai, Shen Ling, Shi Zhiqin, Wang Jianmin, Xu Xianglin, Yan Qing, Yuan Yuhong, and Zhang Xiangrong. In Indonesia, I am especially grateful to Nurul Bazirah, Vinsensio Dugis, Eman, Iqbal Felisiano, Frans Limahelu, Maradona, Andree Maramis, Ronny Maramis, Peter Mahmud Marzuki, Irjuniawan Radjamin, Lieke Radjamin, Dwi Rahuyu Kristianti, Emma Senewe, Joko Susanto, Sartika Soesilowati, Bambang Suheryadi, Basis Susilo, and Muchammad Zaidun. In addition, I am forever grateful to all those who selflessly agreed to be interviewed or granted me access to courtroom proceedings or case records in both countries, and who unfortunately must remain anonymous here.

I must also gratefully acknowledge my very deep debts to Ninik Lunde, who has expertly trained generations of far better students than me in Indonesian language at the University of California–Berkeley for twenty-five years, as well as to all of the teachers and staff of COTIM 2004 at Sam Ratulangi University's Unit Pelaksana Teknis (UPT) Bahasa, without whom I could never have learned Indonesian sufficiently to undertake this research. More recently, I also had the serendipitous opportunity to learn Dutch (at least sufficiently to access some important written sources for this project), taught to a small group of us at Northwestern University by Alexandra van Oeteren in 2016–17. Language teaching and learning are too often undervalued, but without words we are all doomed to wander the world in silent ignorance.

Finally, much has changed in the intervening twelve years since I began this research. For instance, China replaced Hu Jintao with Xi Jinping in 2012 and convened the much-ballyhooed "Fourth Plenum on the Rule of Law" in October 2014. Indonesia also experienced a leadership transition (from Susilo Bambang Yudhoyono's administration to that of Joko Widodo in 2014) and has seen the great intensification of ethnic and religious intolerance, manifested in a degradation of rule by law in parts of its the legal system – as on display, for example, in the political prosecution of Jakarta Governor Basuki "Ahok" Tjahaja Purnama in 2016–17. Though such events have not reshaped either country's legal regimes fundamentally, they can prevent parts of my work from being up-to-the-minute and I must accept blame for anything that might be out of date by the time it is published. As with physics, the speed at which history moves is dependent upon one's perspective. In this spirit, I dedicate this book to Charlotte, who, for the first time in her life, can now finally know me no longer to be working on it.

INTRODUCTION

> *How is it that in all these years no one has come seeking admittance but me? ... No one but you could gain admittance through this door, since this door was intended only for you. I am now going to shut it.*
>
> (Kafka 2005: 198)

This book examines legal institutions in Chinese and Indonesian contexts where the law is often assumed to be weak or unimportant. By categorizing legal regimes along multiple dimensions of politics and day-to-day functioning, rather than along a simple continuum, and then unpacking the micro-level internal dynamics of each type based on over two years of field research between 2006 and 2014, we can begin to understand what makes law work and how it governs interactions between states and societies, as well as between citizens themselves, in diverse authoritarian and developing country settings. Yet, a tendency to minimize law in the study of politics in these countries has imbued even many of the most perceptive insider analyses.

"The sum of justice in this country amounts to nil!" proclaimed the head of a rural district court in Indonesia when interviewed in October 2014, arguing that formal rules and structures were of little utility in promoting anything other than basic dispute resolution. Fourteen years earlier, an eminent Chinese legal scholar – and future dean of Beijing University's Law School – famously dismissed both teleological notions of China's "progress" toward a Western-defined "rule of law" and any notion that rural Chinese citizens understood or cared much about formal laws or juridical processes (朱 2000; Ji 2009: 134–5). Both close observers offer reasoned and powerful critiques of a prevailing conventional wisdom that as formal legal knowledge and practice spread throughout their populations, diverse states' legal norms and structures would begin to converge toward a common standard rule of law. But both also remain trapped by a normative and ideal-typical – ultimately, Anglo-American – rule of law; one that occludes other forms of systematic legal knowledge or practice.

My step is to retreat from this simplistic conceptualization to think about how law actually works in citizens' lives and in society at the grassroots. This lets us see that farmers, workers, and small business people are often very well-informed, even deviously savvy, in their use of formal law and legal structures. But, more importantly, legal institutions promote and protect specific political and social relationships – frequently very different ones from those usually implicitly thought to underpin a rule of law, though no less meaningful, legitimate, or systematic – even as they themselves are founded upon the basis of political decisions and power relations.

CHICKENS, FERTILIZER, AND LEGAL REGIMES

Sometimes the ways small private actors harness the power of public legal institutions can reveal much about the relations those institutions support. In 2006, a businessman imported a cargo of fertilizer into the Indonesian port of Surabaya, a bustling city of three million people and capital of East Java, with the intent to sell this on to farmers in his home region of Kupang, on the island of Timor in the far Southeast of the country. Everything appeared to be in order and the goods landed in Surabaya without incident. Soon after, however, he was arrested after a competitor reported his allegedly illegal importation of cargo intended for sale. The fertilizer was impounded and the businessman forced to undergo a lengthy trial in Surabaya. When I was able to observe part of his trial and interview him and his lawyers in 2010, the outcome was far from certain and the poor businessman had to commute regularly between Kupang and Surabaya (a three-hour flight), all the while facing the potential of a devastating conviction and lengthy prison term. The case hinged on technical measurements of the volume of fertilizer and possible minor issues with the customs documentation, but it was unmistakably an instance of mobilization of the coercive power of criminal law in the service of a private actor – his clever and well-connected, though unscrupulous, business competitor.

In a locally well-known story (told to me by several lawyers in Chengdu in 2006), a farmer in Southwest China's Sichuan Province contracted to sell hundreds of live chickens to another farmer in the East Coast province of Shandong. Payment was received successfully, but the Sichuan farmer never sent the chickens. After several notices, the Shandong farmer had no choice but to file suit for breach of contract. The Sichuan farmer did not contest the suit and a judgment was duly issued against him, ordering him to pay back the money or turn over the chickens. After several attempts, a team from the court's enforcement division (执行庭) appeared at his farm several months later to seize the chickens (and presumably transfer them on to the farmer still waiting in Shandong). To the officers' surprise, the farmer had already crated the chickens and prepared them for shipment. He even explained that the court costs and whatever other fees he might owe would amount to far less than the shipping costs he would have had to pay out of pocket had he sent the chickens on schedule, not to mention his additional income from several months' worth of eggs laid by the hundreds of chickens he had yet to send. The seemingly naïve farmer in Sichuan had expertly manipulated the Chinese civil litigation system to his advantage, even by forfeiting the suit.

These stories of legal system failure or abuse are certainly not unique to Indonesia or China. Nor are they necessarily representative of all aspects of those countries' legal orders. But they do speak to what is often perceived as a less-than-perfect rule of law: dependable and transparent accountability, consistently enforced through legal structures and institutions, whether in business disputes, criminal trials, or rectifying administrative wrongs. Simply acknowledging that developing authoritarian or newly democratic countries lack what European or American scholars would consider rule of law is not particularly illuminating, as indeed the judge and professor referenced earlier noted. Neither are endless hair-splitting conceptual debates over whether or not we can admit that such counties might have "thick," "thin," "socialist," or some other hyphenated or partial rule of law. It is far more interesting to analyze how courts and legal institutions actually work outside the classic Western democratic core.

While many have addressed issues of legal reform, mostly from a formal and normative perspective focused on writing new rules, and others have examined popular perceptions of or engagement with the law, few have analyzed quotidian judicial politics in non-democracies and new democracies in the developing world from an institutional perspective.

This book examines courts and legal institutions in China and Indonesia, the world's largest and fourth largest countries and largest authoritarian and newly democratic states, where little research has been undertaken on this or related topics. I offer a novel conceptual and theoretical framework for understanding the interplay of politics, society, and the legal system across a wide variety of contexts. I do this through the conceptual lens of legal regimes, which I define as frameworks of relationships between institutions and actors that structure the politics of the application of legal rules and the social effects of that application.

RULING BEFORE THE LAW

Another classic story offers guidance on where to begin. "Before the Law" is a parable related to Joseph K by a sympathetic priest he encounters in the Cathedral, soon before his execution at the conclusion of Franz Kafka's masterful allegory of legal politics, *The Trial*.[1] In the parable, a man from the countryside seeking justice is compelled by an imposing gatekeeper to wait outside the mystical "Door to the Law" for most of his life. Soon before expiring, he convinces the gatekeeper to reveal a nugget of cruel wisdom – the door was intended only for this one man and only he could ever have entered through it. States and political orders likewise arrive at legal regimes via their own individual paths. All states follow different routes to different doors, that they may or may not enter, but their wanderings represent similar quests; for certain pathways lead to specific legal regimes and those regimes have much in common with each other, even across national and temporal boundaries. Before we can access what lies within the legal system, we need first to understand how the ways a country is ruled shape the contours of its legal regime.

[1] My approach to this parable differs somewhat from that offered by Ewick & Sibley (1998) in their typology of "before the law, with the law, and against the law," as well as those of many others in the broader law and society tradition, who tend to see the story from the perspective of access to justice and with questions in mind regarding how individuals and social actors remote from the legal system approach powerful and often aloof institutions. Indeed, my perspective is closer to the examination of law as being "in force without significance" (Agamben 1998: 49–51, referencing Kant's concept of the "pure form of law") and, yet, also existing in a multitude of highly differentiated forms, each with distinct and often contradictory power over specific subjects or in particular situations (Agamben 1998: 49–58).

Rule of law is a concept much debated in modern social science and throughout history. Perhaps the most parsimonious and clear definition is of a system in which all agencies and officials are subject to a principle of "legality" (or at least to the rules that they themselves make) and in which citizens are able to know and to test that principle and officials' adherence to it (Berman 1983; Merryman 1985). Of course, neither China nor Indonesia has met such a standard in any straightforward way at any time since 1949. If we allow for a less teleological or normative concept, we can get much more mileage for the analysis of how law rules and is ruled rather than simply measuring all systems against an explicit or implicit standard template. I suggest a new conceptual framework, *legal regimes*, that differs from dominant ideas about rule of law, yet nevertheless specifies principles around which different legal orders are organized in a wide range of diverse contexts.

Such macro-level concepts are best illuminated when translated to the actual functioning of courts and legal institutions at the grassroots. Rather than engage in an abstract, and dangerously abstruse, pure discussion about rule of law or legal regimes, I seek to get beyond constitutions and supreme courts to compare the relationships between law and politics as expressed through the work of basic-level courts in two important countries. By analyzing how Chinese and Indonesian courts have adjudicated criminal and civil cases since 1949, I explain core interactions of citizens with the legal system and of the legal system with other parts of the state and political order. In doing this, I also address several larger empirical questions and theoretical debates.

In most political contexts across all countries, criminal law is the primary mode through which the state exercises its monopoly on legitimate violence. Civil law serves as the state's framework for governing interpersonal relations and economic transactions. Both are thus key, in ways that extend far beyond debates over concepts of the rule of law, to crafting the political and social arenas inhabited by citizens. As the most influential remaining Communist state and largest majority Muslim nation, respectively, China and Indonesia have an importance beyond even their size. They have legal systems rooted in different subsets of the Continental Civil Law tradition that also carry specific historical legacies of state socialism and colonialism that share many common features with a variety of other countries around the world. Understanding the shape and dynamics of this arena in China and Indonesia helps substantially reorient research on law and society in nondemocratic, newly democratic, postcolonial, and other developing countries.

By examining how ground-level courts and legal institutions function in China and Indonesia, we can bring a new perspective to the study of law and society and judicial politics. This book also contributes significant new data to the understanding of Chinese and Indonesian politics and constitutes the most comprehensive political analysis to date of either country's legal system at the grassroots, where citizens most often interact with state judicial power. This renewed micro and empirical emphasis, combined with a more flexible conceptual and theoretical approach, should facilitate further fruitful analysis of legal systems beyond advanced industrial countries and the Anglo-American Common Law tradition, even as it also fills in crucial gaps in our knowledge of Chinese and Indonesian politics.

BACKGROUND AND SIGNIFICANCE

Most research in political science has traditionally centered on activities and actors remote from the legal system. When addressed, the analysis of courts and other legal institutions in politics is usually confined to supreme or constitutional courts (Shapiro 2008). Other fields, notably anthropology, law, and sociology, have paid more attention to the wider politics of legal systems, but literatures in these disciplines have also had their limitations. Sociologists and anthropologists have frequently concentrated on social perceptions of the legal order or judicial processes by those outside the system, examining the functions of courts themselves only when this affects popular access to or attitudes toward justice. Legal scholars have often tended toward the other extreme, confining their analyses to formal written rules governing judicial conduct, rather than engaging in more direct empirical studies of the behavior of legal actors and institutions.

Scholars across all fields have disproportionately concentrated their research on the United States and other countries whose legal traditions are rooted in English Common Law, very often with a narrow lens trained on constitutional decisions of the US Supreme Court (Shapiro 1989, 2008). With relatively few exceptions (including recent studies of Latin American and Middle Eastern countries, e.g. Brinks 2007; Moustafa 2007), research on legal systems in the Civil Law tradition has centered on relatively stable democracies in Continental Europe (e.g. Merryman 1985) and, to a lesser degree, Japan (e.g. Oda 2009).

Though it has been over thirty-five years since Martin Shapiro's seminal work on the comparative political analysis of courts and legal institutions (Shapiro 1981), relatively few researchers have examined courts in developing, authoritarian, or newly democratizing countries.

Most studies of the role of courts and legal institutions in the process of democratization have restricted their attention to constitutional courts (e.g. Ginsburg 2003), while research on courts in authoritarian contexts is even less developed. Indeed, only since about 2005 has the analysis of authoritarian legal institutions become fashionable, with a general view to explaining how legal reform can legitimize authoritarian control or promote market reform and economic development (e.g. Clarke 1996b; Moustafa 2007; Moustafa & Ginsburg 2008). Especially notable is that recent scholarship has tended to place civil litigation at the core of its analysis, despite the fact that criminal law remains a crucial mechanism of social and political control, as intended when the legal infrastructures of many non-democracies were first developed at key moments of regime consolidation (Jowitt 1992: 88–95; Solomon 1996).

China imported much of the Soviet legal system in 1949 (particularly in the realm of criminal prosecution), but grafted this onto an already relatively well-established legal order that had been cemented in the Qing Dynasty legal codes and modified by the German and Japanese-influenced Republican legal system adopted after 1911. The hodgepodge of city-states, sultanates, and traditional kingdoms that eventually declared independence as a united Indonesia in 1945 functioned according to myriad systems of customary law (later termed *hukum adat*) before the imposition of Dutch law (*hukum Belanda*) beyond Batavia under colonial rule in the nineteenth century, thereby creating a system of overlapping legal orders that persists in some ways up to the present day (Lev 1972; 2000c; Bedner 2001) in an extreme example of what has been termed institutional layering (Mahoney & Thelen 2010). Since 1979, China's leaders have struggled to reform and strengthen the country's legal system, while bringing it under increasing central control. Indonesia, since 1998, has attempted to rationalize and bolster legal institutions, while offering them greater local autonomy, in order to increase public trust in government (especially local government), support democratization, and enhance the legitimacy of the national state in the context of rapid and thorough-going devolution of central power to provincial and other regional authorities.

To make sense of these developments and trajectories in Indonesia and China, traditional rule of law paradigms make for blunt tools indeed. Neither of these countries ever established anything commonly recognized as the rule of law. But neither can we describe their legal systems simply by its absence nor by retreat to concepts such as rule by law. Likewise, we would not gain much by clinging to rule of law subtypes to analyze Indonesia's or China's presumed partial rule of law development.

CONCEPTUAL FRAMEWORK AND MOTIVATING QUESTIONS

Legal regimes are shaped first by the interaction of social groups and individuals with the state, and then by the interaction of states with legal institutions. Specifically, there are two basic dimensions to legal regimes: (1) the level of openness or changeability of the polity (or constellation of politically empowered social actors) and (2) the degree and manner of intervention into the legal system's handling of specific cases by other state institutions or empowered actors. Though neither is easy nor simple to measure, they are both less unwieldy and more elucidative than other aspects of legal orders. Based on these two dimensions, which are not directly part of the outcomes we want to study, we can build a typology of legal regimes, as outlined in Figure I.1.

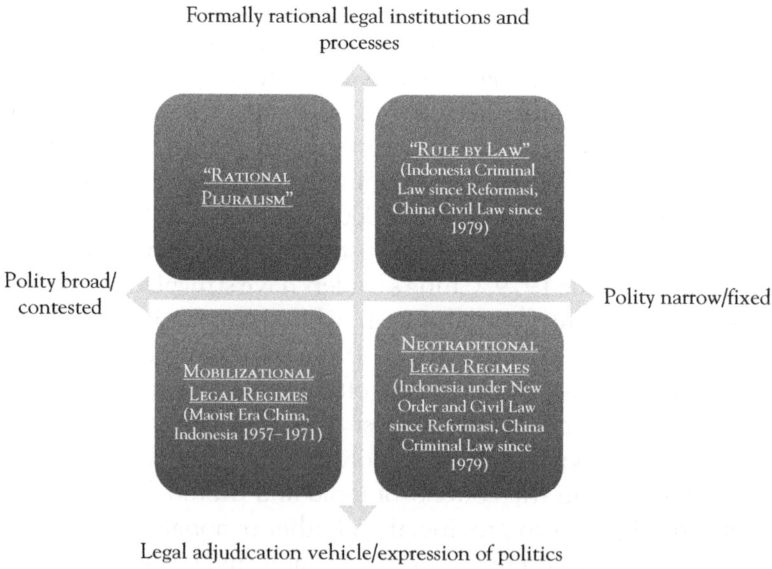

Figure I.1 Legal regimes

Where the polity is pluralistic and open and other parts of the state do not interfere in the work of legal institutions, we can observe a kind of rational pluralism that likely approximates commonly held understandings of a rule of law. In such legal regimes, courts and other legal actors are independent, citizens have access and influence in the political system, and there is a minimal gap between social and legal norms. This is the order many seem to assume exists (at least as an ideal-type) in well-functioning democracies with powerful and independent legal systems that apply the law consistently and without bias to all who seek justice.

Where the polity is open or in flux, but there is heavy interference in individual cases by other state institutions or extra-legal actors, we see mobilizational legal regimes. Here, powerful new players coming to the fore in the political arena use state institutions as tools for refashioning legal systems to support the new orders of power and social relations they hope to establish. If single actors dominate, such legal regimes may become charismatic. If multiple actors contend over protracted periods, these regimes can be quite violent and unstable. Such regimes are common in countries undergoing extreme political change or which have recently undergone such change and have yet to establish more regularized structures of power and authority.

Where the polity is closed and fixed, but legal institutions handle cases relatively free of interference, legal regimes promote a "rule by law" order. Legal institutions are relatively independent, consistent, and legitimate, yet their work at root supports entrenched political and social hierarchies and relationships. Such regimes are common in developmentalist states, where conservative authoritarian rulers prioritize predictability in transactions and the lowering of costs. They also help bolster the legitimacy of unelected or otherwise non-validated political elites, even in nominally democratic contexts.

Finally, where we see closed polities and widespread intervention into specific cases by nonlegal actors, neotraditional legal regimes dominate. In such regimes, established conservative hierarchies actively use their political power to ensure that the legal system reinforces their dominant positions in wider social and political realms. Such orders are common in colonial and postcolonial states, as well as in authoritarian countries with consolidated structures of power, far removed from any revolutionary upheaval. They help preserve the positions of those in power, but do not improve the state's legitimacy or generally facilitate market economic development.

As shall be further elaborated in the chapters to come, China was characterized by a mobiliztional legal regime throughout the Maoist period (1949–76); since 1979, it has had a hybrid legal regime (neotraditional in the criminal arena and rule by law for civil dispute resolution). Indonesia was marked by a neotraditional legal regime during the Liberal Democracy period (1949–57), which then gave way to a mobilizational regime during Guided Democracy and the early years of New Order (1957–c. 1971). During Suharto's heyday (1974–98), Indonesia had a neotraditional regime in both civil and criminal law, while since *Reformasi* (1998) it has had a hybrid that is the converse of China's – rule by law for the criminal justice system and neotraditional in the civil arena. These regimes were shaped by the political and social realities of their times and places but also exerted important and distinct causal influence upon their countries' political and social systems.

Simply categorizing these national-level cases is a major step forward and contributes much to understanding how states, citizens, and social groups interact. But, beyond this, I also seek to parse the varieties of micro-level state-society relations under different legal regimes in the context of criminal prosecution and social control versus civil litigation's emphasis on providing consistent dispute resolution. Furthermore, I examine the dynamics of institutions and adjudication specific to the distinct structural settings of urban and rural areas.

COMPARING CHINA AND INDONESIA AND COMPARING WITHIN EACH

At first glance, Indonesia and China may not seem readily comparable. Asia's largest continental nation and the world's largest archipelago, one of the world's least religious societies and a country in which everyone must belong to an official religion, a nominally still-socialist state and an emerging democracy with a long history of military dictatorship do not appear to have much in common. This, however, is precisely part of the appeal. Both China and Indonesia came into being in their contemporary forms within months of each other, in October and December 1949, respectively. Both are large and complex societies with vast regional differences and sharp distinctions between their rural and urban areas. Both also have had very similar levels of per capita income, even as Indonesia surged ahead in the 1970s and 1980s, before China moved ahead economically after Asia's 1997–8 financial crisis. The two countries are sufficiently similar to be comparable, yet different enough to provide an array of clear contrasts.

These contrasts are useful because of the way I apply legal regimes to the study of the two countries. Rather than having fixed and monolithic legal regimes, both Indonesia and China have been characterized by multiple legal regimes over time and even in different areas of the law or in different subnational contexts. Holding constant national-level political structures and dynamics lets us shed light on how civil and criminal law, for example, can be characterized by different legal regimes within the same country. Similarly, urban and rural courts often work differently in both countries, given disparate economic and political resources. Yet looking across the two cases also exposes which political variables exert consistent influence and helps rule out otherwise seductive, yet spurious, explanations rooted in idiosyncratic aspects of one or another political system. Looking comparatively *within* each of the two states adds nuance and accuracy, while comparing *between* the two countries enhances parsimony and generalizability.

The advantages of most-similar systems designs for subnational comparative analysis are well established (e.g. Snyder 2001; Hurst 2009, 2010). By holding constant many potential independent variables, we can see more clearly the influence of those with differing values across subnational regions or institutions (such a method has been widely and well employed in the study of Chinese politics, e.g. Whiting 2000; Tsai 2002). Less appreciated is the potential of combining such within-country analysis with a most-different systems design to nest the subnational research within a larger cross-national comparison. Such an additional step provides an additional test of hypothesized causal relationships, as similar causes can be matched with similar outcomes across cases that are otherwise quite disparate.

Comparing civil litigation with criminal prosecution, courts in cities with those in rural areas, and specific time periods with others, allows for several vital dimensions of subnational comparison in Indonesia and in China. Looking across these two distinct national contexts offers an opportunity for exactly the sort of previously under-explored nesting strategy just discussed. By examining different areas of the law in both urban and rural settings over time and across both China and Indonesia, I endeavor to build a theory of law and politics outside the democratic and wealthy core that is both more nuanced and more generalizable than what has been possible in previous studies.

Before dissecting the anatomy of legal regimes, it is necessary to pin down their conceptual shapes and specific theoretical utility. This is the task to which the next chapter turns.

CHAPTER ONE

UNDERSTANDING LEGAL REGIMES

The law may ... be seen simply in terms of its own logic, rules and procedures – that is, simply as law. And it is not possible to conceive of any complex society without law ... there is a difference between arbitrary power and the rule of law. We ought to expose the shams and inequities which may be concealed beneath this law. But. . .the imposing of effective inhibitions upon power and the defence of the citizen from power's all-intrusive claims, seems ... an unqualified human good. To deny or belittle this ... is to throw away a whole inheritance of struggle about law, and within the forms of law ... law has not only been imposed upon men from above: it has also been a medium within which other social conflicts have been fought out.

(Thompson 1975: 260, 266–7)

I have had many times the initial apprehension of the objective coverage of a case by a rule. . .[But]. . .From the inside, what happens to my initial experience of the rule as objective is radically contingent. . .Rule application is something that does happen, but it is never something that has to happen ... If you tell me that law is rules, or that there is always a right answer to a legal problem, I will answer with these cases in which my experience was that law was indeterminate, or that I gave it its determinate shape as a matter of my free ethical and political choice ... The rule may at any given moment appear objective, but at the next moment it may appear manipulable. It is not as I apprehend it from within the practice of legal argument, essentially one thing or the other.

(Kennedy 1987: 157, 165–6)

INTRODUCTION

How do we assess the dynamics of relations between law, politics, and society? What attributes lead states to structure legal systems in particular ways? Under what types of conditions do courts and legal institutions adjudicate either the exercise of legitimate state coercion through criminal prosecution or the resolution of disputes between individuals or organizations through civil litigation in particular ways? To look at these issues in China or Indonesia we need a general conceptual and theoretical map for thinking about how societies and states shape legal institutions' behavior and how that behavior affects relations between citizens and the law and between legal institutions and other parts of the state. Previous research on comparative law and society has made great strides, but does not yet offer a ready template to help guide my research.

Most early scholarship on law and politics was grounded in the study of Anglo-American Common Law systems. There have been several divergent clusters of research on law outside this traditional core since the mid-twentieth century. At first, scholars began investigating European Civil Law systems in the earliest ventures into comparative analysis. Gradually, some began to build upon this to develop a large and vibrant literature on comparative "legal traditions," including Civil, Socialist, and Islamic, alongside Common Law. Later, interest developed in specific areas of law and politics in nondemocracies, postcolonial nations, new and emerging democracies, and weak or failed states. Among the strongest work in this last tradition are studies of comparative constitutionalism and judicial review, as well as analyses of "rule by law" and research on what can be characterized broadly as "transitional justice." None of these traditions, however, provides a comprehensive framework that allows us to analyze key aspects of law and politics in China or Indonesia.

Legal regimes are created by societies and states depending on how easy or difficult it is for social groups or individual or organized interests to gain political influence or power and how readily and in what manner nonjudicial state institutions or empowered actors intervene in legal institutions' handling of specific cases. We can use the framework of legal regimes to map out types of law–state–society relations that can then guide research into the political and social dynamics of both criminal and civil adjudication in urban and rural areas of China and Indonesia over time. After assessing the contours of previous scholarship, this chapter lays out the legal regimes framework and explains how it guides the empirical analysis to follow, as well as its potential utility for research further afield.

GENERAL CONTOURS OF PRIOR SCHOLARSHIP

Relevant prior scholarship on comparative law and politics can be divided into several strands. First, general comparative analysis of legal families or traditions has contributed much to our understanding of how specific institutions – like courts – function within each and how the relations between legal institutions and other parts of political systems and societies can vary across them. Studies of institutions and politics within specific legal traditions, and especially within the Civil Law tradition, are extremely useful for setting the present study in its proper general context. Many scholars have also examined law and politics with an aim of explaining aspects of economic development, political authoritarianism, democratization, or other types of institutional frameworks or change. Such scholarship informs any project seeking to compare legal systems and their relation to political or social orders. After examining each of these strands, we can identify remaining lacunae in the literature more clearly.

Research on Comparative Legal Traditions

Students of comparative law and politics distinguish between a variety of legal traditions or families, within which national-level systems clearly have more in common than they do with systems in other families. Most agree that there are at least four main families: Civil Law, Common Law, Socialist Law, and Religious Law (David & Brierley 1985). Civil Law refers to those systems in some sense founded upon the law of the Roman Empire (especially as codified in the *Corpus Juris Civilis*, published by the Emperor Justinian in 533 CE, or which later imported core elements of the French *Code Napoléon* or German law codes, especially as established in the late nineteenth century *Bürgerliches Gezetzbuch*, which itself was largely derived from the Napoleonic Code). Common Law encompasses all those systems tracing their origins to English Law as established on the basis of custom and common practice during the reign of King William I, after his conquest in 1066, even as multiple other systems of law (Canon, Norman, Roman, etc.) continued to hold sway over elements of British criminal investigation and civil dispute resolution throughout much of the Middle Ages (Strayer 1986: 423–4). Socialist Law refers to those systems implemented in countries that experienced socialist revolutions during the twentieth century and is often seen to take the law of the Soviet Union as its main basis. Finally, Religious Law is something of a catchall category, including all systems based explicitly on religious texts (e.g. Islamic *Shari'a* Law) as well as others more loosely based on customary ethical or philosophical principles (e.g. traditional legal orders in tribal societies, or what is discussed in Chapter 2 as *adat* in Indonesia).

Moving beyond such general characterizations, scholars probed the internal workings of systems within specific families, as well as across them. Martin Shapiro's seminal analysis of courts across what he called the Civil, Common, Chinese, and Islamic traditions (Shapiro 1981) sets the standard for how to examine courts in different political, social, and historical contexts. A number of other scholars also developed typologies to categorize different aspects of legal systems, mainly to contrast Common and Civil Law (e.g. Damaska 1991). Within the Civil Law tradition, John Merryman and others have probed the distinctions between Roman, Canon, and Commercial law and explained how these earlier codes and frameworks formed the foundation of the fuller development of modern legal systems in Europe as they were later influenced by the French Revolution and the development of "legal science" (Merryman & Perez-Perdomo 2007). As we shall see in Chapter 2, the common contours of the Civil Law tradition inform many aspects of both the Chinese and the Indonesian legal systems. Scholarship on the Socialist legal tradition is also important, however.

Students of Socialist Law emphasize that it is generally similar to the Civil Law tradition, but with the important addition of class struggle and revolution as organizing supreme principles, to the service of which all other rules and structures must conform. In practice, most analysis of Socialist Law has focused on legal development and politics in the Soviet Union (USSR). John Hazard set the tone early on, focusing on the early days of the USSR and the manner in which divergent strands of thinking had influenced the building of legal systems beyond the USSR, including in China (Hazard 1960, 1965). Later analyses continued to look at this early period (Burbank 1995), but also focused in on developments during the Stalin era (Solomon 1996), as well as the Khrushchev years and beyond (Berman 1963; Barry, Ginsburgs & Maggs 1979; Solomon 1997), before the field began to shift away from emphasis on a Socialist legal tradition and toward a tighter focus on Russian law and politics, extending into the post-Soviet era (Hendley 1996, 1997, 2017; Gans-Morse 2017). One may also question the degree to which anything like a coherent Socialist Law tradition ever existed, as well as whether it has continued to influence legal institutions or practice in China since the 1980s.

Research on Law, Development, Authoritarianism, and Democratization

A great deal of research has focused on questions of law and economic development. At root, these studies ask what legal protections or provisions are necessary to facilitate certain types of economic development (Ginsburg 2000), with most following Hayek (1944, 1982) and generally agreeing on the need for an efficient and predictable legal system to reduce arbitrary state intervention, uncertainty, and transaction costs (Posner 1981, 2014). As championed by scholars in the New Institutionalist movement in economics and law, this perspective stresses that strong legal rules and consistent predictable enforcement are necessary for the development of efficient markets and higher growth (e.g. North 1961, 1990; Williamson 1985). Some others suggest, to the contrary, that there is little need for a well-functioning formal legal system to support economic growth (e.g. Kang 2002), sometimes seeking to underscore a noneconomic – perhaps moralist or Kantian – theoretical basis for the development of private law (e.g. Weinrib 2012a, 2012b), sometimes citing the case of China as counterexample to earlier claims without necessarily challenging their philosophical underpinnings (e.g. Clarke 2003; Allen, Qian, & Qian 2005).

In a related strain (e.g. Olson 1993), studies of law and democratization, as well as transitional justice (e.g. Teitel 2000), have sought to explain how reforms to legal systems can help support the liberalization of political institutions or processes, alongside the protection or extension of political rights. Tom Ginsburg's 2003 study of judicial review in new democracies offered a framework for understanding how countries seeking to become democratic after long periods of authoritarianism could use powerful constitutional courts to check unbridled government authority (Ginsburg 2003). Much of his later work has also centered on explaining the role of constitutions and constitutional courts in promoting durable democratic change (e.g. Ginsburg, Elkins, & Melton 2009; Ginsburg 2010). Some others have looked to broader trends of the judicialization of politics (Stone Sweet 1999, 2000; Shapiro & Stone Sweet 2002; Hirschl 2004) as possible forces for democracy promotion (e.g. Dressel 2015). Still others, like Meierhenrich (2008) and Massoud (2013), have emphasized the legacies of authoritarian or inchoate legal systems when analyzing domestic and international efforts to promote new, more stable and democratic, institutions. Indeed, a whole industry has sprung up around the analysis of efforts to promote "rule of law" around the world or to promote democratization through legal reform in particular countries, especially in the wake of calamitous or genocidal civil strife or conflict (e.g. de Greiff & Duthie 2009; Hayner 2010; Olsen, Payne, & Reiter 2010; Hinton 2011).

The past couple of decades have also witnessed an explosion of research on law and authoritarianism. Some have looked at authoritarian states' use of law as an instrument of government action (Tamanaha 2004: 91–3) – one that can legitimate and regularize, as well as constrain, that action. Some of these theories posit a "rule by law" (Ginsburg & Moustafa 2008), under which authoritarian governments' actions are made more predictable and legitimate, transaction costs and uncertainty are reduced, and conflict is brought under state-centered and state-dominated frameworks, even if rulers are not always subjected to the law's full control. Others have gone further, suggesting that authoritarian governments can willingly and consciously constrain their own behavior through a "partial rule of law" in order to facilitate easier governance or more efficient economic growth (Wang 2015). Still others have analyzed the ways in which authoritarian states have deployed a superficially liberal discourse of law to give political cover to actions of illiberal authoritarianism (Rajah 2012). Thus, adherence to formal rules, rigorous separation of powers and at least nominal judicial independence can, somewhat counterintuitively, help bolster state attempts to restrict freedom of speech and of the press, contain protests and demonstrations, severely punish vandals and other petty criminals, and generally strike fear into a populace under a very high degree of surveillance and social control in a place like Singapore. Rule of law, or a retreat to legal formalism, in other words, can be used to enshrine and perpetuate political and economic power relations that are fundamentally inequitable (Neumann 1942, 1986: 6, chapter 16; Mattei & Nader 2008; Meierhenrich 2008). Finally, a few scholars even go so far as to suggest that creeping ideas and practices of "liberal legality" can emerge even under harshly authoritarian political systems like Egypt's or Kuwait's, given the right mix of institutional arrangements and political incentives (Brown 1997).

Persistent Gaps and Remaining Lacunae

Though scholarship has blossomed in the general field of law and politics, many significant gaps remain. For example, though much empirical work has been done on courts and legal institutions in other contexts (e.g. Shapiro 1981; Jacob et al. 1996; Epp 1998; etc.) – generally outside the Civil or Socialist legal traditions – less work has focused on China, Indonesia, or developing countries in general. That which has, has mostly centered on the analysis of supreme courts or judicial behavior (e.g. Helmke 2004; Pompe 2005; Hilbink 2007), with some more recent attention to corruption and the rule of law and to issues of law and economic development (e.g. Kang 2002; Moustafa 2007; Wang 2015). Generally missing from these analyses, however, is an historically informed focus on basic-level institutions and adjudication.

Importantly, most previous studies have tended to view legal systems as independent, rather than dependent, variables – as causal factors helping to lead to economic or political outcomes, rather than as outcomes to be explained in their own right. Thus, we often pay a great deal of attention to whether or how law facilitates or hinders economic development, protects or undermines individual liberties, promotes democratization, or preserves authoritarianism. But we have paid much less, and overall far too little, attention to how law or legal institutions are shaped by politics – and less still to the dynamic and iterative relationships between politics, law, and society across time.

This book sets out to fill some of these gaps. Specifically, by looking at legal regimes as products of political and social arrangements, I hope to add to our understanding of how politics can shape law. By examining the "second-order" causal influence of legal regimes on state–society relations and conflict resolution among citizens, I will improve our grasp of how legal orders, once established, structure other important political and social processes. By looking beyond supreme or high courts and focusing on local-level basic courts, I will increase our knowledge of how justice actually operates on the ground in previously underresearched contexts. By comparing across time and between both urban and rural areas, I will contextualize previously uncritical generalizations about courts or legal systems in China, Indonesia, and beyond.

LEGAL REGIMES

Differentiating Legal Regimes from Rule of Law

Conceptions of the rule of law have garnered much attention and debate for a very long time, even well before Berman or Merryman offered the definitions I quoted earlier. Reacting against Plato's illiberal ideal of the "philosopher king" (Plato 1991), Aristotle (1984) argued that laws must reign supreme over any human ruler. Cicero advanced a similar position to bolster the institutions of the Roman Republic (Cicero 1928). Locke (1690) and Montesquieu (1778) also saw legal rules and institutions as key to promoting good governance and preventing abject tyranny. Yet, it was not until Allen "A. V." Dicey, an Oxford historian and legal scholar, wrote about it in the context of British constitutional debates in the nineteenth century (Dicey 1889) that rule of law came to concern the core of English language scholarship on law and politics.[1] Shortly thereafter, Max Weber and Émile Durkheim emphasized formal legal rationality (though of a sort not necessarily compatible with Dicey's conception, rooted as it was firmly in the Common Law tradition) as an essential attribute of any modern state or political system (Durkheim 1978; Weber 1978, 1995: 338–43).

Since the early twentieth century, two basic streams of thought have emerged: a substantive perspective that sees rule of law as rooted in particular social or political arrangements (e.g. Weinrib 1987, 2012a), versus a formalist view that sees specific legal rules as the foundation of the rule of law (Tamanaha 2004: 91–2). Each camp can be further subdivided into "thicker" and "thinner" variants, with the thin formalists arguing that a rule of law is achieved so long as governments act through some sort of formalized legal rules and thick substantivists maintaining that only with full democracy and social and economic equality can we even begin to contemplate a rule of law (Tamanaha 2004: 91). These sorts of debates sometimes take on an unfortunate normative character, with reprobative brickbats hurled at opponents by members of all camps.

Indeed, to borrow a phrase, the operationalization of rule of law has remained rather "dicey" (Rajah 2012: 37–9), as normative arguments have been put forward while specific metrics remain opaque, sometimes leaving scholars to lament that we are reduced either to an empty formalism or a facile assumption that all adjudication is hopelessly politicized and merely a product of broader power relationships (Weinrib 1987: 61, 65–7). In practice, we are often left with an adaptation of US Supreme Court Justice Potter Stewart's formulation (in a ruling on hardcore pornography): "we can't really define rule of law,

[1] For more on the history of scholarship and debates on the rule of law, see Tamanaha (2004).

but we know when we do or do not see it in operation in Country X." (Stewart 1964).

Besides the moral hazard of slipping into normative name-calling, efforts to measure the rule of law (e.g. Ginsburg 2011) have sometimes been prone to succumb to what could be termed an endogeneity trap. To assert, for example, that the presence of certain legal rules implies a rule of law, and then also that the lack of a rule of law implies the absence of those same rules, and finally that a failure to adopt those rules will necessarily prevent the development of a rule of law, is tautological reasoning. Alleged causes of an outcome are measured by looking at aspects of the outcome itself. Without recognizing this sort of problem, too many scholars, governments, and international institutions define benchmarks uncritically and then assess countries in relation to imagined "objective" rule of law standards (Serban 2015: 204–5).

To steer clear of both the Scylla of fuzzy normativity and the Charybdis of tautological measurement, we must set aside the loaded concept of rule of law for purposes of dispassionate and systematic analysis. Rather than trying to rank legal systems by how "good" or "bad" they are – or by how closely they align with an explicit or implicit Anglo-American ideal type – we ought to group legal systems into categories defined by aspects of politics and the relationships of political institutions and actors to the work of the legal system, rather than by substantive or formal dimensions of law itself. The concept of legal regimes accomplishes this task and allows for a better characterization and categorization of legal orders and systems.

Legal Regimes: Outline of a Concept

The most basic definition of a legal regime is a system or framework of rules governing some physical territory or discrete realm of action that is at least in principle rooted in some sort of law. Often the concept has been applied to specific areas of law, relating to American labor relations (e.g. Estlund 2002) or environmental protection of the Polar Regions (e.g. Joyner 1999), for example. Much of this work, in turn, ties closely into political science scholarship in international relations, especially that which emerged in the 1980s under the banner of "regime theory" (e.g. Krasner 1983), emphasizing the development of shared rules, norms, and conventional practices that help shape actors' expectations and behavior across national jurisdictions or between states in the international arena.

Lauren Benton, over a decade ago, offered the clearest recent application of the concept to the study of law and politics, focusing on "patterns of structuring multiple legal authorities" (Benton 2002: 3). Tellingly, her main point is also to assess the interplay of legal systems, philosophies, and authorities in a specific kind of international context – legal pluralism in the age of imperialism and colonization. Benton's core questions revolve around how European powers negotiated specific kinds of indigenous law or systems of norms at different world historical times and against the backdrop of different legal and political orders in the metropole. In a different vein, John Cioffi used the basic idea of legal regimes to critique previous scholarship on corporate governance and the assessment of the rule of law outside advanced industrial economies (Cioffi 2009).

While these are consequential points on important topics, the concept as deployed so far is of limited utility for my purposes here. I am less interested, for example, in understanding how the Dutch came to prioritize certain aspects of European or *adat* law or why the Chinese Communist Party made specific choices about which portions of the Republican Code to expunge or leave on the books than I am in getting to the bottom of the ways in which aspects of Chinese or Indonesian politics shape a general legal order, the functioning of which, in turn, has implications for broader dimensions of state–society relations and political change. Unpacking the concepts of legal regimes and sovereignty from a slightly different angle brings this into sharper relief.

Indeed, if we view legal regimes through a more clearly non-Weberian, lens, we can see the horizontal dimension of the typology presented in Figure I.1 as whether or not a given state has a coherent sovereign, and the vertical dimension as the degree to which any sovereign (or would-be sovereign) moves to declare exceptions in the realm of legal adjudication. Thus, when a coherent unitary sovereign is present, and that sovereign allows the legal order to operate more on the basis of norms and rules than decisions and exceptions, we see a rule by law. When such a sovereign exerts the force of exceptional decision with some regularity, neotraditionalism is present. When no sovereign is present and the legal order operates by norm rather than decision, we see formally rational pluralism (an unsurprisingly rare outcome). And finally, when no sovereign is present, but one or more would-be sovereigns move to assert their positions through appeals to charismatic or revolutionary authority and to claim the right of exceptional decision, mobilizational legal regimes can be observed.

Building on the work of Rousseau, Hobbes, and others, Carl Schmitt famously argued that, "sovereign is he who decides on the exception" (Schmitt 2005: 5). Citing the work of Jean Bodin (a sixteenth-century law professor at the University of Toulouse), he further maintained that the sovereign must be unitary, able to act to suspend laws or political commitments without any checks or accountability to other actors or processes. If this unity could not be guaranteed, "sovereignty would thus become a play between two parties: Sometimes the prince and sometimes the people would rule, and that would be contrary to all reason and law" (Schmitt 2005: 9). This view of sovereignty as indivisible also can be traced back to *The Social Contract* and *Leviathan*, since, "Sovereignty is indivisible for the same reason that it is inalienable. For the will either is or is not general; it is the will either of the whole body of the people, or of a part only" (Rousseau 1986: 26), and, "For what is it to divide the Power of a Common-wealth, but to Dissolve it; for Powers divided mutually destroy each other" (Hobbes 1985: 368).

It is possible that a state lacking a sovereign may also lack any legal order at all. This would be a true case of the *bellum omnium contra omnes* that theorists like Hobbes and Schmitt feared so gravely. More likely, we might find an order in which a constitutionally limited or otherwise silent sovereign, one which Schmitt might deride as a state seeking to reduce politics to a "monstrous" debating club (Schmitt 2005: 25–6, 63, 2007: 28), gives way as much as possible to the operation of a formally rational legal system, operating on the basis of norms and steady rules rather than exceptional decisions. Such rational pluralism is also very close to the ideal seen by many rule of law theorists, but it is not present in the cases I have studied and is likely much rarer across the world than many would like to believe or hope.

In a state where one or more would-be sovereigns seek to establish themselves, but none has yet prevailed, we can observe mobilizational legal regimes, in which one or more actors seek actively to impose sovereignty through exceptional declarations and decisions, to assert an unlimited authority, to call a legal order into being by producing and guaranteeing a situation in its entirety, and to lay claim to a "monopoly to decide" (Schmitt 2005: 12–13). The successful imposition of such charismatic authority restores an equilibrium of normality in which mobilizational legal regimes can no longer function. Unsuccessful attempts allow continuing contestation and the further deployment of mobilizational regimes.

Legal regimes in states with Schmittian or Hobbesian sovereigns are easier to categorize. The sovereign either allows the legal order to operate without recourse to exceptional decisions or it does not. Where it allows legal institutions to operate normally, we see a rule by law regime. Where the sovereign feels obliged frequently to decide to suspend normal legal processes or protections, to exert nonlegal power over law, it does so in order to clarify and maintain a consistent friend–enemy distinction, and thus to preserve vital elements of political order (Schmitt 2007: 26). Specifically, according to Schmitt, all states must decide upon public enemies, *hostes* not *inamici*, who are to be excluded from the polity, confronted, and if need be destroyed, in order to constitute and preserve the political order and the very integrity of the state (Schmitt 2007: 28–30). This means that there will be some individuals or groups to whom the law specifically does not apply, who are rendered as some form of *homo sacer* – made to stand outside all law, secular and religious, human, and divine, such that their lives are not valued either as potential murder victims or as valid sacrifices (Agamben 1998: 73–4). When the sovereign frequently acts to draw such distinctions, almost always in the interests of preserving established hierarchies and power relationships, we can see neotraditional legal regimes in action.

Examining the typology of legal regimes from these different perspectives serves several purposes. It helps broaden the theoretical and analytical foundations upon which my main arguments rest. It addresses critiques of the entire rule of law project and literature – which I have already criticized for its close adherence to conservative and Common Law principles – that have come from many quarters (including some fundamentally illiberal ones). And, finally, it affords us a more complete and coherent platform from which to consider the conceptualization of various legal regimes and to categorize those on which I was able to collect data in China and Indonesia.

In the end, legal regimes are frameworks of relationships between institutions and actors that structure the politics of the application of legal rules and the social effects of that application. Legal regimes are defined by two key dimensions of politics, rather than by any provisions of formal or substantive law. As suggested earlier, and building on Damaska's two-by-two framework (Damaska 1991), legal regimes take shape along two dimensions: how open or changeable the polity is and the degree and manner of intervention by nonlegal state institutions or

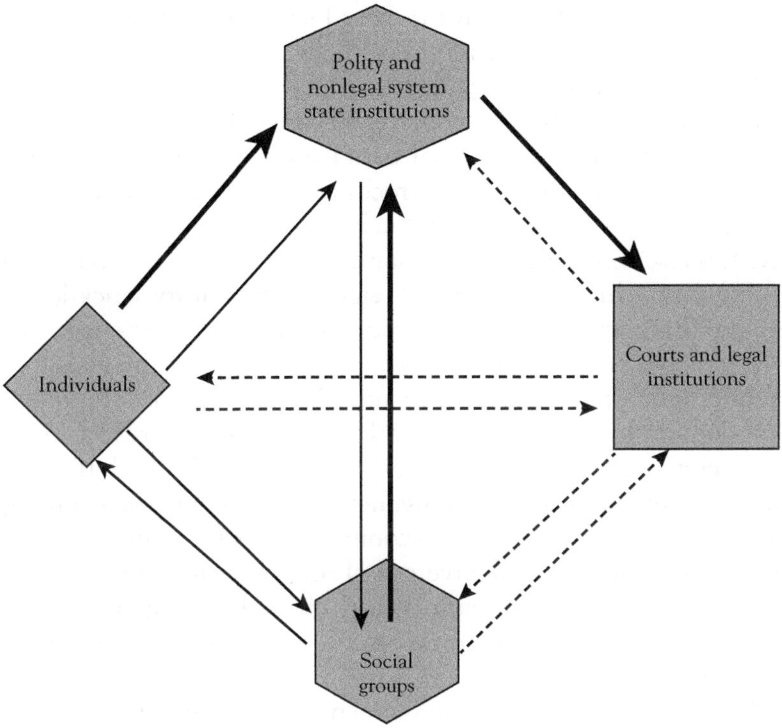

Figure 1.1 Causal dynamics of legal regimes

political actors into the legal system's adjudication or handling of specific cases. Political variables exert causal influence over legal regime outcomes. But legal regimes, in turn, exert causal influence over important dynamics of state–society and intrastate relations.

Specifically, individuals and social groups exert influence over the constitution of the polity and nonlegal system state institutions. These institutions then exert influence over the manner in which courts and legal institutions are constituted and engage in adjudication. The structure and functioning of courts and legal institutions, in turn, exert influence over the polity and nonlegal system state institutions and also interact in important ways with social groups and individuals, helping shape other aspects of politics as well as important dynamics of state–society relations. In Figure 1.1, the thick solid lines thus represent primary causal influence. The dotted lines show what sorts of causal relationships come into play once the primary influences have essentially done their work. Finally, the thin solid lines show causal influences and relationships that I will not attempt to analyze or explain, but that are important nevertheless.

Having defined legal regimes as at least in large part products of political arrangements, it is seductive to conclude that law and adjudication are merely epiphenomenal, or at least in a subordinate position – in other words that rules and processes matter little in the face of political power or social change. Such a position, while clear and consistent, is also too facile. E. P. Thompson, in the final chapter of *Whigs and Hunters* – his book about an eighteenth-century crackdown on deer poaching in Southern England – struggles with the role of law vis-à-vis economic and political power relations. What he ends up saying, after much perambulation around the topic, is that the relations of production help produce legal rules and forms that reflect material class hierarchies and power politics; but, once established, these legal rules and forms, rather than being mere superstructure, play important roles in structuring ongoing class conflict and social relations. My position on the somewhat reflexive causal role of legal regimes is similar, though less faithfully Marxian. Politics shape legal regimes, but once in place legal regimes structure political and social relationships and contestation.

This causal two-step, building on Thompson and placing law at an intermediate stage of the chain rather than at the end or the beginning, is an essential innovation over most previous perspectives and allows us to grapple with more complex arguments and empirical reality with greater agility. It also allows me to take into account the fundamental insight of many scholars of what we might term critical legal studies (e.g. Kennedy 1987): that not only the content of rules, but also the manner in which they are applied to specific cases, is largely a function of political preferences, choices, and constraints faced by judges.

Rulemaking and the structuring of the judiciary are outcomes of fundamentally political processes and conditions (the structure of the polity, or whether or not there is a coherent unitary sovereign). Once we understand this, we can then examine rule application and adjudication not to assess whether or not it is objective by any universal standard (as it is highly unlikely ever to be in any country or system), but rather merely to gauge the manner and degree of direct intervention into the process by actors outside the formal legal system; that is, to what degree and in what manner can we regard the adjudication process as formally rational on its own terms (or to what degree the legal order operates according to norms rather than decisions).

In this blending of a social science perspective on "law in action" with more traditional approaches to the study of law and politics and a sustained attention to the insights of more critical perspectives, my approach aims to occupy the terrain staked out recently by the so-called New Legal Realism, especially in its "big" or "broad tent" formulations (McCann 2016: xviii; Mertz 2016: 6–8). Specifically, I aim to take power as a central concept, focus on the recursive relationship between law and society, examine how legal systems and structures interact with social and political hierarchies, and integrate the perspectives and experiences of individuals and institutions near the bottom of the hierarchy in ways that inform theory, blending more traditional top-down ideas with a more bottom-up empirical focus and perspective (Klug & Merry 2016: 1–4; Mertz 2016: 6–7). Such an approach seeks to follow the example set by Nick Cheesman's pathbreaking study of law and politics in Myanmar (Cheesman 2015), in which he manages to relate broad conceptual debates about the nature of law, society, and the state with astute observations about law and politics over 200 years in Myanmar and careful analysis of numerous, mostly previously unavailable or unexamined, individual criminal cases.

Utility of Legal Regimes for Understanding Complex Realities

Legal regimes can be used to characterize a broader set of complex realities than many otherwise useful and popular concepts. Rule of law and rule by law, for example, are both more limited. Without adding clumsy and cumbersome adjectives or qualifiers – epicycles and exceptions worthy of a Ptolemaic astronomer – we can only use them to describe or analyze a narrow band of the range of possible legal orders. Everything else is necessarily beyond the conceptual pale. Similarly, classifying legal systems according to legal traditions provides scant help for those seeking to compare within or between them. Pioneering work like that of Shapiro or Merryman may have hinted at how to compare across traditions, but for these authors most variation seemed always a product of differences between the traditions of interest (almost always Common versus Civil Law), even while most other authors restricted their analyses to a single tradition. Scholars of legal pluralism, federalism, and other special arrangements have perhaps made more substantial gains, but their studies are too often restricted to the examination of formal legal rules rather than legal structures or institutions in action.

Legal regimes let us compare both within and between legal traditions. They also facilitate comparisons at the subnational level – allowing us, for example, to comprehend the legal order in the American South by accounting for that region's much less open polity and the stronger tendency of nonlegal institutions to intervene in the adjudication of specific cases there (Gibson 2013). They also let us explore how a particular kind of political or social organization or arrangement – oligarchy, for instance (Winters 2011) – can exert important influence across a wide range of legal traditions and state structures to bring much greater uniformity to their legal orders than might otherwise be expected. Finally, legal regimes also offer us a way to get beyond broad national-level phenomena and relatively blunt, if weighty, conceptual tools like judicial review (e.g. Ginsburg 2003) or secularism and constitutional design (e.g. Jacobsohn 2003) to examine the way law actually works at the grassroots; but then also to aggregate back up again in a way that facilitates comparison at the national level or beyond. This is because each category of legal regimes follows a broadly consistent set of political, institutional, and social causal phases and relationships.

In legal regimes in which the polity's composition is open, unsettled, or contested, law will usually be accessible to a broader segment of the population. Where contestation is the order of the day, political contests will play out in legal arenas, especially when nonlegal actors intervene deeply or frequently into the adjudication of cases. In legal regimes where the polity's composition is settled and fixed, law is likely far less accessible to the general citizenry and much more likely at least to appear apolitical. This is true even when political actors intervene frequently and substantially in adjudication.

Formally Rational Pluralistic Regimes

Though this is an empty set for the countries and time periods I am looking at, it is important to outline what this sort of legal regime looks like. In rational pluralist regimes, the legal system can be mobilized by previously disenfranchised or abused social groups in support of their newfound power within the polity (McCann 1994). In short, law supports polyarchy (Dahl 1972) and pluralism. Conversely, it is not susceptible to being hijacked by entrenched interests to repress aspirant members of the polity because nonjudicial actors do not intervene in specific cases (they are either incapable of doing so, prohibited from doing so, or simply refrain from doing so). So long as the polity is both relatively free of high-stakes conflict and open to new entrants, legal institutions remain competent and willing to adjudicate cases consistently and without interference, and no sufficiently powerful social group successfully upsets the applecart, such an order can be a happy equilibrium indeed. Democracy, pluralism, equality, access to justice, legal rationality, and judicial consistency – all are maintained in mutually reinforcing harmony. Yet such legal regimes are as rare as they are seductive, products of very specific moments in history and political arrangements. Less happy regimes – prone to conflict and instability – are far more common, even when polities are open and accessible.

Mobilizational Legal Regimes

In a mobilizational legal regime, like Maoist China or Indonesia during Guided Democracy and the early years of New Order, contenders to political power make use of the law as much as possible, intervening in specific cases whenever they can to gain any advantage available. When the polity is open, yet politics stay calm and genteel, relaxed pluralism prevails and all interest groups have equal access to the law as a tool for achieving equality and efficacy. But, when open or contested politics become a fight to the death, or even when the stakes are raised such that losers cannot be assured a peaceful retreat from power, all-out struggle, rather than compromise, becomes the order of the day (Tsou 1976). Incentives to intervene in the process of adjudication far outweigh any desire to maintain judicial independence, formal rationality, or institutional legitimacy – "intrigue always unites the crimes of her perfidious treachery" (Robespierre 1794: 20). Equality and justice become less important than domination and survival – that is, one must dominate or risk one's very survival – during periods of revolutionary upheaval or systemic instability. Such periods can go on for quite some time – indeed, such arrangements are often more long-lived than the kinds of political conditions that facilitate rational pluralism – but they are by definition unsettled as well as unsettling, always shifting and in conflict, never staid and constant.

Under such political conditions, law is not merely a tool of politics, but becomes a vehicle and arena of social upheaval and political reordering – as Neumann says of the legal system of the Third Reich, "law is nothing but an *arcanum dominationis*" (Neumann 1986: 298). Unlike in any other arrangement – in which law is almost always conservative (Garlan 1941: 3) – the law becomes both a venue for transformative upheaval and an often brutal revolutionary force in itself. Such conditions are inherently unstable and fluid and the one force that can reliably bring order – rather than state collapse – is charismatic authority (Weber 1978: 241–5; Andreas 2007). Yet, the assertion of this authority is neither assured nor, in the short-term, stabilizing – as Neumann also reminds us, "the whole machinery of the law stands exclusively at the service of the Leader [Hitler], in order to transform, as rapidly as possible, his will into legal forms. We cannot, therefore, ascribe to the National Socialist State the basic principles of a *Rechtstaat*" (Neumann 1986: 296).

Would-be charismatic leaders also fail much of the time, and when they do they can sow even greater upheaval in their wake (Weber 1978: 1114–5). When they succeed, their transformative influence (Jowitt 1987) brings *increased* politicization of law and adjudication, at least in the short run, as they remake society in the image of the polity they have reconstituted – "genuine charismatic justice does not refer to rules" (Weber 1978: 1115). Only after a time, as charismatic authority begins to become routinized and institutionalized (Weber 1978: 246–51, 1121–3), do successful charismatic interventions into the legal system begin to promote more regularized adjudication, as they transition through phases Ken Jowitt has termed "consolidation" and especially "inclusion" (Jowitt 1974, 1975).

Nonlegal actors still intervene, to be sure, but their intervention becomes more predictable. Eventually, the polity either returns to a struggle reminiscent of a Hobbesian state of nature or begins to solidify into a stable set of hierarchical power relations, for, "it is the fate of charisma ... to recede with the development of permanent institutional structures" (Weber 1978: 1133). The routinization of charisma in legal regimes, therefore, either fails or ushers in a new regime, one that is almost always either neotraditional or rule by law (or, in some cases as discussed below, a hybrid of the two). Unstable conflictual polities, punctuated by revolutionary charismatic interventions that eventually degenerate back into less ideological conflict or give way to more stable, fixed, and closed polities and more institutionalized legal orders are thus the main narrative of mobilizational legal regimes.

Rule by Law Regimes

Rule by law regimes, such as those we see in Indonesian criminal law since *Reformasi* or Chinese civil law in the Reform era, exist in states with fixed and closed – often authoritarian – polities where nonlegal institutions and actors refrain from excessive intervention into the adjudication of specific cases. There are two main advantages to such regimes. First, they offer the "calculable adjudication and administration" (Weber 1995: 277) that many scholars have identified as necessary for the development of efficient or rational markets. By creating predictability and at least perceived impartiality, or at a minimum dependable and consistent partiality, in at least some parts of the legal system, they allow economic actors to forge contractual relationships with relative confidence and reduce uncertainty and transaction costs for those seeking to engage in any type of meaningful exchange. But the second advantage is perhaps even greater: they offer a degree of routinization, regularization, and transparency that can help prevent splits from reemerging within the polity while also providing at least a potentially high degree of popular legitimacy. These advantages come at a price, however: the autocrat (or oligarchic ruling elite) must tie its hands (Wang 2015) and refrain from excessive intervention into the adjudication of specific cases.

Sometimes this price proves too high to pay. Some rulers fear legal challengers too much to permit even the remote possibility of any emerging. Where rulers are insufficiently secure in their position to refrain from intervention or legal institutions are too weak to function reliably (or at all) without the intervention of nonlegal political actors into the adjudication of specific cases, neotraditional legal regimes will prevail. One can find the two regimes in hybrid combinations, however – with, for example, a neotraditional regime in place for criminal law and a rule by law regime maintained for commercial law – that allow elites to maximize advantages of rule by law regimes in some areas while maintaining the power-preserving aspects of neotraditionalism in others.

Neotraditional Legal Regimes

Neotraditional legal regimes – as we see in Indonesia under Liberal Democracy and New Order (as well as in criminal law since *Reformasi*) and in Chinese criminal law in the Reform era – maintain established hierarchies by allowing nonlegal actors, drawn from a closed and fixed polity, to intervene heavily into the adjudication of individual cases. Those with power wield it through the law, intervening in individual cases when necessary, explicitly to keep others from attaining power or even slightly more equal status. Unlike rule by law regimes, neotraditional legal regimes tend to proliferate when stable elites have reason to believe they may be under threat. For when longstanding elites believe themselves secure in their position, they have incentives to embrace the predictability and legitimacy offered by a rule by law regime.

Neotraditional legal regimes are often a key feature of colonial administrations, as some astute officials of such systems have observed, though their existence and importance can sometimes be masked by the presence of features of a rule by law or even rational pluralism in certain segments of the legal system (governing the economic transactions of the colonizer, for example). Indeed, J. S. Furnivall (a famous British colonial officer in Burma), in his comparative study of the British administration of Burma and the Dutch administration of what became Indonesia (Furnivall 1956), argues that Dutch legal pluralism and a combination of "direct rule on western lines" with indirect rule "through native chieftans" (Furnivall 1956: 279), allowed for a system in which social order could be maintained, produce and labor could be cheaply extracted, and the property rights of the colonizer and "comprador elites" (Evans 1979) could be protected.

Anticipating other important arguments in social science (Polanyi 1957; Huntington 1968), Furnivall maintained that a crucial factor behind Dutch success was the use of law and legal pluralism to constrain the political participation of Indonesians or their entry into the polity, limiting both political instability and the social dislocation caused by the imposition of what he saw as a market-facilitating rule of law (which was really closer to a rule by law regime) in places like Burma, such that: "Two basic principles of British colonial policy are the rule of law and economic freedom, whereas Dutch colonial policy has aimed at imposing restraints on economic forces by strengthening personal authority and by conserving the influence of custom ... Dutch rule has, in great measure been successful in softening the impact of the modern west on native social life" (Furnivall 1956: Preface, 263). Other than colonial regimes, neotraditional regimes are most common in authoritarian states that have long-established political systems and relatively secure and stable elites – though not quite so stable and secure as to countenance a rule by law order.

Neotraditional regimes can be blended with rule by law regimes in different geographic regions or across different areas of the law. For example, in states where certain territories or regions are deemed at risk of insurrection (but, crucially, are not yet in full rebellion or otherwise in any situation such that the constitution of the polity is actually contested), neotraditional regimes might prevail in those territories, even though a rule by law dominates elsewhere. The same dualism could be applied to different segments of a population – as, for example, the Dutch sought to do in the East Indies – with rule by law available to colonists, commercial elites, or favored ethnic groups, and a neotraditional regime for everyone else. Likewise, there are situations in which a state may seek the legal certainty and stable property rights offered by a rule by law regime in civil (especially commercial) law, while simultaneously maintaining a neotraditional regime in criminal or family law to ensure tighter social control. Such hybrid arrangements can help maintain traditional clientalism, while simultaneously facilitating the entry of essential parts of developing or peripheral economies into international markets, staving off the upheaval that has often accompanied such integration (Scott 1976).

USING LEGAL REGIMES TO GUIDE EMPIRICAL ANALYSIS

I use legal regimes to guide my empirical analysis of complex local and subnational realities, across time and between China and Indonesia. Specifically, criminal (public) and civil (private) law in both countries can be grouped into mobilizational, neotraditional, and rule by law regimes in different periods since 1949. In some cases, there are hybrids, with neotraditional regimes in the criminal law arena and rule by law regimes governing commercial or civil law, or vice versa. The precise character of each regime is expressed somewhat differently, moreover, in rural versus urban settings. Finally, I exclude family and administrative law from my analysis. I do this first because these realms of law are extremely specialized and subject to particular research restrictions. Family law stands out as the most morally and normatively loaded area of law and serves a special function of social control, despite being nominally a subset of private law in most contexts. In China, family law case records and proceedings are sealed to protect the litigants' privacy and reporting in secondary and scholarly sources is scant (though some have focused on this area recently and it is clear that family disputes are the most common of civil suits – see Diamant 2001; Michelson 2007a). Most Chinese political actors and theorists of civil law also consider family law distinct, in large part because the associations between parties are neither voluntary nor equal (Chen 1995: 51). Family law, likewise, is influenced strongly in the Indonesian case by religious norms and very often adjudicated (for Muslims, in any case) by stand-alone religious courts, especially after 1970. The purpose of administrative law is also special – to rein in unruly agents by allowing citizens to alert distant principals to their bad behavior. There are exceedingly few administrative cases filed in either China or Indonesia. Administrative litigation has also only been possible in China since the early 1990s, while in Indonesia administrative suits are handled through special purpose-designed courts. For these reasons, I confine my analysis to criminal law and nonfamily civil law.

Distinguishing between Public and Private (or Criminal and Civil) Law

Many authors have noted in multiple contexts that law governing relationships between citizens and the state (especially criminal and administrative law), often called public law, is fundamentally different in its aims and organizing principles from law which governs relationships between individuals or non-state organizations (for example, tort law, contract law, and family law), often called private law. Public law is concerned most essentially with regulating the state's application of violent or coercive power – what could be termed its "legitimate domination" – to individuals or private entities (Neumann 1986: 20). Indeed, even in the realm of US criminal adjudication (often presumed by many to encapsulate the sedate and norm-based operation of the rule of law), Robert Cover astutely observed that, "The judges deal pain and death" (Cover 1986: 1609), since, "Legal interpretation is (1) a practical activity, (2) designed to generate credible threats and actual deeds of violence, (3) in an effective way" (Cover 1986: 1610). Private law is fundamentally concerned with facilitating certain kinds of social relationships (stable and honest business partnerships, transparent transactional contracts, monogamous families, etc.) and discouraging others (e.g. making contractual promises one cannot keep, negligence regarding consumer safety, bigamy, or libel) (Neumann 1986: 21). Within private law, family law is in many ways a special case. It governs the definition, structure, maintenance, and dissolution of the most basic social units – families – and thus functions more in the manner of public law than does, say, commercial or tort law.

The basic political logic and social implications are thus different for public and private law. It is through public law that states and polities fend off challenges and maintain order (Pound 1942), but through private law that they foster the development of markets or other economic arrangements they see as preferable or efficient (Hart 1994: 40). Failure to distinguish between these two areas of law can obfuscate one's view of the legal regime in play, especially in many cases of what I have called "hybrid" regimes. In such cases, we may see a very clear neotraditional regime in private law and what looks like a rule by law regime in public law, or vice versa. In fact, such hybrids may be more common than "pure" examples of either type. Acknowledging the different political roots and social implications of each type of law allows us to observe such regimes more clearly and to categorize them more accurately.

It is very rare that we might find hybrids of rule by law and mobilizational regimes. Indeed, mobilizational regimes are more prone to ignore one or the other type of law almost completely. When charismatic authority is successfully asserted and states have sufficiently functional institutions, public law may be used to enforce reigns of terror upon perceived enemies or challengers. But when states are weak or sufficiently powerful leaders absent, feuding factions within the polity may be apt to fight out their battles in the arena of private law – or to attempt to reshape portions of private law to suit their agendas, while public law's coercive apparatus may become enfeebled or even lie moribund in the absence of coherent direction from above.

Finally, the history of particular countries can sometimes show a long-term bias for public or private law. As I discuss in Chapter 2, this is true to some degree for both China (which has often favored public law) and Indonesia (which has placed more stress on private law). Thus, when examining the legal regime or regimes present in any given state, we must look separately at both public and private law systems and institutions, before we can assess them together, because of the fundamentally different political dynamics that underpin each and the divergent types of social effects each can produce, as well as idiosyncratic features of specific country contexts. Failure to disaggregate in this way can lead to misperception and inaccurate categorization.

Distinguishing between Urban and Rural Justice Systems

In both China and Indonesia, and likely across many developing countries, the principal divide is between urban and rural areas. This is true for many areas of social, economic, and political life, as well as for the structure and functioning of legal institutions. These institutional differences are key to understanding why legal regimes play out differently, at least in terms of some of their effects, in urban versus rural settings. Urban courts and legal institutions are likely to have vastly more economic resources at their disposal, to be more secure in their political position, to be staffed by judges and other officials of higher status and holding more prestigious qualifications, and to be much more visible to elites and other observers, both within and beyond a country's borders. Rural courts and institutions tend to be short-staffed, to be administered by less qualified – or even completely unqualified – judges and officials, to be chronically underfunded and short of resources, to suffer from a lack of status and clout, and to be overlooked by both domestic and international elites and observers.

But what does that matter? Such differences should not change the underlying elements of the legal regime. We cannot observe, for example, a neotraditional regime throughout the cities and a mobilizational one in the countryside. While they do not affect the core attributes of a national-level legal regime, urban–rural divides can and often *do* exert tremendous influence over the specific ways in which legal regimes manifest themselves on the ground and the social and political effects they have in the broader society.

For example, interventions by nonlegal actors into the adjudication of specific cases (whether in a neotraditional or mobilization regime) are much more likely to be coordinated and consistent in urban areas, but less efficacious and subject to being hijacked by the idiosyncratic interests of local strongmen in rural hinterlands (Migdal 1988). Also, perhaps perversely or counterintuitively, the social and political stakes in play are often *higher* in rural settings than in urban ones. Because relatively little social conflict or repression reaches the formal institutions or courts in the countryside, that which does is frequently only observable in a subset of the most intense, meaningful, or politically charged cases. Finally, actions of national-level states to reform or change the legal system can have profoundly different effects on the ground in urban versus rural contexts. One vivid example of this can been seen in how mass campaigns in China during the 1950s upended an urban justice system left more or less intact after 1949, but breathed new life and clout into many rural courts that were just being constituted in many parts of the country (Hurst 2011). It is thus vitally important, when assessing national-level legal regimes, to examine both urban and rural areas with some sensitivity to these important differences of economic, social, and political background and effects.

THE LOGIC OF COMPARISON AND RESEARCH APPROACH

The Indonesian and Chinese legal systems differ in many important ways. But they are ultimately two individuals of the same species – or at least two species of the same genus. The structure of institutions and the basic rules that govern them provides a foundation for the activities of a variety of players and a baseline setting that can be challenged through reforms or other changes. Over time, China has tended to build new rules and systems more or less from a clean slate, following episodes of political or social change. Indonesia has traditionally layered new features and functions on top of the accumulated basis of existing laws and institutions. Legal system development can also follow a more punctuated or fluid, revolutionary or evolutionary, dynamic – and both countries show examples of each type during different phases of their histories.

Both Indonesia and China have experienced wrenching political change and regular upheavals across their legal systems since the early twentieth century. Both have also evolved along a path that could be characterized as broadly within a "civil law tradition." Yet, in many ways their histories are rather divergent – not simply because of the two countries' different geographies or the different political ideologies of their leaders or political orders. The *basic approach* to reform or remaking of legal institutions over a century or more of upheaval is as distinct in each county as are the earlier roots of its legal apparatus. Their current forms are also, of course, rather distinct.

Indeed, Indonesia and China represent perhaps the outer limits of comparability between countries, even as their common features allow for side-by-side comparison of components of their legal systems within each country. Comparing different parts of the legal order within each country allows us to understand how legal regimes actually operate, while comparing across these particular two countries opens a window into the generalizability and necessary antecedent conditions for the development of particular legal orders *precisely because of the extreme differences between them.* Comparing either China or Indonesia with other countries, such as Russia, India, Vietnam, South Africa, Brazil, or Nigeria, for example, would likely not yield similarly fruitful results. Indeed, most other potential comparator cases share certain key attributes with only one of my cases (e.g. a socialist legal tradition or an experience of being colonized), but many also differ in critical respects from both of them (e.g. having a common law system or being a federal state), making the sort of analysis I am about to outline much less feasible.

Internationalizing Subnational Comparison

Chinese Politics has remained remarkably isolated from the rest of comparative politics, while scholarship on Indonesia, and Southeast

Asia more generally, has been much more successful at speaking to broader audiences. Yet, even the most celebrated works from the field's heyday (roughly 1965–85), as well as more recent hits (e.g. Slater 2010; Vu 2010) can be criticized for perhaps moving too quickly up the ladder of generality and sometimes glossing over important subnational variation (for a recent exception, see Buehler 2016). The critical task looking ahead is to scale up insights from careful subnational work (like that which has characterized the best of the China field) so that they can help advance broader claims and debates, as the best work from the Southeast Asian literature has done.

Some of the most methodologically attuned China specialists have advanced a case for not subjecting China to cross-national comparison. Allen Carlson, Mary Gallagher, and Melanie Manion have argued that China does not bear many similarities to other socialist countries and cannot, therefore, be compared easily against this group. Second, citing my work and that of others, they note that significant subnational variation requires nuanced and careful analysis before cross-national comparative studies could do justice to the complexities of China's political reality. Finally, they maintain that persistent problems of data quality and availability restrict researchers in any attempt to gather cross-nationally comparable data (Carlson, Gallagher, & Manion 2010: 4–7). All of these are valid points if we presume that comparisons of China with other countries will be in the form of whole-to-whole examinations of national-level cases.

Indeed, this penchant to eschew cross-national comparative analysis of China apparently stems from the fact that most in the China field and beyond have assumed that small-n cross-national comparisons tend to (or ought to) involve the paired or structured comparisons of states at the national level. Even in prominent recent work that professes to celebrate subnational comparative analysis, Dan Slater and Daniel Ziblatt confine their most important theoretical and methodological discussions to extolling the advantages of controlled comparisons of states at the national level (Slater & Ziblatt 2013). Large-n cross-national analyses, comparing scores of countries in a dataset using quantitative techniques, hold even less appeal for those who care deeply about the accuracy and internal validity of arguments about specific national cases.

Colleagues working on other parts of the world have sought in recent years to compare subnational units across states (e.g. Gibson 2013; Sinha 2015). While most of this work has centered on subnational political units – largely in federal systems – some of the best recent research has started to look beyond such neat divisions, for example at subnational political economic regions across states (e.g. Boone 2014) or at specific portions of the political or economic order across states (e.g. Naseemullah 2017). It is this kind of comparison of political economic regions, subnational social or ethnic groups, or of specific portions of the political apparatus or economy that is potentially most fruitful for those looking to compare across large nonfederal states, especially in the developing world. Doing this requires two choices, however: first between inductive and deductive comparison *within* each country and then between several possible strategies for comparing *across* countries.

Inductive analysis entails selecting several subnational cases pretty much at random, or based upon where the researcher can best secure access, and then, after compiling extensive data on each case, suggesting types or categories based upon observed variation between the cases. Little need to be established or assumed about the representativeness or external validity of the case study findings. While hypotheses about larger classes or groups of cases can be generated, they cannot be tested or evaluated. This method also cannot suggest what may lie beyond the range of observed variation and categories. Inductive analysis may thus not be the optimal choice.

In deductive subnational analysis, the researcher must select cases to be representative of some larger set according to some framework theorized *a priori*. Once cases are selected and analyzed, the researcher can advance claims about the classes or subsets of cases they represent. Perhaps more importantly, this method is especially useful for suggesting hypotheses about the limits of generalizability of any claims made – that is, about the antecedent conditions or background variables required for them to operate. It is these meta-hypotheses, as much as the subnational causal claims, which can be usefully tested by engaging in similar or analogous subnational analysis in another national context (Hurst 2009). The difficulty lies in the necessary first step of selecting representative cases – which is not feasible in all research contexts.

After deciding between deductive and inductive analysis, a choice must also be made between "general insight" comparison and at least two possible two-step comparative strategies. General insight comparison involves the derivation of general hypotheses from the subnational analysis of cases within one country. This has always been the most common strategy for moving beyond the borders of a single state in subnational analysis (Slater & Ziblatt 2013: 10–11). Once some argument about subnational variation or causal patterns is established for Country A, it can be phrased in general terms, "replacing proper names with variables" (Przeworski & Teune 1970), and transported to other national contexts for evaluation.

A "traditional" two-step comparison involves subnational comparison first, followed by national-level comparison of the country studied to some other country or set of countries. Essentially, this strategy amounts to using subnational comparison to derive general claims about one country as a whole – analyzing several parts to map the contours of that whole – and then comparing the whole against that of some other country or set of countries. The disadvantage of this strategy is that it assumes that a valid part-to-whole mapping is possible (Snyder 2001). If we cannot know anything meaningful about China *qua* China, then we cannot compare China as a coherent unit with some other country also taken as a coherent unit. The baseline problem of overgeneralization about each country case is not resolved and the advantages of subnational analysis are eroded.

"Millian" two-step comparison first uses Mill's method of difference (Mill 1843: 455–60) to control x-variation and engage in side-by-side subnational comparisons of outcomes and processes separately within one country *and* within another country, running what amounts to two most-similar systems designs (Przeworski & Teune 1970) in parallel. Then, subnational cases or processes that appear analogous are matched across national contexts and Mill's method of agreement (Mill 1843: 454–5) is applied to evaluate whether similar causal logics hold across different country cases – essentially a type of most-different systems design (Przeworski & Teune 1970) in the second step. This method has the very significant advantage of first controlling x-variation to discern patterns and to formulate hypotheses about the antecedent conditions required for these to operate, and then controlling y-variation to test the necessity of these hypothesized antecedent conditions.

Comparing subnational phenomena across cases has become a popular strategy among China researchers (e.g. Solinger 2009; Read 2012; Repnikova 2014). I suggested some years ago the utility of comparing regions (Hurst 2009: 143), though this has not yet been taken up widely. Comparing institutions may actually be more practical than comparing regions and more useful than comparing phenomena.

For example, looking at subnational braches or other microlevel arms of the state, such as local courts or police, should make it clearer which dimensions of x-variation can be held constant and which cannot. By restricting one's focus to subnational institutions, the researcher can have a clearer sense *a priori* of his or her cases across a broad range of potential independent variables, and spell out much more accurately and cleanly on which causal dimensions they vary and which factors can indeed be held constant.

The Method Applied

To study legal regimes in China and Indonesia, I use a combination Millian two-step and traditional two-step comparative method. Selecting urban and rural areas to give as broad a cross-section of contexts within each country as possible (while holding national-level variables constant), I look over time at how courts and legal institutions functioned, regarding both public and private law, in each place. Aggregating up to the national level, I am then able to outline the legal regimes in play in each country during specific time periods. In this basic form, my method resembles the traditional two-step. Still, the fact that legal regimes are disaggregated to public and private law and into different time periods in each country helps me use more of a Millian two-step, in that neither China nor Indonesia is given a single fixed score for "legal regime type." Comparing legal regimes operating in either public or private law at specific moments in time thus amounts to a comparison of subnational elements of politics rather than overarching national types.

Data and Empirical Approach in Light of Prior Research

No research begins *tabula rasa*. There are rich traditions of scholarship that have accumulated on law and politics in both Indonesia and China, though these have not addressed all of the concerns that inform my study. This book aims to offer a more comprehensive and macro-oriented perspective than most prior empirical research, while at the same time offering much richer close-to-the-ground data and micro-analysis than most prior theoretical work, bringing the two strands together and making contributions to both. This book's principal theoretical contributions have already been discussed, but its new empirical offerings should become clearer after a brief review of prior work on Indonesian and Chinese law and politics.

Prior Research on China

The seminal work on Chinese courts was Jerome Cohen's study of the criminal process (Cohen 1968). Others followed this up with updated and increasingly comprehensive studies of the Chinese legal system as a whole (Lubman 1999; Potter 1999, 2001; Peerenboom 2002; Zou 2006; Liebman 2007; Li 2014; Blasek 2015). Many of these works took sides in a macro debate about China's relative progress (or lack thereof) toward some form of "rule of law," and whether or not such progress should be measured against an implied American ideal type. Thankfully, this debate has quieted down as scholars have observed Donald Clarke's advice (Clarke 1998–1999) and moved beyond relatively empty conceptual arguments.

Susan Trevaskes has recently offered a more focused analysis of mass campaigns and the criminal process, mainly in the Baotou Intermediate Court, in Inner Mongolia, during the 1980s (Trevaskes 2007). Woo and Wang (2005) presented a similar study of civil adjudication in three intermediate courts (one in each of three Southern Chinese provinces). A few recent books have set out to trace the contours of criminal (e.g. McConville et al. 2011; He 2014) or civil (e.g. Woo & Gallagher 2011) adjudication in China. Finally, there has been some significant scholarship on very specific issues such as the enforcement of civil judgments (Clarke 1996a; Peerenboom 2001; He 2009) or informal aspects of the penal system (Seymour & Anderson 1999; Biddulph 2007; Sapio 2010). What has been missing so far is sufficient systematic political analysis of just how courts function as institutions and how this affects Chinese politics as a whole.

Bin Liang's book (Liang 2008) uses case observations, interviews, and statistics to analyze Chinese legal reforms since the 1990s. His study suffers from some shortcomings, however, including his looking only at urban courts in two quite atypical cities (Beijing and Chengdu), and that his analysis does not advance any larger theoretical agenda. So far, there have also only been a few attempts at analyzing the politics inside Chinese courts (e.g. Liu 2006a; He 2011, 2012). While a good starting point, this work is still far from comprehensive and would benefit greatly from analysis across Chinese regions and up and down levels of the judicial hierarchy.

Since the early 2000s, a debate has emerged over whether judicial independence (or lack thereof) and the use of mediation and other alternative dispute-resolution mechanisms in Chinese courts affect the integrity of the legal system or trajectory of legal development.

Some, like Carl Minzner, have argued that efforts to prioritize mediation (especially since 2009), while enhancing political top-down monitoring and possibly control of judges, have amounted to a "turn against law" and serious retrograde motion in terms of China's progress toward any form of rule of law (Minzner 2011). Others, like Randall Peerenboom, have countered that mediation and judicial supervision, while they do impede any ideal of judicial independence, actually help improve the functioning of the Chinese legal system and make courts more reliable and less corrupt (Peerenboom 2006, 2010). Other, more recent, examinations of judicial behavior have been more equivocal in terms of grand conclusions, while often emphasizing the demoralizing aspects of judges' work (Stern 2010; Kinkel & Hurst 2015) – though a few analyses have examined links between judges' professionalization and the market for legal services in large cities (Kinkel 2015). All told, the question of just how courts function has not been settled in any authoritative way by scholarship on judges and their professional incentives and constraints.

Analyses of the legal profession have attacked this question from a more oblique angle, examining the role of lawyers, law firms, and legal aid groups in bringing change through litigation and other social and political activities (Alford 1995; Gallagher 2006; Liu 2006b; Michelson 2006; Alford 2007; Stern 2011; Givens 2013; Liu & Halliday 2016). Few scholars, however, have looked directly at the work of lawyers in the courtroom or their impact on judicial decision-making. Some others in the same broad tradition have studied the professionalization of judges, while others have examined the impact of activities within the legal system on the perceptions or attitudes of those outside it (Diamant, Lubman, & O'Brien 2005; Gallagher 2006, 2017; Landry 2008). But, despite the richness of these literatures, they have limited relevance to the issues I seek to address.

Two important new books have also been published on the politics of the Chinese legal system. Rachel Stern's study of environmental litigation (Stern 2013) and Yuhua Wang's analysis of China's construction of a partial rule of law (Wang 2015) share several essential attributes. Stern argues that, in a context of political ambivalence, lawyers – as newly private actors since 2000 – have strategically and skillfully pressed the boundaries of legal reform by helping ordinary citizens sue polluting private and state-owned firms. Wang argues more expansively that local courts make progress toward predictable and noncorrupt behavior when large concentrations of foreign firms (as politically unconnected actors possessing vast sums of mobile capital) press for a level playing field in the economic arena (for a somewhat similar argument about firms of different ownership promoting divergent paths of institutional development, see Fuller 2010). Stern's analysis is qualitative and revolves around a decidedly political set of relationships and considerations, whereas Wang's is mainly quantitative and hinges on an economic logic. Both books, however, are decidedly ahistorical (beginning from the mid-1990s or early 2000s without much attention to anything prior). Both focus exclusively on areas of private law and civil litigation. And both treat the functioning of legal institutions as an outcome to be explained rather than an explanatory variable.

Prior Research on Indonesia

The scholarly literature on Indonesian legal politics and institutions is less developed than that on their Chinese counterparts. Daniel Lev remains the seminal author in this still nascent field. His work provides an exceptionally vivid and incisive description of the transitions from Dutch colonial rule to Liberal Democracy and from Liberal to Guided Democracy (Lev 2000a, 2000b).[2] Of particular use for my purposes is his analysis of how general patterns of state–society relations are expressed in citizens' specific encounters with legal institutions (Lev 1972). Adriaan Bedner more recently added an impressive discussion of the evolution of Indonesian legal institutions up until the end of the New Order period (Bedner 2001). Since 1998, several Indonesian scholars (including the former Chief Justice of the Constitutional Court) have also produced substantial works on the relationship of law and politics across key periods of their country's history (Mahfud MD 1998; Saragih 2006), though these have tended to focus more on legislation and the politics of rulemaking than on the functioning of legal institutions like courts.

Many studies specifically of courts have clustered around the Supreme Court (Pompe 2005), Islamic religious courts (Lev 1973b; Bowen 2003; O'Shaughnessy 2009 – the last notable for her extensive use of individual case records from several courts in Yogyakarta), religious politics as played out in court cases (Crouch 2013), and the

[2] *Legal Evolution and Political Authority in Indonesia* (Lev 2000) is a volume comprised of eight articles and book chapters, originally published between 1962 and 1998, that collectively comprise the core of Daniel Lev's seminal contribution to the study of law and politics in Indonesia.

implementation of local traditional customary law known as *adat* (Li 2001; Davidson & Henley 2007). A smaller number of studies have explicitly examined the interrelationships between state and customary law, including the manner in which *adat* can sometimes be used in state courts and the possibility of forum shopping between state and *adat* venues (von Benda-Beckmann 1984). Few have paid sufficient attention to the legal profession or the politics of judges. Though some have examined the use of courts for larger social purposes (e.g. Susanti 2008), analysis of the role of basic level courts throughout the provinces in the context of Indonesia's rapid democratization has with few exceptions (e.g. von Benda-Beckmann & von Benda-Beckmann 2013) been almost completely absent.

With relatively few exceptions (e.g. Bertrand 1995; Buehler & Tan 2007; Buehler 2008), most political scientists have remained focused on national or provincial levels of elite political debate and contestation. Refocusing research on a lower level of analysis will promote greater understanding of the micro-foundations of Indonesian politics within and beyond the legal system. In fact, much can be learned from the rapidly expanding literature on local governance and autonomy in post-Suharto Indonesia (Kingsbury & Aveling 2003; Schulte Nordholt & van Klinken 2007; Erb, Faucher, & Sulistianto 2009), though these studies have too often disaggregated down only to the provincial level and have rarely focused on judicial institutions (for an exception, see Feener 2013).

My Empirical Approach

Between 2006 and 2014, I completed field research in twenty-two urban and rural localities: Chengdu, Deyang, Luzhou, Meishan, Nanchang, Jiujiang, Jingdezhen, Shangrao, Guangzhou, Dongguan, Shenzhen, Ji'nan, Liaocheng, Surabaya, Kediri, Lamongan, Tuban, Pamekasan, Sidoarjo, Manado, Minahasa Utara (Air Madidi), and Minahasa (Tondano) – as well as more limited work (mostly library research plus a few interviews) in Beijing, Shanghai, Jakarta, Hong Kong, and Singapore. Primary field work involved collecting case files and court documents (both current and historical), observing trials and proceedings, and interviewing judges, lawyers, prosecutors/procurators, parties to cases, and other relevant officials or actors (e.g. secretaries of Communist Party political and legal affairs committees). This overall breadth and depth of field research across multiple provinces in both countries is likely the most comprehensive to date.

There are issues of uneven data quality and availability, however. In general, much more data of much higher quality are available in China than in Indonesia. Of course, the relative utility of archival versus observational data collection also varied across the two counties. China utilizes a version of what might be called a "day-in-court" procedural system, in which trials take place mostly in short single sessions and archives of case files are mostly closed. Indonesia follows an extreme version of what could be called a "piecemeal trial" system, in which trials play out over numerous hearings separated by months or years, but archives and case files are more open (on the contrasting systems, see Damaska 1991: 51–3, 62). Observational data were thus more valuable and easier to collect in China, while certain kinds of archival data (such as case files) were easier to obtain and relatively more revealing in Indonesia.

In selecting the field sites and collecting data in specific courts or on specific cases and issues, I was guided by two general principles. First, I sought to gather data on as wide an array of cases, in as many different settings, and across as many time periods as possible in both China and Indonesia. Second, I aimed to select cases and sites that were at least broadly representative of the times and places from which they were drawn (to the degree that I could assess their representativeness from available secondary sources or general information). Within these two broad guidelines, however, I was forced – like all others who do intensive field research – to follow my contacts and resources to some degree, pursuing an *ad hoc* inductive approach to the agglomeration of data gathered in places where I was able to go and from sources I was able to access.

CONCLUSION

To sum up, previous scholarship on law and politics has too often been fixated on an ideal type of rule of law. This has sometimes caused it to be inflected with a normative teleology. Other scholarship that emphasizes rule by law, transitional justice, law and economics, law and democratization, or other perspectives, has tended to offer conceptual toolkits that are too narrow for my purposes here. Using a new conceptual lens offered by legal regimes allows us to understand the politics of legal institutions in authoritarian and developing country contexts more fully and accurately.

Legal regimes are structured by politics along two dimensions: the degree to which the polity is open/in flux or closed/stable and the degree to which nonlegal institutional actors intervene in the adjudication of specific cases. Conceiving of them in this way allows us to measure and categorize legal regimes without resorting to use of judicial outcomes as a metric. It also lets us see more clearly exactly how political arrangements affect the functioning of courts and legal institutions in different settings.

Distinguishing between public law (mainly criminal) and private law (civil, commercial, etc.) helps us understand the specific dynamics of legal regimes in each area of law as well as the different ways in which certain types of legal regimes can be mixed in specific settings – e.g. neotraditional regimes at work in the criminal arena alongside rule by law regimes in the civil sphere. Furthermore, distinguishing between urban and rural settings helps us see how the specific on-the-ground dynamics of a legal regime operate and also to assess the exact social, economic, and political effects of particular patterns of court or legal institutional functioning more precisely.

In this book, I am looking at legal regimes in China and Indonesia since 1949, across both criminal and civil (nonfamily) law. Based on extensive field research in both urban and rural areas of several provinces in each country, I draw on a comprehensive new set of data, including firsthand observations and interviews, case files and court documents, other archival sources, and secondary sources, to engage in what I would term a hybrid traditional–Millian two-step comparison. That is, I first hold national-level variation constant, to engage in comparative analysis of local courts in specific regions of each country. I then aim, however, simultaneously to aggregate up to broader national-level patterns and to compare specific components of the legal system at particular moments in time across countries. Such an approach is difficult and has rarely been attempted, but it promises many advantages for both the present study and future research.

Before discussing the details of how each legal regime has operated in Indonesian or Chinese local courts, we need a broad historical understanding of the evolution of each country's legal regimes. Chapter 2 summarizes the histories of legal development in China and Indonesia and explains how different legal regimes took root at different times and in different areas of law in each country.

CHAPTER TWO

AN HISTORICAL OVERVIEW OF INDONESIAN AND CHINESE LEGAL REGIMES

The skillful carpenter, though able to mark the inked string with his surveying eyes and calculating mind, always takes compasses and squares as measures before his marking; the great genius, though able to accomplish his task with swift move, always takes the law of the early kings as the ruler before his accomplishment. Thus, if the inked string is straight, crooked timbers will be shaved; if the water-level is even, high gnarls will be planed down.

(Han Fei 1939: 45)

It shall be permissible to acquire for oneself, and to retain, those things which are useful for life . . . [arms] are used by the just man for defence and [lawful] acquisition . . . [thus] . . . we can conclude that private wars are justly waged by any person whatsoever.

(Grotius 1950: 10, 30, 62)

INTRODUCTION

The historical trajectories of legal development and legal regimes in Indonesia and China diverge sharply, even as they are ripe for comparison, as noted in the preceding chapter. China's maximalist state has long used a unified legal apparatus chiefly as a tool of social and political control (on this overall historical arc see Dutton 1992). Indonesia's minimalist state has sat atop a much more fragmented, often explicitly pluralist, legal order that has functioned largely to preserve the private material interests of aristocratic, colonial, and later other elites. This chapter traces these longer-term histories and outlines the general institutional and political contours of the Indonesian and Chinese legal systems as they have evolved since 1949.

China is perhaps the oldest unitary state in the world. First brought under centralized control by Emperor Qin Shihuang (秦始皇) in 221 BCE, its original legal order was founded on the autocratic and severe, yet impartial, application of precise statutes, as advocated by Han Fei (韩非) and other Legalist (法家) philosophers. Maintenance of political authority through brutal, yet consistent, criminal punishment of any transgressive or subversive acts was the paramount goal and ultimate purpose of the law: "Thus the intelligent ruler neglects no reward and remits no punishment … men of real merit, however distant and humble, must be rewarded; those of real demerit, however near and dear, must be censured" (Han Fei 1939: 35). The law can thus be a supremely useful tool for the state to shape society and force conformity from the powerful and meek alike:

> The law does not fawn on the noble; the string does not yield to the crooked. Whatever the law applies to, the wise cannot reject nor can the brave defy. Punishment for fault never skips ministers, reward for good never misses commoners. Therefore, to correct the faults of the high, to rebuke the vices of the low, to suppress disorders, to decide against mistakes, to subdue the arrogant, to straighten the cooked, and to unify the folkways of the masses, nothing could match the law. (Han Fei 1939: 45)

This relatively unified, internally coherent, and inflexible character that has imbued Chinese law from its earliest days has made piecemeal or pluralistic reform much harder, even in much later historical periods. In the context of a maximalist state, focused on preserving the political power of its ruling elite, change in Chinese legal history tends to come in abrupt breakpoints.

Indonesia's experience could not be more different. Though the Sriwijaya (c. 850–1100 CE) and Majapahit (1293–c. 1500 CE) Empires brought much of the archipelago under somewhat unified control prior to the arrival of the Dutch in the early 1600s, these functioned in a manner more akin to leagues of trading mini states than coherent political entities. Each region, ethnic group, religion, and social class thus developed its own legal norms and adjudication practices. Legal pluralism was present even before a coherent political order existed to enshrine it.

Dutch colonialism was founded on the basis of the pursuit of private wealth – legal institutional development was secondary. Indeed, Hugo Grotius, at the time a brilliant twenty-year-old attorney retained by the Dutch East India Company (*Vereenigde Oost-Indische Compagnie*, or VOC), was evidently prepared to set aside his very lawyerly personal motto (*Ruit Hora*, Time is Running) to devote 1603 and 1604 to writing a 400-page scholarly treatise on this and related subjects, *De Iure Praedae Commentarius*, that he never published. The VOC's case, in which it called upon Grotius's services, revolved around the seizure in Johor of a Portuguese merchant ship, the *Santa Catarina*, by Captain Jacob van Heemskerck (for details of the case and Grotius's involvement in it, see van Ittersum 2003, 2006: chapter 3; Borschberg 2011: 42–3, 48–50). One of Grotius's larger theoretical purposes in his treatise was to justify private war, waged to secure private property or commercial advantage, even if it should undermine the legal coherence or political authority of states (or at least if by necessity it were to take place in the absence of coherent or efficacious public state authority).

Under a minimalist state, centered on protecting the economic advantages of a commercial elite, the Indonesian legal system presumed from the beginning a remarkable degree of pluralism, and opted consistently to layer new rules and structures onto the complex webs of multiple existing ones. Indeed, as Grotius explains,

> In cases where [the laws] can be observed simultaneously, let them [all] be observed; when this is impossible, the law of superior rank shall prevail ... that which concerns one's own good is preferred to that which concerns another's good; the greater good to the lesser, and the removal of a major evil, to the promotion of a minor good. (Grotius 1950: 29)

In such a context, change in Indonesian legal history has tended to unfold gradually over lengthy periods, at least relative to China's experience (for an excellent general overview of the history of Indonesian law see Lindsey & Santosa 2008).

Despite these differences, indeed in some senses even because of them, Chinese and Indonesian legal histories and development are eminently comparable. China's home-grown maximalist state and law contrast with Indonesia's minimalist state and law imposed by European colonialism; time-honored insistence on absolute uniformity and consistency of law in China can be juxtaposed with Indonesia's traditional acceptance of legal pluralism; and the use of law as a tool for the state to mold society in China stands opposed to the frequent deployment of law and state institutions in the service of private interests in Indonesia. By tracing the pathways – glacial evolution and wrenching revolution alike – through which legal traditions and institutions have evolved in both countries, the roots and contours of their legal regimes come into sharp relief.

CRISIS, PUNCTUATED EQUILIBRIUM, AND THE STUDY OF LEGAL INSTITUTIONS

To understand the evolution of legal systems in China and Indonesia, a broadly historical institutionalist perspective is most helpful. Though many have examined a variety of outcomes through this lens, Ruth and David Collier's study of Latin American politics and labor pacts (Collier & Collier 1991) is especially informative. Their argument revolves around political bargains struck at important moments of instability, which brought the incipient labor movement into the polity and structured the future development of party systems and political orders across a wide range of countries. Their suggestion that change in one part of the political system at a critical juncture could have wide-ranging long-term effects departed from the earlier work of others like North (1982), who focused on shocks exogenous to the states he examined, or Moore (1967), who was more interested in revolutions and their relationship to deep structural shifts like the commercialization of agriculture. My argument is that broad systemic crises and their resolution at critical junctures, both before 1949 and after, helped structure the specific development of legal systems in China and Indonesia.

The specific domains of legal institutions developed along relatively stable trajectories, interrupted by periods of intense change. Unlike the theory of punctuated equilibrium in American politics advanced by Baumgartner and Jones (1993), my framework holds that the punctuation points are both predictable (they are periods of generalized political crisis and instability) and often protracted (they can last for many years or even decades). Once in place, legal system equilibria are fragile and vulnerable, should a more generalized crisis again ensue. When and if a more stable broad political order can take root, we can expect legal institutions in countries like China and Indonesia to settle into long-term stable arrangements, as did their counterparts in England, the United States, France, and elsewhere in the second half of the nineteenth century. Yet, even in volatile political contexts like Indonesia and China, the high costs of systemic change lead to relatively more static legal regimes during most periods, even when generalized low-level instability is the order of the day, punctuated by sharp changes in direction at moments of crisis or overall political change in a kind of "soft" path-dependency (Meierhenrich 2008: 50–3).

Both China and Indonesia have seen recurrent political crises since their moments of liberation in 1949, despite very different histories and challenges prior to that point. Broadly speaking, both countries took steps toward consolidating at least a weak equilibrium in their legal systems during the 1950s; both experienced extreme chaos from the late 1950s through to at least the end of the 1960s; both then managed to cobble together a stronger equilibrium by the end of the 1970s; and finally both faced another round of crisis (China between 1989 and 1992, Indonesia between 1997 and 1999). From this point onwards, their trajectories diverge further, with China building a revamped version of its 1980s equilibrium and Indonesia still struggling to arrive at a new point of stability after attempting more radical change with *Reformasi* and since.

THE DEVELOPMENT OF THE CHINESE LEGAL SYSTEM BEFORE 1949

China in 1949 was far from being a blank slate. Extensive criminal and civil legal institutions had existed for centuries. In fact, the Qing Codex (大清律例, first published upon the Qing's seizure of power in 1644 and revised multiple times over the following 265 years) was among the most comprehensive non-Western legal codes at the turn of the twentieth century (Ch'ü 1961) – and it was only the most recent and comprehensive Chinese law code; the oldest surviving complete code was promulgated under the Tang Dynasty, a full millennium before the rise of the Qing, in around 624 CE. The Revolution of 1911, however, broke what had been at least a relatively stable equilibrium, leaving urban courts in flux and rural ones often barely functional (for a different view, see Huang 2001).

Though hampered by political divisions and a lack of state capacity after the 1911 Revolution, the Nationalist (國民黨, or GMD) government, along with many regional warlords, took significant strides toward building "rational" and "modern" institutions and systems of rules, many inspired by Japanese and German examples (Xiao-Planes 2009). But two important continuities were the foundation of the system in inquisitional, rather than adversarial, processes and a preference for clear lines of hierarchical control over lower-level institutions.

By the time the Chinese Communist Party (CCP) began formulating and implementing its own order, China's legal system was already a mix of imported and indigenous concepts, rules, and structures, in which power was exercised in regionally differentiated ways by a relatively weak judiciary. Law in the countryside had receded, leaving the cities as redoubts of coherent legal practice surrounded by a barely governed hinterland. It was thus after the CCP had been driven from Shanghai and other cities that it crafted its own courts and other institutions in earnest in its base areas, notably in the Jiangxi Soviet and later in Yan'an.

From November 1931 until October of 1934, the CCP established and administered the Chinese Soviet Republic (中华苏维埃共和国, or CSR), headquartered in Ruijin (瑞金, a county town in Ganzhou, Jiangxi Province) and dominated by Mao Zedong, Zhu De, and the rural guerilla wing of the Party, who had by 1928 come together in the Jinggangshan (井冈山) mountains along the Jiangxi-Hunan border after unsuccessful uprisings in the large cities of Changsha and Nanchang (Lötveit 1973). Often referred to as the "Jiangxi Soviet," the CSR government set about establishing a distinctive legal order that formed the basis for much of what emerged after 1949 (Mühlhahn 2009: 159, 162). Specifically, it passed a number of important laws during its brief existence, including a law on counter-revolutionary crimes, a constitution in draft outline form, a law on organizing political power, a general criminal law, a land law, a labor law, and a marriage law (吉安法院志 2002: 149). More than 70 percent of criminal prosecutions in the CSR, at least during one two-month period in 1932 for which comprehensive data are available, were for counter-revolutionary crimes (江西省志 1996: 94). Of the remainder, a high percentage involved official corruption by CSR officials or agencies (吉安法院志 2002: 151). Civil cases appear to have focused heavily on land disputes and family issues, with the latter interestingly being more widely adjudicated and developed as an area of law than the former (吉安法院志 2002: 243–4).

Despite the heavy emphasis on counter-revolutionary crimes, the identification of class enemies, and the rooting out of corruption, a viable system of criminal adjudication did grow up around the prosecution of thefts and malfeasance, even if the number of cases tried each year was far smaller than after 1949. Indeed, from as early as May 9, 1931, a basic criminal law was promulgated, defining at least thirty-six offenses (江西省志 1996: 96). Corruption cases were elaborated in a new regulation (order, 训令, number 12) issued on December 15, 1933 – cases involving the theft of more than 500 yuan were punishable by death, those involving sums of 300–500 by between two and five years in prison, those involving 100–300 by six months to two years in prison, and those involving less than 100 by a maximum of six months' forced labor (江西省志 1996: 96). Cases (at least those involving serious crimes or corruption) were then adjudicated according to these principles.

For example, in one case, a shopkeeper conspired with five others in his food shop to murder a woman who had resisted his attempted rape. He did kill her on August 13, 1932, for which he was tried and sentenced to death (江西省志 1996: 96). In another case, the chief accountant of the Ruijin County finance bureau was found to have embezzled more than 2000 yuan through various means in 1934. After conviction and a special review by the temporary government (临时中央政府人民委员会), his death sentence was carried out by firing squad (江西省志 1996: 97). A rudimentary system of judicial supervision, and for the appeal and review of incorrect cases (错案) by higher authorities (including the Temporary Supreme Court, 临时最高法庭), even evolved over the course of 1932 and 1933 (江西省志 1996: 97–8).

After the Long March interrupted the CCP's legal construction project, the Party leadership set about refining its institutions of social control and adjudication in the Yan'an Base Area (YBA, 延安基地区, or, more broadly, the so-called Shaan-Gan-Ning Border Area – 陕甘宁边区 – both hereafter collectively referred to as the YBA) after about 1938. Some of the laws passed in the CSR came in for criticism, especially the labor law (张 & 孙 2011) and the laws and regulations governing counter-revolutionary crimes and criminal law more generally (Dutton 2005). Though a softer or more moderate line was taken in defining the Party's goals, the adjudication and enforcement process was rationalized and intensified. Specifically, the so-called rectification campaigns sharpened the coercive dynamic underlying this move to impose a new set of political structures and social values (Mühlhahn 2009: 165–7). Despite hardening lines, however, regularization of legal institutions and processes advanced rapidly, both in the handling of "enemies" and counter-revolutionaries and in the adjudication of more routine disputes (Dutton 2005: Chapter 2).

Looking in more detail, we see that the legal institutional development process begun in the CSR did not simply continue at a steady pace, but actually shifted into a higher gear (杨 & 方 1987). While headquartered in Yan'an, the CCP issued new laws and regulations governing the base areas that covered important areas of criminal law, land tenure rights and redistribution, marriage and family, and criminal and civil procedure (韩 1995: Vol. 1, 9–13). Most of these new provisions were enacted between 1942 and 1947, such that a set of at least proto-institutions and rudimentary rules and procedures existed and could later be applied more or less "off the shelf" by local authorities upon the CCP takeover in 1949.

While the CCP was busy struggling to establish workable rules and institutions in its mountainous base areas, the Nationalist (GMD) government was left to assemble codes from what remained of the Qing Codex and the early Republican attempts at revision. On the criminal side, the Empress Dowager (慈禧), stunned by the events of the Boxer Rebellion and still sheltering in Xi'an, had called upon the bureaucracy in 1900 to suggest criminal law reforms, in answer to which a group of provincial officials and military leaders, spearheaded by none other than Yuan Shikai (袁世凯, who was to assume power after the 1911 Revolution), put forward a progressive official, Shen Jiaben (沈家本) to design a new legal order (Meijer 1967: 9–10). Shen's proposed new code and procedures drew upon the European Civil Law tradition and then-current Japanese law, as well as his own ideas, but few changes were implemented, as his backers fell into disfavor until Sun Zhongshan (孙中山, or Sun Yat-sen) pushed through the new code in its entirety after the 1911 Revolution (even though his government was powerless to enforce it) (Meijer 1967: 101, 119). Reforms on the civil side followed a similar trajectory, with comprehensive changes enacted after the Revolution, to be implemented fully only after the mid-1920s.

The GMD also inherited the legacy courts of the Imperial system and grappled with the task of transforming these into a "modern" judiciary worthy of the republic it was struggling to establish. The Imperial Qing Law on Organizing Courts, adopted in 1910 (on the eve of the Republican Revolution in 1911), provided for the establishment of China's first stand-alone judicial institutions in a now-familiar "four-level courts, three-level trials" framework, which was at least partially implemented by 1912 (Xu 2008: 41–3).

Under the 1910 law, courts of the first instance were to be established in every county, with district courts in every prefecture, high courts in each province and a Supreme Court in the capital. Trials were to be heard first in either district courts or courts of the first instance and then could be appealed twice, up to either the high court or the Supreme Court. By 1914, however, Yuan Shikai's republican government had decided to dismantle courts of the first instance due to lack of funds, and to focus on courts at the district level and above, returning the day-to-day administration of justice at the grassroots to county magistrates and local government offices (Xu 2008: 63–5). Even in some key urban areas, this relative vacuum of formal institutions allowed informal structures of power and authority, including secret societies and criminal syndicates, to play important roles in everyday justice and social order (Martin 1996).

Once in power across most of the country, the GMD government under Chiang Kai-shek (蒋介石, Jiang Jieshi) set about trying to institutionalize the legal system and formalize its workings more fully. In 1927 and 1928 the GMD government enacted laws and regulations defining counter-revolutionary crimes and on the punishment of "local bullies and evil gentry" (Xu 2008: 92–6), which indubitably served as something of a model for the similar laws passed by the CCP in the CSR a few years later. Finally, in 1932, the GMD enacted its own Law on Organizing Courts, which abandoned the four-level courts principle, merging courts of the first instance and district courts, while maintaining the goal of establishing a court in every county (Xu 2008: 101). Of course, most counties were never able to establish courts, even in wealthy areas such as Zhejiang and Jiangsu, and the administration of justice at the lowest levels remained in the hands of county magistrates (Xu 2008: 101–2). At the same time, the government pressed for greater regularization and formalization of procedures, especially in urban courts, with mixed results (蒋 2011). Most efforts to build or reform judicial institutions seem to have stalled with the Japanese invasion and occupation of most GMD controlled areas in 1937, to be taken up anew by the CCP after the conclusion of World War II and the Chinese Civil War.

Yet another source influenced efforts at building a modern Chinese legal system in the pre-1949 period: foreign law. This was codified and practiced in the concessions – most comprehensively and systematically in Shanghai's International Settlement. Even though temporary courts had existed there long before, on April 1, 1930, a formal district court was established for the International Settlement (technically a basic-level court in the Jiangsu Province system), which the GMD government had hoped it might one day incorporate into its legal system, and by so doing force it to apply Chinese law (姚 2011:

70–1). Ultimately, on the near-eve of the Communist takeover, none other than the great Roscoe Pound, visiting Nanjing in 1948, was sufficiently confident that coherent and functional institutions of legislation and adjudication were in place under the GMD government that he focused almost exclusive attention on calling for the greater development of indigenous Chinese doctrines of judicial interpretation and legal philosophy in light of the GMD Constitution and law codes, as well as in accordance with Sun Zhongshan's Three People's Principles (三民主义) (Pound 1948).

CHINESE COURTS AND LEGAL INSTITUTIONS, 1949–1978

After the CCP victory, China's mobilizational legal regime was active mainly in the area of criminal law. Mao claimed charismatic authority until the end of his life (after which Hua Guofeng tried at least briefly to take up his mantle), while other sundry contenders entered and left the political stage. Courts and legal processes were tools of political mobilization and arenas of struggle and conflict.

Once in power after 1949, the CCP set about establishing or rebuilding rural courts and reconstituting urban ones. The preferred means to accomplish both tasks was the mass campaign (Bennett 1976). Yet, before the campaigns began, we can observe a surprising degree of continuity in the court system, especially in urban areas, by looking at individual cases that ran directly up to or straddled the CCP takeover in 1949. I was able to track down records of four such criminal cases in the Sichuan Provincial Archives in Chengdu when I visited in Summer 2013 (for more on the character and utility of such case records, see Ma 2015: 20–30). In the first such Case (SC.1949.1), a relative of a Mr. Luo Huangmin was beaten to death in Pi Xian (郫县) county town just outside Chengdu on March 25, 1949. The court in Pi Xian tasked its investigation office (郫县地方法院检察处) to look into the matter, but decided not to prosecute the two prime suspects. Mr. Luo petitioned the Sichuan Higher-Level Court to review the case and correct the injustice. In response, the Pi Xian court sent a letter to the Higher-Level court on May 10, 1949, explaining the complex circumstances of the fight in a tea house where Luo's relative had died, as well as the social relationships and interactions of the parties involved. It concluded that there was insufficient evidence to prosecute due to unclear witness testimony and incomplete records of what had actually occurred. The High Court agreed with this conclusion, but changed the legal reasoning slightly, in a decision issued to Luo on June 11, 1949. The degree to which this case followed basic procedures and norms of the GMD system, and the similarities it bears to many cases discussed in Chapter 3 from the post-1949 period are remarkable, as is the fact that the courts at both the county and provincial levels were operating so smoothly, even as the government was in its final months.

The murder trial and sentencing of the Chengdu merchant Liu Guoyu (who shot and killed a woman he had had a dispute with), which resulted in his being convicted and sentenced to five years in prison after he had confessed in the face of physical evidence (including bullets) and witness testimony describing the victim screaming and fighting with her assailant, shows similar continuities (Case SC.1949.2). The Provincial High Court again took up the case on appeal and upheld the lower court's decision, with Liu starting his sentence on May 9, 1949. Similarly, the open-and-shut case of drug dealer Han Zhangmin (Case SC.1949.3) – whose client had killed another person after having smoked his product – was tried in Peng County (彭县, now called 彭州, also just outside Chengdu) and evaluated on appeal through a by-the-book process in July and August 1949, painting a picture of local and high courts operating pretty much as normal as the GMD regime was collapsing.

Finally, the long-running case of the young Mr. Zai (Case SC.1949.4), convicted of murder in Guanghan (广汉) in eastern Sichuan in 1946, shows how the GMD courts all the way up and down the hierarchy kept operating to the very last. The twists and turns of the appellate process began in 1946, after Zai was originally convicted in Guanghan. He appealed this decision and on October 25, 1946, the Sichuan High Court asked the Guanghan court formally to send a prosecutor to Chengdu to handle the case. Then, on November 16, the High Court delayed the case until February 1947, citing the complex nature of the facts and a desire to give the defendant time to prepare. After a prosecutor was again summoned from Guanghan on January 9, the defendant asked for the case to be delayed on January 16 because he was ill. He then received another six-month delay (also to recover from his illness) from March to September 1947, at which point the high court overruled the Guanghan court and acquitted Zai of all charges due to what it said were gaps in the physical evidence and flaws in the prosecution's reasoning. Finally, the prosecutor appealed to the Supreme Court branch in Chongqing (最高法院重庆分庭) in late October 1947. The Supreme Court formally rejected the appeal on April 23, 1949, and issued a decision to the prosecutor on August 9. In the end, the Sichuan High Court recorded the decision and closed the file on the case on October 3, 1949 – two days after Mao had ascended to the rostrum in Tiananmen to proclaim the founding of the People's Republic of China (PRC).

One case file from 1947 (Case SC.1947.1) provides a good illustration of rural justice being administered by administrative agencies in lieu of proper courts, even under GMD rule. The Justice Office (司法庭) in Danba County (丹巴县), a relatively remote, mountainous, largely ethnic Tibetan area in western Sichuan, had to make do with limited resources and personnel in trying Mr. Wang for what it termed "theft banditry" (盗匪) in June 1947. After being convicted, Mr. Wang appealed to the Sichuan High Court in Chengdu, which rejected his case on the basis of his appeal failing to meet standards for redress. But the important point is that even several years before the CCP rose to power, we can see justice sections or offices dispensing criminal justice for "banditry" across more isolated rural areas (a pattern that will be discussed at length in Chapter 3). Over all, the lack of a sharp break in the legal system's everyday work in 1949 is worthy of note, even as we focus on the important macro-level transition that did indeed occur.

Land Reform (1950–2), the Campaign to Suppress Counter-Revolutionaries (1950–2) and the Three-Anti (1951) and Five-Anti (1952) Campaigns all pumped resources and breathed life into moribund or defunct rural courts, while simultaneously shaking up urban courts and purging many GMD holdovers from their personnel ranks (韩 1995: Vol. 1, 218–21; Hurst 2011: 80). In 1954, China ratified its first post-revolutionary constitution (Tiffert 2009) – Chapter 2, Section 6 of which outlines the role and structure of the court system – and shortly thereafter enacted The Organic Law of the People's Courts of the PRC, establishing the court structure we know today: basic level courts (基层法院) in every county or urban district, intermediate courts (中级法院) in every prefecture or city, high courts (高级法院) for every province, and the Supreme People's Court (最高人民法院) at the top of the system in Beijing.

The vast majority of cases – both civil and criminal – should be initiated at the basic level, with one appellate hearing possible at the intermediate level (though this principle was not fully enshrined or respected until after 1979). Certain cases involving foreigners, high-ranking officials, key state-owned firms, or especially complicated issues or serious crimes may be initiated at the intermediate level (though this too was made much clearer and has been much more consistently adhered to since 1979), with an appellate hearing possible at the high (i.e. provincial) level. The Supreme People's Court was to play the primary role of a court of final appeal in cases with national implications, as well as to set guidance over the legal system generally. It was not meant to function as a constitutional court or locus of judicial review in any manner familiar in a Common Law context.

In a system that persists today, within each court, civil and criminal divisions hear cases of each type and most cases are heard by panels of three judges (合议庭). On each panel, a presiding judge (审判长) oversees the procedure of the trial, while a "principal adjudicating judge" (主审法官) (who may or may not be the same person as the presiding judge) is responsible for managing the panel's internal deliberations, drafting the decision document (判决书), and answering for the outcome and reasoning should there be an appeal or "supervision" (监督) (for more on the supervision system for civil cases, which also permits procurators to challenge civil verdicts, under a system called 民事抗诉, see 应新龙课题组 2011). Also within the court, an adjudication committee (审判委员会) is empowered to take charge of the process in any given case and oversees the work of the court's judges in general. Court staffing (including the appointment of court leaders) is overseen at each level by the CCP's political and legal affairs committee (政法委 – a subcommittee of the CCP Party Committee), while court finances are allocated by the corresponding fiscal authorities of the local government (财政局 / 厅 / 部).

The new regime lagged in drafting a full criminal code, which was not published until 1979 (Chen 2013: 3–4). A civil code did not follow until 1986, after an even more contorted series of abortive drafting attempts (Chen 1995: 35–48), although the Republican Code had been abolished officially from 1949 (though many elements and ideas remained important by convention) (Chen 1995 33–4). Overall, though, public law – and especially criminal law – was privileged over private or civil law (excepting family law) in early attempts to replace the GMD framework with something new. In this endeavor, the CCP built upon the foundations it had laid in the CSR and YBA, but it also sought conscientiously to import much of the Soviet legal system from the USSR. Indeed, top Chinese universities sent large cohorts of students to study in the Soviet Union during the early 1950s, some also invited Soviet faculty to lecture in China, even as numerous criminal law documents and academic studies were translated from Russian into Chinese and widely distributed (陈 2009: 13–17).

The development of many institutions and practices that became hallmarks of the PRC legal system was also influenced by study of the Soviet Union in the early 1950s (陈 2009: 70–3). Leonid Gudoshnikov, a prominent Soviet scholar, published a book on Chinese law and courts in 1957 that praised the CCP's studious application of what he saw as good socialist legal principles and practices (Gudoshnikov 1959). Among other things, he noted that land reform and campaign politics had both transformed society and strengthened the institutions of law and justice during the first seven or eight years of Communist rule (Gudoshnikov 1959: 82–119). Other Soviet analysts seem to have taken similarly laudatory positions (Berman 1970: 318).

By 1957, the outlines of a new equilibrium had begun to emerge, both in criminal law and other key areas such as family law (Diamant 2001). Law was politicized, to be sure, both on a consistent basis and in a heightened way during mass campaigns, but the basic functions of courts had begun to stabilize. Moreover, there was some degree of convergence and homogenization between city and countryside (Diamant 2001). Criminal law was still prioritized over civil dispute resolution, with the exception of family law. Contracts and agreements between state firms, government agencies, and other economic entities were overseen and regulated by bureaus of notaries, but minimal efforts were made to create robust or enduring judicial institutions or legal mechanisms for dispute resolution (Lubman 1970).

The campaigns of the early and middle 1950s, especially the Campaign to Suppress Counter-Revolutionaries and the Campaign against Waste, helped invigorate new courts and institutions in the countryside, while the Three-Anti and Five-Anti campaigns brought a degree of politicization to urban courts' work that disrupted their earlier quotidian (Hurst 2011). The Anti-Rightist Campaign of 1957, however, had a much more dramatic impact in cities and set the tone for the Great Leap Forward (GLF) that was to follow (Hurst 2011: 80–1; 韩 1995: Vol. 1, 515–21). Indeed, it was in 1957 that Soviet commentators began to show a certain "impatience" with the slow pace of codification of Chinese criminal law. By the mid-1960s, they had arrived at a consensus that China had all but turned its back on any path leading to socialist legal development (Berman 1970: 319–22).

Incipient mechanisms and rules for civil law and contract adjudication, too, were perceived to have fallen even further down the agenda by 1958 and to have been prioritized less and less during the 1960s (Lubman 1970: 248–55).

The GLF threw this new order back into crisis in 1958. During the GLF years (roughly 1957–62), all institutions became politicized. Courts and police focused heavily on the prosecution of counter-revolutionary crimes and much ordinary business was pushed to one side. Most strikingly, a significant spike in social and political violence marked a sharp contrast from the creeping institution-building of the early and mid-1950s. As Chinese politics generally descended into severe crisis, the legal system continued to function but followed suit in being wracked with conflict and politicizing the law, in a way that ironically brought urban and rural justice systems together (Hurst 2011: 82–6).

Courts and other legal institutions in the aftermath of the GLF scrambled to regain the incipient equilibrium achieved in the mid-1950s. Commissions were established to review excessive or wrongful prosecutions (see, e.g., 人民司法社论 1962; 最高人民法院 1962; as well as the several more substantive articles that follow both of these in special journal sections), as well as to reconstitute court, procuratorial, and police personnel rosters that had been decimated by the turmoil. Across many rural areas, a very high percentage of political convictions and sentences were revised or overturned, even posthumously (Hurst 2011: 83). Urban areas, however, continued to be plagued by renewed campaigns (the Four Cleanups and "New Five-Antis") that prevented significant steps toward re-establishing a trajectory toward equilibrium (Hurst 2011: 85).

These short-lived efforts were cut off in the summer of 1966 with the start of the Great Proletarian Cultural Revolution (CR) (for details of national-level attacks on the legal system and great purges within it between 1967 and 1970, see 韩 1995: Vol. 2, 610–15). Many scholars and politicians, both inside and outside China, mistakenly assert that the legal system completely ceased functioning from 1966–78 (e.g. Liu & Halliday 2016: 20–1). In fact, courts and other institutions remained in operation and were disrupted less severely than they had been during the GLF. Yet any trend toward regularization across the board was indubitably interrupted (韩 1995: Vol. 2, 589–90), especially in courts that saw their formal caseloads decrease markedly (e.g. 韩 1995: Vol. 2, 664–7). Rural areas continued to see greater institutionalization during the CR years, but urban institutions were severely impacted and any moves toward reducing political intervention into the adjudication process were reversed in both contexts.

Only after Mao's death in 1976, and the solidification of a stable hierarchy within the polity in the wake of Hua Guofeng's decisive move against the "Gang of Four" less than a month later, was there any chance to adjust the underlying dynamics of the legal system. In fact, even after Deng Xiaoping had outmaneuvered Hua to take power in late 1978, legal reform was far from his mind. This changed quickly, however, as those around him came to see legal system reform and development as essential to their broader agenda.

The Maoist Era Chinese polity was a coalition of those social groups and leadership factions empowered at any given moment, along with Mao Zedong himself. There were some who were explicitly excluded, such as leaders out of favor and social groups like former landlords and capitalists, along with certain categories of intellectuals and professionals (e.g. "rightists"). This polity presided over a set of institutions that were, paradoxically, powerful and coherent while also extremely unstable. These actors and institutions were not shy – in fact they almost felt compelled by the logic of political conflict – to intervene directly into the adjudication of individual cases in all levels of courts. In basic-level courts, which focused heavily on criminal trials rather than civil dispute resolution, this meant that individuals from empowered groups faced a different sort of justice than individuals from disfavored groups or backgrounds accused of the same crimes. It also meant that the process of adjudication differed substantially from one time period to the next, as the makeup of the polity shifted, as well as even from case to case, as one influential actor or another temporarily gained the upper hand. Courts and the legal process were both products of mobilizational political contestation and important tools in the shaping of political outcomes in many social contexts.

THE CHINESE LEGAL SYSTEM, 1979–2001

Over the first two decades of the Reform Era, the coalition forged by Deng Xiaoping in the late 1970s was ensconced as a stable ruling elite. This elite was seldom leery of intervening directly in the criminal adjudication process when it deemed it necessary to ensure political survival or social control. But it also prioritized the construction of market institutions that required authorities to demonstrate a general pattern of nonintervention into formally rational civil adjudication processes (especially as related to contracts or commercial law), creating a new hybrid legal regime.

Once Chinese politics had stabilized more generally after the purge of the Gang of Four and the return and rise to power of Deng Xiaoping by December 1978, reform of the legal system quickly became a top priority. In 1979, a new Criminal Procedure Law was enacted, followed by a Civil Procedure Law in 1986 and an Administrative Litigation Law in 1989. Also during the 1980s, important legislation on contracts, bankruptcy, and defining (or refining the definitions of) key concepts and aspects of both criminal and civil law came into effect. The 1986 General Principles of Civil Procedure for the first time established a civil procedure law in the People's Republic, defining such ideas as "legal personhood" and spelling out, albeit in rudimentary terms, what sorts of organizations or entities could be considered legal persons and what this meant for their dealings in the civil law arena (Chen 1995: 90, 94–100). Incipient reforms in the direction of expanding the influence of civil law and making the criminal process less political came to an abrupt halt in 1989.

Indeed, after the wave of student protests culminating that spring was violently repressed in June 1989, the reform project as a whole was placed into suspended animation for several years. A campaign of prosecutions for counter-revolutionary crimes – the first on such a scale since at least the Socialist Education Campaign of the early 1960s – quelled any discussion of meaningful liberalization of criminal law. Civil law, meanwhile, did not develop nearly as quickly as it had begun to during the late 1980s, due to the generally stagnant economy and often retrograde direction of market reforms. If the planned economy was indeed re-ascendant, in other words, what was the use of redefining economic or "commodity" social relationships in law? Very little headway was made during these few years, even in resolving debates over whether civil and "economic" law should be separate, and whether there could ever be such a concept as "private law" in a Chinese context (Chen 1995: chapter 7).

After several decades of crises too frequent to allow a new order to take hold, the institutional foundations of a new equilibrium were well-established by just before Deng's Southern Tour. Following this landmark trip in the Spring of 1992 by China's nominally retired paramount leader to economic centers in the country's Southeast, the general trajectory of market reform was settled. The legal order based on the new laws of the 1980s was free to take hold. An easing of the campaign politics that had dominated much of criminal adjudication during the 1980s (particularly through the "strike hard" movements that I discuss in Chapter 5) also helped further stabilize the political situation, a stabilization reflected in the conduct of legal processes and the establishment of norms in the legal system. A substantial revision and clarification of the Criminal Procedure Law in 1996 also helped cement this trend. Yet, criminal and civil law remained on fundamentally different paths, toward the edification of neotraditional and rule by law legal regimes, respectively, despite a superficial appearance of possible convergence.

Throughout the 1990s, many areas of civil law were expanded and clarified, and adjudication was made more transparent. This pertained to corporations and corporate governance, property rights and ownership, commercial transactions, product liability, contracts, and torts. Some of this new legislation was enacted in the run-up to China's negotiations and eventual entry into the World Trade Organization in 2001, but much of it was debated and proposed as early as the 1980s, following earlier landmark reforms. Commercial law, especially as it related to the private sector or foreign firms, was one of the first areas to experience significant reform. Law relating to labor contracts, state firms, and property rights was overhauled more slowly. Adjudication and implementation were also made more transparent and predictable, first in larger cities and coastal areas, and only later in rural and inland localities, where varieties of "local protectionism" remained important barriers for far longer (Wedeman 2003). But the general direction of change was toward a more predictable, efficient, and transparent system with rapidly decreasing intervention or interference in the adjudication process by nonlegal actors.

The criminal apparatus did not enjoy such focused or efficacious change, at least not in the direction of removing extra-legal actors from the adjudication process. China's Criminal Procedure Law was overhauled in 1996, instituting a new trial process (one that gave far more initiative to the procurator, rather than the presiding judge, and which in some ways at least made it easier for the accused to defend him or herself). Importantly, this revision was also intended to limit the role of the adjudication committee (审判委员会, a committee within every Chinese court that has explicit authority to intervene in all aspects of adjudication by the three-judge panel) and enhance the independence of judges (Chen 2013: 90). The Criminal Code was revised a year later, more clearly classifying crimes into different varieties and spelling out elements that would need to be proven for conviction. This update also essentially removed counter-revolutionary crimes from the list of offenses for which one could be prosecuted.

After Deng Xiaoping's rise to power, political stability and economic development were prioritized above all else. The Reform Era polity was composed of a relatively much more stable coalition of developmentally minded cadres, technocrats, and newly emergent business elites and entrepreneurs. This coalition has remained remarkably durable, even to the present day. Specifically excluded from the polity have been workers, leftists, and intellectuals and professionals vocal in their desire for a more liberal or democratic political order. During this same period, state and other institutions were set on a much more stable footing, in line with the general goals of restoring state capacity and preserving social order. Finally, as market-oriented economic development was a top priority, a legal apparatus capable of predictable tripartite dispute resolution was also highly desirable, at least for handling commercial and contract cases. The polity thus increasingly constrained its own intervention into specific civil cases.

When it came to criminal prosecutions, however, the stable authoritarian polity emphasized social control above all else and continued to intervene at least as deeply and frequently into individual cases as had been the norm during the Maoist Era, despite significant reforms to the laws on the books. In basic-level courts, more and more civil disputes were adjudicated without outside intervention and in predictable ways, even as criminal trials remained subject to pervasive and determinative intervention. Market players could compete in a relatively equitable and transparent arena, despite criminal defendants having to consider their political status and the interests of powerful extra-legal actors when contemplating their fate. Law and the legal order were essential to China's successful construction of a market economy, but also played a vital role in the maintenance of its particular – increasingly regimented – authoritarian political stability and social control.

CHINA'S LEGAL SYSTEM SINCE 2002

China in the new Millennium has generally continued the patterns of law and politics observed in the earlier Reform years. The same basic coalition has remained in power and, if anything, increasing state capacity and preemptive repression have combined with China's deepening integration into the world economy to reinforce the further development of its hybrid legal regime, with neotraditionalism steadfast in criminal law and rule by law taking deeper root in civil law.

With China's arrival onto the world stage and ongoing internal social tensions, the Party's leaders perceived that law must be made to serve several relatively new functions. First, in commercial and civil law, China faced new pressure to conform to international norms and the expectations of foreign corporations and governments. This was especially true in areas such as intellectual property protection and contracts. Second, alleged excesses of criminal law had to be reined in if the CCP was to reduce negative attention from abroad. The same impetus was at least partially behind moves to bolster areas of law and regulation such as environmental protection. Third, the rights of aggrieved social groups – e.g. workers and farmers – had to be protected more thoroughly (at least on paper) in order to ward off social upheaval, but in a manner that did not challenge the fundamental power of the Party or state.

The solution was to tighten oversight of lower courts and judges, allow for more appeals in cases of serious crimes or severe sentences, and *increase* the degree to which those responsible for criminal adjudication were subject to intervention from court leaders, adjudication committees, and the political and legal affairs committees of the CCP (政法委) at corresponding levels (Zhu 2010; Li 2016b). All the while, adjudication of civil disputes continued to become less and less politicized and more and more technocratic and transparent. In this spirit, the Criminal Procedure Law was revised once again in 2012, in an effort to make less likely the mishandling of cases in ways that damaged social stability. This was ensured through both greater respect for the openness of the process and the basic rights of the accused and through the clearer definition of categories of cases subject to nonlegal intervention and the mechanisms through which such intervention could take place. It aimed to make a neotraditional legal regime a bit less capricious, but also more effective and forceful in the defense of entrenched authority.

Meanwhile, civil law has become increasingly complex and comprehensive, moving much closer to becoming a transparent system for technocratic dispute resolution, even as judges become ever more wary of actually making any decisions and more and more cases are shunted toward mediated settlements (Minzner 2011). A specific law on torts and liability was passed in 2009 and came into effect in 2010, further clarifying the way in which a wide variety of civil cases ought to be handled. Special courts and agencies have been established, which can often work together to rein in those who continue to exploit loopholes and gaps in the regulatory framework of China's market economy (Mertha 2005). As more suits are filed over issues like labor rights and benefits, product safety, trademarks and patents, and even simple contracts and commercial transactions – and especially as these suits have come to be decided in more predictable, consistent, and transparent ways – the overall civil law system has moved substantially to deepen its rule by law regime.

Further revisions to various statutes have been important, but the overall trajectories of both civil and criminal law reform have been relatively fixed since the end of the 1990s. Indeed, all four five-year plans for legal reform promoted by the Supreme People's Court (1999–2003, 2004–8, 2009–13, and 2014–18) have reinforced the basic dynamics of civil law moving toward a rule by law regime and criminal law remaining a neotraditional regime. Without deep, structural change to the criminal system it is hard to envision how it could function without the strong influence of nonlegal state actors in the adjudication process (as shall be discussed more fully in Chapter 5). Similarly, the reinsertion of political interference into the civil adjudication process could endanger economic growth and institutional development; yet only a fundamental reordering of the polity could push the system from a rule by law toward a rational pluralist regime (as will be discussed in Chapter 4).

The main differences between the post-2002 order and the earlier Reform period have been of degree rather than kind. Oligarchs and magnates have replaced smaller-scale entrepreneurs in the polity, while technocrats no longer stand out among CCP cadres, and leftists have almost completely exited the stage. Meanwhile, ongoing legal reforms have made further strides in codifying the polity's self-restraint from intervention in civil cases, while advancing technology and the practice of "stability maintenance" has made politicized social control an easier-to-achieve outcome in the administration of criminal justice. China's legal regime remains intimately bound up with its evolving model of economic development, tightening social control, and authoritarian political durability.

THE DEVELOPMENT OF THE INDONESIAN LEGAL SYSTEM UNDER THE DUTCH

The construction of a legal system was not a top priority for the VOC as it extended its rule over Indonesia in the seventeenth century. Indeed, before about 1650, the company acted more as adventurer than sovereign, launching trade missions without any confidence in a secure long-term political position in Southeast Asia (Ball 1982: 4–6). It was only in 1619 that Batavia (now Jakarta) was established as the official *rendezvous* of the VOC in Southeast Asia, after the victory of Jan Pieterszoon Coen, who had been regent in Banten (near the northwest corner of Java), in a complex series of disputes and battles (Gaastra 2003: 40–3). Only after such a base had been established – by necessity close to the Straits of Sunda and Malacca – could the VOC contemplate broader colonial ambitions in the region. After the Dutch capture of Malacca and the signing of the Treaty of The Hague with Portugal in 1641, the VOC's lasting influence throughout the archipelago began to expand in earnest. Between 1650 and 1750, the VOC extended its administration over many areas of Java and Madura, as well as other enclaves in other parts of the archipelago – especially in Sulawesi and Maluku.

The earliest formal judicial institution of colonial legal governance was the Council of Justice (*Raad van Justitie*), established in 1642 under the Statutes of Batavia, the first codification of colonial law for the archipelago (Ball 1982: 17–18, 31–2). Though the statutes were meant to apply to "natives" (*inlanders*), "foreign orientals" (*vreemde oosterlingen*), and Europeans alike, there were some stipulations and exceptions made for cases in which Chinese (referred to here as *Chineezen* rather than *vreemde oosterlingen*) or natives would be held to more stringent standards than Europeans (De Bussy 1918: 14). Despite the general applicability of the Statutes *de jure*, in practice the *Raad* focused its jurisdiction over cases directly affecting the VOC, in which at least one of the parties was a company employee, and as an appellate court for other serious cases. A significantly less formal venue, the Court of Alderman (*Schepenbank*) was established in 1620 and had jurisdiction to settle disputes (and later criminal cases) involving non-Dutch (especially Chinese) foreigners, Dutch citizens not employed by the VOC, and local residents (Ball 1982: 21–2).

Both the *Raad* and the *Schepenbank* were limited in their jurisdiction to Batavia and immediately surrounding territories. Even within the capital, though the Statutes of Batavia were revised and thoroughly updated in 1766 (Ball 1982: 33–5), institutional development was slow prior to the nineteenth century. Beyond the capital, the administration of justice remained the responsibility of local kingdoms (e.g. Mataram), regency chiefs (*bupati*) or – especially in larger cities like Surabaya, Semarang, or Makassar – of VOC-appointed governors, with much less formal institutionalization (sometimes through semi-formal traditional venues), until local government courts (*Landraden*) were established in core areas in 1747 (Ball 1982: 57; Lutiko 2013: 27). More far-flung areas had no such institutions, however, even if they were nominally under VOC control, and the *Landraden* functioned unevenly (at best) where they did exist.

By as early as 1690, the financial position of the VOC in Batavia had eroded to the extent that over the following ninety-year period it came to rely very heavily on subsidies and payments from Amsterdam to sustain its trading capital, though even with these net losses nonetheless eventually mounted substantially (Gaastra 2003: 129, 132). In fact, some of this problem had even earlier roots, as the VOC's offices in all parts of Indonesia except Sumatra had operated at a loss during decade from 1670–80 (Gaastra 1989: 80–1), and financial exigencies prompted debates among the directors over the payment of dividends during the same span (Gaastra 1989: 114–15). By 1749, the VOC decided to appoint the sovereign (*stadhouder*), King Willem IV, as chief director (*opperbewindhebber*), who nominally stood above the company's erstwhile board, the so-called Gentlemen Seventeen (*Herren XVII*). This was an hereditary position that would pass to his heirs and it tied the state more closely to the company's slowly declining fortunes (Gaastra 2003: 163–4).

With losses mounting, the VOC fell upon a crisis with the start of the Fourth Anglo-Dutch War in 1780, when the company found itself barely able to defend Batavia, often unable to send or receive shipments reliably and safely, and unable to secure either financial or military assistance from the Dutch government (Gaastra 2003: 164–6). Ultimately, the VOC was nationalized, a new "Batavia Republic" was formed, and a twenty-one-member "Committee for the East Indies Trade and Possession" was constituted in December 1795, taking effect on March 1, 1796 (Gaastra 2003: 170). With its formal bankruptcy on January 1, 1800, the rule of the VOC came to an end. Under its rule, the territory under direct or indirect colonial control had expanded greatly, but the legal institutions in place beyond Batavia remained rudimentary at best.

After the bankruptcy and dissolution of the VOC and transfer of colonial sovereignty to the Dutch government on January 1, 1800, a period of instability ensued in both Indonesia and the Netherlands. The following thirty years were marked by the Napoleonic Wars in Europe and French and British colonial interregna in Indonesia from

1806 to 1815, and concluded with the rebellion of Prince Diponegoro and the Dutch victory in the Java War (1825–30). During this period, there was much debate over the course of Indonesian legal development (Lev 2000: 14–15), but relatively little was implemented in terms of either codes or institutions. Once back in control, however, the Dutch colonial government undertook a series of relatively radical economic and institutional reforms, which went hand-in-hand with substantial legal development and codification, aiming to make the colony both economically and politically sustainable.

After reestablishing order, the Governor General, Johannes van den Bosch, instituted what became known as the Cultivation System (*Cultuurstelsel* or *Tanam Paksa*) (Fasseur 1992: 26–32), which required all villages on Java to devote at least 20 percent of their land to the cultivation of commodity crops such as sugar (Fasseur 1992: 86–91; Bosma 2007, 2013: 92–5) and coffee (Breman 2010: 211–27), to be turned over to the government for export, or else compel their inhabitants to labor on government projects or plantations for sixty-six days per year. In addition to its well-documented effects of social disruption across rural Java (Geertz 1963: 62–82), the Cultivation System greatly facilitated the extension of political control and institutions beyond Batavia, up until it was abolished in 1870 (Bosma 2007). This included the reinvigoration of the *Landraden* (Ball 1982: 233–4; Pompe 2005: 29–31).

Key to this was the promulgation of a code of procedure, called the *Indisch Regelment* (sometimes also called the *Inlandsch Regelment*), for cases involving non-Europeans in Java and Madura (Lev 2000: 17–18). The new code was supplemented outside Java by the similar, even more pared-down Outer Islands Legal Regulations, or *Rechtsregelment Buitengewesten* (Lev 2000: 73, fn. 5). A notable feature of the legal system was the persistent division of its jurisdiction among legally defined ethnic groups, with one set of laws and adjudication venues for Europeans, another for "foreign orientals," and a third for "natives" (Hooker 1978: 194–5), distinctions which carried over into civil dispute resolution as well as criminal law.

As one might imagine, civil dispute resolution had – since Grotius and the first conflicts with Portugal – been at least equally, if not more, important to a commercial and extractive colonial venture than questions of crime and punishment. Civil procedure and commercial law were contrastingly slow to develop in Europe, however, having been formalized in more-or-less their contemporary forms only during the Napoleonic Era. In the Netherlands, King Lodewijk Napoleon (younger brother of the French Emperor) began the process in 1809, with comprehensive codes of civil law (*Burgerlijk Wetboek*), civil procedure (*Wetboek van Burgerlijke Rechtsvordering*), and commercial law (*Wetboek van Koophandel*) adopted in October 1838. Very soon thereafter, discussions ensued over how to roll out the new laws in Indonesia and to which populations across the Archipelago they would apply (Brondgeest 1897: 1–7). Eventually, in the culmination of a process that began in the 1840s, a Civil Code (*Burgerlijk Wetboek*) was implemented by the early 1890s that applied differentially to Europeans, Chinese residents, "foreign orientals," Muslims (and among these differentially to those residing in different parts of the Archipelago or coming from different foreign countries), "native Christians" (especially those living in certain Residencies in Sulawesi and Maluku), and other "natives". Essentially, the comprehensive code applied to Europeans and some non-European foreigners, while portions of it could be applied in certain matters involving people from other populations. Outside the formal code, customary law (*gewoonterecht* or *adat*), as well as Islamic (*Shari'a*) law, was to be applied in most cases not involving Europeans or their interests.

By 1900, after key areas of the outer islands (especially Sumatra) had been brought more tightly under colonial government control and Dutch strategy transitioned to the so-called "Ethical Policy" (*Ethische Politiek*), the legal system was also extended and improved at the local level, especially across Java. A new focus was placed on the codification and formalization of indigenous customary law, on providing local citizens with dispute resolution venues, and eventually on the creation, in 1914, of courts of the first instance (*Pengadilan Landgerechts*) for minor criminal matters, operating under a unified legal code applicable to all: European, native, or other (Government Printing 1914; Hooker 1978: 189; Lev 2000: 16). A comprehensive criminal code, known as the *Wetboek van Strafrecht voor Nederlandsch-Indië*, was established by royal decree (No. 33) on October 15, 1915 (De Bussy 1918: 1–6). While this code was meant to apply universally, it is not clear how widely it was implemented either beyond Java or among non-European populations.

Efforts were also made to establish *Landraden* in every regency (*kabupaten*) and, by 1939, there were at least seventy-five operating across Indonesia (twenty-eight of them chaired by Indonesians) (Lev 2000: 16, fn. 4). Alongside this institutional intensification, a serious campaign, influenced by the scholarship of Dutch academics such as Cornelis van

Vollenhoven and his student Barend ter Haar, was launched to catalogue and codify as much customary (*adat*) law as possible from every part of the country, so as to provide more regularized and formalized procedures and rules for its use in adjudication (Hooker 1978: 192–3; Lukito 2013: 25–9). Though neither of these projects was completed before World War II, they did help lay the groundwork for a legal order in which clearly codified law could be applied through consistent and competent institutions across the entire, far-flung Archipelago. Though an extreme version of legal pluralism remained a hallmark, the Dutch colonial order had managed to construct a rough-cut legal system that could serve as a model for postindependence jurists and political leaders, at least in theory, though both codes and institutions would be shaken, divided, and reconfigured under Japan's military occupation.

INDONESIAN LEGAL INSTITUTIONS DURING THE JAPANESE OCCUPATION, 1942–1945

Upon their occupation of Indonesia in 1942, Japanese authorities dismissed most Dutch officials, including judges and prosecutors (Zorab 1954: 49) – often imprisoning them and appointing Indonesians in their place – closed the *Raad van Justitie*, abolished the more complex procedural codes applicable to Europeans and in appellate cases (Zorab 1954: 49–51), and adopted a version of the Native Regulations (which had only just been revised in 1941 and which were known as the *Herziene Indonesisch Regelment* or HIR) as a uniform national code applicable to all (Lev 2000: 73–4). These sweeping reforms were not implemented uniformly across the Archipelago, however, and critical variations across time, place, and area of law helped structure the Indonesian legal system for many years after the war ended.

The Japanese military government divided Indonesia between three commands: one administered by the 16th Army from Batavia for Java and Madura, a second administered by the 25th Army in Singapore for Sumatra (with its headquarters later moving to Bukit Tinggi in West Sumatra), and the third a naval command for all of Eastern Indonesia based in Makassar (Zorab 1954: 5–6; Han 1961: 2). The civil code was not significantly revised or eroded under any of the commands (Zorab 1954: 55), though adjudication and enforcement were obviously hampered during the occupation. In the Java and Madura Command, all laws and structures in place before the occupation were first decreed to remain active as of 1942, while the new authorities focused their efforts on simplifying and unifying legal institutions and preparing a possible new criminal code (Wignjosoebroto 1994: 183).

A new criminal code, known as the *Gunsei Keizirei* (translated from the Japanese by Zorab as *strafwetboek van het militaire bestuur*, or "criminal code of the military administration") was proclaimed on June 1, 1944 (Zorab 1954: 57). This new code applied at least to Java and Madura and, though little appears to be known about exactly what was implemented on the outer islands (Zorab 1954: 9–10; Han 1998: 444), it seems likely that similar moves were made to implement the same code or something similar there (but almost certainly with less impact or enforcement on the ground). The code simplified procedures and created a uniform system of criminal justice applicable to all residents of Indonesia equally, regardless of race, religion, or ethnicity (Zorab 1954: 55–6) – the only exception being Japanese nationals, who were generally exempted from all Indonesian jurisdiction, and required to abide only by the laws of Japan under a general principle of extraterritoriality (Han 1961: 14).[1]

The Japanese occupiers also streamlined the complex and pluralistic Dutch colonial system of legal institutions, creating three levels of courts: unifying lower-level authorities into a revamped version of the *Landraden*, which became courts of the first instance at the regency/*kabupaten* level (that later would come to be called *Pengadilan Negeri*); reopening a new version of the *Raad van Justitie* in every province (which later became known as high courts, or *Pengadilan Tinggi*) and restricting their role to hearing cases appealed after first hearings in courts of the first instance (rather than allowing certain ethnic or national groups direct or exclusive access); and establishing a single national-level court of final appeal for all classes of people and types of cases, which became the Supreme Court (eventually known as the *Makamah Agung*) (Zorab 1954: 49; Lev 2000: 39; Rosadi & Desmon 2012: 58–9, 63–4).

An institutional system almost exactly like that in Indonesia today (Han 1998: 417–18), applicable to all inhabitants universally, was in existence and ready to be taken up more or less "as was" by Sukarno and his new government at independence, at the end of World War II (Wignjosoebroto 1994: 184). Despite this, the ongoing war against the Dutch and the British after 1945, along with the uneven character

[1] For a more detailed discussion of the substance of the Japanese-issued criminal code and its implementation, see: Han (1961: 7–16); Zorab (1954: 56–64).

of social revolution and institutional transformation, prevented any immediate or consistent application of coherent rules or structures across the archipelago until well after the defeat of the Japanese (Kahin 2003; McMillan 2005).

THE INDONESIAN LEGAL SYSTEM IN THE EARLY YEARS OF INDEPENDENCE, 1945–1957

The continued dominance of colonial era elites helped ensure that Indonesia maintained a neotraditional legal regime in the area of civil adjudication during this period, as the powerful intervened freely into the settling of disputes to protect their privileged positions. A lack of state capacity meant that the operation of the criminal apparatus was hampered, concentrating political violence outside the purview of legal institutions.

When Sukarno proclaimed independence on August 17, 1945, he declared that all laws then current in the newly formed Republic of Indonesia would remain valid, unless they contradicted the Constitution or were explicitly replaced by the new government. This meant that the Japanese criminal code (eventually revised somewhat and translated to become the *Kitab Undang-Undang Pidana*) and the court institutions that went along with it were adopted across the areas controlled by the Republic in a process that lasted until 1947, by which point they were in place across most areas of Java (though not in Jakarta), Madura, and Sumatra (Han 1961: 19–27). During the same period, however, in the area of the Archipelago reoccupied by the Dutch (including Jakarta, as well as most of Eastern Indonesia), the pre-War *Wetboek van Strafrecht voor Nederlandsch-Indië* was revised, updated, renamed, and adopted as the law of the land as the *Wetboek van Strafrecht voor Indonesië* (Han 1961; chapter 2). When sovereignty was transferred on December 27, 1949, there were thus two separate criminal codes (with different courts and institutions attached to them) in force across different parts of the country (Han 1961: 1) – while in some localities there was uncertainty and dispute as to which system applied. This inconsistency and division persisted throughout the 1950s, despite attempts by Sukarno and others to rectify the situation.

Rather than inheriting a relatively coherent legal order and tradition like China's, Indonesia was left to grapple with at least three contending legacies – of Dutch colonial law (which was maintained for civil dispute resolution, though the *Burgerlijk Wetboek* was re-branded as the

Kitab Undang-Undang Perdata), traditional or "customary" law (*adat*), and Islamic religious law (*Shari'a*). The Japanese occupation authorities had done much to bequeath a more unified system of rules and structures in criminal law to the new Republic than might otherwise have been the case, but these could not even be rolled out across the whole country (Alisjahbana 1966: 70–7). Older debates among Dutch scholars (such as those between the "Leiden School" and the "Utrecht School" in the nineteenth century) fueled conflict within the Indonesian legal system, even for decades beyond formal independence – to the degree that "the national identity conceived for Indonesians, in the long, hard struggle to disengage from the Netherlands, was informed by ideas more Dutch, in origin, than aboriginal" (Burns 2004: 221). Even after transitioning further away from its Dutch roots, Indonesian law continues to grapple with its legacies (Massier 2008). The legal system today is still subdivided between "Dutch" (*Belanda/Sipil*), customary (*Adat*), and religious (Islamic/*Shari'a*) codes and institutions. Even this, though, is more unified than the myriad systems of law and adjudication that had existed before the Dutch and Japanese created the outlines of a coherent order across the sprawling colony (Lev 1972: 248).

Despite its leaders' best efforts, Sukarno's government during so-called "Liberal Democracy" (1949–58) was never able to consolidate a truly cogent or consistent set of legal institutions or practices. Some blamed the Constitution of 1950, which divided power between a weak executive and a fractious parliament. Others pointed to the inconclusive results of the election of 1955, which brought four disparate main parties (Sukarno's Nationalists, two very different Islamic parties, and the Communist Party) into a relatively evenly divided parliament. But lingering divisions and lack of clarity in the legal system emerging from colonial rule and wartime occupation certainly played a role.

Despite these ongoing struggles, a basic system of courts (that in many ways was inherited from the Japanese at the end of World War II) was put in place and remains in place to this day. Though formalized mostly by Law 14/1970 (to be discussed later in this chapter and in Chapter 5), the outlines of the system were already in general operation long before then. Indeed, Sukarno's new government decided to modify the court system as unified and simplified by the Japanese only slightly, putting in place a basic three-level model in the late 1940s, even before gaining full control of the country's territory (Wignjosoebroto 1994: 191–3).

Courts of the first instance (*pengadilan negeri*) exist at the regency/*kabupaten* level – at first introduced in more densely populated areas only, but since the 1970s across the entire archipelago. All cases are heard first in these courts, which are divided into civil and criminal sections. Cases are heard by panels of three judges (*majelis hakim*), with a presiding judge acting as chair (*ketua*) and as the primary author of and signatory to the decision. A secretary-registrar (*panitera sekretaris*, or *pansek*), who tends to remain permanently appointed to his or her court, oversees the court's judges and staff. Nominally, the *pansek* is accountable to the chair (*ketua*) and deputy chair (*wakil ketua*) of the court, but since these leaders often rotate in and out of individual courts and are frequently focused on trying to move up to higher-level positions, the day-to-day operations are often left to the *pansek*.

Above the courts of the first instance are high courts (*pengadilan tinggi*), which exist in every province, whose sole jurisdiction is over appeals brought after first hearings in the *pengadilan negeri*. The internal structure is similar, but most of the judges (to say nothing of court leaders) have their sights set on promotion, rather than lifetime service. At the apex of the system is the Supreme Court (*Makamah Agung*), which functions as a court of final appeal for all cases, in addition to having some very limited roles in adjudicating constitutional questions (though these were obviated by the creation of the Constitutional Court, the *Makamah Konstitusi*, under Law 24/2003).

Despite their best efforts, however, Indonesia's leaders were not able to achieve the degree of unification they had hoped for in the legal system, in part because so much of the fractious and outmoded colonial legal order remained intact (Lev 1972: 257–8; Wignjosoebroto 1994: 207–8). In the late 1950s, as the Indonesian Republic itself showed signs of breaking apart under the strain of regional rebellions (e.g. Permesta and Darul Islam) and increasingly open and violent conflict between Islamists, the military, and communists, various legal institutions and actors began to grapple for position, influence, status, and access to resources. Thus, courts and judges were pitted against lawyers, who in turn struggled against police and prosecutors, who were so busy fighting each other that they could not unite against courts or lawyers (Lev 1972: 261–71). By 1957, the degree of dysfunction was so deep that it had almost become its own type of perverse stability.

During the Liberal Democracy period, Indonesia's polity was stable but impotent. Sukarno remained at the center in theory, but the circle of politically empowered actors was dominated by holdovers from the pre-Independence order – religious leaders, large landowners (many hereditary nobility or notables), intellectual and professional elites with strong ties to the old colonial system, and a rotating cast of other self-appointed revolutionary or progressive leaders. Smaller players came onto the stage and exited, but the core remained in place, even as this coalition proved unable to govern the country effectively. Institutions, weak under the Dutch and strained by war and occupation, were neither meaningfully reconstituted nor fully revived during most of the 1950s. Attempts to breathe new life into the machinery of the state, as with the 1955 elections, almost invariably disappointed and sometimes led to still greater weakness and instability. The criminal justice system barely functioned and anyone with the capacity to do so routinely intervened into the adjudication of civil disputes. At the basic level, local notables, religious and economic elites, and others who had held sway under the Dutch continued to exercise significant discretion to influence the process and outcomes of cases. Those from weaker social elements were at a decided disadvantage as a neotraditional legal regime helped prop up a creaking yet persistent economic, social, and political hierarchy.

THE INDONESIAN LEGAL SYSTEM THROUGH CRISIS AND TRANSFORMATION, 1957–1974

With the collapse of parliamentary democracy in 1957 and Sukarno's assertion of charismatic authority in 1959, Indonesia entered a mobilizational legal regime. Continued institutional weakness, however, meant that its operation was largely confined to the sphere of civil dispute resolution rather than criminal law. When Suharto supplanted Sukarno's leadership, the cast of leading characters changed but the political drama's basic plot and genre remained unaltered during the early years of New Order, with those claiming power using law as a tool to act against enemies in the absence of competent institutions or stable elites.

The Communist Party of Indonesia (PKI) had become the largest and strongest single force in civilian politics by the time of the regional elections in 1957 (Lev 1966: 9). Meanwhile, the failure of the other major parties (PNI, NU, Masyumi, and others) to form a cabinet (whether under the leadership of Prime Minister Ali Sastroamidjojo, Vice President Muhammad Hatta, or President Sukarno himself), combined with armed rebellions in Eastern and Western Indonesia, led to the declaration of a national state of siege and martial law, even as the parliamentary government collapsed in March 1957 (Lev 1966: 15–16). This elevated the political position of the military as a whole, increased the power of local and regional military commanders throughout the country, and augmented the influence and expanded the leverage of key national military leaders like Major General Abdul Haris Nasution. Both the PKI and the military were upstart actors with very keen interests in securing places in the polity and near the top of its pecking order of power. With the legal system open to political intervention at all levels since before 1945, the fractured and unstable polity allowed a neotraditional regime to give way to a mobilizational one – though one far less predictable or tamed by charismatic authority than its counterpart in China. The political deadlock between the PKI, the military, and the traditional ruling parties proved unsustainable over the intervening years (Singh 1959).

One of the last major pieces of legislation to be passed before Sukarno seized power was Law 73/1958, which sought to unify the criminal law system by invalidating the *Wetboek van Strafrecht voor Indonesië* and declaring the *Kitab Undang-Undang Hukum Pidana* to be in force across the entire country (including Jakarta, all of Sumatra, and Eastern Indonesia) as of September 29, 1958 (Han 1961: 60). Despite problems with the wording and implications of this law, the stage was set for a new critical moment, one in which Indonesia's legal system could be pushed in a new and more unified direction through mobilizational political intervention.

In many ways, the full transition to "Guided Democracy" on July 5, 1959 – when Sukarno unilaterally decreed a return to the Constitution of 1945 and effectively made himself dictator atop a centralized authoritarian order – was intended precisely to engineer a critical juncture, break the institutional stagnation, and put Indonesia on a path toward some sort of equilibrium, albeit an authoritarian and "revolutionary" one driven by the force of Sukarno's charismatic authority. In particular, Law 19/1964 explicitly set aside any idea of separation of powers or judicial independence and afforded Sukarno broad latitude for configuring the institutional structures of the judiciary and interfering in their work (Ikatan Hakim Indonesia 1965; Saragih 2006: 89; Butt 2008: 347).

Yet perhaps the most important substantive legal development during the Guided Democracy period was the passage of the Agrarian Law of 1960 (*Undang-Undang Pokok Agraria*, UU.5.1960), which allowed tenants and farmers much greater scope for advancing claims to land ownership and facilitated adjudication of claims to land not formally titled by the Dutch during the colonial era (Wignjosoebroto 1994: 212–15). Prior to this, the colonial Agrarian Law of 1870 divided all land into the categories of "free" and "unfree." Free land could be appropriated for settlement or by the state. Land that had been cleared and was occupied by indigenous Indonesians was considered "unfree," but was not registered formally and rights over it were governed by customary law (*adat*). Land owned or occupied by Europeans was to be registered formally and governed by the Civil Code (Hooker 1978: 188, 206–7). The 1960 Agrarian Law thus threw open the door to litigation and the reassignment of land tenure rights over land not covered by the formal registration system. This meant most land outside major cities (especially on islands other than Java – with a few exceptions, such as established, formally registered plantations, particularly on Sumatra and Sulawesi) and even some important parcels in urban centers became legally contestable.

At least in theory, dictatorial direction by the revolution's "president for life" (Sukarno was established officially as *presiden seumur hidup* by resolution of the People's Consultative Assembly in 1963) should have helped push the legal system toward greater coherence – in other words, Sukarno at least expected his assumption of such powers to draw the critical juncture to a close and establish a new equilibrium trajectory "for the pressing interests of the Revolution, the dignity of the State and the People, or the interests of society" (Lev 1972: 268). The 1964 Judges Law (*Undang-Undang Pokok Kehakiman*, UU.19.1964) even gave explicit powers to the president to intervene in the adjudication of individual cases (Wignjosoebroto 1994: 229). Instead of coalescing neatly, however, politics under Guided Democracy came to be dominated by a tense and unstable standoff between the military and the PKI. As the PKI developed its own independent military capacity with presidential approval (and allegedly also with assistance from China) and more right-leaning generals took on increasingly important roles within the military hierarchy, a decisive battle appears in retrospect to have been almost inevitable.

Guided Democracy thus proved to be the crisis that provoked change rather than the definitive culmination of such change. A coup d'état (launched by PKI-linked military officers who called themselves the "Movement of the 30th of September," GESTAPU in its Indonesian acronym) and counter-coup (coordinated by officers and troops of the

Strategic Command, KOSTRAD, under General Suharto) during a six-month period of high crisis from September 1965 to March 1966 brought the conservative Suharto to power as leader of the New Order military regime. By forcefully crushing the PKI (killing hundreds of thousands of its members and suspected sympathizers) and elevating the more conservative elements of the armed forces to power, the coup helped break the impasse that had long been festering in Indonesian politics. Once ensconced in control of the state, Suharto and his lieutenants set about trying to cement a coherent and stable legal order such as Indonesia had never before had. A series of landmark laws enacted from 1966 through the mid-1970s helped accomplish this to some extent, even as the political situation remained fluid up until the early 1970s.

First, there came a series of directives (*ketetapan*), issued by the People's Consultative Assembly (*Majelis Permusyawaratan Rakyat*, or MPR) between March of 1966 and late 1968. An early directive (Ketetapan MPRS No. IX/MPRS/1966) gave the force of law to Sukarno's so-called "Letter of the 11th of March" (*Supersemar*), which many have claimed he signed under duress, authorizing Suharto to take any necessary steps to restore political and social order. Subsequent directives disestablished Sukarno as president for life, banned the PKI and the use of Marxism-Leninism as an ideology, stripped Sukarno of his powers as president, legitimized and formalized Suharto's ascent to the office of president, and called upon the new government to hold elections by 1971 (Saragih 2006: 105–6). These directives succeeded in placing a praetorian fig leaf over Suharto's brutal military coup d'état. More importantly, and perhaps without explicit intent, they also helped establish the basis in law for the institutions that more formal legislation was to shape and nourish in the first half of the 1970s.

The first key act was Law Number 14 of 1970, which overturned the Guided Democracy legal order, refined the definition of legal institutions and their roles, and helped pave the way for a significant infusion into courts and prosecutors' offices of new fiscal and personnel resources (Saragih 2006: 111). Article 10 of Law 14, in particular, enshrined the by-then familiar three-level hierarchy of secular courts and delineated the lines of jurisdiction between these and religious courts. Customary *adat* institutions retreated to a limited and supporting role. The Supreme Court (*Makamah Agung*, or MA) was to be both the constitutional court and court of final appeal for all ordinary cases. Below the MA, each province was to have a high court (*pengadilan tinggi*) that would function primarily as an appellate court. Each regency (*kabupaten*) or regency-level city (*kotamadya*) would then have a basic level court of the first instance (*pengadilan negeri*). The law also codified the basic adjudication procedures that, again, had already been in widespread use. The institutional base was thus set, just as the relatively fixed hierarchy of the polity had begun to stabilize. Law and legal institutions in these early years of New Order came to be viewed by the ruling junta as important for promoting national development and as a tool for social control, but decidedly less as a vehicle for the promotion of progressive social change than they had been under Guided Democracy (Wignjosoebroto 1994: 226–34).

During Guided Democracy, Sukarno had asserted himself as a charismatic leader, yet had failed to become ensconced in the role as Mao had. He brought together a coalition of certain military factions, the PKI, his own Nationalist Party, and smaller disparate elements. This polity proved unwieldy, however, due to both internal struggles and its inability fully to exclude other powerful actors who opposed it (including other military factions and religious and landed elites). The Guided Democracy polity governed through institutions that remained inchoate, even as it sought to reshape many of them in important ways. With the criminal justice apparatus still largely ineffectual, civil adjudication became a critical arena for the settling of political scores and the shaping of what Sukarno, the PKI, and others hoped might be a new social order. Land disputes and other cases over substantial capital or property became particular targets of significant intervention for both local and national-level power-holders. In basic courts, this meant a systematic bias in favor of peasants, small business owners, and other elements of "small society" (*rakyat kecil*), as against landowners, capitalists, and old elites. Enforcement was difficult at best, and intervention inconsistent, but the politicization of processes and outcomes was clear.

This same logic held during the years after the coup and countercoup of 1965–6. Suharto came to replace Sukarno, while religious elites (especially from the *Nahdlatul Ulama*, or NU), landowners, capitalists, and right-wing military factions took the places of the PKI, left-leaning militarists, and others within the polity. This new coalition was as weak as the previous one, however, and Indonesian institutions were no stronger in 1966 than they had been in 1957. Suharto unleashed a lethal wave of mass violence against his opponents (real and imagined), but this took place almost entirely outside the legal arena of criminal justice. Civil dispute resolution remained politicized, just as under Guided Democracy, but this time the intervention came from resurgent conservatives, religious and economic elites, and militarists on the right. In basic-level courts, adjudication favored those seeking or supportive of Suharto's restoration of old elites, in both process and outcome. In both highly unstable and critical moments of contemporary Indonesian history, a full-throated but relatively ineffectual mobilizational legal regime was key first to dismantling and replacing the old social order and then to restoring and revamping many parts of it.

THE INDONESIAN LEGAL SYSTEM UNDER NEW ORDER, 1974–1998

Once a ruling elite had solidified around Suharto, this group of empowered actors could set about using the legal system to protect and advance its interests. This meant frequently intervening in the criminal process to repress real or potential regime opponents, as the institutions of state coercion became stronger and more coherent. It also entailed using civil litigation skillfully to preserve rents and other advantages, as well as to capture new economic and social gains.

After elections in July 1971 brought the Suharto-backed Golkar (a political party in all but name that was officially meant to be a sort of corporatist "functional groupings" – the literal meaning of its full name, *Golongan Karya*) to power and stabilized a relatively fixed membership and hierarchy within the Indonesian polity generally, a number of new laws were passed to help solidify the new neotraditional equilibrium in the judicial system and beyond. Most important among these was Law Number 5 of 1974 (UU.5 1974), which spelled out the configuration and proper functioning of central, regional, and local government institutions (Mahfud MD 2009: 268–79). Coupled with this legislative push, New Order also invested vast new resources in the physical infrastructure and human capital of the legal system in an effort to extend its penetration beyond the core urban areas on Java. Projects ranging from schools to airports and highways abounded. Most notable here, however, was the extension of courts, police, and other formal legal institutions to areas of the country – e.g. Papua, parts of Kalimantan and Maluku, etc. – that had previously known none.

Accompanying the extension of institutions and the reinvigoration of human capital investment in the legal system was a drive to standardize implementation and adjudication practice across the archipelago.

During the 1970s, nearly every province was directed to publish a gazetteer of its High Court and the basic-level courts of the first instance within its jurisdiction (e.g. *Pengadilan Tinggi Palangka Raya dan Wilayah Hukumnya*) – which now form a rich resource of data on the legal system during the first fifteen years of the New Order regime. As courts, prosecutors, and police came to know more about one another's work cross-regionally, they came to act more and more similarly, converging on a model of adjudication.

A marked decline of civil litigation in the early 1970s, combined with a general easing of "backlash" cases aimed at redressing adjustments made to economic and property relations during the early to mid-1960s, ushered in a neotraditional equilibrium under New Order that saw frequent political intervention into the criminal process when needed, and minimized the use of the civil justice system, even in cases of simple commercial, contract, or property disputes (the vast bulk of this system came to be dominated by inheritance and family law). For more than twenty years, Indonesians could rely upon the criminal system to instil fear and to punish those whose actions threatened the interests of established ruling elites, while the civil system sat relatively disused. Indeed, by the mid-1990s, a prominent Indonesian scholar could confidently proclaim that "legislative law, over the entire history of the development of the New Order regime, has become a legitimated (in a formal-juridical manner) controlling force in the hands of the government, and has never reflected the concept of justice" ("*hukum perundang-undangan sepanjang sejarah perkembangan pemerintahan Orde Baru telah menjadi kekuatan kontrol di tangan pemerintah yang terlegitimasi (secara formal-yuridis), dan tidak selamanya merefleksikan konsep keadilan*") (Wignjosoebroto 1994: 247).

As a prominent lawyer, with more than forty-five years of experience, explained when I interviewed him in Surabaya in February 2013, the key principle for judges and lawyers during the period was to ensure outcomes in line with elite interests, especially as communicated by General Ali Murtopo (and by those who followed in his footsteps in the 1980s). Judges could have their careers ended and lawyers could meet with informal rebukes or consequences (even disappear) if they resisted. Such discipline only worked so long as the authoritarian basis of the regime endured.

With New Order stabilized and Suharto's personal hold on political power secured after about 1974, Indonesia's polity settled on a coalition of military factions, business elites, and traditional leading social elements (e.g. landowners and religious leaders) aligned with Suharto. At the same time, Indonesian institutions took on greater coherence and capacity than at any time since before World War II. The authoritarian polity acted stridently in its own particularistic interests, economically and socially as well as politically. Pervasive intervention into both criminal and civil adjudication, both to preserve political stability and to protect rents and other material advantages for the powerful, was the order of the day. At the grassroots, this meant that criminal defendants faced differential processes and outcomes based on their social and political status, while parties to civil disputes had to navigate a labyrinth of influence, corruption, and coercion along an uncharted path to an uncertain destination. The one constant was that those closest or most valuable to Suharto and his immediate circle were protected in both arenas, as a paradigmatic neotraditional legal regime supported both authoritarian stability and entrenched economic and social privilege. What followed its disintegration in 1999 was neither a fractured polity nor a more universally transparent or independent adjudication process. Rather, Indonesia came to embody a new kind of hybrid legal regime, with democratization ushering in a rule by law in the criminal arena while a stable elite held fast to its privileged economic and social position through the persistence of neotraditionalism in civil law.

INDONESIA'S LEGAL SYSTEM SINCE *REFORMASI* AND DEMOCRATIZATION, 1998–2017

Democratization tied the hands of elites from intervening broadly into criminal cases for purposes of repression. But the old New Order elite has been slow to exit the scene politically, economically, or socially. In the absence of comprehensive social or institutional change, members of this holdover elite have taken full advantage of opportunities to intervene into the resolution of civil disputes to maintain their social and economic positions.

Ultimately, by the late 1990s, New Order's economic development model had begun to break down. The Asian Financial Crisis of 1997–8 greatly hastened its demise. With Suharto out of power and his brand of authoritarian developmentalism discredited, Indonesia groped for a new basis on which to establish a credible and functional set of legal institutions. Democracy and decentralization quickly became the foundational concepts driving a new massive push of legislation, roughly from 1999 through 2009 (Hosen 2003).

These new laws covered everything, from decentralization of fiscal authority, to electoral reform (notably switching to a system of direct elections for chief executives, including the President), anti-corruption, environmental protection, and labor rights. Notably, Law Number 4 of 2004, later revised and passed again as Law Number 48 of 2009, sought to clarify and refine the definitions of judicial institutions and authority rooted all the way back in Law 14 of 1970 and Law 5 of 1974. The roles and micro-level facets of some key institutions were redefined, but overall little changed in their basic structure, despite the entry onto the scene of new institutions without clearly defined roles or scopes of authority.

The new institutions and loci of authority created by this legislative barrage were still far from settling into any true new equilibrium as of late 2017. Rather, they still appeared fraught in their day-to-day operations. Many, including the anti-corruption commission and court, face an uncertain future. Others, like the Constitutional Court, have yet to carve out clearly defined jurisdictions and norms of practice. Indonesia's institutional morass also provides opportunities to those who would use the law to tighten access to the polity by, for example, curtailing free or transparent elections and shielding politicians from legal accountability.

On the whole, however, the main effect of democratization has been to remove direct authoritarian repression from the menu of state options in the lion's share of criminal cases. The criminal system as a whole has become far more transparent, open, and predictable, as will be further discussed in Chapter 4. While far from perfect, and still subject to serious abuses, such as in the criminalization of civil disputes mentioned in the introduction, it has come to be governed by a rule by law regime. The civil system, meanwhile, remains subject to frequent political intervention in the adjudication process for all types of cases, even as the frequency of litigation has increased, as will be covered Chapter 5.

Suharto has been gone from the political scene for twenty years, and most members of his family are no longer important players. Yet inveterate New Order elites continue to dominate the *dramatis personae*, to the exclusion of new entrants. The leader of the old coalition has been removed and the manner in which it can govern has been constrained by democracy, but the composition of the polity remains in place. Direct intervention into most phases of the criminal process is no longer an option, but it remains the order of the day to bend civil dispute resolution to serve the interests of the socially advantaged and the economically well off. In local courts, criminal defendants can rely on a set of formally rational processes and relatively predictable outcomes, even as parties to civil cases continue to face a New Order style labyrinthine morass. Indonesia's hybrid legal regime continues to be vital to maintaining its seemingly peculiar blend of democracy and entrenched economic and social stratification.

CONCLUSION

Though the historical roots and pathways of institutional development of the Chinese and Indonesian legal systems are in many respects quite different, there are core aspects in which they are comparable. Comparing across time periods and taking account of differences between civil and criminal law, as well as between urban and rural areas, allows us to analyze the legal regimes present in components of each country's legal system at specific points in time in relation to one another. This subnational disaggregation actually promotes a cross-national comparison that goes beyond simple side-by-side analysis of national-level means or types.

This chapter has provided the basic historical overview necessary to allow for that sort of analysis. After laying out how each country's legal regimes have developed and how they are constituted in different structural contexts and substantive areas, we can now move on to begin to analyze the micro-level dynamics of legal regimes, starting with a look at mobilizational regimes in each country.

CHAPTER THREE

LAW AND REVOLUTION: MOBILIZATIONAL JUSTICE AND CHARISMATIC POLITICS

> *The law must speak with all its energy, especially to the organs of it. The power of the government must be felt to keep all parts of it in harmony with the law ... It is necessary to annihilate both the internal and external enemies of the republic or perish with its fall; - then, in this situation, your first political maxim should be, that the people are guided by reason, the enemies of the people driven by terror alone ... The government in a revolution is the despotism of liberty against tyranny ... The law of self-preservation, with every being whether physical or moral, is the first law of nature. Crime butchers innocence to secure a throne and innocence struggles with all its might against the attempts of crime ... To punish the oppressors of humanity is clemency; to forgive them is cruelty ... Imagination cannot picture all the excesses of which the hypocritical counter-revolutionaries have been guilty to stigmatise the cause of the revolution.*
>
> (Robespierre 1794: 9, 10, 11, 14, 19)

INTRODUCTION

Two examples of mobilizational legal regimes are present in the countries and time periods I study: China from 1949 to 1979 and Indonesia from about the end of 1955 (or certainly 1957) to 1971 (or 1974). In the Chinese case, Mao Zedong's successful imposition of charismatic authority, immediately upon the Communist takeover, fundamentally upended what remained of the legal system after decades of war and civil strife. Indonesia's experience presents a sharp contrast. There, the breakdown of stability in the Indonesian polity (which sat atop its neotraditional legal regime) that accompanied the 1955 elections was followed by Sukarno's failed attempt to impose charismatic authoritarian leadership under "Guided Democracy" from 1959 to 1965, as well as the later degeneration into open conflict that was settled only once Suharto's New Order was firmly ensconced in power, by about 1974. Of course, in both countries, the story also played out differently in urban and rural areas and in regards to criminal and civil law.

In China, criminal law reigned supreme throughout the Maoist period. Civil law, in fact, was neglected to the point that little was even codified or litigated outside family law. Criminal law rules and procedures, though also scantily codified, became increasingly regularized and predictable, in spite of continuing political turmoil and social upheaval. In Indonesia, private law was the main arena of contestation – as can be seen from battles over agrarian reform, property rights, and other forms of civil litigation. Throughout most of the mobilizational period, the state was too weak to enforce the law in significant matters of crime and punishment and the often lethal application of state (or other political) violence frequently took place entirely outside the legal realm – often in secret and almost always without even a veil of judicial process. These different trajectories endowed mobilizational legal regimes in each country with distinct features and facilitated specific effects, as this chapter will discuss.

In terms of urban-rural divides, China's relatively intact urban legal institutions were repeatedly besieged and undermined by waves of political mobilization, while weak, incipient institutions in rural areas were able to harness the resources and energy of political campaigns to strengthen themselves. In Indonesia, the civil law issues in play centered on the redistribution of land and capital. Indigenous urban elites were left relatively untouched by legal challenges and expropriation, even as foreign-held assets and firms were nationalized and Chinese-Indonesians were harassed or dispossessed in several phases between the mid-1950s and 1965. In rural areas, the story was very different, as Sukarno and various allies – not least the PKI – pressed for meaningful land reform. This challenged the entrenched power of traditional elites in a way that capital appropriation in the cities did not, making the rural areas the primary loci of mobilizational legal contestation.

The sources available for this period are of mixed quality. In Indonesia, few court records survive from Guided Democracy or the years prior to it, while secondary sources are also thin on the ground. Enough material exists, however, to trace the basic contours of the evolving legal regime at this critical time. For the most part, I rely on what can be gleaned from gazetteers and the few records I was able to compile, in addition to secondary sources.

In China, records are much better and gazetteers cover the Maoist era in great detail. Secondary sources abound, though many have, in my view, misinterpreted important dynamics of the legal system. Central to my work, therefore, are gazetteers and other sources from around the country, in addition to a stream of county public security bureau (PSB) records to which I was able to gain access.

INDONESIA

As discussed in Chapter 2, electoral politics finally began in Indonesia in 1955. The results, however, proved anything but conclusive and led to serious splits in the ruling coalition as well as pressure from powerful outsider groups. The roughly equal vote shares garnered by Sukarno's Nationalist Party (PNI), the syncretic Islamist Nahdlatul Ulama (NU, with its large base on Java), and the more orthodox/modernist Islamist Masyumi (with more support in urban centers on the "outer islands" – especially Sumatra and Sulawesi) plunged the uneasy cooperation between Sukarno and his more conservative Vice President Muhammad Hatta into crisis. It also fractured the parliamentary coalition between those three main parties, as Masyumi refused to cooperate in the formation of any grouping that might include leftist or communist parties, while the NU and the PNI sought to salvage what they could of the old order.

At the same time, the Indonesian Communist Party's (PKI) surprisingly strong showing, especially in the key provinces of Central and East Java, emboldened D. N. Aidit and other PKI leaders to press for the party's inclusion in (or at least much stronger and more legitimate influence on) government. The army, unnerved by both the PKI and Masyumi, and protective of local economic interests and rent-seekers (especially in areas of the outer islands with strong export-commodity sectors), sought greater influence to block what it saw as both right-wing and left-wing extremists and to limit what it perceived as the destructive power of the central government to disrupt profitable local economic orders in places like Sumatra and Sulawesi. Intervention in critical outer island regions would also prove necessary, from the army's point of view, in order to preserve national unity and prevent outright separatism.

After Sukarno's attempted assertion of charismatic authority with his decree of return to the 1945 Constitution on July 5, 1959, he moved to implement an explicitly authoritarian strategy of governance after his Independence Day speech on August 17 of the same year. The legal system lurched toward a new form of upheaval, driven largely by attempts at land and property rights reform. Though Law 73/1958 had just unified the criminal system, most conflict around these issues played out in the civil arena.

After the abortive coup d'état, attempted by some elements of the PKI and their sympathizers on September 30, 1965, General Suharto seized power from Sukarno, solidifying his control with the so-called Order of March Eleventh (*Surat Perintah Seblas Maret*, often abbreviated as *Supersemar*) in early 1966. Still, it took at least five years for Suharto's New Order regime to stabilize itself in power. During this time, many backlash actions made use of the still reeling legal system to address perceived wrongs and redistributive initiatives taken during Guided Democracy, as Suharto scrambled to assert sovereign control over the polity as a whole.

Paucity of Data on Urban Suits and Criminal Cases

Surprisingly, records of urban criminal cases for the Guided Democracy period proved extremely difficult to come by in my research. It seemed there were not many criminal cases at all, and extremely few that showed any substantial degree of politicization. As we know from prior research (e.g. Muradi 2014: 26–30), the police were very weak during this period, their power largely sapped by political struggles between political factions, the PKI, the military, and local elites. Still, it seems slightly surprising that so few of the cases that made it into the criminal justice system would show obvious markers of the heightened political drama of the day.

But one such political case did unfold in Manado, capital of North Sulawesi Province, several years prior to the formal start of Guided Democracy, in 1955–56 (Case 394/Pid/1955/PN.MDO). A Chinese-Indonesian couple, officially recorded by the court as foreigners (*orang asing*) though they had long resided in Indonesia, failed to register the birth of their son (who had been born in 1953) as required by law and were found to be two years delinquent. The court ruled that they had committed a criminal offense and imposed a fine of Rp.5000 (equivalent to about US$754 in 1955, roughly the level of Indonesia's annual per capita GDP at the time), which could be converted to fifty days in prison if not paid in full or on time. The couple appealed directly to

President Sukarno for a pardon (*grasi*), a petition that his office brusquely rejected almost four months to the day after it was filed, on March 23, 1956, leaving the stiff fine in place. Almost all other urban criminal cases I could uncover from the period – whether in Surabaya, Manado, or in smaller cities – were simple thefts (of items like wristwatches or bicycles) or beatings resulting from street fights. Unfortunately, I could find no comprehensive statistics for any courts of the time, and thus cannot assess how common specific types of cases were in particular places. I was also unable to gather data on civil suits in the urban areas where I sought data. For most of my analysis, therefore, I must rely on what I found in rural areas of East Java and North Sulawesi.

Rural Criminal Cases

Of my rural fieldwork sites, the most complete records of case files for the period are from Pamekasan, in the eastern part of the island of Madura in East Java Province. There were, of course, a number of simple criminal cases in rural settings as well. Several cases in rural Madura, for example, were handled easily by a functioning court in Pamekasan, even at the height of early the 1960s' disorder. In one case, a forty-nine-year-old farmer was sentenced to six months in prison after admitting that he had broken into a neighbor's house and stolen plates, teacups, and other valuables (Case 102/Pid/1962/PN.PMK). In another case (Case 103/Pid/1962/PN.PMK), a fourteen-year-old girl was caught burglarizing her neighbor's house and stealing a similar collection of valuables, but escaped any punishment beyond having to return the stolen items because of her young age. Finally, a thirty-seven-year-old farmer was sentenced to nine months in prison after being convicted of assaulting (*penganiayaan*) his neighbor and stabbing him with a knife, causing significant injury (Case 60/Pid/1962/PN.PMK). These criminal issues were routine, as indeed were all those in the small number of cases I was able to collect from this period. This suggests that the criminal system, despite recently having been brought under a nationally uniform code, remained too weak to take on anything beyond simple trials for simple crimes like theft of goods from someone's house or attacking a neighbor.

Rural Civil Suits

Compared with the dearth of criminal cases, there was a relative abundance of civil suits brought to courts in rural areas during Guided

Democracy. Specifically, there were a great many suits over land, as well as inheritance and divorce, with relatively few relating mainly to other matters. If we look at some of the early Guided Democracy land tenure suits, we can see the influence of changing political conditions, as well as the evident weakness and indecision of the courts at pivotal moments.

In one case from 1959, for example, one man sued another, claiming he had been illegally occupying his house and making use of twenty-five trees on his land and other valuables since 1954 (Case 200/Pdt/1959/PN.PMK). The defendant, in turn, produced testimony and affidavits – though no original formal documentation – to support his claim that he had purchased the land, the house, and its contents from others who had held formal title (i.e. registration) in separate transactions in 1932 and 1952. In this case of one person's word against that of several others, the court dismissed the suit and charged the plaintiff Rp.41 in court costs.

In a more complicated 1959 suit (Case 236/Pdt/1959/PN.PMK), five sons of a deceased merchant sued the occupant of land they claimed rightly belonged to their late father, but had been illegally occupied by others. The suit was complex because the father had himself been involved in a legal dispute with the land's occupant, winning a decision from the Pamekasan court in 1957 that should have granted him title. The other party appealed to the provincial high court in Surabaya, however, which took until 1959 to issue a decision confirming the lower court's ruling. Just before that appellate decision was received, however, the old merchant died, leaving it to his sons to sue once again after the losing party argued that he had a duty to relinquish title only to the original litigant, not to his heirs. The sons won their suit and the court ordered the occupant to hand over the land and pay court costs of Rp.46.

The documentation of suits over disputed land claims is less complete for cases during the period 1960–5, but what records *are* there show that the court frequently showed preference for the interests of tenants and of claimants to new land rights. In one 1962 case (Case 38/Pdt/1962/PN.PMK), one farmer sued another over land claimed by the former but occupied by the latter. The court's first hearing of the case was in September, but on October 9, 1962, the defendant (a thirty-year-old farmer) was taken into police custody for alleged (and unspecified) criminal offenses (which the documents suggest might likely be handled through a summary, i.e. *sumir* or *pidana rol*, process) and detained at least until the end of that month. The civil process did not advance during his prosecution and it is unclear from the file whether it was ever taken up formally again.

In a similar case two years later (Case 06/Pdt/1964/PN.PMK), one farmer sued his neighbor, saying that he had purchased a parcel of land from the neighbor for Rp.12,000 in 1962, but that the seller had never ceased occupying that land or allowed the buyer to take possession (in the interim it had also been discovered that the land was valuable for salt production). The plaintiff sought what for the time and place were quite high damages of Rp.100,000 and dozens of motions and counter-motions were filed by both sides at multiple court hearings well into 1965. Right around the time of the Gestapu Coup, however, the file runs dry and no documentation of further actions by the court or any conclusion of the case is included. In another 1964 case (Case 42/Pdt/1964/PN.PMK), the Pamekasan Court dismissed a suit seeking to relitigate a land title dispute that had just been decided in 1963. The court threw out this new suit, suggested the plaintiff (who had lost his land in 1963) was likely guilty of fraud, and ordered him to pay costs of Rp.1211 in November, 1964.

In a more complex case that also lasted almost right up until the end of 1965 (Case 94/Pdt/1964/PN.PMK), a plaintiff sued, claiming he had purchased a parcel of land in 1941 from the father of a woman (defendant 1 in this case), who had herself recently been involved in other litigation over title to the same land. The plaintiff claimed that, although he had purchased the land in 1941, he did not register it in his name until 1948 because the Japanese occupation and subsequent war of independence had disrupted such quotidian bureaucratic services as land registrations. Meanwhile, another man (defendant 2 in this case) claimed to have purchased the same parcel of land from defendant 1's father in 1920. Defendant 2 knew that the plaintiff had been occupying the land since 1942, but had somehow been able to get it registered in his name in 1952 (duplicate registration certificates had been issued to different people, apparently – one in 1948 and the other in 1952). Defendant 1, however, was able to get a court order issued in 1963 declaring that the parcel of land was "vacant" and should belong to her, after winning a civil suit for its title against defendant 2. The plaintiff's 1964 suit, seeking to nullify the claims of both defendants and grant title to him, was dismissed by the Pamekasan Court on March 17, 1965, leading him to appeal to the Provincial High Court in Surabaya. That court concurred with the lower court and upheld the original ruling in a decision issued on August 30, 1965.

Backlash lawsuits, brought by those who had lost land after 1955 (particularly during Guided Democracy), became far more common in Pamekasan after 1965, and the court came more predictably to rule in favor of those seeking to restore or enforce old land claims. In one such case (Case 92/Pdt.G/1966/PN.PMK), the plaintiff claimed that a parcel of land was his rightful inheritance from his mother, who had died during World War II. The testimony of many witnesses, including the village chief, confirmed that the plaintiff's mother had indeed owned the land since Dutch colonial times. She then leased the land to a sharecropper (who was eventually to become the defendant in this case) during the Japanese occupation. After she died, the land was registered under her son's (the plaintiff's) name in 1951. The defendant claimed, however, to have legal rights to the land under the Agrarian Law because he had worked and lived on it for more than twenty years and the plaintiff had not (at least in recent years) sought to enforce the old sharecropping arrangement. The court ruled for the plaintiff and ordered the defendant to vacate the land immediately and turn it over to the plaintiff on December 1, 1966.

Upon appeal, the High Court in Surabaya upheld the lower court's decision on May 29, 1967, but for a different reason – saying that it had no jurisdiction to decide what amounted to a land reform case under Law 109/1964 and dismissing the appellate suit, while advising the losing party to seek redress from the central-level special court for land reform (then still in effect) in Jakarta. The pendulum had swung in a more right-wing direction (indeed, the inscription at the top of every decision document had even changed, from "In the Name of Justice," *Atas Nama Keadilan* to "For the Sake of Justice Rooted in God the Almighty," *Demi Keadilan Berdasarkan Ketuhanan yang Maha Esa*), even though the legal system was more timid than ever in terms of asserting its jurisdiction or authority.

The court also became more resistant to claims against alleged illegal occupation of land by local elites – provided they had been reasonably long-standing. In one case (Case 98/Pdt.G/1966/PN.PMK), a plaintiff claimed that another man had illegally seized land that was rightfully his during the Japanese occupation. The village chief – in office since at least 1942 – testified in support of the defendant's claim to ownership (the land was apparently never registered formally and no certificate of title was presented). The court accepted the defendant's evidence, rather than the plaintiff's more populist assertions, and dismissed the suit in November 1966. Not satisfied, the plaintiff appealed to the High Court in Surabaya, which also dismissed his case in May 1967.

In Case 61/Pdt/1968/PN.PMK, a man sued his neighbor – to whom his mother had given a parcel of land as collateral – for return of the land in question, now that he could repay the money she had borrowed from him more than twenty years earlier. The defendant and the plaintiff's mother had made an agreement in the late 1940s, when she was sick and in need of medicine, that the neighbor could take possession of a plot of land she owned in the village (large enough to be worked in a morning – *luasnja sepagi hari kerdja* – and worth about Rp.15,000) in exchange for Rp.70 to pay for her medical expenses. Now that her son had gathered the funds to pay the neighbor what his mother owed him, he argued, he should have been able to get the land back. Further, since it had been more than seven years, he maintained the land should be due back to him even without any payment (as the neighbor's enjoyment of it for that long would have already provided him with sufficient compensation to repay the loan).

The neighbor, however, refused and claimed that his exchange of money for the right to occupy the land constituted a sale and that the land was therefore now his. Three witnesses testified. The first, a relative of the plaintiff, said he did not know anything about the details of the case. The second, a former village leader, said that when he had been in office, the defendant had come to him to report that he was going to purchase the disputed land from the plaintiff's mother for Rp.70, that this sale had indeed been completed in 1947, and that he had witnessed the stamping of the sale documents. Finally, the current village chief testified that there was no need to file special reports on the sale of land, but only to notify the village chief if the officially registered landowner was to be changed (which it had been in this case, from the plaintiff's mother to the defendant, in 1947). The sale documents were also submitted to the court as evidence, leading the Pamekasan court to dismiss the suit in February 1969. Not satisfied, the plaintiff appealed to the High Court in Surabaya, which took two years to consider and reexamine his case, before rejecting the appeal in June 1971. After this, there was a lapse in communication between the parties and the court, until the Pamekasan Court issued a notice in 1973, confirming that the plaintiff in the case had died and informing the defendant that he could still appeal to the Supreme Court in Jakarta should he wish to.

Backlash land reform cases proliferated outside Java as well. The Tondano Court, with jurisdiction over the Minahasa Regency in the highlands of North Sulawesi, saw many such suits after the 1965 coup and before 1971. In Case 87/Pdt/1968/PN.TDO, a man sued for return of plantation land in Tomohon that he claimed was rightfully his but had been seized by the Japanese during their World War II occupation of Indonesia. During the war, he claimed, the Japanese military planted the land with high-quality coffee (*kopi robusta*), further increasing its value. Another (apparently poorer) villager assumed occupancy and control over the land when the Japanese left in 1945 and never relinquished it. After the suit was filed, a "case examination team" (*tim pemeriksa perakara*) was constituted in the village and spent two days in February 1968 surveying the land, recording exactly what was planted on every square meter, and interviewing the district head (*ketua kecamatan*). They were unable, however, to come to any definitive determination about who held formal title to the land or exactly what had happened to it between 1942 and 1945. The court did appear to deem the evidence sufficient to rule for the plaintiff (even though the decision document is missing from the file), but does not seem to have been able or willing to enforce its decision – for, in 1982, the same plaintiff sued once again for enforcement of the decision in the original 1968 case.

In another 1968 case that seems to have encountered decision and enforcement problems (Case 184/Pdt/1968/PN.TDO), a sixty-five-year-old farmer filed suit over a land sale concluded in 1953. At that time, the plaintiff had agreed to sell a parcel of land to his neighbor (the defendant in the 1968 case) in exchange for a cow and a promise to dismantle, move, and reassemble his house for him. He claims that the defendant turned over the cow in poor condition (sickly and thin) and failed to rebuild his house properly (leaving it unfit for habitation). The plaintiff originally filed a suit against the defendant in 1954, but no decision was ever issued and the case seems to have disappeared into the chaotic politics of the court during the transition to Guided Democracy a few years later. In 1964, after the original buyer had sold the land in question to someone else, the plaintiff filed a new suit against him and the new buyer (recorded as Case 222/Pdt/1964/PN.TDO, though documents are missing and the original case file has been lost). Hearings did not begin in that case for three years, however, with three taking place between March and August 1967. That case, too, quickly evaporated into the apparent chaos of the court. Then, in 1968, the plaintiff filed yet another suit, but no judge was assigned to the case – and no other action was taken by the court – until March 1975. Hearings were then scheduled for April 1975, and letters of summons were sent to the parties. The file contains no record of the proceedings ever beginning, however, and it seems likely that the plaintiff may have died before his case was actually taken up.

In yet another case that appears to have been litigated multiple times without a decision (Case 151/Pdt/1968/PN.TDO), a woman sought the return of rice fields (both dry and wet, *ladang* and *sawah*) that she claimed were rightfully hers by virtue of inheritance. According to the plaintiff, she inherited the lands in question in 1949 and 1952. She then had to go to Makassar (in South Sulawesi) for treatment of a heart condition in 1958. While she was there, conditions in Minahasa deteriorated, because of the Permesta Rebellion, to the point that she could not return (*keadaan di Minahasa adalah kacau diakibatkan oleh karena pergelakan* [sic] *Permesta sehingga Penggugat tidat dapat kembali ke Minahasa*). Though she had not yet fully recovered and conditions were still chaotic, she returned to her home village in 1961 when her husband died. There she discovered the defendant occupying the disputed lands, claiming that he had purchased them from her late husband.

She immediately filed suit in Manado over the veracity of the land registrations (recorded as Case 663/Pdt/1961/PN.MDO) and appears to have won (though full records are not included in the Tondano court's file or available in Manado). She maintained that the original land registration was in her name alone and thus that any sale to the defendant would have been fraudulent (likely fabricated by the defendant himself upon her husband's death). After filing suit in 1968, she made these arguments and presented documents from 1949 and 1952 showing the land in her own name only (not her husband's or jointly between the two of them), as well as a letter of instruction from the Manado court based on the 1961 case. The defendant produced a bill of sale for the disputed land and called several witnesses from the village to testify that he had indeed bought the land from the plaintiff's husband legally and openly. At least nine hearings were held in the case, between August and November 1969. But, the court does not seem ever to have reached any decision and there are no records in the file of further legal action or enforcement, suggesting that the court lacked either the power or the political will to restore the plaintiff's land tenure rights.

In a final example from Tondano (Case 04/Pdt/1968/PN.TDO), a man sued several of his relatives for occupying land (planted with wet-field rice) that he claimed his parents had willed to him before their deaths. His other relatives (the defendants) argued that the land had been sold, given, or deeded to them in a series of transactions in 1955, 1957, and 1962, producing documents to bolster these assertions. The plaintiff, however, was able to point to a Dutch land registry from 1914, showing that the land had belonged to his grandparents, and then to documentary evidence of its transfer to his parents and thence to him. The Tondano court very quickly ruled in his favor and issued a decision on June 10, 1968, ordering his relatives to vacate the land and relinquish the title to him. That was when political wrangling began and external actors appeared to intervene. The defendants appealed to the High Court in Manado in early 1969, but the court did not issue a decision back to the parties until 1978, apparently sitting on the politically sensitive (though legally reasonably straightforward) case for nearly a decade. The eventual appellate decision upheld the original Tondano ruling, but there were still more problems with enforcement. Finally, in 1986, the plaintiff's daughter (as his heir, following his death) petitioned the Tondano Court (*Permohonan Executie*), asking that the 1968 decision be enforced.

In other parts of the country, there are even examples of cases from decades later with roots that go back to this era of backlash against land reform in the late 1960s. Two cases from rural Kediri (in East Java), for example, show this pattern clearly. In Case 52/Pdt.G/1984/PN.Kab. KDR, six siblings, all children of a woman who had died in 1956, sued the occupant of a plot of farmland they claimed had belonged to their mother and thus to them. Before she died, the plaintiff's mother had leased the land to a man in 1952. After her death, he continued to occupy the land, dismissing complaints from the woman's family. He died in 1970 and left the land as inheritance to his son (who became the defendant in the 1984 case). In 1972, one of the woman's children threatened to press a more formal claim challenging the new occupant's right to be on the land. His response was to apply for an official certificate of land ownership and registration, which he received in his name in 1975. He was able to present this at the 1984 trial, where he also called the village chief (*kepala desa*) to testify that he had always lived on the land, as long as anyone in the village could recollect. Perplexingly, the court never issued a decision in the case, and also never recorded any documents suggesting it was settled out of court. Most likely, it seems, either the plaintiffs dropped or withdrew their claim or the court simply failed to rule on the case over sensitive land issues, even decades after the political situation had been settled.

The second Kediri case (Case 39/Pdt.G/2001/PN.Kab.KDR) was even more sensitive and complex. Six elderly farmers sued their former village chief and district head (*kepala desa* and *camat*), the Ministry of Health, and three other farmers. The plaintiffs asserted that land, which had belonged to them, had been unlawfully occupied by two other farmers (ancestors of two of the defendants in the 2001 case) in 1960 and 1961. To back up their claims of ownership, the plaintiffs submitted hand-written and worn registrations and sale documents from 1954 and 1956 that showed their families in possession of the land in question. After occupying the land, the two other farmers sold it (illegally, the plaintiffs claimed) to the village chief in December 1963, who received financial assistance for the purchase from the district head. At trial, the defense submitted a formal bill of sale (*akta jual-beli*) from the 1963 transaction, as well as registration documents and land dispute adjudication decisions from 1967 and 1968 to show it had actually been owned and occupied by the village chief.

The two farmers who'd occupied the land in 1960 and 1961 died suddenly in 1965 or 1966 (*meninggal dunia pada jaman Gestapu*, as per the explanation in the file), very likely, it would seem, murdered or "disappeared," perhaps as suspected leftists or PKI sympathizers (the Communist Party, after all, was very active in Kediri, as was NU, and thousands on both sides were killed there during the turmoil of the mid-1960s). The village chief held onto the land – and his post – until 1990. In 1989 and 1990, he completed the sale of the disputed land. Most of it was sold to the Ministry of Health for the construction of a community clinic (*puskesmas*). The remainder was sold to another farmer (the third farmer defendant in the 2001 case).

The court sided with the defendants and issued a decision rejecting the suit in its entirety and ordering the plaintiffs to pay court costs of Rp.561,000 on October 15, 2001. The history of this one parcel of land encapsulates the political struggles and social upheaval of several decades as played out in the civil adjudication system of rural Indonesia. The plaintiffs lost their land during the high tide of land reform and Guided Democracy. The village chief took advantage of his position as a local power-holder at another tumultuous time a few years later to ensure he could acquire and retain title to it. He then sold it before retiring, to the national government and another farmer – actors powerful enough to defend their claims in court relatively easily, even after *Reformasi*.

But there were also many civil suits from the period that were not obviously political in nature (indeed, some cases, such as Case 02/Pdt/1971/PN.PMK, a disputed sale of a house, were even settled through mediation or out-of-court agreements). Many of these involved simple contracts or occurred when disputes erupted over common property among family members in the aftermath of divorce or death. In Case 01/Pdt/1959/PN.PMK, the Pamekasan Court ruled that four plaintiffs had not received the land inheritance they were entitled to from their father (who died in 1948), based on land registration documents, wills, and letters. The court ordered the land to be surveyed and redivided among them.

Another inheritance dispute (Case 105/Pdt/1959/PN.PMK) hinged on issues of gender equity and proving that there were no other heirs than the deceased's wife. The couple had been married since 1927, but the Post Office in neighboring Sampang (where her late husband had deposited all of their cash assets before he died in March, 1959) refused to release any funds to the widow and would not explain whether this was due to doubts over whether there could be other heirs or simply because Postal officials were unwilling to release funds directly to a woman. The court quickly ruled that the couple had been childless – and thus that no one else could claim the funds – and ordered the Post Office to release all of the money to the widow.

Many cases involved the disposition of property following divorce. In Case 54/Pdt/1959/PN.PMK, a couple had divorced in 1958, but continued to contest ownership of their house and some of its contents (especially an armoire and the stove). The husband said he had built the house and acquired the possessions with his labor and money. The wife argued that the house was built on land that she had owned before they were married and that some of the funds to purchase the furniture had been hers as well. The court decided (in October, 1959) that the husband could claim two thirds of the value of the property in question, while the wife was entitled to one third (Rp.2400) as compensation – or could instead return the stove, armoire, and other goods in question. One somewhat surprising case (Case 177/Pdt/1959/PN.PMK) involved a woman who had apparently been betrothed to a man since

1929 – some years before she was even born. They were married, but divorced in 1955. Upon their separation, her ex-husband took their house, most valuables, and several wet-fields (*sawah*) that she said had belonged to her family. The court rejected the woman's suit, ordering her husband only to pay the court costs she had incurred.

Some routine cases were really just simple contract disputes, involving issues like rental of a toy cabinet (*lemari mainan*), for example (Case 09/Pdt/1959/PN.PMK). In this case, a man agreed to rent the cabinet from his neighbor for Rp.50/month, starting in August 1958. These payments were to be put toward the eventual purchase of the cabinet for Rp.750. The renter apparently had stopped paying, however, and then claimed when confronted that the cabinet was now his, so his neighbor took him to court. The court found, though, that clear records had not been kept, that the defendant had already paid the plaintiff at least Rp.650, and that there had never been a clear written agreement on the lease or purchase terms, so the suit had no validity – i.e. the defendant had already purchased the cabinet *de facto* and the suit was dismissed. Case 03/Pdt/1962/PN.PMK saw a man sue his friend, to whom he had lent some gold jewelry in 1960, for the return of his property. The court very quickly issued a judgment ordering the defendant to return the jewels or compensate the plaintiff with cash equal to their value (Rp.280).

Concluding Thoughts

Even from the sparse data available, we can observe that in Indonesia's unstable political environment of state weakness and leadership uncertainty during Guided Democracy and the early years of New Order, social groups and actors mobilized to pursue civil litigation to advance their economic and social claims or protect their political power and privilege. Many of the civil disputes revolved around land tenure claims and land reform, as well as later around conservative backlashes against the redistributive mobilization of the early 1960s. Criminal law lay largely unused, as organs of state coercion apparently failed to organize criminal justice for political or most other ends. Those cases that remained in the system tended to be largely routine prosecutions of petty criminals. Despite reforms that aimed to bolster the criminal law apparatus, the lack of cases suggests it remained largely irrelevant to most social actors (though to be confident in this claim would require collection of more comprehensive data than I could obtain). Overall, Sukarno's failed and Suharto's still inchoate attempts to impose charismatic authority perpetuated disequilibrium and contestation, between about 1955 and 1974, that allowed competing social and political actors to mobilize portions of the legal system as instruments of their broader discord during the period.

The situation in China, however, was markedly different, as Mao Zedong managed to keep hold of the mantle of charismatic authority for most of the period from 1950 to 1975. Criminal law there became a weapon of repression to be deployed against class enemies, regime opponents, or factional rivals, even as the civil dispute resolution apparatus remained woefully under-developed and almost entirely unused.

CHINA

The overall story for China during the Maoist Era is of recurrent charismatic interventions by Mao himself into the high-stakes battles raging throughout the period over the constitution of the polity. Each intervention proved decisive in the short term, but none fully settled the underlying contests. Still, in such an environment of pervasive intervention into the adjudication process by nonlegal political actors, the fact that the basic institutional structure never fractured completely meant that legal system regularization and development continued (at least up to a point), despite all the political and social turmoil, and that criminal law remained the primary area of law to be mobilized. This general trend played out quite differently in urban and rural areas, however.

Urban Areas

In urban China, functioning courts and other legal institutions that already existed when the Communists took over in 1949 were disrupted and subverted during the early 1950s and again repeatedly over the next twenty-five years. Although personnel changes and purges were frequent, judicial decision-making was heavily politicized, and there were frequent episodes during which institutionalization appeared to stall or reverse, an overarching trend toward creeping regularization persisted up through the 1970s. Even if one could imagine urban courts and procuratorates ending up stronger and more regularized in 1979 had they not endured the previous three decades, they were indisputably more competent and formalized institutions upon the advent of reform than they had been at the moment of the CCP's takeover, as a mobilizational regime eventually gave way to a neotraditional one.

I have written before, based on its gazetteer (成都市锦江区法院志 1999), about the disruptions caused by Maoist campaigns to the work of the court now called Jinjiang District Court in Chengdu City, but also of how that court's work gradually became more regularized (Hurst 2011: 84–6). The patterns described there are not unique to that locality. In Baotou, Inner Mongolia, for example, the disruption caused to that city's political classes and institutions by the CCP's victory was jarring. The new authorities established a special criminal court for the suppression of counterrevolutionaries that operated from June 1950 until October 1951 and prosecuted 940 cases, including 432 of spying, 33 against "political bandits" (政治土匪), 34 rapes, 9 murders, 31 cases related to the activities of "reactionary party groups" (反动党团), 17 against "evil landlords," 218 for membership in secret societies and cults, 40 against "reactionary officials" (反动官史), and 126 for other counterrevolutionary crimes. Verdicts were reached in 886 cases, leading to 159 people being put to death, 19 sentenced to life imprisonment, 226 sentenced to time in prison, 234 remanded to the masses for supervision or education, and 246 being deported to other areas (2 people also died of illness while incarcerated) (包头法院志编纂委员会 1990: 10). A highlight of the campaign was a mass rally in April 1951 – attended by 50,000 people (out of 90,000 total residing in the city at the time) – to sentence several high profile counterrevolutionaries (包头法院志编纂委员会 1990: 11).

Kunming City, capital of Yunnan Province, in Southwestern China, saw crackdowns against counterrevolutionaries in 1951 and 1955, as well as early versions of "strike hard" campaigns against criminals in 1954 and 1957, reducing crime to very low levels and infusing the courts with power to enforce social order (云南省昆明市中级人民法院编 1994: 49). There, counterrevolutionary cases during the early 1950s were separated into three categories: those considered serious threats to the revolution or involving public security officials were tried by military tribunals, those involving landlords or rural land reform were handled by the people's tribunal in Kunming County, while all others involving urban residents were tried in the city people's court. During the first campaign to suppress counterrevolutionaries in 1951, Kunming City People's Court tried 676 such cases, while 3,389 were handled by military tribunals (云南省昆明市中级人民法院编 1994: 53). Some of these more serious counterrevolutionary cases were adjudicated with much attendant spectacle: for example, two defendants accused of organizing a fishing cartel and harming fishermen's income were struggled against, tried, sentenced to death, and immediately executed at a mass trial organized by the labor union in a sports stadium and attended by more than 20,000 people in April 1951 (云南省昆明市中级人民法院编 1994: 52–3, 57). A further 2,163 counterrevolutionary cases were tried during the second campaign, between 1955 and 1957 (云南省昆明市中级人民法院编 1994: 60).

Upon the launch of the Anti-Rightist Campaign in August 1957, the courts of rural and suburban Kunming first began taking special measures to struggle against and crack down on landlords, rich peasants, and other "counterrevolutionary elements" (云南省昆明市中级人民法院编 1994: 67). When the Great Leap Forward began in 1958, courts in both urban and rural areas began processing dramatically higher numbers of counterrevolutionary cases, even in comparison to those brought under the Anti-Rightist Campaign a year earlier – 2207 compared to 592 (云南省昆明市中级人民法院编 1994: 68). So excessive was this high tide that in 1961 and 1962, corrective campaigns were undertaken to reinvestigate most of these cases, before the years between 1962 and 1965 were largely given over to recovering the integrity of the courts' functioning and personnel (云南省昆明市中级人民法院编 1994: 68–9).

Data on Kunming courts during the Cultural Revolution period are paltry, but the gazetteer notes that courts as formal institutions were suspended (and replaced by case adjudication teams – 办案组 – under the military-backed revolutionary committee) from September 1968 until June 1973, and 80 percent of cadres working in courts were sent to "May 7th Cadre Schools" or forced to work in factories or rural communes. Still, during the ten years from 1966 through 1976, Kunming courts (and adjudication teams) tried 5039 criminal cases (including 641 against counterrevolutionaries), reaching verdicts in 2526 of these (including 253 against counterrevolutionaries), though nearly 70 percent of the counterrevolutionary cases were later found to be flawed and invalidated (云南省昆明市中级人民法院编 1994: 70).

Even less obviously political offenses were adjudicated in similar fashion. For example, throughout the 1950s, Kunming courts tried a total of 3205 cases against drug offenders (addicts and dealers). But more than 1300 offenders were prosecuted through a special drug court expedited process in 1952 under a targeted campaign, and the number of drug trials actually dropped precipitously with the start of the Great Leap Forward (from 472 in 1958 to 39 in 1959) (云南省昆明市中级人民法院编 1994: 84). Criminal cases across the board jumped tremendously in number in 1958, with 4777 non–counterrevolutionary cases being taken up by the courts in that year alone with the launch of the Great Leap (云南省昆明市中级人民法院编 1994: 91), before the numbers of cases declined markedly as more were presumably handled outside the formal legal system during the Cultural Revolution. Overall, we see a clear story of Kunming's courts and legal institutions disrupted by campaign politics between 1950 and 1957, upended by the Great Leap Forward, and then thrown into disarray by the Cultural Revolution, despite a brief respite in the early 1960s.

In more heavily urbanized Anshan, an industrial city in Northeast China's Liaoning Province, a people's court was fully functional in 1949, but in the first year or so of the People's Republic, it adjudicated very few cases against counterrevolutionaries – only eight, versus 371 for theft and 264 for arson (王玉琴主编 1996: 69, 73, 81). After the start of the campaign to suppress counterrevolutionaries, however, the city held a mass rally in May 1951 (attended by nearly 80 percent of local residents), after which more than 2500 citizen reports and denunciations flooded in, resulting in 600 criminal trials of counterrevolutionaries by the end of the year (王玉琴主编 1996: 69–70). Nearly 500 more cases against counterrevolutionaries were tried during the second suppression campaign (from 1955 until early 1957), followed by another 498 in 1957 under the Anti-Rightist Campaign (王玉琴主编 1996: 70).

In one example of such a case, a former prison warden for the GMD in Xinjiang was accused of killing more than 250 people in the course of the Chinese Civil War and sentenced to fifteen years in prison (王玉琴主编 1996: 70). With the beginning of the GLF, the number of cases against counterrevolutionaries also soared in Anshan, reaching 3691 in 1958, more than six times higher than the 1957 total, before falling rapidly in the early 1960s (王玉琴主编 1996: 70). Meanwhile, trials for theft increased markedly during the Great Leap Forward period, reaching a high of 1549 in 1960–1, with especially high rates of theft from urban work units, often perpetrated by youths, throughout the 1960s (王玉琴主编 1996: 74). Fraud cases – almost always related to the illicit privatization or stripping of public assets from work units – also spiked dramatically during the 1960s (王玉琴主编 1996: 83).

Turning to the Southeast Coast, Foshan City, a suburb of Guangzhou in the Pearl River Delta, saw a similar pattern of politicized adjudication during most of the Maoist era, even though its courts were subsumed by the Revolutionary Committees from 1967 to August 1972

(佛山中级法院 1991: 25). Indeed, cases against alleged counterrevolutionaries constituted an inordinately high percentage of the total in Foshan courts, ranging from a low of 5 percent in 1975 all the way up to 50 percent in 1959 (佛山中级法院 1991: 31). Still, ordinary crimes were prosecuted and tried reasonably normally. For instance, the case against a Mr. Liang, accused of attempting to murder three women in his neighbor's household (successfully killing one of them and seriously injuring the other two) after the youngest had refused his marriage proposal in 1962, was adjudicated without incident or overt political intervention in 1966, resulting in a death sentence for the defendant (佛山中级法院 1991: 34–5). Finally, subsequent reviews, instituted to help restore the court's integrity, voided convictions in fully 42 percent of cases from the campaign to suppress counterrevolutionaries in the early 1950s and just under 60 percent of those from the Cultural Revolution period (佛山中级法院 1991: 39–40).

Sanming City, in Fujian Province, also saw high numbers of counterrevolutionary cases during the campaigns of the 1950s (冯开方主编 1993: 68–71). Then, during the Cultural Revolution, extreme leftism led to anyone who had ever uttered a politically incorrect sentence or expressed dissatisfaction being prosecuted for counterrevolutionary crimes. Even trials for ordinary crimes were influenced by political movements, with much higher rates of prosecution in the 1950s than in the 1960s or 1970s – though many cases were also handled outside the formal legal system during the Cultural Revolution (冯开方主编 1993: 72).

Trials for theft of state property also saw a noticeable increase during the Cultural Revolution years (冯开方主编 1993: 82). The way crimes were judged and criminals sentenced also varied based on political currents. For example, an activist worker from Sanming Iron and Steel (a large state-owned enterprise) got into an altercation with a migrant from the countryside near the Sanming bus depot late at night on December 26, 1967. The worker summoned a group of armed activists who beat and shot the migrant and several of his companions, killing one and seriously injuring four others. Yet, the worker who had instigated the whole brawl was sentenced only to five years in prison. In a similar incident from the late 1970s, two men who had instigated a brawl near the bus station that ended with two victims being stabbed to death and one other seriously injured were sentenced to death for their offenses (冯开方主编 1993: 77). The political climate of the Cultural Revolution protected the activist worker in the first case, while the conservative restoration of the late 1970s led to the later offenders being treated far more harshly.

Qinhuangdao City, in North China's Hebei Province, saw 2207 cases against counterrevolutionaries during the 1950s, roughly 480 between 1960 and 1979, and only 13 after 1980 (河北省秦皇岛市中级人民法院 1993: 140–1). During the same period, the courts there tried a total of 438 murder cases (288 during the 1950s, 87 during the 1960s, and 63 during the 1970s) (河北省秦皇岛市中级人民法院 1993: 153–4). Similarly, there were roughly 1000 cases of rape tried in Qinhuangdao during the Maoist period (533 in the 1950s, and about 490 in the 1960s and 1970s) (河北省秦皇岛市中级人民法院 1993: 156). Nearly 1100 counterrevolutionary cases were brought during 1950 and 1951 alone – many against alleged "evil tyrants" (恶霸), spies, or members of reactionary groups – in which nearly a third of those convicted were put to death (河北省秦皇岛市中级人民法院 1993: 144). Another 256 counterrevolutionary cases were brought during a second campaign period in 1955, though less than 7 percent of those convicted in this round were sentenced to death (河北省秦皇岛市中级人民法院 1993: 146). Then, starting in 1959, during the Great Leap Forward, courts in Qinhuangdao began to try cases of "historical" counterrevolutionary offenses dating back to well before 1949 (河北省秦皇岛市中级人民法院 1993: 148–9).

Still, these city-level accounts don't tell the full story of the politicization of urban courts and legal institutions' work during the Maoist era, in part because these cities also contained large rural hinterlands. To get a fuller picture, we need to look at district court sources, like the gazetteer for Chengdu's Jinjiang District Court mentioned earlier. For example, in Shijiazhuang City, capital of Hebei Province, Chang'an District Court adjudicated fifty-five cases against counterrevolutionaries between its founding in 1958 and 1980, but fifty-two of these occurred during the Great Leap Forward years of 1958–60 (石家庄市长安区人民法院编 1994: 55).

The gazetteer even gives an example of one such case, against a Mr. Wang, who in the "difficult times" of 1960 was said to have cursed revolutionary leaders, defamed the Party, and written reactionary statements in a public place. For this, he was convicted and sentenced to five years in prison in 1961 (a decision upheld even after additional reconsideration, 复查, by the court) (石家庄市长安区人民法院编 1994: 55). Looking at other types of crimes, rape and sexual assault cases peaked in the 1980s (石家庄市长安区人民法院编 1994: 57),

while the incidence of theft cases in the 1958–66 period was roughly one tenth that of the 1980s (石家庄市长安区人民法院编 1994: 63). Still, there were some economic crimes prevalent during the Great Leap Forward era. For example, in a case of fraud, a local official swindled residents out of more than RMB2700 by claiming he could take their money and purchase then-scarce goods (including wristwatches and bicycles) on their behalf (石家庄市长安区人民法院编 1994: 65).

Qincheng (now called Qinzhou) District Court, in Gansu Province's Tianshui City, in Northwestern China, also saw high numbers of counterrevolutionary trials during the early 1950s. For example, two defendants in their twenties, one from Tianshui City and the other from the nearby countryside, were both brought to court in early May 1952, on charges of having belonged to reactionary societies (including the Chinese Youth Academic Research Society, 中国青年学术研究会, and the Just Spirit Academic Research Society, 正兴学术研究会). They were both convicted, sentenced to death, and executed on May 23 (天水市秦城区人民法院编 1993: 42). After a greater emphasis on cracking down against economic crimes and any actions that might undermine socialist development during the first five-year plan, a renewed focus on counterrevolutionary crimes permeated the court's work during the Great Leap Forward, when even crimes like stealing food or complaining about shortages were taken to be "counterrevolutionary" offenses (天水市秦城区人民法院编 1993: 47–9).

In an example of how the court's views of economic activities changed with the times, a twenty-seven-year-old Mr. Zhang was convicted in 1958 of wrecking the management of the planned economy and sentenced to ten years in prison. His crime was to sell cabbages, turnips, bean sprouts, sweet potatoes, and other vegetables, as well as noodles and tofu (all of which were then in extremely short supply), at various places on the outskirts of town. Later, in August 1962, his case was reevaluated by the court and his conviction was allowed to stand, but it was determined that he should be released early from prison. Finally, in 1987, the court took up his case again – this time ruling that he never should have been convicted of any crime (天水市秦城区人民法院编 1993: 50–1).

The Qincheng court was militarized under the oversight of the Revolutionary Committee from early 1968 through 1972, but criminal cases continued to be adjudicated – 345 were tried during those several years, including ninety-five for counterrevolutionary crimes and 103 involving economic crimes (天水市秦城区人民法院编 1993: 52–3).

Ordinary crimes were still prosecuted in these extraordinary times – for instance, in the case of a thirty-three-year-old Mr. Li, who had been "sent down" (下放) to Tianshui from his home in Henan Province (天水市秦城区人民法院编 1993: 55–6). Li was originally sentenced to five years for rape in 1969, but then had his sentence extended by another two years after he escaped from detention before his verdict had even been announced. While serving his sentence under mass supervision (交群众执行), Li found his way on the evening of April 22, 1970 to a working-class household in an alley in Qincheng District. There, he lay in wait for the seventeen-year-old woman who lived there to return home, and then strangled and beat her to death when she did, stealing clothes, shoes, and a bicycle from her house before fleeing and returning to his home in Henan. After being caught in Henan and returned to Tianshui for trial, Li was convicted by the Qincheng Revolutionary Committee on May 6, 1970 and sentenced to death. Li appealed to the Gansu Province Revolutionary Committee, which upheld the verdict and sentence, and he was executed on May 8.

Rural Areas

In rural areas, by contrast, courts and other legal institutions were mostly nonexistent in 1949. My earlier work has discussed how the district court in Yunnan's Zhenxiong County became increasingly institutionalized by harnessing the resources and political energy of campaigns (Hurst 2011: 81–4). As I will discuss Jiangxi's "County P," later in this chapter, there is less need to talk in detail here about many rural counties based on their court gazetteers. But looking quickly at even a small sample shows that the situation across many rural areas was rather like that in Zhenxiong – courts hardly existed on the ground in 1949, campaigns injected much-needed resources and clout during the 1950s, and trends of capacity-building and toward regularization persisted, even at the height of politicization during the Cultural Revolution and Great Leap Forward.

In Sichuan's rural and mountainous Qingchuan County, a functioning court was taken over by the CCP upon its rise to power in 1949. In the early 1950s, many counterrevolutionary crimes were prosecuted, leading to 403 trials in the sparsely populated county between 1950 and 1952. There were also campaigns to round up guns and ammunition from potentially dangerous reactionary elements, resulting in the seizure of more than 1000 handguns and 3700 bullets. Finally, in 1955, a new campaign against counterrevolutionaries involved two mass adjudication rallies, in which roughly 30,000 people participated (青川县人民法院法院志编写组 1988: 44–5).

Later, during the Cultural Revolution, other issues emerged. For instance, several local residents – allegedly old landlords – formed the "China Political Equality Party" (中国平政党) in May of 1966 and recruited roughly twenty members. This party even formed subregional committees and was said to have used the chaotic atmosphere of the moment to acquire weapons and ammunition and conspire to rebellion (图谋暴乱). A case was brought against the party's leaders in October 1968, however, and in July 1970 the two leaders were sentenced to immediate execution by firing squad, while other members were given suspended death sentences or lengthy prison terms (青川县人民法院法院志编写组 1988: 45).

Even as all these counterrevolutionary and political cases were unfolding, though, far larger numbers of ordinary criminal cases were being adjudicated by the Qingchuan Court – 2462 between 1950 and 1958 alone (青川县人民法院法院志编写组 1988: 47). In a simple theft case that escalated into a brutal murder and arson during the acute food shortage of the Great Leap Forward (and of which a photograph is included in the gazetteer), a farmer surnamed Zheng went to help his neighbor, Mr. Liu, repair his pigpen on April 12, 1958. While at his house, Zheng observed that the Liu family evidently still had some grain stored. On the night of April 16, Zheng then took a wooden club and other supplies and went to Liu's house, telling his neighbor that he had an emergency. Zheng then set Liu on fire and beat him with the club. Once Liu lay unconscious on the ground, Zheng stole as much grain as he could carry and set fire to Liu's house.

Returning to the house later and seeing that Liu was still alive, Zheng again tried to burn his house down. At that point, Liu came to and ran into the burning structure to rescue his six-year-old daughter and retrieve his belongings. After he had reemerged, however, Zheng beat him to death. For these crimes, Zheng was taken into custody on April 18, tried, and sentenced to immediate execution by firing squad on June 7 (青川县人民法院法院志编写组 1988: 51). Liu's hoarding was not seen as a political problem or a viable justification for Zheng's violent crimes, despite the intense mobilizational climate in 1958. Numerous other cases of rape, murder, theft, and assault proceeded through the court relatively routinely, even in periods of extreme upheaval or desperate conditions like the Great Leap Forward and Cultural Revolution.

At heightened political moments, notably between 1950 and 1956 (when such cases comprised 19 percent of the total handled by the Qingchuan Court), cases of corruption and other "economic crimes" were especially important ways in which wrongdoing by powerful actors was exposed and through which political battles were fought (青川县人民法院法院志编写组 1988: 57–8). In one example, a middle-school accountant forged receipts and embezzled procurements meant for the building of the school during the Great Leap Forward, amassing more than RMB4000 in ill-gotten gains. For this he was sentenced to eight years in prison in 1961. In another case, an overseer at a logging depot in the county took advantage of lax enforcement during the Cultural Revolution to establish a corrupt circle of roughly fourteen people, who then forged receipts, sold ration coupons, and otherwise skimmed more than RMB10,000 in illegal income between 1969 and 1972. The ringleader was sentenced to fifteen years in prison and a heavy fine in October 1972. Overall, we can see a pattern of political contestation from within the polity playing out especially strongly during the early 1950s, the Great Leap Forward, and the Cultural Revolution, and then a certain type of political backlash, especially during moments of greater stability in the polity like the early 1960s (and after 1978), that took the form of reviewing (and often overturning of judgements in) large numbers of "flawed" or "mistaken" cases (青川县人民法院法院志编写组 1988: 67–9).

These same general patters can be found across rural areas of China, from Guangdong and Fujian to Hebei and Shanxi, during the Maoist era. A fractured polity fought some of its political battles through the legal system, but in ways that added to the institutional capacity of rural courts and the regularization on the judicial process (even in the small minority of counties that had functional courts before 1949, as with Qingchuan in the example just discussed), rather than disrupting intact legal orders or stunting the development of courts and other institutions, as occurred in many cities.

Cases from the County P Public Security Bureau

An ideal (yet usually unavailable) source for the study of criminal law, especially in a context like Maoist China, is PSB case records, for these encompass both trials held in courts and extrajudicial legal processes (such as reeducation through labor, *laojiao* 劳教)[1] commonly employed during the period, in addition to trials conducted during intervals of militarized control of the courts during the Cultural Revolution. As we shall see, many *laojiao* cases involved petty crimes, but many also appear to have been related either to specific political campaigns (e.g. the Anti-Rightist Campaign) – in which *laojiao* punishment seems to have been the favored outcome of "struggle sessions" – or to migrant workers' deprivation of urban residency status (see also Mühlhahn 2009: 215–19).

The archives of the PSB of "County P," a rural area in the northern part of Jiangxi Province, provide just such a set of sources, which I was able to access in September 2013 at Shanghai Jiaotong University's History Department, where many files were compiled and are kept. The files I was able to review cover the years 1950–72. As far as possible, my sampling of cases was broadly representative, based on what we can observe across other basic-level court jurisdictions in the region. For example, in Wannian County, another rural area in northern Jiangxi quite similar to County P in most respects, the general pattern of cases during the period supports my sampling of cases from County P, in terms of both how many cases were drawn for each year and the rough allocation between different sorts of crimes (万年县法院志 2003: 149–50).

No formal court existed in County P before 1949, though a people's court (人民法院) was established in 1952 (according to its gazetteer and official website). During Land Reform (1950–3), before a court was functioning, "mass adjudication" (公审) or adjudication through the "justice section" (司法科) of the local government was the norm for most cases. Such rough and ready legal institutions were at least in theory under the loose supervision of a people's tribunal (人民法庭) (萍乡市中级法院 1995: 61–3; 万年县法院志 2003: 113; Mühlhahn 2009: 180–1). These tribunals were themselves established hastily after 1949 under directives from above, and their implementation in rural Jiangxi does not seem to have been comprehensive (江西省人民法院 1951). As in many localities, the County P Revolutionary Committees

[1] "Re-education through labor" (*laodong jiaoyang*, 劳动教养, or *laojiao* for short) is a sort of parallel track, administered by Public Security Bureaus directly, without recourse to judicial processes or courts (Seymour & Anderson 1999; Belkin 2000; Biddulph 2007; Mühlhahn 2009; Sapio 2010). The County P files offer an important window onto the workings of this system. Though the *laojiao* system had supposedly been phased out by 2015, it was an important factor in criminal justice during the Maoist Era – and especially in the 1960s.

assumed at least some level of control over the court during much of the Cultural Revolution, beginning in 1967 and continuing through at least 1972. It is for this reason that case decision documents (判决书) from this period are stamped with the seal of the county's revolutionary committee. Still, it appears that the court continued to function in many ways as it had before, in contrast to what has been asserted by some other scholars (e.g. Mühlhahn 2009: 235).

We can look across time periods to examine the highly politicized cases from Land Reform in contrast to the expectedly somewhat more routinized administration of justice during the First Five-Year Plan (1953–7) (Cohen 1968: 10–17). We then see an abrupt shift with the Anti-Rightist movement, the advent of the *laojiao* system, and the Great Leap Forward. The heightened mobilization of those years never fully calmed throughout the rest of the 1960s and the Cultural Revolution, though the types of crimes did change (with more routine cases being more prevalent between about 1962 and 1965 and more overtly political cases more common after 1966).

Land Reform Cases

In 1950, two typical cases against a landlord and an alleged bandit were handled through mass adjudication and the justice section. In Case P 1950.2, the defendant,[2] who had earlier been a school teacher in the provincial capital of Nanchang, was accused in general terms of mistreating tenant farmers and agricultural workers in his village. After testimony was received from several witnesses, he was officially stripped of his political rights and given the class label of "unlawful landlord." The County P Revolutionary Committee reconsidered his case in 1969, but the file does not contain documentation of the ultimate result. In Case P 1950.1, the defendant was accused of killing several villagers, including a Red Army veteran and a worker, and of sexually abusing at least one woman, on the basis of collectively written reports signed with the fingerprints of nearly a dozen witnesses. The County P People's Government (presumably the justice section, but it appears it did not yet have its own seal or letterhead) sentenced him to three years in prison and another three years of labor.

Two other cases from 1950 also involved alleged GMD agents. In Case P 1950.3, a local official stood accused of assisting the Nationalist

[2] All names of County P defendants and witnesses have been deliberately omitted to protect their privacy (especially as some are likely still living).

Army during the Civil War and acting as a GMD spy later. There was testimony from several witnesses and the presentation of several maps of the area, showing how troops had benefited from the intelligence he provided. This case is especially revealing because it was first handled by a special agency for the discipline of public servants rather than any judicial organ. The file contains a document from labeled as "江西省XX[3]分区行政督察专员公署刑事判决" (criminal decision of the Jiangxi Province XX district office for the administrative supervision of commissars). This administrative agency had sentenced the accused to three years in prison, followed by one year of labor, on September 4, 1950. Many other actors felt that punishment was too light, however, and sent directives to the County P People's Tribunal and PSB calling on them to punish him more severely. The provincial department of public security even sent a notice to the County P PSB demanding that it to look into the case (查明处理) and emphasizing the strong case against the defendant, whom it termed a GMD special intelligence agent and "despicable person." Sure enough, after gathering additional evidence, including a letter from the relevant township secretary, the tribunal issued a decision document in January 1951, convicting him and sentencing him to be stripped of his political rights and immediately executed.

A thirty-six-year-old defendant in Case P 1950.4 had been the head of the local civil affairs section, but was said to be secretly an agent of the GMD and to be working alongside an even more powerful spy. The two defendants were both said to have recruited local shopkeepers to join "reactionary organizations" during the early 1940s and then to have abused positions of power, attained after 1949, to aid the GMD. Both were convicted, deprived of citizen rights, and stripped of all their personal property – yet no prison or labor sentence was imposed.

In a somewhat similar case (Case P 1951.1), the defendant was accused of "political banditry" for allegedly helping organize the Nationalist Youth League (三青团) during the 1930s and generally working for the "reactionary regime." He was initially tried through mass adjudication, with a statement, signed (with fingerprints) by over 300 people, claiming that he had beaten at least three people to death and another, signed by approximately 115 people, saying he was an "evil landlord." A subunit (分庭) of the County P People's Tribunal

[3] I cannot name the district, as doing so could reveal the location of County P. So I have redacted its name to "XX".

first sentenced him to life in prison on February 26, 1951. Just over two weeks later, the full tribunal changed this sentence to death on March 12. After this, a period of uncertainty ensued, during which other actors petitioned the tribunal to impose the harshest possible sentence, while the court demurred from enforcing the one from March. The same administrative agency that had earlier argued for leniency in an apparently more serious case (Case P 1950.3) this time demanded harsher treatment in a letter dated June 8, 1951. The tribunal, after deliberation and clear internal division (some members are recorded as having favored a sentence of just six years in prison), affirmed the death sentence on July 20.

The first ordinary cases begin to appear in my sample in 1952 (for example the relatively straightforward cases against a man who admitted having sexually assaulted a woman he met while walking down the road – Case P 1952.1 – and against a thief who admitted to several offenses – Case P 1952.5), as the new People's Court began to hear cases in a more regularized fashion. It is also the first year in which sentences to labor reform (劳动改造) were routinely imposed. The issue of contestation over sentencing by nonjudicial actors remained important, however, as can be seen in a case of three convicted rapists in which the court, bombarded with missives from outside agencies like the Women's Federation, struggled to agree on equitable sentences for all the defendants (Case P 1952.6).

There were, of course, still many overtly political cases, in many of which investigation and sentencing also appear to have been problematic. One example is the prosecution of an alleged spy for blocking land reform, sexual, and other violence, and the murder of a Red Army veteran (Case P 1952.4). Though this file does not contain information on his sentencing, the initial investigation was conducted by a nonjudicial Party small group (县委内部政治清理领导小组) and this small group is listed as the official complainant (原告人) in the case. In another political case, the sixty-year-old leader of a secret society (同喜社) was sentenced, apparently first to life in prison, for leadership of a reactionary organization. The County PSB later petitioned for a shortened term, however, given his advanced age.

First Five-Year Plan Cases

In the early stages, some trials had still not switched over completely to the new County P People's Court, and the tribunal and "mass adjudication" system remained in effect for at least some political cases.

In one such case (Case P 1953.2), a forty-nine-year-old member of the old local gentry was convicted of aiding the GMD, as well as pretending to be a revolutionary so as to be able to continue oppressing the people. He was sentenced to three years of labor reform in a decision issued by the tribunal. Most cases, though, do seem to have switched over to the court's judicial process.

For example, three young workers accused of organizing anti-government labor actions in their production unit in February 1954, were tried and convicted of "wrecking" and sentenced to one year of labor reform through an orderly process (Case P 1954.1). Even a case that amounted to a political takedown of an entire family with old GMD connections for counterrevolutionary crimes proceeded smoothly (Case P 1955.1). A fifty-five-year-old member of the family fell under suspicion because of his long military service record under the GMD. After 1949, his main offense was said to be resistance to the household registration system and refusal to register (破坏户口管理), for which he was sentenced to three years of labor reform. Meanwhile, his thirty-three-year-old younger relative was convicted based on his record of abuse of women before World War II and his resistance to land reform in the early 1950s, even after the final divisions of land had been agreed upon, for which he was sentenced to five years of labor reform followed by three years' deprivation of political rights.

In an even starker example, a forty-three-year-old monk was convicted of fraud in 1955 for refusing to pay taxes and otherwise failing to conform to mandated standards of conduct (Case P 1955.2). He had originally been sentenced to two years of labor reform for abusing the people during the land reform campaign politics of 1950, and then apparently returned to his old ways after his release in 1952. Records indicate he came back under investigation in 1954, not for fraud, but for being a "bad element," before he was tried a year later. In this case, it appears the state took some pains to make a deeply political case appear ordinary, at least procedurally.

There were also, of course, some more straightforwardly political cases (e.g. Case P 1955.4). In one of these (Case P 1956.1), a high school educated villager was convicted of being a counterrevolutionary and sentenced to two years in prison. On October 13, 1956, perhaps because of prison overcrowding, or maybe for political reasons, the court changed its judgment and handed him over to be disciplined by the masses (改判交群众制) for one year. After that, the unfortunate convict was subjected to much harsher and longer-term punishment, meticulously documented by the PSB in the rest of the file on his case. Many of his fellow villagers came to the PSB to inform on or denounce him during the Great Leap Forward, usually for exhibiting a bad attitude or failing to concentrate during mandatory evening political study sessions, but occasionally for more serious offenses like selling grain ration tickets (粮票) to several neighbors for cash. In a few instances, villagers even put up big character posters (大字报) and criticized him openly.

In another fraught case (Case P 1957.1), a forty-five-year-old farmer was sentenced to five years in prison in December 1957 for having been a member of a GMD paramilitary organization before 1949 and for cursing the CCP cadres (calling them "worse than bandits") after liberation. In 1956, he then also allegedly proclaimed repeatedly that the GMD was about to return from Taiwan, even shouting when he saw an airplane in the sky that the invasion had begun. He was transferred from prison to labor reform in June 1958, and was then repeatedly denounced by other inmates, who informed on him for his criticism of the Great Leap Forward, for his saying that he did not trust reports of higher grain production, for commenting on the attractiveness of women he saw in the camp, and for shouting angrily in the fields, "What kind of People's Livelihood is this, we are hungry all day through to the evening!" (一天饿到晚，什么民生主义！). More than forty other inmate informers testified to his over-eating, stealing food, or complaining about shortages. Finally, in another case, a fifty-five-year-old farmer was sentenced to four years in labor reform for stealing pottery, food, and tools from warehouses belonging to local agricultural producers' cooperatives, which he allegedly opposed politically (Case P 1957.7).

In some cases, simple crimes took on more dimensions through sentencing based on class or political background. For example, Case P 1957.2 involved a Communist Youth League member, who had helped the Party greatly, being convicted of obvious theft of valuable goods. His light sentence (two months of labor reform) was a direct result of his political status and experience. In a more egregious example (Case P 1957.3), a poor peasant was given a death sentence, suspended for two years, for beating his wife to death. In 1959, Chairman Mao's special order (毛主席特殊令) of September 9 helped the intermediate court decide to reduce the sentence to fifteen years in labor reform. Though he performed well in labor reform during the early 1960s, leading the intermediate and higher courts to further reduce his sentence to thirteen years (again citing his class background, as well as his good behavior), he came under some criticism during the Cultural Revolution for, among other things, complaining that reading Mao's writings gave him a headache. Despite this, however, the Revolutionary Committee and a specially appointed research committee recommended his even earlier release in 1971 and 1972. Perhaps ironically, the file documents that he took up employment as a farmer in his old labor reform unit upon his release in July 1972. In Case P 1954.2, a farmer received a harsher sentence for theft than he might have otherwise because of his suspect political background from before 1949.

Looking at more clear-cut cases involving ordinary offenses, one of the few examples of a successful "citizen prosecution" among my sampled cases was a manslaughter prosecution by one villager of another, who admitted to killing the wife of yet another man while embroiled in an argument (Case P 1953.1). After being convicted, the defendant began to serve his three-year sentence in labor reform in September 1953. Several documents on file from his detention indicate that he behaved well in labor reform and was at least considered for early release, before being released and returning home on schedule in 1956. In another case (Case P 1957.4), three people preparing moonshine liquor got into an argument. During the argument, one hit one of the others, causing injury, and was convicted of intentional injury and sentenced to two months in prison. Similarly, a twenty-nine-year-old farmer was convicted and sentenced for stealing fertilizer from a public management department and taking it away by boat (Case P 1956.2). Several theft cases are generally similar (e.g. Case P 1954.3), including one involving theft from the public granary (Case P 1955.5).

Finally, there are some cases in which prisoners serving time committed additional crimes in labor reform camps. For example, in Case P 1957.6, a thief had his sentence doubled, from three years to six years, for (among other things) complaining about the "grass-boiled gruel" he was given to eat (吃各草煮稀饭只见草而见不到饭). After he resisted and reacted negatively to the new sentence, the court doubled it again – to twelve years. In Case P 1955.3, a thirty-nine-year-old villager, originally sentenced to two years for failing to adjust his mindset from the old regime, escaped from labor reform, only to be recaptured and given an extended sentence.

Great Leap Forward Cases

The Great Leap Forward was the period of the greatest and most intense politicization of justice in rural China – even more so than the

Cultural Revolution. Still, by looking in detail at a wider array of cases in County P, we can observe more complex dynamics. Specifically, even while many cases were politicized and there was a definite surge in prosecutions for political offenses, many ordinary cases became more regularized. Also, as will be discussed separately later, the Great Leap years saw the first significant use of extrajudicial administrative detention by the PSB. Finally, many of the political cases actually related substantially to issues from before 1949.

Cases 1958.1, 1958.6, 1959.7, and 1959.8 were all prosecutions of alleged former GMD agents or elites for political offenses dating back to before 1949. In some instances, recent statements or acts seemed to have been used as excuses for prosecution (e.g. more recent thefts in Cases 1958.6, 1959.7, and 1959.8). But the prevalence of such "historical" political cases is surprisingly high, especially given the extreme political tension and mobilization of the moment, which presumably could have led to more contemporaneous charges.

Remarkably, many of the most obviously political cases were handled according to the most scrupulous procedures, even at the height of the Great Leap Forward. In Case P 1959.6, for example, the PSB filed an official request with the procurator to detain the suspected "bandit," and the procurator filed official statements of prosecution with the court, which then issued a very clear and properly written decision sentencing him to life in prison (though he was released from labor reform in 1981, after twenty-two years, according to other documents in the file).

In an illuminating political case with its roots in the years after 1949, a forty-six-year-old rich peasant was convicted of defrauding two brothers, who had received the defendant's old house during land reform, in order to reacquire the property in 1957 (Case P 1958.9). For this he was initially sentenced to seven years of labor reform, which the court revised just a few months later up to nine years (because of his supposed lack of remorse). In Case P 1961.2, a thirty-three-year-old from a landlord family was sentenced to one year of labor reform for "selfish behavior" (which apparently consisted of moving in with his girlfriend without being married). In Case P 1962.1, a twenty-seven-year-old farmer was sentenced to nearly four years of labor reform for stealing and selling grain ration tickets.

There are some surprisingly routine petty cases that ran through the court system, even though the number of *laojiao* cases increased substantially during this time (e.g. Case P 1959.9). In Case P 1958.2, for example, a villager was sentenced to two years in labor reform for fighting with and injuring two others. Case P 1958.7 deals with a fifty-four-year-old villager caught stealing tools and machines from an agricultural producers' cooperative. He had earlier been convicted of theft several times in the early 1950s, and after this latest incident even went so far as to say the cooperatives were bandits (合作社是土匪). After a routine trial, which even involved two jurors alongside the presiding judge, he was sentenced to one year of labor reform.

As in earlier years, several cases involved crimes committed while defendants were incarcerated in labor reform camps. In Case P 1958.4, for instance, a twenty-one-year-old worker from Nanchang serving in labor reform in County P plotted with two other prisoners to escape, and had his sentence extended after being caught. A twenty-three-year-old illiterate farmer from County P was caught stealing clothes and a towel in labor reform and had his sentence extended by five years (Case P 1958.5). Finally, in Case P 1958.8, a fifty-year-old career criminal escaped from labor reform and went on the lam for one month, during which time he stole a variety of items and assaulted at least one person. After being recaptured, his sentence was extended by five years.

As noted, the Great Leap Forward era was the first time large numbers of *laojiao* cases had appeared in the County files. Though some encompassed only mundane offenses (e.g. Cases P 1959.2 and P 1959.1), many involved highly politicized crimes. For example, in Case P 1960.5, a seventeen-year-old villager was sent to *laojiao* for six months (later extended to three years) for unspecified reactionary speech and actions. In Case P 1961.2, a forty-one-year-old housewife was sent to *laojiao* for two years for complaining about food shortages caused by the Great Leap Forward. She had earlier spent three months in labor reform in 1951 after being caught stealing, bringing her under increased suspicion a decade later. Case P 1960.6 involved a thirty-six-year-old man from a landlord family in County P, who had been working for the Shanghai Labor Bureau as a mid-level official. In 1958, he was said to have criticized the Anti-Rightist Campaign and generally spoken out against the CCP's policies on intellectuals and education, claiming that, "in twenty years, we'll all be illiterate." He decried the repression of speech during the campaign as well, asking "what kind of petty democracy is this? People are not allowed to speak!" (这是啥小民主？是不让人讲话！) and said the atmosphere resembled the "second generation of Ah Q" (啊Q第二代).[4] Notably, he also decried the injustices of the household registration system in regards to labor, saying it was unfair to keep peasants out of the city (防止农民进城，这是不公平的). He was branded a rightist and sent to *laojiao* in August 1960. Finally, in 1964, the Jiangxi *laojiao* management bureau (江西省劳动教养管理局) issued a statement removing his "rightist hat" (右派分子帽子) and also approved his release that May.

Many political cases still revolved around issues from before 1949. For example, Case P 1959.4 was the prosecution of an old GMD cadre, who said he had joined and participated in the Nationalist Party because it gave him opportunities (including attending university). The forty-four-year-old landlord was sent to *laojiao* for three years, where other inmates informed on him for eating too much and for behaving badly in front of other inmates (though this does not seem to have affected his release date). Case P 1958.3 centered on a forty-five-year-old worker – and CCP member – sent to *laojiao* in County P. Most of his alleged misdeeds occurred before 1949, but he was also said to have taken other workers' rations for himself during the mid-1950s. His sentence was extended twice before his release in May 1962, though the file documents that he was still closely monitored by the PSB until at least 1966. Case P 1959.3 involved an old GMD Army veteran, who had stolen food and alcoholic beverages from villagers before 1949, resisted land reform, finally resisted collectivization in 1959, and was branded a "bandit." For this, he was sent to *laojiao* for five years. Case P 1959.10 involved the punishment of a forty-eight-year-old ex-GMD member (indeed the main evidence against him in the file was his GMD registration card from 1948) partly through *laojiao*, but mainly through supervision by the local police.

In Case P 1961.1, we see an example of the use of *laojiao* in an otherwise petty case to return a migrant worker to the countryside. A twenty-one-year-old poor peasant from County P was sent to Nanchang to be apprenticed at a state-owned steelworks, where he even joined the Communist Youth League, following the collectivization of his village. He was caught stealing ration tickets from the cafeteria, however, and sent to *laojiao* back in County P (on a military-owned farm) for eighteen months in 1961. After his official release, he stayed on to work

[4] This is a reference to Lu Xun's classic 1922 novella "The True Story of Ah Q" (阿Q 正传), a preeminent literary critique of traditional Chinese society in the early twentieth century.

at the farm from 1962 until a report during the Socialist Education Campaign in late 1965 concluded he should be sent back to live with his family in their commune in early 1966.

In a tragic example of the use of *laojiao* during a political campaign to return rural migrant workers to the countryside, in Case P 1960.1, a nineteen-year-old woman, originally from County P, arrived in Nanchang in January 1960 to take up work at a state-owned fishing equipment factory. She was said to have been a poor worker, to have had sex with her boyfriend outside marriage, and to have generally engaged in bad behavior. Her most egregious offense, however, was stealing articles of clothing from other workers (valued at a total of over 68 RMB). After stealing clothes on April 29, she fled the factory and did not return to the work unit until the next morning. She was made a prime target at a special meeting convened by the district PSB on May 2, to struggle against bad people and actions (向坏人坏事作斗争). At the end of the meeting, she was taken into custody by the PSB and sent to *laojiao* back in County P. According to a clinic report, she died of complications from uncontrollable bleeding on November 30, 1961, while in *laojiao*, at age twenty.

Finally, some seemingly routine cases played out in an extreme economic and political environment. For instance, a twenty-six-year-old illiterate peasant was caught stealing shoes, clothes, and cloth from his neighbors, along with sweet potatoes and turnips from the communal mess hall during the Great Leap Forward (Case P 1959.5). He was sent to *laojiao*, initially for a two-year term, but his sentence was extended several times for bad behavior and he had not been released as of mid-1964 (the date of the last documents in the case file). In Case P 1960.3, a forty-seven-year-old illiterate farmer was sent to *laojiao* for just over three years for stealing food and ration tickets. In Case P 1960.4, a nineteen-year-old poor peasant was sent to *laojiao* for three years for stealing shoes. All of these events unfolded against the backdrop of severe shortages caused by the Great Leap Forward. In another case indicative of the times, a County P native, who had been sent to work for a state-owned company in Beijing, was sentenced to *laojiao* in Beijing for alleged sexual harassment (Case P 1960.2).

Cases from 1963–1965

Most of the cases I was able to sample from the relatively brief 1963–5 period, between the end of the Great Leap Forward and the start of the Cultural Revolution, were processed not through the courts, but through administrative detention (*laojiao*). Still, many cases involving ordinary offenses proceeded through formal prosecution by the procuratorate and careful application of clear and formal rules by the court in its decision documents, despite obvious ongoing politicization. For instance, a thirty-six-year-old poor peasant was convicted of murder after sleeping with the wife of his neighbor, who later killed himself after the adulterous dispute could not be resolved through mediation (Case P 1963.4). The neighbor, a miner, had been away at work at the time. For this crime, the accused was sentenced to four years of labor reform (and while there he was struggled against during the Socialist Education Campaign). In a similarly neatly handled case (Case P 1963.5), a thirty-one-year-old poor peasant was convicted of sexually assaulting two women and stealing soy beans from the production team's supplies in the summer of 1962. He served five years in labor reform and was released in 1968.

In a less serious example (Case P 1963.1), a twenty-five-year-old migrant from County P was sent to *laojiao* for five years after being caught pickpocketing passengers on a Nanchang bus. After completing his sentence, he stayed on to be employed at his *laojiao* unit until March 1978. Strangely, though the defendant was sent to *laojiao* (not prison or labor reform), his case was handled by the County P Court (rather than the PSB directly).

In perhaps the most intriguing case from the period, a thirty-nine-year-old rich peasant was convicted of class reprisals after beating a neighbor and causing injuries (Case P 1965.1). His family had apparently suffered during land reform at the hands of the victim's family (in fact, some of the documents imply that his father may have been killed in the early 1950s because of the actions of the neighbor). Then, in August 1964, the neighbor's waterwheel broke, causing a flood in a field for which the defendant was responsible. The next day, when the waterwheel had not been repaired, he threatened to destroy irrigation works in the neighbor's field. The neighbor responded by asking that he leave the production team, at which point he attacked him. The court sought testimony from a doctor as to the exact severity of the victim's injuries. The defendant's confession was recorded in a much more precise and orderly form than had been common in earlier cases and the court decision document was very professionally written and prepared. He was sentenced, however, not to prison or labor reform, but to *laojiao* for five years. Upon his release in 1969, he remained employed at the *laojiao* unit until September 1977, when he at last returned to his family home.

There are also many political cases in which *laojiao* was employed (e.g. Cases 1963.2, 1965.2, and 1966.1). In Case P 1964.1, a thirty-eight-year-old from a landlord family was struggled against and sent to *laojiao* during the Socialist Education Campaign. His alleged offenses included stealing and manipulation of supplies, but the main issues in the case appear to have been purely political. Case P 1965.4 was the *laojiao* investigation (and apparently very lenient punishment) of an elementary school teacher in County P, who allegedly looked down on rural students and taught reactionary versions of history. There are many examples of *laojiao* being used to punish ordinary petty crimes (e.g. Cases 1963.3, 1964.2, and 1965.3). For instance, a twenty-six-year-old thief was sent to *laojiao* for five years in Case P 1959.1. He was later released, but fell under renewed suspicion and coercive control during the Socialist Education Campaign in 1966.

Finally, in another such case (Case P 1966.6), a railway worker in Nanchang, originally from the County P, was swept up in the "Four Cleanups" Campaign in his work unit in 1966 (just before the start of the Cultural Revolution). Deemed by the Railway Bureau Party Committee to be a semi-landlord style rich peasant based on his actions from before 1949, he was made to "wear a hat" for this, and was sent to County P for "mass-supervised labor" (a less formal type of *laojiao*). Eventually, the Railway Bureau Party Committee decided, in December 1975, that he had been a model worker in supervised labor and had committed no further crimes. Still, the committee reasoned, his long absence from work was tantamount to resignation from his railway post and abdication of his urban household registration.

Cultural Revolution Cases

Little scholarship has been done on the Cultural Revolution era in Chinese law (but for a relatively comprehensive and nuanced overview of the criminal justice system during the Cultural Revolution, see 韩 1995: Vol. 2, Chapter 5). As mentioned earlier, there is a tendency among many scholars to write off the entire decade from 1966 to 1976 as completely lawless and chaotic. While it is notable that Revolutionary Committees assumed at least *de jure* control over court functions after 1967, and Party Committees, along with specially-constituted "small groups" took up much of the work of investigation and evidence gathering (especially in political cases) (for more on these, and how they could overstep their authority and even engage in illegal acts, see 韩 1995: Vol. 2, 617–19, 621–2, 669–70), the basic criminal process was not upended by the Cultural Revolution, at least in County P. Indeed, in one relatively routine case of a forty-year-old farmer's illegal cultivation of private plots and secret raising of small animals, in which the original decision document was issued officially by the Revolutionary Committee (Case P 1968.1), a later review of the convict's status in labor reform (in 1975) referred to the case as having been adjudicated according to proper procedures by the County P People's Court, suggesting the change may have been in name only.

In an early ordinary case that the file does not document through to trial or punishment, a thirty-three-year-old poor peasant stabbed his neighbor after a dispute on October 31, 1966 (Case P 1966.2). The defendant was investigated by the Party Committee of his commune as well as by the County P PSB. He himself had also filed a citizen prosecution with the County P court that August against the man he eventually killed, alleging that he had "become corrupted with my wife" (与我妻搞腐化). After a long series of alleged affairs between the victim and the defendant's wife, which could not be resolved through mediation by production team cadres, things came to a head when the defendant, who happened to be sitting under a tree near the entrance to the village toilets, overheard the victim speak to someone else inside the latrine about murdering him with a knife. The authorities did investigate the charges, and even interrogated the eventual victim on August 9, but nothing appears to have been concluded before the actual killing (and the end result of the legal process is not documented in the file).

In another case without documentation of conviction or punishment, a forty-four-year-old man was said to have engaged in violent acts against poor peasants in cooperation with his landlord father and grandfather (Case P 1966.5). In a report by the brigade (大队) Party Committee, he is said to have forcibly taken one person's house and beaten another man to death before 1949. He was also charged with six sets of misdeeds since liberation, among them: threatening land reform cadres when his family was labeled "landlords," poisoning pork that sickened many people, beating up two villagers and stealing a pair of shoes from one of them in 1950, distracting his workmates picking lake grass in 1962 by saying they should have stayed at home and eaten better instead of starving by the lakeshore, accusing the production team leader of being responsible for the deaths of his wife and children from malnutrition and starvation during the Great Leap Forward, selling his own house and then wrongfully moving into the house left vacant after his brother had been executed for being a counterrevolutionary, and generally being disagreeable with other villagers. The Commune Party Committee investigated further, interrogated the defendant, and interviewed a series of witnesses in early 1966, after the brigade committee had asked "judicial organs" (司法部门) to take the case up for prosecution. But it is not clear what ultimately became of the case against him.

In a routine case (Case P 1966.3), a twenty-eight-year-old man from County P was convicted and sentenced to five years in labor reform for stealing nine truckloads of wood and arranging to transport them to Nanchang for illicit sale. In another case (Case P 1967.3), a sixty-year-old "hooligan" (流氓), who had been in repeated trouble for stealing grain during the 1950s, was arrested for stealing a water buffalo (水牛) from the commune's paddock in August 1966. In light of his past transgressions, he was given the relatively harsh sentence of five years in labor reform, from which he was released on time in 1971.

Other ordinary cases from this period were clearly influenced by political conditions. For example, in Case P 1972.2, a twenty-eight-year-old poor peasant, sent to work in a state-owned factory as part of the Third Front Project, stole supplies on various occasions (including lamps, sheets, glass, oil, electrical machines, door handles, batteries, umbrellas – even bedpans from the workers' clinic and fire hoses and extinguishers from the dormitory). He sent all these goods back to his family in County P.

In an ordinary case that took place under extraordinary conditions, a "barefoot doctor" was convicted by the PLA Legal Committee (中国人民解放军江西省P县公安机关制事管制小组, a subcommittee of the County P Revolutionary Committee that was overseeing the court at the time) of sexually assaulting a fifteen-year-old girl multiple times, including at least once inside the clinic (Case P 1967.4). The university-educated defendant had engaged in improper sexual relations with two different married women in the past, but these matters had been handled internally in his brigade. In another case of "ordinary" sexual depravity, a thirty-two-year-old middle school teacher was convicted and sentenced to five years of labor reform for violent and sexual acts against twelve of his students (Case P 1968.2). A review of his labor reform status just before release in 1973 also referenced the County P People's Court as having decided his case according to law, even though the original document was issued by the PLA Legal Committee (and stamped by the Revolutionary Committee). After being caught, he was tried and sentenced to labor reform and, upon his release in 1975, he went to work for a *laojiao* unit for two years until 1977. Other cases also involved stealing grain from public reserves or supplies from state-owned factories or projects (e.g. Cases 1970.1 and 1970.2). Another such case involved a thirty-seven-year-old poor peasant who had stolen coal from a Third Front project, but had also previously been involved in an illicit sexual affair with a married woman (Case P 1971.1). All of these were processed pretty much routinely through the Revolutionary Committee.

Case P 1969.1 is a case that crosses the boundary between ordinary and political crimes. A fifty-five-year-old pharmacist from a landlord background was said to be profiteering off of privately reselling drugs from the public pharmacy. When a student exposed these crimes in a big character poster (大字报), the pharmacist retaliated by setting fire to several houses and the public health office. One house was destroyed and three people suffered injuries. The pharmacist was convicted in a decision document issued by the Revolutionary Committee and sentenced to death; a sentence which was suspended for two years, to be spent in labor reform. Later, in 1973, the Jiangxi Higher-level Court reviewed the case and commuted his sentence to life in prison because of his good behavior. While the crimes were not overtly political, the manner of exposition and retaliation appears to have been at least strongly influenced by the unique political environment and mobilization of the Cultural Revolution.

In another such case, a medical assistant, who had committed several past abuses, was treating a female patient, a youth rusticated from Shanghai (Case P 1972.1). While in the exam room, he asked her to remove all of her clothes and began groping her, claiming he was a CCP member, a Korean War veteran, and otherwise beyond reproach. He then entered into a sexual relationship with the patient (which certainly seems from the tone of the accounts in the file to have been forced). After the original patient's older sister came to visit her, he assaulted the sister and began an "evil triangular love" (三角恶爱) with the two of them. In light of his past record, and because the victim was a rusticated youth who deserved special protection, he was sentenced to fifteen years of labor reform (to be released in 1986).

There were several almost stereotypically political cases. In one of these, a twenty-two-year-old poor peasant was convicted and sentenced to two years of "mass supervision" in a decision issued by the Revolutionary Committee in June 1969 (Case P 1969.2). His primary offense was apparently writing several pages of counterrevolutionary ramblings, in which he made veiled and open statements wishing death to Mao Zedong and proclaiming opposition to the revolution. In a more complex case, three members of one family, all in their twenties – brother 1, brother 2, and brother 1's wife – were prosecuted both for being of a bad class background and for allegedly making political statements and errors during the Cultural Revolution (Case P 1969.3).

Their recent transgressions, at the time of their trial in 1969, included making negative remarks about having to hang a portrait of Mao in the doorway of their house (which they derided as "formalism"), making fun of other leaders pictured with Mao (saying they looked like "toadies," 拍马屁), resisting using Mao's words in their performances (they were performers in a Maoist Cultural Troupe), listening to prohibited radio broadcasts from Taiwan and the Soviet Union, making fun of people spontaneously shouting "ten thousand years to Chairman Mao" (毛主席万岁) in the street by saying that no one could live that long (一个人能活到一百岁就算不错), and insinuating that the real reason for Liu Shaoqi's downfall was his wife Wang Guangmei's relationship with Mao's wife Jiang Qing. All three were sentenced to "mass supervision" through labor and the decision over whether or not to place "counterrevolutionary hats" on them left to the masses in the commune.

There were cases in which administrative channels were used to target petty criminals. A relatively dramatic *laojiao* case (Case P 1967.1) involved a man suspected of theft, investigated initially by a commune "Cultural Revolution Committee of Poor and Lower Peasants" (人民公社贫下中农文化革命委员会). A similar committee at the brigade level had initially collected evidence against the suspect in the routine theft case. Once the commune committee's report was completed, the suspect was turned over to the County P PSB for punishment through the *laojiao* system. In another case, a thirty-two-year-old former soldier was convicted by a military committee of causing injuries to several patients, and even killing a child by administering the wrong dose of medication to her, in 1966 (Case P 1966.4). Before that, he had served five years in prison for sexual assault, before being assigned as a medical worker upon his release in 1963. After his 1966 conviction, he served two years on a military labor reform farm, before being released in 1968.

Sometimes *laojiao* was used to strip workers of urban residency. In one such case, the forty-eight-year-old defendant, whose class background was listed as "urban poor" and who had been employed at a power plant in Jingdezhen for many years, lost his urban household registration and was sent "home" to County P, where his family had come from originally (Case P 1967.2). Officially, he was deemed by an internal investigation committee in his work unit to have engaged in myriad suspicious acts, almost exclusively prior to 1949. He was then sent to County P for indefinite mass supervision. Strictly speaking, this case does not appear to have been processed through even a perfunctory *laojiao* review by either the Jingdezhen or County P PSB.

Concluding Thoughts

While civil adjudication remained undeveloped, Chinese criminal law was deployed frequently as an important instrument of political and social mobilization and contestation during the Maoist era. Though some previous research has depicted this time period as essentially lawless, legal institutions operated and exercised important and powerful functions throughout the 1950s, 1960s, and 1970s. They operated rather differently in different periods within the Maoist era, however, and their roles played out quite distinctly in rural versus urban areas. In the former, campaign mobilization sometimes brought resources and clout that otherwise were absent, while in the latter, the same movements undermined otherwise more functional and independent agencies. On the whole, the high-stakes political struggles of Chinese politics under Mao were clearly reflected in the politicized mobilization of criminal justice, even as the legal regime inched toward greater regularization and institutionalization.

CONCLUSION

As Robespierre, perhaps the original architect of a mobilizational legal regime in the modern world, summarized the failures of ordinary law in extraordinary political and historical contexts: "The revolution is attempted to be carried out with cavils, as business in a court of justice is conducted. Conspiracies against the public are treated as law-suits of private persons. Tyranny kills and liberty pleads; and the code framed by the conspirators is the law by which they are judged" (Robespierre 1794: 14). Mobilizational polities and the would-be charismatic leaders who head them are leery of anything that smacks of a staid and conservative legal order, under which existing power-holders can manipulate seemingly objective institutions, norms, and processes to their advantage – the whole point, after all, is to subvert existing power relations through exceptional means and tactics.

Still, perhaps ironically, it is when the exercise of charismatic authority is most successful that mobilizational legal regimes become most regularized, especially when prior institutions are weak or inchoate, as they were in much of rural China in 1949. When institutions – prior to whatever break leads to an open and fractious polity – are strong and their holdovers remain intact, mobilizational legal regimes are detrimental to any attempts to rebuild coherent legal institutions or processes, as in urban China. Another aspect of state strength helps differentiate between primarily criminal and primarily civil law mobilizational regimes.

Mobilizational legal regimes are more likely to focus on criminal law when they exist in a postrevolutionary moment of consolidation, in which a reign of terror is useful (even seen as necessary) for attempts to cement a new political order or to strike against enemies not yet defeated or ejected from the polity. The "cavils of private law" are cold comfort against the hot winds of Thermidor, when only the full coercive power of the state holds any meaningful sway. Hence, the very fragility and uncertainty of the basic contours of the polity and the high stakes in play can lead to a prioritization of criminal law and a neglect of civil law. But aggregate state strength can also be seen as having the opposite effect.

When states are stronger than powerful private interests, criminal law can become appealing in mobilizational contexts. But where states are weaker and private interests stronger, mobilizational legal regimes can work through the civil law process to advance redistribution (with outside political intervention into the rulemaking and adjudication processes as needed). Chinese peasants had no need of suing their local landlord in the early 1950s when they could expropriate his land by force (and convict and kill him if he resisted – or even if he didn't), with the full backing of the ideological and violent power of the state. Rural poor Indonesian citizens during Guided Democracy enjoyed no recourse to such visceral methods – they had to wait it out in the courts as they pursued politicized litigation under the new rules of the 1960 Agrarian Law.

Suharto's counterrevolution could not be forestalled – it came just the same, even though it, too, was weak and inchoate for its first eight years or so. The weakness of the mobilizational legal regimes in Indonesia, and their corresponding focus on civil, rather than criminal, law, gave them a fundamentally different character than their counterparts in China. This difference played out in other respects as well.

In urban areas, where prior institutions tend to have been stronger, more robust mobilizational regimes threaten their integrity and drive the system further away from predictability or regularization. But in rural areas lacking such an institutional base, the more robust the mobilization regime, the more it tends to promote the basic integrity, regularization, and predictability of the system, facilitating the potential implementation of a rule by law or rational pluralist order, should one of these become preferable or necessary.

CHAPTER FOUR

RULE BY LAW: AUTHORITARIAN LEGITIMACY AND LEGAL EFFICIENCY

> *Fundamental law and the diffusion of authority were incompatible with political modernization. Modernization requires authority for change. Fundamental changes in society and politics come from the purposeful actions of men. Hence authority must reside in men, not in unchanging law.*
>
> (Huntington 1968: 101)

> *Once rulers, or other parties, understand the utility of law and instruments of law enforcement, they can use them as administratively efficient tools to control behaviour and to secure relative stability, order, and peace in the ordinary affairs of life . . . This does not mean that such rulers place themselves and their own activities under law, which is a distinguishing characteristic of true rule of law . . . It means instead that, for reasons of control, efficiency and administration – and for its value in ordering human affairs and resolving conflicts – power holders may cede decision-making in certain areas of human affairs to neutral decision-making under law, provided creating and enforcing law does not threaten regime power or interests. Rule by law, if applied to property and contract rights and if truly free of power holders' interventions, can also provide a foundation for economic and social development.*
>
> (Goodpaster 2007: 127–8)

INTRODUCTION

Rule by law legal regimes have been widely remarked upon and studied across the existing literature. But they are also perhaps the most rare in the world. It is not every closed hierarchical polity that can restrain itself from intervening in the process of adjudication. In fact, I would venture to say that *no* ruling coalition within such polity could likely remain on the sidelines across *all* types of cases. If it did, it would risk abdicating its position at the apex of the political, economic, and social order.

What we find in Indonesia since *Reformasi* is a hybrid regime in which nonlegal political actors and social elites have removed themselves (or been ejected) from the criminal adjudication process through genuine and deep (though in important ways still partial) democratization. Though many critics have made the charge (with some justification) that Indonesia's democracy is hollow because elites remain entrenched or because of interventions into the civil adjudication system, the criminal apparatus is today remarkably free of political interference (once the process is initiated – any intervention tends to take place before it starts, to keep cases out of court or to criminalize civil disputes such that defendants are improperly charged). There are still of course, some exceptions, especially when top leaders become defendants (e.g. the sensationally political prosecution of Basuki Tjahaja Purnama, a.k.a. "Ahok," for alleged "blasphemy" in 2016–17). Such cases tend, however, to be exceptional in most criminal justice systems, whether they involve the Governor of Jakarta or the President of the United States.

In China since 1978, an impressively calculating and careful authoritarian regime has managed to craft a civil rule by law regime such that transaction costs and uncertainty are reduced and economic growth is fostered, even if a small set of relatively inconsequential cases can remain subject to intervention by at least local powerholders. One example was a 2009 case I observed at trial in rural Liaocheng (Shandong Province), in a court so poorly resourced that the judges could only hear cases in the mornings because they had to work tilling fields and cultivating vegetables behind the courthouse every afternoon (though they set down their gavils, the judges worked outside while still wearing their court-issued trousers, while they took off their uniform shirts to wield their hoes and spades in undershirts or shirtless). The suit involved elderly villagers suing their children for financial support that had not been forthcoming – and was decided in the plaintiffs' favor apparently because the village Party Secretary had written a letter to the court appealing to the judges' sense of traditional morality. But, to ensure its hold on power, the Party has not given up the capacity to use the criminal system for repression of potential enemies or challengers. In fact, successful ongoing operation of rule by law in the civil sphere has helped promote and sustain the performance legitimacy of the still very much authoritarian CCP, allowing it to maintain a neotraditional regime in the criminal apparatus.

CHINA

Though some readers may disagree with my decision to characterize civil adjudication in the reform era as a rule by law regime (e.g. He

& Su 2013; Ang & Jia 2014), this is in fact in keeping with at least one major strand of the extant literature. Indeed, authors like Randall Peerenboom see Chinese law in the current era as becoming in many important respects more reliable, transparent, predictable, or "fair." Whether the professionalization and accountability of the legal system on which such a transformation depends occur due to the political influence of foreign investors (Wang 2015), the relative strength of local private markets for legal services (Kinkel 2015), or some other set of factors (Balme 2010), matters less than the fact that there is indeed a discernable trend toward a rule by law order (in contrast to a slide back toward politicization or a "turn against law" observed by Minzner and others). Critically, *none* of the scholars who perceive an emergent rule by law regime in China focus on the criminal apparatus – every argument for the "rationalization" or professionalization of Chinese law is centered on the analysis of the *civil* litigation system (and with good reason, as will be discussed in reference to the criminal system in Chapter 5).

Civil Law in Rural Areas

Across rural China, civil adjudication became dramatically more predictable and routinized from the early 1980s through to the late 1990s. By looking at a few localities in some detail, we can see a clear picture of courts emerging as venues in which parties could rely upon their cases being heard and decided according to clear and well-known rules, and as institutions that might even be able to enforce civil judgments. We can also see courts looking frequently to use mediation as a means of avoiding difficult or unenforceable decisions and scrambling to keep up with rapid social and economic change and correspondingly burgeoning case loads. On the whole, though, an increasingly rule by law regime was definitely coming into being during China's first two decades of economic reform.

In Mianyang's[1] Santai County, in the northeastern part of Sichuan Province, civil case filings skyrocketed in the first seventeen years of the

[1] Of course, some may object that Mianyang is largely run as a company town by Sichuan Changhong Electronics Company, a gargantuan manufacturer of televisions, batteries, and other products that dominates the local economy and many aspects of politics and society, thus hopelessly predisposing courts there to local protectionism. Such critics should look to recent published cases in which Changhong has not triumphed, such as Mianyang Intermediate Court's Civil Case 172 (2013) (which I thank Jonathan Kinkel for bringing to my attention).

reform era, from 200 in 1979 to 2309 in 1996, with the additional twist that only about half of all cases concluded after 1990 were mediated (三台县法院志编纂领导小组编 1999: 115). This court also, notably, adjudicated nearly 600 land disputes in its civil division between 1950 and 1956 (三台县法院志编纂领导小组编 1999: 112), in contrast to the prevailing mostly criminal and mass-adjudication model of land reform and its aftermath described in Chapter 3. From the start of the 1980s, however, the varieties of cases and adjudication mechanisms used to resolve them evolved rapidly.

For example, the Santai Court was suddenly inundated with housing-related disputes in 1980 and 1981 because, in its own words, the implementation of new housing policies and clarification of property rights after the Third Plenum in 1978 allowed citizens the right to sue for restitution of their housing. The flood of new cases alarmed the county Party Committee, so it commissioned a comprehensive report from the court on how to reduce their numbers. And indeed the number of cases duly declined consistently starting in 1982 (三台县法院志编纂领导小组编 1999: 129). Many of these suits related to land transactions and agreements from the Republican Era (1911–49). Others were based on transfers of housing rights during land reform in the early 1950s, as in the case of a Mr. Jiang versus a Mr. He, which was adjudicated in 1980. Jiang claimed that He's house had originally been his family's lineage hall. Upon investigation, the court found that He and several of his relatives had been given the hall to live in during land reform in 1951 because their family lacked adequate housing. Jiang's claim was thus deemed baseless, as the court upheld the thirty-year-old redistribution (三台县法院志编纂领导小组编 1999: 130).

In a 1987 case with similar origins, the court ended up dividing several houses and cash between three brothers, even though one of them had purchased five houses in his township both for his family to live in and to use to run a candy business in 1949. The business was then taken over by the state in 1955 and two of the brothers had moved to villages to work as farmers, but some parts of the family's claim to the property remained valid (三台县法院志编纂领导小组编 1999: 130). Several cases noted in the Santai court's gazetteer also related to transactions and sales of houses or property that had previously changed hands during the Great Leap Forward years or to cases of property that had been left in the care of friends or relatives during that same era (三台县法院志编纂领导小组编 1999: 131).

In a related development, there was also a spike of land tenure disputes, especially during the late 1980s. Many of these related to boundaries of land holdings, while others revolved around managerial authority. One such case, which was eventually resolved in 1984 after previous attempts at mediation in 1969 and 1971, involved an orchard with 250 fruit trees in one of the county's villages. As cooperatives expanded and then collectivization proceeded during the 1950s, management of the orchard shifted from a family, to the village cooperative, to a production team (生产队). The brigade (大队), however, sought to extract high levels of grain output from the team, setting unreasonable production quotas, even though the orchard took up a large tract of the village's land (which then could not be used to grow grain). Eventually, the village assumed responsibility for the orchard and the quotas were adjusted to be more equitable (三台县法院志编纂领导小组编 1999: 137–8). Collective ownership was maintained, but its terms and institutions were adjusted in accordance with the spirit of reform and the logic of the market.

Suits related to the payment of debts (债务案) – including those related to leases and contracts – were especially problematic, as it was only in 1984 that the Supreme People's Court issued a decision, implemented by the Santai Court, prohibiting the filing of such claims in relation to obligations incurred before 1949 (三台县法院志编纂领导小组编 1999: 133). Prior to that time, a large number of difficult-to-resolve disputes with roots in the Republican era had poured into local courts. In subsequent years, rules on time limits, interest, and other aspects of such cases were also clarified (and in most cases tightened). But the number of debt collection suits filed continued to rise sharply, from just 3 in 1979 to 564 in 1996, making these the most frequent type of disputes other than divorces (三台县法院志编纂领导小组编 1999: 114).

Among the difficulties of adjudicating these cases, as the gazetteer explains (三台县法院志编纂领导小组编 1999: 133–4), were how to assign responsibility to the different parties, on what terms or schedules debts should be repaid when no formal agreement or contract had been made between the parties in advance, and how much interest or other penalty (if any) should be levied on late payments. The general practice of the court seems to have been to assign responsibility equally among all debtors in cases where a debt was incurred in common, to require payment of interest or penalties roughly equal to what the principal would have earned had it been deposited in a savings account at the local bank at the time the debt was incurred, and to require repayment of debts upon the issuance of a judgment, except where doing so would present an undue hardship. Meanwhile, as villagers became more accustomed to contractual lending relationships, these issues became less murky, even as the numbers of cases surged and enforcement likely continued to be difficult.

In fact, enforcement of civil judgments was a persistent problem in Santai well into the 1990s. After the establishment of the people's court, only a single official tasked specifically with enforcing judgments was sent to the court in 1958, and that person was recalled and sent to another locality so he could be with his spouse in 1960 (三台县法院志编纂领导小组编 1999: 231). After that, it was not until 1984 that any enforcement personnel or division were established in the court, and plaintiffs had to rely on spotty enforcement by Party or other government organs, even though the court had been petitioning the county Party Committee specifically for such resources or personnel since at least 1963 (三台县法院志编纂领导小组编 1999: 231).

After the enforcement division began operating, with one official assigned to it, from January 1985, it was referred a total of 1401 cases for enforcement by the end of 1990 (a rate of roughly 234 per year) (三台县法院志编纂领导小组编 1999: 231). In 1990, seven new officers were added to the enforcement division, even as economic disputes needing enforcement began to get much more numerous and complex, and the court made great efforts to avoid common problems in enforcement like local protectionism (in its own words, "自觉克服地方保护主义") (三台县法院志编纂领导小组编 1999: 234–5). Then, between 1993 and 1996, a number of additional reforms were undertaken to improve the court's capacity for effective and equitable enforcement of civil judgments (三台县法院志编纂领导小组编 1999: 236–7), even as the issue remained vexing and apparently was not fully resolved.

Cases from the Yushan County Court, in northern Jiangxi Province's Shangrao Prefecture, show evidence of similar general patterns, even though its gazetteer is less detailed than Santai's. In one 1991 case, for example, a woman and her grown daughter suffered minor injuries in a brawl with their neighbors, after the neighbors' child had eaten some watermelons growing on their property (玉山县法院志编纂委员会 1999: 119). After listening to the case and considering that the two families had been in conflict before (over fruit trees and also over a "methane pond," 沼气池), the court decided the neighbors should pay compensation for the plaintiff's medical bills, as well as her daughter's medical expenses and lost wages. The judges were attempting to resolve what amounted to a tort before a concept of torts had been fully articulated in Chinese law, drawing on some background ideas and assumptions regarding "fairness" and "reasonableness" to do so, while also taking care to comply with established laws and guidelines.

In a more fraught 1990 case, a villager joined several of his neighbors who had been contracted to work on a railroad construction project in Jingdezhen. Because of badly laid stones, one of the rails fell onto the plaintiff's leg and broke his bone. He sued his employer for medical expenses and lost wages, but even after the adjudication committee pressed him, the person in charge of the construction site would not accept responsibility to pay any compensation (经审判委员会讨论决定，李XX不予承担本案赔偿责任) (玉山县法院志编纂委员会 1999: 119). The court ultimately decided to impose the burden of compensation upon the two coworkers who'd brought the plaintiff to the site, shrinking from asserting a legal principle of liability or imposing a remedy of the sort that might seem reasonable in light of stricter or clearer labor laws and workplace safety regulations. What's more, the judges were unable to reach a decision on their own and had to rely on the adjudication committee. Though cases were being adjudicated in closer adherence to then-extant regulations by the early 1990s, political influence, the adjudication committee, and economic clout still could certainly sway outcomes – at least some of the time.

In the early 1990s, the Yushan court also made efforts to settle cases in which individuals or companies (i.e. legal persons, 法人) owed money to each other. In most of these, recalcitrant borrowers appeared to have given in to the pressure of a trial and agreed to mediated settlements under which they repaid what they owed (玉山县法院志编纂委员会 1999: 120–1). Similarly, a variety of real estate transaction cases, such as a 1992 disputed home sale, were settled through court mediation after suits progressed toward trial (玉山县法院志编纂委员会 1999: 122). Finally, a number of disputes between neighbors began to be adjudicated during the same period. These included suits over water control and water damage, as well as a particularly colorful 1992 case (also concluded with a court mediated settlement) in which a man sued his neighbor for constructing a toilet right next to his window, obstructing the path in front of his house with vehicles and household items, and blocking the sunlight with other building projects in his yard (玉山县法院志编纂委员会 1999: 127–8). All in all, Yushan's experience suggests a rising tide of lawsuits, from seventy in 1979 to 203 in 1992 (玉山县法院志编纂委员会 1999: 133), across an increasingly wide array of economic and social areas, adjudicated in more and more transparent and predictable ways linked ever more closely to the letter of the law, and with an expanding use of court-initiated mediation.

Even in a sparsely populated majority-Uyghur rural area outside Kashgar, in far-Western Xinjiang, we can see rapid expansion of the court's civil dispute resolution capacities in the reform era, while the overall caseload remained low. Although its civil division was established in 1953, the Yuepuhu County Court had focused almost exclusively on family and divorce cases before the Cultural Revolution and only began hearing many other disputes after 1980 (岳普湖县史志办公室 2004: 265–6). Over 90 percent of all civil cases there were resolved through mediation, but the numbers of economic and non-family personal disputes rose sharply in the 1990s – both in absolute terms and as a proportion of all civil cases (岳普湖县史志办公室 2004: 268–70). This trend clearly accelerated after the government took a series of measures to emphasize economic dispute settlement starting in 1997 (岳普湖县史志办公室 2004: 274–5). In fact, by 2002, the court was hearing almost as many debt, liability, contract, and "compensation" (赔偿, basically a way of conceptualizing at least some types of torts before the more complete codification of tort law in 2009 – see Lin 1989) cases as it was adjudicating disputes over divorce or inheritance.

In one illustrative 1994 compensation case that would have been handled through the criminal process or possibly mediation (if any remedy were to be applied at all) during the Maoist era, a Uyghur villager took a loan of RMB30,000 from the county's rural credit cooperative to build himself a brick house. After he had collected the cash, he was standing around in front of a pub when he encountered some friends who invited him to drink with them. While drinking in the bar, the villager entrusted the money to one of his friends, but it had gone missing by that evening. He and his friend went to the police station to report the loss and the manager of the credit cooperative wanted to file a criminal complaint, yet the civil adjudication process was able to resolve the case quickly and efficiently (and, so far as the gazetteer reports, fairly according to all parties) (岳普湖县史志办公室 2004: 275–6). Formal legal rules may not have been clear or complete, but the principles of efficiency and equity guided the court to a speedy and effective resolution in accordance with the law, such as it existed on the books at the time.

Direct observations in Sichuan in 2006 show how a rule by law regime continued to develop in the new millennium. In Case MS.Civ.2006.1, which I observed at trial in a rural county court in Meishan (in Southern Sichuan) in April 2006, and which was presided over by a panel of three young judges, a woman who had lost her hand and sustained other injuries in an automobile accident sued her husband's employer. The plaintiff's husband was a truck driver, whose employer dispatched him in summer 2005 to deliver a truckload of ice cream to Chongqing, pick up other products there, and return with these to the county in Meishan. The company did not suggest or provide a relief driver, although it was a long journey over mountainous terrain. The driver's wife decided to accompany him as a passenger. On the return trip, just after passing the Fuling Toll Station, they got into a serious accident, in which the plaintiff lost her hand and sustained other serious injuries.

The police investigation of the accident concluded that it was caused by her husband being an "exhausted driver" (疲劳驾驶). It was also revealed that he had failed to take any breaks or to rest during the previous segments of the journey, despite company policy and legal regulations requiring him to do so. In the end, the court assigned 10 percent responsibility to the woman herself (for choosing to travel as a passenger on her husband's work assignment, in violation of company rules and safety regulations), 45 percent responsibility to the company (for failing to provide a relief driver for such a long trip), and 45 percent to the plaintiff's husband (for failing to take required breaks or rest periods and causing the accident). Since the company was not seeking any damages (e.g. to recover the cost of damage to the truck), the decision resulted in the plaintiff receiving more than RMB500,000 from her husband's employer in damages to cover her medical bills and as compensation for her emotional distress and physical disability.

The verdict was routine, but the process through which it was reached was instructive. I had the opportunity to interview all three judges almost immediately after they had issued their decision and they explained that their deliberations had been difficult and contentious. The letter of the law was vague as to exactly what risks one assumes when hitchhiking or traveling as a non-paying passenger. At least one of the judges thus felt initially that perhaps the plaintiff should bear more than 10 percent responsibility. At least one judge also thought at the outset that the driver was more than 45 percent responsible for causing the accident through his driving errors and decision not to rest, even though he knew the rules well. In the end, the decision was a compromise reached with the intent of protecting a "weak social element" (弱势群体, the plaintiff who had lost her hand) and in the general spirit of "fairness" (公正). The judges all claimed that they felt no pressure from the adjudication committee, the court president, the CCP political and legal affairs committee, or any government agency. But their reasoning and the compromise they reached suggested that they did indeed prioritize social equity and stability over legal reasoning, at least in some ways. Their process could still be formally rational, in accordance with well-known and established customary or political norms, even as it diverged from some specific implications of codified rules.

In Luzhou (eastern Sichuan) Intermediate Court, I observed the appellate phase of a civil case (Case LZ.Civ.2006.1) in which social concerns also surfaced as a factor. A man involved in a traffic accident sued the driver he said had hit him, and hired a lawyer to do so. The case was never tried, but with the lawyer's help (including her spending RMB1300 to travel to another city to engage in negotiations) the man received an out-of-court settlement of RMB17,000. The lawyer then asked him to give her RMB3700 (22 percent) of what he had received, as agreed in their contract. This was in addition to the RMB5200 in legal fees he was also obliged to pay, as per the contract. He refused to pay any of it. So his lawyer filed suit against him. She won the suit in the first instance hearing, with the basic-level court ruling that she was indeed owed RMB5200 in legal fees *plus* RMB3700 as her share of the settlement funds. The man was still not happy, however, so he appealed the decision to the Intermediate Court.

There, the man argued that he had already paid his lawyer RMB1700 for her expenses earlier (RMB400 more than she claimed to have received or been due). He also maintained that his lawyer had told him their contract required him to pay RMB1500 in legal fees and then RMB3700 as a share of the settlement money – for a RMB5200 total. If he had understood otherwise, he would never have signed a contract with her or accepted her representation. Finally, when he tried to pay her something (right around Chinese New Year), he found no one at the lawyer's office. He thus felt he should pay only about RMB600 in legal fees, as this was reasonable and all he could afford. The court ruled that the lawyer's understanding of the contract was correct, but that she could not expect the man to pay her everything he owed – and that she should thus accept RMB600 in legal fees, in addition to RMB1500 as her share of the settlement. I was not able to ask the three judges why they'd come to this decision, but the fact that it happened on appeal to the urban court (rather than at the basic level in a rural setting) is perhaps telling of some degree of outside influence extending beyond the most basic levels.

In a rural county of Luzhou, a seventy-year-old retired cadre was run over by two farmers riding motorcycles when she was crossing the street. Represented by a lawyer, she filed suit (Case LZ.Civ.2006.3) against the farmers in the county court, seeking RMB17,000 in damages to cover her medical expenses and four months of recovery, plus RMB30 per day for her emotional distress during the 120-day period. An important point of contention was the level of compensation for emotional distress. Here, both sides presented previous court rulings to bolster their arguments. The plaintiff cited a Supreme People's Court decision in a similar case saying that RMB30 per day was a reasonable standard for such compensation. The defendants pointed to a 2005 decision from the local county court saying that RMB30 per day exceeded local economic conditions and was too high a rate. The judge suggested that a mediated settlement might be possible (and more efficient than moving to a formal judgment) and both parties agreed. The trial then moved to a mediation phase in which the defendants offered to pay the plaintiff 90 percent of everything she was asking for, but her lawyer refused out of hand.

This appeared to shock the presiding judge, to the point that he called for a recess to discuss the matter with the plaintiff and her lawyer without the defendants in the room (though others in the audience – including me – were allowed to remain). During the recess, the judge explained to the plaintiff's lawyer that it was unlikely he could give his client 90 percent of the damages she was seeking in a formal ruling and inconceivable that she could do any better than that. A formal ruling would also entail higher court costs that could not be reasonably imposed on the defense (especially in light of their generous settlement offer). The plaintiff's lawyer explained that his client needed a formal court ruling for insurance purposes (i.e. her insurance would pay some additional compensation for medical expenses and recovery – beyond any damages won – but only if she could present a formal court decision). The judge then called the defense back into the court and issued a formal decision, ruling that the defendants should pay the plaintiff 90 percent of the damages she sought and also should be responsible for RMB900 of the roughly RMB1000 in total court costs for the case. After the trial, I was able to interview the judge, who explained that if there had been no mediation phase, he probably would have awarded the plaintiff only about 65–70 percent of the damages she sought, but would have required the defendants to cover 100 percent of all court costs.

Across a variety of rural contexts, civil dispute resolution moved closer and closer to a rule by law pattern, in which powerful nonlegal actors stayed out of the adjudication of individual cases and predictability increased. This was true even though social concerns, general (nonlegal) ideas of "equity," a baseline preference to settle disputes by arbitration whenever possible, or efforts to promote "stability" entered explicitly and often into judges' decision-making. That courts managed to grapple with such a flood of so many new kinds of disputes as occurred from the mid-1980s onward without recourse to overt politicization of civil justice is also testament to the force of the government and Party's agenda to promote greater transparency and efficiency of the legal system after 1979. Similar trends in urban areas were, if anything, more pronounced. The formal written rules and statutes were not always applied exactly as one might expect upon reading them, but consistent and predictable patterns of dispute resolution and rules of adjudication were used and direct interference into the work of courts and legal institutions by other actors was minimal.

Civil Law in Urban Areas

A number of scholars have argued that many areas of Chinese civil adjudication have become more predictable, transparent, and have come to be handled in at least somewhat closer accordance with formal and written rules, particularly in urban areas (Pei et al. 2010). As Randall Peerenboom observes, China's leaders by the early 1980s perceived a need to develop a market economy based on legal rules and institutions

(Peerenboom 2002: 55; see also Chen 1995). He further argues that significant progress was made in the first fifteen years of reform, in terms of both institution-building and the creation of a "culture of legality," especially in commercial and civil areas of adjudication required to enhance the legal system's "certainty and predictability demanded by investors" (Peerenboom 2002: 221). Yuhua Wang, as noted earlier, has picked up on Peerenboom's basic exhortation to explore the uneven regional distribution of rationalizing reforms and predictability in relation to the concentration of certain kinds of foreign direct investment; but he takes as a starting point that there has indeed been substantial movement in that direction since 1978 (Wang 2015). Even Fu Hualing and Richard Cullen, while criticizing what they perceive as China's backsliding toward greater emphasis on mediation, point out that civil adjudication has been at the center of a sea change in legal reform that has brought much greater institutional autonomy and procedural predictability and transparency (Fu & Cullen 2011; see also Howson 2010).

Indeed, there is ample evidence of the development of a rule by law regime in urban civil adjudication to be found across court gazetteers from around China. For example, the basic level court in Qiaoxi District, in the central part of Shijiazhuang City, capital of Hebei Province, established a team responsible for civil adjudication in 1978, with six judges assigned to work on cases. It then established a more formal civil section (民事审判庭) in 1982, with ten judges assigned to work under its director (庭长). Finally, by 1993, after several reassessments of its personnel numbers, the section had one director, two deputy directors, three judges, and one clerk. Meanwhile, in the fifteen years covered by the gazetteer, 4,319 civil cases were adjudicated by the Qiaoxi Court, meaning the case load (roughly thirty to forty-five cases per judge per year) was much higher than in most rural areas, but not atypical of a major urban setting (石家庄市桥西区人民法院编 1994: 53). Some of the cases involved new categories of disputes that were rare or unheard of before market reform, even though more than half (2,491) were family law cases (石家庄市桥西区人民法院编 1994: 53).

One new category involved arguments over housing, both rights to real property and rental or landlord-tenant disputes. There were more than 500 of these disputes in Qiaoxi between 1978 and 1993 (石家庄市桥西区人民法院编 1994: 57). In one such case, the court had to decide on the ownership of a house that had been purchased in 1950, but later came to be disputed. After careful investigation, the court found that the records kept at the time listed only one owner, even though three people had made the purchase collectively. The plaintiff and defendant thus had equal claims to the property, even though only the defendant's name was recorded on the old documents as the owner (perhaps, as the gazetteer hints, the plaintiff was left off because she was a woman). The judges were thus able to use discretion to ensure that an equitable and enforceable judgment was reached, even if the letter of the law had to be interpreted somewhat liberally (石家庄市桥西区人民法院编 1994: 58).

Many new kinds of cases, especially those related to payment of debts, proved difficult to adjudicate. In cases where debts were incurred through oral agreements, these had to stand in for written contracts (口头协议代替书面合同) (石家庄市桥西区人民法院编 1994: 60). In such cases, the court was hard pressed to get to the truth of the matter, as one party would simply refuse to admit that any contractual relations existed, while the other would then be left without any leg to stand on (空口无凭) (石家庄市桥西区人民法院编 1994: 60). In one 1991 case that the court saw fit to cite as an example in its gazetteer, one man sued his former business partner for repayment of RMB3950 related to expenses they'd jointly incurred. Even though the defendant admitted that he owed the money, he later refused to pay it (claiming he had never incurred the debt) and the plaintiff had to seek forcible enforcement (强制执行) from the court, which was eventually successful (石家庄市桥西区人民法院编 1994: 60) – which seems truly exceptional, considering the initial suit was resolved through court-led mediation.

Over the course of the 1980s, and especially through the early 1990s, the court substantially ramped up its enforcement capacity and tactics, gaining powers to seize assets and funds from businesses as well as individuals (石家庄市桥西区人民法院编 1994: 99–103). Yet there were still cases of spectacular difficulty – including some in which unclear civil procedure and other rules made enforcement especially problematic.

In one such case, a leather shoe factory in a rural county in Hengshui Prefecture (adjacent to Shijiazhuang) defrauded a Shijiazhuang state-owned enterprise (SOE) based in Qiaoxi out of nearly RMB24,000-worth of materials in 1984. After many attempts to reach an administrative remedy or informal settlement, the SOE filed a claim in the Qiaoxi Court in 1989. The court tried to call the leather shoe factory director to appear, but he refused multiple times, requiring that the case be decided in his absence (缺席审理). After issuing a judgment against him in July 1990, the court was unable to collect payment for the SOE and the local court in the shoe factory's home county was not of any help either. Thus, in June 1992, the Qiaoxi Court's enforcement division organized a five-member team to travel to the county in Hengshui and extract payment from the factory director. When they arrived, the director refused to see them and tried to leave the scene. At that point, a melee ensued, in which the director's wife and brother-in-law beat the officers and brought forth a mob that kidnapped and then beat and tortured two of the officers for nearly three days, while the remaining three managed to get back to Shijiazhuang and organize a rescue operation.

Finally, in July 1993, with the help of the Hebei Province Political and Legal Affairs Committee and the Political and Legal Affairs Committees of both Hengshui and Shijiazhuang, the court managed to have criminal charges pressed against the shoe factory director, his wife, and his brother-in-law. They were also investigated by the CCP's Discipline and Inspection Commission and made to pay fines and restitution as well as the original debts (石家庄市桥西区人民法院编 1994: 105–8). The extreme difficulty of enforcing even what seemed a routine judgment against a local boss in another area (and the fact that the case took a decade to resolve) is illustrative of the challenges of transitioning to a rule by law regime. That the dispute found its way into the home court of the plaintiff, rather than the defendant, is also indicative of still inchoate civil procedure rules and norms, as well as the likely obstacles to adjudicating the dispute in the home court of the leather shoe factory, which would likely have been subject to substantial local protectionism.

In Chengdu's Jinjiang District, the basic-level court heard more than 20,000 civil cases between 1979 and 1997. While the largest share were family disputes, cases over debts, real estate, and compensation/torts represented sizable and growing fractions of the total throughout the period (成都市锦江区法院志 1999: 174). What's more, the percentage of cases resolved through mediation, while never less than about 35 percent, was never so high that judicial adjudication could be crowded out (成都市锦江区法院志 1999: 175–6), despite very high and rapidly growing case loads. As some new types of cases, big and small, began to crop up, the court sometimes found itself having to step in to help citizens seeking remedies against powerful work units and institutions.

In a 1997 medical malpractice case, a woman had gone into labor and went to her work unit's hospital (职工医院) in the district. While performing a caesarian section on her, doctors managed to sever part of her small intestine (小肠切断), causing intestinal fluid to leak into her abdominal cavity for eighteen hours (肠液流入腹腔达18小时之久). This led to serious injury, infection, and life-threatening complications. Though she was but one individual and her work unit was large and powerful, the court decided the case in her favor and mandated the payment of significant damages. In a smaller case from 1996, the court ruled for a plaintiff – a customer – who sued the Chengdu Number One Department Store (the largest in the city) after it had wrongly imposed a RMB40 fine upon her for handling merchandise without purchasing it. The court's decision required the store to refund the fine and offer a formal apology (赔礼道歉) (成都市锦江区法院志 1999: 187). Also of note, especially in the 1990s, were the burgeoning numbers of disputes related to commercial debts (of which there were 167 by 1997), which often involved complex triangular relationships between creditors, businesses, and customers (成都市锦江区法院志 1999: 188–9).

Real estate and property disputes grew sharply in number, with the Jinjiang court processing 582 such cases during the 1980s and 1,546 between 1990 and 1997 (成都市锦江区法院志 1999: 190). In a typical case from 1984, the court adjudicated a suit brought by a woman who claimed ownership of a house in the district that had been occupied by another couple since 1964, when the woman had leased it to them. In 1968, she had borrowed RMB120 from her tenants because she was facing economic hardship and they drew up a lending agreement (借条). By 1984, when she sought to evict the tenants and move into the house herself, they argued that they had purchased the house from her by lending her money she never repaid and refused to leave. The court ruled for the plaintiff, allowing her to take back her house, but requiring her to repay the RMB120 along with RMB700 in deferred maintenance costs for the house during the period of tenancy (成都市锦江区法院志 1999: 191).

Some real estate cases involved disputes over demolitions and relocations (房屋拆迁纠纷) and could be contentious. For example, family members armed with long knives and cleavers threatened court officers who sought to enforce a decision evicting them from their residence to make way for redevelopment in a 1997 case. Only after repeated attempts and special procedures did the court manage to enforce its judgment (成都市锦江区法院志 1999: 192–3).

Some localities faced particular issues in civil litigation, specific to their history or geography. Many real estate disputes in Xiamen, a vibrant city on the southeastern coast of Fujian Province – and a central node of emigration to Taiwan and Southeast Asia between roughly 1600 and 1950 – took on a distinct character. "Overseas Chinese" (华侨), mainly from Taiwan and Southeast Asia, owned more than 60 percent of the city's real estate as late as 1956 (厦门政法志编纂委员会 1996: 441). A great many of the more than 3,200 disputes adjudicated by the court during the 1980s, therefore, involved claimants from Taiwan or Southeast Asia asserting property rights rooted in ownership before the 1950s (厦门政法志编纂委员会 1996: 440).

In one such case, a Chinese-Indonesian couple filed suit in 1982, while visiting relatives in Xiamen over Chinese New Year, seeking restitution of their rights to half-ownership of a large eighty-two-room building in the center of the city. The principals, who had built the structure and divided ownership, were long-since dead. The owner as of 1982 was able to present a certificate from the land reform era of the early 1950s, showing that he had complete ownership, while the couple from Indonesia had no similar documents to support their claim. After more than two years of intensive investigation, including interviews with local cadres, elderly neighborhood residents, and various relatives and descendants of the original builders in the 1920s, the court decided the couple's claim was valid and awarded them a 50 percent ownership stake in the building – a decision upheld upon appeal to the Fujian High Court (厦门政法志编纂委员会 1996: 442).

In another case, a Mr. Yang fled to Taiwan before 1949, leaving a relative to look after his property. When he returned to Xiamen in 1989 seeking to reclaim it, he ended up having to file suit against his kin, who had claimed during land reform that they'd owned the property since the twenty-ninth year of the reign of the Guangxu Emperor (1903), and had produced documentation to that effect. The district court of the first instance ruled against Mr. Yang. But on appeal the Xiamen Intermediate Court found, upon further investigation, that the relatives' documents did not match the exact address of the building in question and awarded ownership to Mr. Yang. In gratitude, he presented the court with a cotton flag he brought from Taiwan, inscribed with calligraphy reading, "Solemnly Enforce the Law, Turn Your Heart to it Inside and Out" (严肃执法，内外心向) (厦门政法志编纂委员会 1996: 442–3). The irony, of course, is that the property may well have not been subject to being claimed back at all, had the relatives not maintained their claim for all those years while Mr. Yang was in Taiwan.

A similar pattern was apparent in a variety of cases I observed in 2006 across urban areas of Sichuan. Adjudication was predictable and transparent and, where practice diverged from written rules or was based on political or social imperatives, it was still coherent and clear to all parties – and, perhaps most importantly, all sides seemed to anticipate the ways in which such informal or unwritten norms would be applied. Social stability and basic equity needed to be preserved, while courts' power and resources were limited (and thus incentives for mediation and clearing cases quickly were substantial – a point also made powerfully by a civil court judge I was able to interview in Guangzhou in 2009), but this was all commonly known and procedure was generally consistent and complied with basic norms.

In Case CD.Civ.2006.1, for instance, a laid-off worker in her forties sued her employer for payment of her pension. When I observed this trial at a district court in Chengdu in April 2006, presided over by a single judge, about eight or nine of the woman's former coworkers were in attendance, along with two law students from a local university. The plaintiff had been laid off in 2005, but she had signed a contract with her employer in the late 1990s that she maintained guaranteed her pension benefits (Hurst & O'Brien 2002; Hurst 2009: 77–81; Frazier 2010). Then, in 2001, her old firm split into "core" and "noncore" companies. The core company became a publicly listed corporation, while the noncore components became a private limited liability company. After losing her job, the plaintiff was told by the core company that responsibility for all social benefits belonged to the noncore firm, while the noncore company claimed that as a private limited liability company it could not be held liable for any promises made before the corporate restructuring in 2001.

Both the core and noncore companies appeared as defendants and their lawyers pointed to provisions of their corporate charters, as well as in the company laws, governing listed and limited liability companies, to argue that they should not be responsible for paying the plaintiff's pension. The noncore firm even said explicitly that requiring such firms to pay all social benefits promised to SOE employees before restructuring would bankrupt most of them and endanger economic reform. When I interviewed the judge after the hearing, she explained that this case was extremely challenging because, in theory, the noncore company should be made to pay, but she believed it legitimately could not do so, leading her to hope for a mediated settlement. She did not, however, suggest that the firms (powerful state actors in their own right), the industrial and commercial affairs bureau, the political and legal affairs committee, the labor union, or any other institutional actors were attempting to influence her decision or its implementation.

In one dispute (Case LZ.Civ.2006.2), it seems my presence influenced the proceedings, at least at the margins. The plaintiff (a bank manager) had lent the defendant (a real estate developer) RMB40,000 in 2005, with the defendant's house as collateral. The defendant did not pay any of the money back by the time of the trial in a district court in Luzhou City (eastern Sichuan) in April 2006. The plaintiff argued that he should receive the money originally lent, plus 3 percent interest for late payment, plus money to cover court costs of more than RMB1000. The defendant said he would repay the money, but that he could not pay right away and should not have to pay interest. The judge pointed out to the parties that no interest rate or payment schedule had been agreed to at the time of the loan and that this meant that no interest could be collected and immediate repayment could not reasonably be expected. He also suggested the parties attempt to find a mediated settlement, perhaps with the money being repaid over one to two months.

The judge then called a brief recess (about fifteen minutes) for the parties to discuss the terms of the settlement privately with him. After the recess, the plaintiff said he could only accept a settlement if the defendant agreed to pay him in full within one month, which he said he could not do, so he asked the judge to issue a ruling. The judge decided that the defendant must pay back the principal within one month and cover all court costs (totaling more than RMB1000). After the trial, I asked the judge why he thought the parties had refused to agree to a mediated settlement, especially since the ruling he issued was so close to what they'd just refused to accept. He explained that during the recess they agreed on the terms but decided also that it would look best to go through the entire formal trial process because I was in the audience.

In Case LZ.Civ.2006.4, the plaintiff (an elderly woman) brought an appellate suit in Luzhou City Intermediate Court against two defendants (a young couple) after having lost a suit to them in the basic-level court in their home county. She had sought to open a majiang parlor (麻将管) on a street in the county town and needed to do some repairs to the storefront. She turned to the tenants living in another property she owned in town (the defendants), who were construction contractors, for the equipment and supplies, agreeing on a price of RMB4000. After the initial repairs had been completed, the landlord of the storefront demanded the woman install a glass door (in addition to the steel grate she'd already purchased from the defendants). She acquired this from the defendants and had it installed. Later, when the defendants asked her to pay an additional RMB2000 for the glass door, she claimed they'd agreed it would be included in the original RMB4000 and she should not have to pay anything more. So the defendants brought suit against her in the basic-level court and stopped paying her rent.

In this lower court case, they had called a witness – one of their cousins – who testified that he had been there when they had agreed with the elderly woman that the glass door would cost an addition RMB2000, on top of the RMB4000 she'd already paid, but neither side had any receipts and there had never been a written contract. At the appellate hearing, the old woman said that witness had never been there and claimed she had a different witness who was there and could testify that the agreement had been to include the cost of the door in the original RMB4000. The presiding judge then called a recess to find the witness and try to get him to testify. It turned out that he was away in Yibin, but was able to speak with the presiding judge by phone. He said he had not been there and had no idea what arrangements the two sides may or may not have had. When the court offered an opportunity for the two sides to negotiate a mediated settlement, the plaintiff said she was willing to do so, but the defendants were not.

Though a ruling was still forthcoming after that set of hearings, I was able to interview the three judges responsible for deciding the case. They explained that the elderly woman was a very frequent plaintiff in appellate suits, which she brought after losing as a defendant in the lower courts. Almost all of these revolved around her refusal to pay for services or goods she'd contracted to purchase. They also said they were very likely to rule for the defendants in this case, but that they would probably not be able to recover the full RMB2000 they were seeking and that they'd have to accept something close to RMB500 or RMB700 – both because they had admitted during the trial that their costs for the door were only about RMB700 and because they'd already withheld about RMB500 in rent. Yet again, social equity and stability concerns appeared to influence the judges' thinking. They all said they had to take into account the elderly woman's poverty and the social implications should she not be able to pay the damages. Should they award the full damages to which the couple might be legally entitled, the court would also be in the uncomfortable position of trying to enforce an essentially unenforceable judgment. But no extrajudicial institution or actor attempted to influence this specific adjudication directly, meaning formal rationality was preserved at least in principle, and the informal norms of social equity and ease of enforcement as they were applied were reasonably predictable to all parties in the small town Sichuan context.

Sometimes, though, social concerns did not factor into judgments. In an appellate hearing of a pension case (Case LZ.Civ.2006.5), a seventy-year-old man sued his former employer (an SOE in his county town) to force it to pay him a pension. He'd lost in the basic-level court and so had appealed, alleging that the lower court had engaged in a form of local protectionism because the enterprise was an important local economic institution. He hoped to get a fairer hearing at the Intermediate Court in Luzhou City (where I observed the appellate trial in April 2006). The plaintiff had stopped working at his factory in 1985, under an arrangement known as "stop the salary, retain the position" (停薪留职, Hurst 2009: 62), which, in theory, entitled him to retain the labor relationship even though he was not working or being paid. He was due to retire in 1994, but no formal retirement (or pension claim) was processed. That was where the stories diverged. The plaintiff argued that he reported back to the enterprise every year until 1990, but was never allowed to process a formal retirement or register for a pension. After that, he was unable to make it back in person, but also never received any notice from the enterprise that his pension rights were to be terminated. The defendants (firm management) claimed that he never returned and only asked for a pension twenty years after he had stopped working there. For nearly thirteen years after he should have been eligible, he never requested a pension or attempted to process a formal retirement from his old position at the firm and, they said, he should have no valid claim now. The court sided with the defendants and ordered the plaintiff to pay RMB400 in court costs, in addition to denying him any pension.

Concluding Thoughts

There is, of course, at least one important facet of China's civil adjudication system that provides a backdoor to intervention by nonjudicial authorities, as mentioned briefly in Chapter 2: civil procuratorial appeal (民事抗诉). Procurators – normally and primarily agents tasked with criminal prosecution – are empowered to file appellate suits in civil cases on behalf of what they perceive to be the public interest as part of their "supervisory" (监督) role in relation to courts. This, along with their retention of seats on courts' adjudication committees (审判委员会), allows for the exercise of substantial influence in the adjudication of specific civil suits, even if these tactics and mechanisms have been applied exceedingly and increasingly rarely since the early 1980s. Unless and until Chinese civil procedure is further reformed to curtail the power of procuracies, this will remain an obstacle toward further solidification of a rule by law order.

Another issue is the bureaucratic oversight and influence of clerks (书记员) and their susceptibility to corruption. One clerk in Chengdu volunteered, in a conversation I had with him in April 2006, that he and his colleagues controlled his court's civil division docket. The clerks thus had great discretion in determining how quickly or slowly suits accepted by the court would actually be heard at trial. This, he said, was probably the greatest power the generally weak and subservient clerks enjoyed. Another clerk in a central Beijing district court, interviewed in August 2006, claimed that in order to get one's case onto the docket at all, a plaintiff needed to bribe one or more of the clerks. This clerk also described what he said was a frequent practice of recording what he called official (正本) and supplementary (副本) transcripts and files of cases (especially civil cases). Only the official transcript and file (which he suggested was usually little more than a Microsoft Word template with names and facts inserted) would be sent to the Intermediate Court in appellate cases or generally be made available for supervision. The much more complete supplementary transcript and file would be retained by the court as an internal record and could be made available to the Beijing High Court (not the Intermediate Court) or the Beijing Municipal Political and Legal Affairs Committee only if specifically requested (which, he said, happened only very rarely).

In all, despite these qualifications, Chinese civil adjudication since the 1980s has evolved into a decidedly rule by law regime. In marked contrast to what we will see of criminal adjudication in the next chapter,

Chinese civil trials are subject to remarkably little intervention from nonjudicial political actors. When such intervention does occur, its application is usually quite predictable and can be factored in relatively easily by all parties as a potential cost or influence in determining their odds of winning. The limited special leverage of the politically powerful or well-connected in Chinese civil justice, therefore, is a wrinkle in its rule by law fabric rather than an attribute that pushes it into being a neotraditional regime.

INDONESIA

It is perhaps surprising to find a rule by law regime in Indonesian criminal adjudication after *Reformasi*, but this is indeed the outcome that obtains across most of the system. A primary effect of democratization has been to render the legitimate application of violence to the citizenry no longer an open arena for the fighting of political battles or naked repression. The police, since the end of the 1990s, have become more competent as they have also been freed from the sorts of controlling influences they used to face from military leadership and political elites (Muradi 2014: 74–5), while the courts and prosecutors have been forced to become dramatically more transparent and accountable in their work of prosecution and adjudication. This is not to say that there is no corruption in the criminal law institutions or that there is no area of criminal law that is still subject to the same types of intervention that were common during the Suharto years. As I will discuss in the next chapter, many civil disputes can be transformed into criminal prosecutions precisely through this sort of intervention and corruption. Aside from these, there are countless charges never brought against especially powerful or influential actors, who can still effectively slow or stop the wheels of justice turning against them. But, on the whole, the transformation from the New Order era to the current legal regime is marked and consistent in both urban and rural areas.

A point of distinction between these two types of settings is mainly in the sort of cases most often brought before the courts. In large cities, there are many cases involving illicit drugs, intellectual property rights, and theft. In rural areas, fights and brawling, sex crimes, and gambling are far more common, relative to other offenses. In sum, the common types of rural cases seem less likely to be subject to intervention or politicization, but rural judges and courts are perhaps more likely to engage in corrupt practices, even in smaller matters. They also, in some instances (though relatively rarely by now) lack the competence to decide even simple cases without recourse to old habits.

Criminal Law in Urban Areas

There were two large cities among my field sites, where I was able to collect data from the post-*Reformasi* era – Surabaya (capital of East Java) and Manado (capital of North Sulawesi). Looking first at Surabaya, it is astounding that of the more than 2900 formal criminal cases (*pidana biasa*, as opposed to summary judgment misdemeanors, *pidana rol* or *sumir*) adjudicated in 2005, a very high proportion related to charges of illicit drug use, theft, gambling, and fraud. Specifically, among the 1160 cases from the year on which I was able to gather detailed information, pretty much at random, 358 (31 percent) were drug-related (281 for "psychotropics" and 77 "narcotics"), 76 (7 percent) were for general fraud (*penipuan*), 43 (4 percent) were for falsification (*pemalsuan*, including 16 for falsification of documents and 3 for falsification of money), 19 (2 percent) were for sex crimes (18 *cabul*/indecency and 1 *perkosaan*/rape), 151 (13 percent) for gambling (*perjudian*), 307 (27 percent) for theft (306 simple theft/*pencurian*, 1 pickpocketing/*pencopetan*), 167 (14 percent) for embezzlement (*penggelapan*), 9 for traffic accidents, 18 (2 percent) for criminal negligence (*kealpaan*), 5 for corruption (*korupsi*), 2 for intellectual property crimes (*hak cipta*), 1 for illegal logging, 1 for unfair competition (*persaingan curang*), and 1 for which I was unable to identify the precise charges, in addition to 2 murders (*pembunuhan*).

A roughly similar distribution appeared to hold for the 4511 cases adjudicated in 2009, based on my review of the court's registers, though I was able to gather detailed information on only a few hundred of those (records were in greater disarray and still incomplete for 2009 at the time I gathered these data in 2010). Overall, the lion's share of criminal cases in Indonesia's second-largest city in the 2000s involved relatively run-of-the-mill offenses. Any politicization or intervention would likely be evinced only in their actual adjudication, which we can assess through the more fine-grained analysis of a variety of 2009 cases.

In Case 2299/Pid.B/2009/PN.SBY, a thirty-three-year-old woman was convicted of drug dealing for illegally selling "Double L," a strong prescription-only narcotic. She obtained the drug from a relative who worked in a pharmacy for Rp.200,000 per packet and then sold it on at double that price. Three witnesses were called to testify against her.

The first, a pharmacist, said that "Double L" was indeed a dangerous prescription drug often abused as a narcotic and explained how the defendant obtained it from her relative. The second and third witnesses were police officers who had caught the defendant through an "undercover buy" they had arranged with her in Sidoarjo (a largely industrial regency just South of Surabaya City) in April 2009. They agreed to purchase 1000 "Double L" pills each from the defendant, but when she arrived with the drugs, they arrested her. At trial, she admitted to the charges and confirmed the details of how she had obtained and sold the drugs and at what prices, as well as the fact that she tried to sell to the police officers. She was convicted and sentenced to twenty months in prison and a fine of Rp.1,000,000 through a very by-the-books, apparently apolitical, process.

In a straightforward case (Case 1509/Pid.B/2009/PN.SBY), an employee of a distribution company in the southern industrial area of Surabaya was convicted of embezzlement (*penggelapan*), after he was caught ordering large quantities of bees' wax (*minyak tawon*) on his employer's account and then selling the product outside the company without paying the employer. All this was demonstrated clearly through documents presented by the prosecutor and the defendant did not even contest any of the facts or interpretation.

In a similarly uncomplicated gambling case (Case 497/Pid.B/2009/PN.SBY), a forty-one-year-old man was accused of essentially helping run a numbers racket in a small street at the edge of the sex-industry district of Doly. The defendant, originally from Bali, was convicted (and sentenced to three months in prison) after two witnesses testified that they would receive regular phone calls or text messages from the defendant or his associates telling them the day's numbers, odds, and other details. The police eventually arrested both witnesses for their gambling activities, who then agreed to testify against the defendant in this case.

In perhaps the most salacious case I encountered in Surabaya that year (Case 738/Pid.B/2009/PN.SBY), a forty-nine-year-old housewife from Malang stood accused of human trafficking (*perdagangan orang*) and facilitating indecency (*cabul*) by serving as a pimp/madam for at least four younger women working as prostitutes. The case was adjudicated in Surabaya because the accused had too many links to local police and judicial officials in Malang and because it had been investigated by a special sex crimes directorate within the East Java Provincial Police (*Polda Jatim*) (thus giving the court in Surabaya, where

Polda headquarters were, jurisdiction). In December 2008, two officers from the unit had information about the defendant's prostitution ring and suspicions that some of the women working for her might be underage, so they set up a sting operation at the *Hotel Pinus* (Pine Tree Hotel) in Malang.

According to their testimony (they were both witnesses at the trial), the officers called the defendant's mobile phone and exchanged text messages to arrange for four prostitutes to arrive at their adjoining rooms at around 4:00 PM on December 4, at a price of Rp.400,000 per prostitute for a two-hour session (they bargained her down, apparently, from the Rp.500,000 she'd originally quoted). At 4:00 PM, one of the prostitutes, "Lia," arrived at one of the officer's rooms and was arrested. She said she worked for the defendant, so the officer asked her to accompany him to the defendant's house. When they got there, they found the defendant receiving other clients who'd called earlier to arrange to meet prostitutes there. She was arrested and, according to the officer's testimony, admitted to making about Rp.4,500,000 per week by pimping four prostitutes. Lia also testified at trial to the same set of facts, adding that she had had an agreement to pay the defendant 30 percent of her earnings as a commission.

Two other prostitutes, "Shelly" and "Rosi," were also called as witnesses and explained how they had worked under similar arrangements and had been arrested by the first officer's partner, who had been waiting in the room next door when they arrived around 4:30 PM and confirmed their narratives in his testimony. Finally, another prostitute, "Lilik," who had been arrested at the defendant's house, explained how she had come to know the defendant through Rosi, her relative, and how she had also worked for about Rp.400,000 per session and given 30 percent to the defendant. All four prostitutes claimed to service about ten clients per week on average and all of them said they were adults over eighteen and had not been physically forced into prostitution.

In her own defense, the accused explained that she did indeed work as a pimp to pay for medicines and doctors' care for her sick parents (she had been administering medicine to her gravely ill mother, in fact, when police arrived at her house). She said she had been running the scheme for about three months and charging between Rp.400,000 and Rp.500,000 per session to clients and taking 30 percent from the prostitutes, whom she said were all between the ages of nineteen and twenty-five (at least as far as she knew). Finally, she confirmed that she had had a call from a mysterious "Mr. Andre" asking for four prostitutes at the

Hotel Pinus on December 4, just before the case had broken open. The court convicted her of facilitating indecency, sentencing her to eight months in prison, but acquitted her on the human trafficking charge since it could not be proven either that the prostitutes were minors or that they'd been forced into prostitution.

Several cases involved the production or sale of falsified university degrees or credentials. In Case 2855/Pid.B/2009/PN.SBY, for example, two middle-aged gentlemen from Madura fabricated a diploma from a Surabaya technical institute to help a local notable win election as their village chief. They were convicted and sentenced to three-and-a-half months in prison, based on the transcripts of police interrogations of ten others connected to the case and testimony establishing that the candidate had never even taken an entrance exam, let alone completed any sort of post-secondary course or degree program.

A more instructive and complex such case (Case 664/Pid.B/2009/PN.SBY) involved an elaborate scheme masterminded by a forty year-old man to sell fake degrees from a prestigious university in Surabaya. The first witness called was a professor from the university, who explained how the defendant met him at fancy downtown hotels to discuss getting transfer students into the faculty of economics and management, such that they would enter just before the final thesis stage. This required the submission of transcripts and grades from a previous university to show that all necessary course credits had been completed. The witness and the defendant devised methods for fabricating all these materials for at least three students and the witness then pledged to ensure successful admissions processing of each candidate for the small fee of Rp.400,000, plus the costs of other bribes (in the case of the student on whom the criminal investigation focused, "Eko," Rp.5 million for one student).

The second witness was the head of admissions at the university's faculty of economics. He testified that the admissions system had two tracks – one in which students applied on their own and another in which their applications were handled by a "coordinating professor." Eko had applied through the second track, with the first witness acting as his coordinator. The admissions head had accepted a payment of Rp.5 million from the professor (Rp.4,900,000 of which he said he deposited into a university account), revised Eko's fabricated transcript to remedy some small problems of missing units and poor grades, and ensured that he could enter the university in April 2008. Because Eko did not complete his thesis by June, however, and had not enrolled in any university classes either, the rector (equivalent to the president of chancellor of an Indonesian university) refused to sign his diploma and allow him to graduate that year.

The final witness for the prosecution was Eko himself. He said he learned of the defendant from a classified ad in the newspaper that listed a mobile phone number. He called the number and arranged to meet the defendant at the food court of a downmarket shopping mall in Surabaya (*Royal Plaza*). He paid the defendant Rp.4 million upfront, with another Rp.4 million due upon receipt of the diploma. After the hiccup with the university rector, the defendant claimed to Eko that he had paid Rp.1,500,000 to the dean of the faculty of economics to ensure the rector would sign Eko's diploma, despite the fact that he'd never been on campus or completed a thesis, and in July 2008, the two met at the food court once again to exchange the diploma for the final Rp.4 million. After Eko's boss learned he'd acquired a fake degree, he called a major newspaper (*Jawa Pos*), which then launched an investigation into the case, eventually inducing the police to become involved as well.

Speaking in his own defense, the defendant said he heard from the first witness about how he could obtain an "instant diploma" (*diploma instan*) for any transfer student who could pay and submit photos along with a high school (SMA) credential. He admitted to posting the ad in the newspaper that Eko found and to meeting him at the shopping center (to avoid attention, he insisted they met at KFC, rather than in the open food court – though, when I visited the mall in 2009, the only KFC was a stand within the food court). He admitted taking Rp.4 million from Eko and to arranging with the first witness (the professor) to have his admission processed. He also bought a fake title for Eko's thesis (ironically, perhaps, on methods for calculating business losses from fraud or default) from someone in an older commercial district of Surabaya and submitted this, along with the other documents for his application. Later, he collected Eko's diploma from the professor when the two met in the doorway of the Ramayana shopping arcade in Surabaya's Bungarasih bus terminal. He then called Eko to set up another meeting at the food court (or KFC) to give him the degree and collect the remaining balance, claiming it was up to the university to assess the academic merit of the fake (apparently totally nonexistent) thesis, the falsified transcript, and other materials. The court convicted him and sentenced him to five months in prison – but, surprisingly, seems to have left the corrupt professor, admissions head, and rector untouched. Politics don't seem to have come into play directly, but a tip-off to the media appears to have been critical in getting this case into the public eye and spurring the police into action.

In a different kind of falsification case (Case 157/Pid.B/2009/PN.SBY), a thirty-three-year-old man was sentenced to a year in prison for issuing fraudulent marriage certificates. The defendant purchased a number of marriage registration books (*buku nikah*) from a friend, identified in court documents only as Hassan, who apparently stole them from local offices of the Department of Religion. Hassan confirmed to police, when questioned, that he had sold the books to the defendant for Rp.60,000 each. The defendant then also got hold of an inkpad and official stamp (*bantalan-stempel*) and would fill out and stamp the stolen books, and issue prayer manuals (*kumpulan doa-doa*) alongside them, for couples willing to pay him Rp.400,000 for the convenience. Surabaya police officers, posing as potential customers, apprehended him and then later confirmed with the Department of Religion that none of the fraudulent marriage books had ever been registered there.

Case 464/Pid.B/2009/PN.SBY involved another kind of falsification – the counterfeiting of currency. In this case, the defendant encountered a man while shopping in Wonokromo, who said the defendant could exchange counterfeit notes with him at a rate of three to one. He agreed to do so and exchanged Rp.500,000 for Rp.1,500,000 in fake Rp.50,000 notes. He then bought a mobile phone from a man (who eventually called police and became a witness at the trial) using the fake bills. After that, he spent the rest of the initial Rp.1,500,000 and went back to exchange more (though at a slightly lower rate, since his ability to spend the counterfeit had been established). He then gave about Rp.200,000 to a *dangdut* singer[2] in a café in Sidoarjo before being arrested based on the phone merchant's earlier tip to police. When arrested, he had over Rp.1,100,000 of the fake currency on his person and at trial he admitted to all the charges, leading to his conviction and sentencing to eighteen months in prison (though the prosecutor had originally asked for thirty months).

[2] *Dangdut* is a style of music and dance, first broadly popularized (especially on Java and among lower-income Indonesians) during the 1970s, which combines elements of Malay, Indian, Middle Eastern, and pop music influences. *Dangdut* songs are typically performed by a single vocalist (who is often also a dancer), backed by a band, and performance venues are sometimes associated with drinking, gambling, drug use, and prostitution.

Looking at Manado, the other large city among my field sites, we see a generally similar profile, but on a smaller scale (in keeping with the much smaller size of the city, relative to Surabaya) – there were only 523 criminal cases adjudicated there in 2005, along with 546 in 2009, mostly for theft and assault, with smaller numbers involving domestic violence and sex crimes. A much smaller share consisted of more complex cases, like intellectual property rights violations and corruption. Some of these, though, came in waves.

In 2009, a number of vendors selling pirated DVDs along a main thoroughfare (Jalan Pierre Tandean, known universally in Manado as "Boulevard") were busted in a series of police raids and crackdowns. In Case 254/Pid.B/2009/PN.MDO, a DVD vendor was arrested with a box of pirated discs. The first three witnesses were the police officers who had apprehended him and processed his case. They explained where and when he was caught, how many DVDs were recovered and what their approximate value was. They also indicated that, when he was caught, the defendant blamed another individual for being behind the pirated goods sales. This individual, who rented counter space in an IT mall, in front of which the defendant was caught, testified that he rented counters to sell DVDs, that he did not know the other informal vendors or the defendant, and that the DVDs being sold (legitimate or pirated) were supplied by the mall managers. The chief mall manager then claimed that he'd known the counter space lessee since he was a boy and that he was actually a key aide to the management in controlling all of the mall's counters. There were no relationships between him and the vendors, though, and he asserted that the other witnesses must have been lying. Another witness, who worked with the counter lessee, testified that she paid him to travel to Jakarta and purchase 1000 DVDs at a time on a regular basis for Rp.4000 per disc (which could then be sold on at the Manado mall for roughly double that price). Then, the prosecution saw a need to call an expert on IT and copyright law, who testified that DVDs are indeed protected by copyright and that there can be no valid license for vendors of pirated goods. He also confirmed the rough street price range of pirated DVDs in Manado. Finally, the accused claimed he was just a vendor, working for the mall managers and those who sent him to buy the DVDs in Jakarta. The court and police were apparently not persuaded to go after the mall managers or the woman who seemed to be the mastermind, instead convicting the vendor of violating copyright law and sentencing him to four months in prison and a fine of Rp.750,000. Several other cases were essentially similar and even appeared to be connected to the same crackdown around the IT mall (Cases 236/Pid.B/2009/PN.MDO; 238/Pid.B/2009/PN.MDO; 240/Pid.B.2009/PN.MDO; 242/Pid.B/2009/PN.MDO; 243/Pid.B/2009/PN.MDO; 244/Pid.B/2009/PN/MDO; 245/Pid.B/2009/PN.MDO). In Case 330/Pid.B/2009/PN.MDO, the defendant received a heavier fine, apparently because many of the DVDs he was caught with contained pornographic films (banned in Indonesia) – so he was selling illegal copies of an illegal product.

In Case 17/Pid.B/2009/PN.MDO, the defendant was sentenced to eleven months in prison for drug possession after he had been caught with a vial of narcotics and a miniscule amount of marijuana (0.1 grams). Urine tests confirmed he had THC in his system, however, and he admitted both to smoking cannabis and to possessing harder drugs.

A weapons possession case (Case 149/Pid.B/2009/PN.MDO) was much more complicated and involved actual violence. Two women were waiting outside a major supermarket on Jalan Sam Ratulangi in downtown Manado, looking for transportation home at nearly 5:00 AM one night in June 2009. After a while, an SUV, driven by the defendant and with his friend in the passenger seat, pulled up and stopped for them. After the women got in, the defendant asked where they were going, and they said to the Tikala neighborhood. Seeing that a motorcycle taxi (*ojek*) had arrived, one of the women got out of the car and onto the motorbike to go home. The defendant and his friend then drove off with the other woman in the back seat. She asked where the defendant was from, and he replied that he lived in Airmadidi, but had just come from a popular (at the time newly opened) combination billiard parlor and discotheque a few blocks away from where he had picked her up. According to police and prosecutors, the defendant and his friend stopped the SUV in a secluded spot and closed all the windows, before the defendant sexually assaulted the victim at knifepoint and robbed her mobile phone and cash. The victim testified at trial to all these basic facts, as did her friend who had taken the *ojek* home (though she, obviously, was not present for the attack or robbery).

A different friend of the defendant testified that he owned the SUV and that the defendant and the friend who'd accompanied him came back to his house after 5:00 AM that night in June. While there, the friend who'd been with him on the drive said the defendant gave him a mobile phone belonging to the victim that he said he had found in the car. The friend later went to Manado's old commercial area (*pasar 45*) and sold the phone for Rp.700,000 – though eventually he had to ask his parents for Rp.1,500,000 to get the phone replaced. But he also described a different series of events before they returned the car. He claimed he'd brought a large knife (21 cm long) into the car with him for protection, that the defendant had been driving when they met the women and continued to drive as far as the bus terminal at Malalayang, on the outskirts of the city, when they switched. When they'd left the city, the friend pulled off the road in a quiet area and both he and the defendant had some sort of sexual encounters with the victim in the backseat. He said there was no use of force or any threats made with the knife, however.

Finally, the defendant testified along the same lines as his friend, but added that the knife was his and also that while his friend and the victim were engaged in sexual activity the backseat, he had opened her bag and stolen her phone and Rp.500,000 in cash. They then took the victim home to Tikala and went to their other friend's house, where the defendant gave his friend the phone, keeping the cash for himself. Later, he apologized to the victim and, he said, gave her Rp.1,500,000 to replace her phone. The court decided that the prosecutor could not prove a charge of sexual assault and, since the defendant had given the victim compensation for her phone and cash, there was no basis to convict him of robbery. But it did find him guilty of possessing a weapon and wielding it inappropriately, sentencing him to fifteen months in prison.

There were some very simple cases, like Case 35/Pid.B/2009/PN.MDO, in which a young woman admitted to stealing Rp.17,000,000 worth of mobile phone accessories and airtime cards from the counter where she was employed, earning her a sentence of five months and fifteen days in prison. Similarly, in Case 375/Pid.B/2005/PN.MDO, a sixteen-year-old boy was sentenced to two months and fifteen days in prison after he was caught running a cock-fighting operation by the side of a road just outside the city. The police officer who had arrested him testified that he'd seen the cockfighting in operation, that the boy had fled when he approached, and that he had caught him with chickens, spurs, and large amounts of cash in small bills in his possession. A second witness saw this unfold and agreed. Finally, a third witness said he'd placed bets on chickens with the defendant and lost, describing also the prices charged for accessories for one's chicken, such as spurs and razor blades.

Not all cases in Manado were so mundane, however. There were several related to election fraud and corruption, as well as several twisted murder cases, and a few very complicated attempts at fraud or theft of land registration certificates or other essential economic or legal documents. Two cases of election fraud were, on the surface, quite similar, though one involved a foreign national and the other resulted in an acquittal on appeal. In Case 159/Pid.B/2009/PN.MDO, a German citizen was arrested for destroying posters in front of the campaign headquarters of a PDI-P candidate for Manado City Council. His claims that his actions were instigated by the arrival of a Golkar candidate for the same post did not sway the court, which sentenced him to six months in prison and a fine of Rp.600,000 – a decision that was upheld on his appeal to the Manado High Court. The defendant in Case 164/Pid.B/2009/PN.MDO, a candidate for the local legislature, had held a campaign event at his friend's house. At the event, some of the guests said they had received envelopes filled with Rp.40,000 in cash and a signed photo of the candidate with his party's logo on the back. They reported this to the election oversight body (*Panwaslu*), officers from which then called the police. The original trial in the basic court led to a guilty verdict and a sentence of six months in prison along with a fine of Rp.600,000. On appeal this was thrown out, however, because the only evidence against the defendant consisted of envelopes turned in by his accusers that contained cash and his photo. No one saw him put the money or pictures into the envelopes or said that they received such an envelope directly from his hands. No one testified to being instructed to stuff or distribute the envelopes either, leading the High Court to reverse the guilty verdict, and even to voice some suspicion that the prosecution could have been politically motivated.

Case 14/Pid.B/2009/PN.MDO was something of a crime of passion, committed during a confrontation that appears to have been remembered rather differently by each of those involved. At about 6:30 PM on September 3, 2008, the defendant was said to have pulled a woman off of a motorcycle taxi (*ojek*) at the Malalayang Terminal, furiously saying that she was his wife and claiming she was on her way to meet another man with whom she was having an affair. The *ojek*-driver (*tukang ojek*, or simply *ojek*) and the man got into a fistfight, which then escalated when several other *ojeks* came running over from their station (*pangkalan ojek*). At some point during the fight, the defendant stabbed the original *ojek* multiple times in the chest, directly damaging his heart and aorta and leading to his death shortly thereafter.

Two of the other *ojeks* who had been involved testified that the defendant had indeed acted in such a manner and stabbed their friend to death. The victim's father said that his son had been an *ojek* and had been at work that day, that he had been called to help his son at the terminal just after the fight, and that he had found him bleeding profusely there and taken him to the hospital, where doctors were unable to save him and he died at 9:30 PM that night. Another *ojek* – not a coworker of the other witnesses – testified that he had taken the defendant to the terminal as a passenger just before the fight erupted, but that he had left to refuel his motorcycle after dropping him off and did not see the stabbing occur. The defendant's wife confirmed that she was the woman pulled off of the motorcycle and explained that she and her husband were having relationship difficulties and he had accused her of having an affair. In fact, though, she was on her way to a village outside Manado, where she was staying with a friend to be away from her husband for a few days to think over their differences. After he had pulled her off the bike and the fight had broken out, she had run away terrified and called for help. She thus did not see the stabbing, but said her husband did not normally carry a knife and that perhaps five to ten additional *ojeks* had attacked him as soon as the fight began.

The defendant admitted to the charges, but clarified that he had found the knife (with a 10 cm blade) on the minibus (*mikrolet*) he had ridden to Manado from his village that day (he did not know whose it was and did not report his find to the driver, but kept the knife instead), and that he had stabbed the victim in what he termed self-defense – he claimed he had been set upon by ten *ojeks*, who had beaten him severely and had hit him with a wooden plank and thus, fearing for his life, he reached for the knife he had happened to find earlier and had kept in his pocket. He was convicted and sentenced to eight years in prison.

Case 313/Pid.B/2009/PN.MDO saw the theft of a land registration certificate in a bid to ensure that a parcel of land could be surveyed and divided anew upon the death of its then-current occupant. Specifically, the defendant was found to have taken and destroyed (or hidden) the certificate after it had been entrusted to him by the victim so that he could examine or photocopy it. According the testimony of eight different witnesses, the defendant had sought to garner a piece of the parcel of land owned and occupied by the victim's father. He had thought he could do this if the certificate were missing or nonexistent upon the father's death because competing claims would then have to be adjudicated and settled through a new survey. The court convicted him of embezzlement (*penggelapan*) and sentenced him to ten months in prison, but did not settle the land dispute (apparently leaving any competing claims to be worked out through a civil suit).

Probably the most complicated and potentially politicized criminal case I uncovered from either city after 2000 was actually rooted in a rural land dispute in North Minahasa (Case 414/Pid.B/2005/PN.MDO). This case, first adjudicated in Manado in September 2005, but then appealed all the way up to the Supreme Court, involved a fifty-two-year-old village chief accused of falsifying land records. Specifically, a parcel of land inherited by one son was to have been divided between him and his brother. At least one of them had also sought to sell portions of the land to others. Meanwhile, two other people had been living on the land, in one case since 1985, when the village chief had sent his deputy to measure the parcels in question. The deputy had recorded the land on which their houses stood as belonging to the occupants, rather than the brother who had originally inherited the whole parcel. This, however, was in accordance with the wishes of his other brother, who had been cultivating parts of the land, who had originally invited the other occupants to live on the land and guard it, and who had been responsible both for reaping the fruits of coconut trees on the land and for cutting down those trees in the past. A number of villagers, all occupants and claimants to the land, and the village secretary and deputy all testified in detail. In the end, the Manado court decided there was insufficient evidence to prove that the chief had knowingly and willfully falsified the land certificates he had issued in 2000 and 2001, and he was acquitted.

The prosecutor appealed to the Supreme Court, arguing that the case did not have to be appealed to the provincial court first and also that the reasoning of the original ruling was badly flawed. Specifically, the prosecutor maintained in his statement of appeal (*memori kasasi*) that the Manado court's claim that the village chief was only discharging his responsibilities as a public servant and was therefore absolved of criminal responsibility did not hold water if the judges could easily see that the defendant had knowingly issued a certificate for land that did not belong to the individuals seeking the certificate. The logic would be the same, the prosecutor argued, as if the chief had issued a certificate to a military or police aspirant stating that he was not married, even though he knew well that the villager in question already had a wife. In a decision issued in January 2008 (Case 407/K/Pid/2007), the Supreme

Court rejected the prosecutor's appeal on procedural grounds, largely sidestepping the questions of whether the chief had a duty to issue only truthful certificates and declining to adjudicate whether undue political or personal influence may have clouded the original measurement and certification of land title or the Manado court's earlier decision.

Urban courts across Indonesia have become increasingly transparent and professionalized over the past several decades. This is obvious in all aspects of their work and communications, from increasingly detailed and updated websites to publicly displayed dockets. The work of criminal adjudication has become less political, however, largely because of improving education levels and closer public oversight of judges. With a more highly trained bench and greater public and media access, urban courts are well positioned to withstand intervention from police or political actors into criminal adjudication. But much more influentially, obvious instances of politicization would incite public anger in major cities, as such intervention is clearly not compatible with even the imperfect and partial form of democracy that has existed in Indonesia since *Reformasi*. The situation in rural areas is broadly similar, but differs in certain respects in light of much greater resource constraints, lower levels of judicial competence and public access, and divergent social conditions.

Criminal Law in Rural Areas

In rural areas, there have been far fewer criminal cases than in cities, and those that have occurred have been mostly routine. In East Java's rural Kediri, for example, a preponderance of cases since 2010 have involved gambling (*perjudian*), with some others of theft, fraud, and assault mixed in – even the occasional murder. Of the 228 rural Kediri criminal cases from 2013 I was able to review in some detail (out of a total of 424 heard by the court that year), 123 (54 percent) involved charges of gambling, 53 (23 percent) were for theft (or sale of stolen goods), 23 (10 percent) were for violence or assault (*kekerasan* or *pengganiayaan*), 1 was for murder, and 4 involved other types of offenses (such as vandalism or drugs). Almost all these cases were open-and-shut.

As a judge described such offenses when I interviewed him in Tuban (another mostly rural area of East Java) in February 2010, "you get caught in the act doing something illegal – in this case, betting on cock-fighting by the side of the road – there is nothing to argue and no need for a complex or lengthy trial." A few of the gambling cases were larger (e.g. Cases 357/Pid.B/2013/PN.Kab.KDI and 379/Pid.B/2013/PN.Kab.KDI), with significant cock-fighting rings being broken up. Of course, one can surmise that police bring many gambling cases when punters grow weary of paying sufficient bribes to keep them at bay. The roots of such cases thus often unmistakably lie in the abuse of power and office, even if their adjudication could not be more unremarkable or workaday.

More informative, perhaps, are the twenty-three cases I was able to review (another 10 percent of the total) that involved charges of fraud, deception, falsification, or embezzlement. Most of these, however, related to dishonest practices by motorcycle dealers, car salesmen, vehicle purchasers who never paid, or employees who skimmed money from cash registers or employers' safes. In a few cases, individuals created fake IDs or driver's licenses, sometimes selling these to others, sometimes using them for their own purposes. All such cases were also easily adjudicated, without exposing any struggles that may have played out within the court over how to handle possible influence from other powerful or political actors.

One case that did expose such tension was that of a forty-four-year-old village chief (*kepala desa*) accused of criminal fraud (Case 358/Pid.B/2013/PN.Kab.KDI). The court clearly wrestled over whether the chief's behavior in handling some administrative affairs rose to the level of criminality. Eventually, the judges ruled that it did not – though they confirmed that he had indeed acted as accused – and suggested that a civil suit (*gugatan*) would have been more appropriate than a criminal prosecution. In other words, the court claimed to have been able to recognize the case as a criminalized civil dispute (a category I will discuss in more detail in Chapter 5) and threw it out. Almost immediately, the prosecutor filed an appeal (*banding*) with the East Java High Court, but the results of the appellate case were not available in the file when I examined it in November 2014.

In rural Sulawesi – in both Minahasa and Minahasa Utara – the overwhelming majority of cases involved assault, frequently with a knife or machete. Alcohol was also often a factor and the incidents tended to take place late at night. There were also, of course, a usual assortment of sex crimes, thefts, and the occasional murder or corruption cases. But, on the whole, cases there were also strikingly routine in their handling. They were also fewer in number, reflecting those areas' much lower populations in comparison with regencies on Java. There were only 160 criminal cases adjudicated in the Airmadidi court in 2013, for example, and only 300 in 2012 in the Tondano court with jurisdiction over the much larger Minahasa regency (covering much of the rural and upland areas of the province).

Looking at the Tondano court, where I was able to review all of the 300 criminal cases it adjudicated in 2012, fully 125 (42 percent) of these were on charges of assault or threats of violence, while 44 (15 percent) involved sex offenses, and 9 were drug-related prosecutions. There were also eleven murder or manslaughter trials (4 percent of the total), and 31 prosecutions (10 percent) for fraud of various kinds, while there were only 25 cases (8 percent) of theft and 17 (6 percent) on charges related to gambling. Most of the remaining 38 trials (13 percent) involved vandalism, human trafficking, or traffic accidents. The prevalence of violent crime, especially in comparison with Kediri's primarily gambling and theft offenses, stands out markedly. Some of this could be due to regional cultural or lifestyle differences – the judges and police I interviewed in Tondano all pointed to the common practice in the region of heavy consumption of powerful moonshine liquor (distilled spirits made from palm wine and usually distributed in old plastic water bottles, known locally as "rat brand" or *cap tikus*, which can contain up to 70 percent alcohol). Inebriation, they claimed, frequently led to sex crimes, fights and assaults, and occasionally murder. It could also be that certain types of violent crimes – e.g. sex crimes, minor drug offenses, or even some types of assault – are not reported or adjudicated as frequently through the formal criminal system in mainly Muslim rural Java as they are in mainly non-Muslim highland Sulawesi. Similarly, gambling appears anecdotally and from my own casual observations to be less common in rural Sulawesi, or at least enjoyment of it is much less public, than it is across Java.

The pattern of charges is even more apparent if we look at the Tondano court's 2001 criminal cases. Of the 207 cases tried that year, 125 (more than 60 percent) were on charges of assault or threats of violence, 12 (6 percent) involved sex crimes, 18 (9 percent) were for theft, and just 6 were for drug offenses. There were also 27 murder cases (more than 13 percent of the total criminal case load) and 11 trials for fraud or embezzlement. Five other prosecutions were on charges of vandalism, criminal liability in traffic accidents, or possession or distribution of pornography. The final three were corruption cases against local officials. Overall, the prevalence of violent crime is still notable, as are the relatively small number of cases in which the court was required to exercise careful or critical judgment on the questions of whether or how outside powerful interests might be exerting any sort of influence.

Focusing in on the three corruption cases, two of these involved allegations of financial misdeeds during the 1998–9 electoral campaign season (Cases 12/Pid.B/2001/PN.TDO & 23/Pid.B/2001/PN.TDO) – which took place against the backdrop of the Asian Financial Crisis and the fall of Suharto's New Order. In both of these instances, officials running for reelection were convicted of embezzling large sums of money (Rp.417 million in one case and Rp.941 million in the other) and spending it on personal investments or luxuries (such as large new houses in the hills). The defendant in Case 12/Pid.B/2001/PN.TDO died after his case was decided, but before the provincial high court could rule on his appeal. This led to a forfeiture of his appellate rights, but also meant he was absolved from his sentence. His heirs, meanwhile, were not required to pay any fines, but only to disgorge the ill-gotten gains he had amassed. The third corruption case related to abuse of power by a fifty-six-year-old village official, who had acquired large tracts of rice paddies and other agricultural land by making use of insider financing deals with local banks (Case 145/Pid.B/2001/PN.TDO). He was required to disgorge these gains and serve one year in prison after his conviction. That traditional elites and elected officials from the New Order era were subject to prosecution in the early years of *Reformasi* suggests that political influence in the criminal process was indeed on the wane, at least in Minahasa, for those holdovers from the old regime who still held vast stocks of social, economic, and informal political power.

There are even stronger indications to be found among some of the criminal cases heard in 2012. In eight of the thirty-one cases related to various types of fraud tried in the Tondano court that year (Cases 03/Pid.B/2012/PN.TDO, 15/Pid.B/2012/PN.TDO, 34/Pid.B/2012/PN.TDO, 35/Pid.B/2012/PN.TDO, 64/Pid.B/2012/PN.TDO, 113/Pid.B/2012/PN.TDO, 114/Pid.B/2012/PN.TDO, & 199/Pid.B/2012/PN.TDO), defendants were acquitted because their behavior had not in fact been criminal. In other words, the court decided to set aside cases (similar to that against the fertilizer salesman, discussed in the Introduction) in which the police and prosecutors were used by well-connected aggrieved parties to mount criminal claims against defendants who more rightly should have suffered only civil suits. In Case 199/Pid.B/2012/PN.TDO, for example, a sixty-eight-year-old woman in the town of Tomohon was accused of fraudulent dealings in a real estate lease dispute. While the court agreed that the defendant's behavior was indeed as alleged, and may not have been particularly fair or kind, it ruled that it did not rise to the level of a crime.

Similarly, in Case 15/Pid.B/2012/PN.TDO, a sixty-four-year-old farmer from a remote rural area was accused of falsifying land ownership certificates when a land transaction went sour. The court decided that there was no evidence of criminal wrongdoing, even if the other party perhaps had some valid claim that the defendant may have abrogated their contract of sale. Finally, in some instances, like Case 34/Pid.B/2012/PN.TDO, the Tondano court of the first instance was persuaded to convict a defendant (in this case a forty-eight-year-old man accused of defrauding his creditors out of Rp.20 million), only to have this verdict thrown out on appeal to the provincial high court in Manado, which was able to recognize an attempt to make private use of the criminal law's coercive apparatus.

In Airmadidi, the relatively new court of the first instance for North Minahasa, founded only in 2008, heard 160 criminal cases in 2011, all of which I was able to review. Of these, 68 (43 percent) were on charges of assault or threats of violence, while 22 (14 percent) were for sex crimes, 23 (14 percent) were for simple theft, and 10 (6 percent) were for murder. There were 16 (10 percent) on other types of charges – largely vandalism – and 21 (13 percent) trials for one sort or another of fraud or deception. While almost all of the trials in 2011 were routine, there were a few cases that required the court to determine whether behavior actually rose to criminal standards and how to proceed in punishing powerful local actors.

In one such case (Case 34/Pid.B/2011/PN.AMD) a fifty-one-year-old official, who actually resided in Manado but worked as head of the Minahasa Utara *kabupaten* government's section on buildings and development, was accused of falsifying numerous building deeds and permits in exchange for bribes. Initially, the Airmadidi court found there was not enough evidence to support a conviction and he was acquitted of all charges. After the prosecutor appealed all the way to the Supreme Court in Jakarta, the verdict was reversed and the Airmadidi court was deemed to have erred. The official was sentenced to four years in prison and a fine of Rp.200 million was imposed. What is not clear from the records I was able to review, however, is what new evidence came to light during the appellate process, beyond the recollections of accusers and witnesses presented at the original trial. It seemed the Airmadidi court was reticent to convict this defendant because it was difficult to establish that he had benefitted personally from the alleged corrupt and fraudulent transactions. Evidently, the Supreme Court applied a stricter standard in judging his conduct.

This was not at issue in Case 80/Pid.B/2011/PN.AMD, in which a village chief (*kepala desa*) was convicted of falsifying land title documents and other records and orders specifically for his personal gain. After prosecutors established the pattern of his actions and the manner in which he had benefitted to the court's satisfaction, the decision was not one with which the judges appeared to have struggled. The fact that this defendant was only a village chief, whereas in the other similar case the accused had been a *kabupaten* official, may also have made a difference, though this cannot be read explicitly from the court records or documents.

Looking at two relatively complicated, yet ultimately unremarkable, trials from 2012 also illustrates the way in which the Airmadidi court adjudicated quotidian criminal cases. In a violent sexual assault and theft case (Case 139/Pid.B/2012/PN.AMD), a thirty-two-year-old man from Bitung was out in the early morning hours of July 23, 2012, with three of his friends in an SUV. Around 6:40 AM, they passed a young woman in Tomohon, who was looking for transportation to her job in Manado. They flashed the lights of the SUV and she got in. After asking her the time, they locked the doors and told her they were taking her to Likupang (in the opposite direction of Manado) to force her to withdraw money from an ATM there. They threatened her and took her handbag. Looking through the bag, they took her mobile phone and then blindfolded her with a pair of her own stockings they had found in the bag. On the way to Likupang, one of the defendant's friends sexually molested the victim (described in graphic detail in the testimony of several witnesses). Then they parked the car near the Likupang ATM, the friend who'd been molesting the victim got out to withdraw money with her card, and the defendant got into the backseat of the SUV, brandished a machete, and sexually assaulted the victim. When his friends in the front seat alerted him to a passing pedestrian who was staring at the rocking car, he quickly stopped. One of his friends from the front seat moved to the backseat and began straightening up the victim's clothes as the third friend returned from the ATM. They drove off, eventually letting the victim out in a wooded area near Airmadidi, before going on back to Bitung with her mobile phone and Rp.100,000 they had taken from the ATM.

The victim testified against the defendant at trial, as did the three friends (apparently in exchange for immunity), leading to his conviction for both rape and violent robbery (*pencurian dengan kekerasan*). He was sentenced to ten years in prison in December 2012 (one of the harshest sentences imposed in any Indonesian case I examined). Though one might argue that less sophisticated rural judges might have been quicker to reach for an easy verdict than their counterparts in the city, it seems actually to have been the unanimity and clarity of testimony from witnesses on all sides of the events that led to a more definitive outcome than in the otherwise quite similar Case 149/Pid.B/2009/PN.MDO discussed earlier in this chapter.

In Case 146/Pid.B/2012/PN.AMD, a fifty-one-year-old school master was convicted of assaulting a child and sentenced to eight months in prison, a fine of Rp.5,000,000, and a year of probation after his release. According to the testimony of several students and teachers, he had made all the students line up outside the school at 7:15 AM on March 6, 2012, so that he could inspect their proper attire and appearance (*kerapihan murid-murid*). After looking them over, he called forward an eight-year-old boy whose hair he said was too long. Taking hold of a pair of large stainless steel scissors, he forcefully cut the boy's hair – so roughly that he sliced open his scalp on the back of his head, causing significant bleeding. Thinking the sentence too lenient, the prosecutor appealed to the provincial High Court in Manado, which issued a decision in March 2013. Somewhat surprisingly, the High Court did not increase his punishment, but "improved" the original ruling to reduce it – to eight months in prison, a fine of Rp.1,000,000, and ten months of probation – citing the need for consistency.

Across rural areas, we can see criminal law operating in a decidedly rule by law model, but with less regularity and apparent ease when compared with urban centers. Rural courts in Indonesia remain badly under-resourced and understaffed. Many rural judges have scant training (or no formal legal training at all). Evidence-gathering and presentation can also be problematic, as police and prosecutors sorely lack resources and training even more than do judges. There also continue to be issues of corruption, especially in the investigation and prosecution of crimes in rural Indonesia. Yet, there appears to be relatively little direct intervention in the adjudication process by politically or socially powerful actors. The judicial process remains one of norms rather than exceptions and retains a high level of formal rationality and basic predictability.

Concluding Thoughts

Indonesian criminal law, both on the books and in the courtroom, changed in very important and significant ways in the wake of Suharto's fall in May 1998. No longer could military, business, or other powerful actors blatantly influence individual cases with impunity. No longer was the criminal apparatus available as a simple tool of brute repression. Reforms to the appointment and oversight of the judiciary, the police, and the prosecutorial system appear to have made some real impact. But, of course, there are some qualifications to be noted.

First, which crimes are investigated and prosecuted and what offenses go unpunished? This may not be random or merely a function of resources and priorities. Drug dealers and pimps may find themselves in the dock only when they stop paying off the right police sufficiently. Similarly, gamblers and cockfight ringleaders may be able to avoid the law so long as they give police or other local bosses a sufficient cut of their profits. The same may even be true of more serious violent crimes. That there may be an "on–off switch" available to the powerful to activate the criminal process or keep it at bay is a significant issue much in the public eye in Indonesia, but a problem difficult to assess through the study of case records or interviews with judges, police, or prosecutors. How cases that were never initiated might have progressed remains a topic on which my work cannot shed more than very limited light.

Second, some aspects of how cases are handled once they get into court may also be an issue, at least in some settings. Those with connections or resources are much more likely to have access to competent lawyers, to be able to mount vigorous and effective defenses, and to pursue appeals should they not be satisfied with trials in the first instance court. These inequalities are present in most justice systems, of course, but they may be more severe in Indonesia than in many other settings. Where they also appear particularly likely to come into play is in sentencing and the conditions in which sentences are served. Wealthier or more influential defendants seem frequently to receive lighter sentences or to be afforded opportunities to serve their sentences in less uncomfortable conditions. While this too is a feature of many criminal justice systems around the world, this dimension of inequality in Indonesia seems especially sharp and is likewise a subject of significant public discussion and anger.

In all, however, we must note that the judicial process itself has become remarkably predictable, consistent, and for the most part free of intervention from nonlegal political or other powerful actors. Once a case is investigated and prosecuted, in other words, few seem to be above or beyond the reach of the law (even if some may be punished a bit less sternly for the same infractions). While the polity remains fully under the control of a stable elite that has run the country for decades, the Indonesian criminal apparatus functions with a high degree of formal rationality and consistency, according to rules and norms rather than exceptions, in a clear example of rule by law legal regime.

CONCLUSION

China's rule by law legal regime in the civil arena since the 1980s and Indonesia's in the criminal sphere since the fall of New Order share a number of important attributes. In both cases, stable hierarchies in the polity take a hands-off approach and allow legal institutions to proceed relatively unhindered and independently with the adjudication process. But they do this for different reasons and the legal regime has different implications and results in each context.

In China, the autocratic state ties its hands (Wang 2015) in terms of the civil (especially commercial) sphere because that comports with its general aim of economic development. Refraining from political intervention in civil cases promotes the goals of lowering transaction costs, making markets more efficient, and inducing greater confidence on the part of investors. By supporting the market's deepening and expansion, this strategy actually enhances the power and legitimacy of the still-authoritarian government and Party, even though no similar policy has been adopted for the criminal system.

In Indonesia, democratization has pushed the extralegal coercive arm of the state out of nearly all parts of the criminal process, though no similar reforms have taken place in civil litigation. What was necessary for basic democratic legitimacy – even regime viability – on the criminal side cannot be mustered on the civil. A wealthy elite could not allow its economic and social position to be challenged through civil litigation, particularly as the repressive capacity of the state to maintain hierarchical order through the law had been curtailed sharply through reform of the criminal system.

Both hybrids appear relatively sustainable, but both depend on the ongoing viability of crucial political bargains to avoid lapsing into fully neotraditional orders. In China, the CCP must continue to deliver high economic growth while also maintaining a strong – even controlling or "commanding heights" – position for the state in the economy. Should it fail to do so, the threat against smooth maintenance of its hold on power could be such that it might need to abandon rule by law in civil law in favor of a more neotraditional arrangement in which active intervention from extralegal actors could prevent devolutionary redistribution away from elites or state firms and agencies or even ensure redistribution *back* to elites and state agencies. In Indonesia, democracy has to remain viable and the populace reasonably contented with the existing social order, even as economic elites remain ensconced. Otherwise, political challenges to elites' positions could provoke a return to older practices of using the criminal justice system as a tool for repression of real or potential opponents.

CHAPTER FIVE

NEOTRADITIONAL SCLEROSIS: LAW IN THE SERVICE OF STAGNANT HIERARCHIES

> *The ancient principles which were decisive for the interlocking of "right" and "law" have disappeared, especially the idea that one's right has a "valid" quality only by virtue of one's membership in a group of persons by whom this quality is monopolized. To the past now also belongs the tribal or status-group quality of the sum total of a person's rights and, with it, their "particularity" as it once existed on the basis of free association or of usurped or legalized privilege. Equally gone are the status and other special courts and procedures. Yet neither all special and personal law nor all special jurisdictions have disappeared completely. On the contrary, very recent developments have brought an increasing particularism within the legal system.*
>
> (Weber 1978: 880)

> *The British raj, sometimes by design but more often by inadvertence, advanced the written, more uniform, and professionally interpreted law of the twice-born castes (*dharmasastra*) at the expense of the parochial, diverse, and orally transmitted customary law of villagers . . . For the most part, the raj initially disregarded, largely through ignorance, the existence of the orally transmitted customary law of villages, castes, and regions. It identified Indian law with the high-culture, literary law inscribed in the classic texts and in so doing unwittingly strengthened it at the expense of the "popular" law of the peasant society.*
>
> (Rudolph & Rudolph 1967: 253, 269)

INTRODUCTION

Neotraditionalism is a somewhat odd concept that has grown out of the Weberian tradition of social science. It is hard to identify almost by definition and can be frustratingly difficult to measure. As I conceive of neotraditional legal regimes, they are marked by high levels of intervention in the adjudication process by actors outside the legal system in contexts of fixed and stable – usually rigidly hierarchical – polities. As I explained in Chapter 1 and as we saw in Chapter 4, neotraditional legal regimes can often be found in hybrid combinations, frequently alongside rule by law orders, but can also exist on their own.

The Chinese and Indonesian cases give us examples of both "pure" and hybrid neotraditional legal regimes. Both civil and criminal law were marked by neotraditionalism under Suharto's New Order regime, once it had been consolidated by about 1974, until it collapsed in 1998. Similarly, though my data are less rich, the period of "Liberal Democracy," from independence until at least 1955, shows reasonably clear neotraditional patterns. But in other instances, we find neotraditionalism existing in hybrids with rule by law regimes, split between civil and criminal law.

Chapter 4 traced the development of a rule by law regime in the civil arena in China after 1978, but a sustained neotraditionalism has been a feature of the Chinese criminal system right up until the present day. Whereas in Indonesia after *Reformasi*, democratization effectively placed a check on political actors' ability to intervene in the criminal process in most cases, even as the polity remained intact and old elites endured unscathed. Democracy has done little to deter Indonesian elites' intervention in civil adjudication, allowing neotraditionalism to persist in this area of law, alongside the rule by law regime that has consolidated in the criminal arena.

INDONESIA

Indonesian law during the New Order period was governed by a neotraditional regime *par excellence* (McVey 1982). Civil law in Indonesia still functions under such a regime today, despite (or perhaps even abetted by) democratization. Finally, a certain – nontrivial – subset of criminal cases in today's Indonesia consist of criminalized civil disputes, as in the story of the businessman and his fertilizer cargo mentioned in the Introduction. Before turning to the present day, however, let us look first at the earliest instances of neotraditionalism in post-independence Indonesian law (prior to 1955), and then to its heyday – indeed a high water mark for politicized law in the service of established social hierarchies anywhere – the period after consolidation of Suharto's New Order in about 1974 until its collapse in 1998.

Criminal and Civil Law from Independence to 1955

The period of parliamentary or "liberal" democracy in the early days after full independence was achieved in 1949 is chronically and severely underresearched among scholars of Indonesian history and politics (McVey 1994). Unfortunately, I can offer little corrective to this deficit, as I was not able to collect comprehensive data from that period at any of my research sites. What is clear from secondary sources, however, is that Indonesian politics of the day were largely dominated by more conservative elements – many linked to Prime Minister Muhammad Hatta – who wished far more to administer a stable hierarchical order based on the continued leadership of old elites than to unleash further social change and upheaval through ongoing revolutionary change (Feith 1962; Sundhaussen 1982: 51–2).

At the national level, though there were no elections, there were at least nine different cabinets that attempted to govern Indonesia between 1949 and 1955 (Finch & Lev 1965). Even with such rapid turnover, however, certain personalities – almost all of them with conservative nationalist and religious leanings – played frequent leading roles. Even Sultan Hamengkubuwono IX of Yogyakarta (the ultimate traditional authority figure) was a frequent cabinet member, serving variously as Minister of Defense, Minister without Portfolio, and Deputy Prime Minister. Though more leftist leaders like Wongsonegoro, as well as federalists and others opposed to the general vision of a unitary state based on traditional hierarchies and patterns of rule (like Ide Anak Agung Gde Agung), began to exert increasing influence, the dominant current was still one of status quo-maintenance through rule by traditional elites in a context of weak, inchoate, and shifting institutions and a general lack of or ambivalence about more egalitarian, consistent, or transparent conventions and norms of political or social activity. This general trend played out in the legal system as well.

Dutch judges were replaced formally in 1950 with a motley assortment of mostly less-qualified nonprofessionals, including law clerks who had been working before World War II, *adat* judges who had been retrained, and recently graduated students (Lev 2000: 81). There were even fewer lawyers, and many who had been trained left the bar to take up government positions (Lev 2000: 173–4, 177). Indeed, most Indonesians with business before a court had to rely on the assistance of rough and ready "bush lawyers" (*pokrol bambu*), who functioned more like back-channel fixers than true advocates (Lev 1973a). Overall, Indonesia in the first part of the 1950s could be characterized as fundamentally a patrimonial political order with relatively weak legal influence (even within the legal system) (Lev 1973a: 21, 2000: 217–18). Even the national police force (*Polri*) – the most basic institution required for the administration of criminal justice or legitimate application of the state's coercive power – was only coherently organized in 1950 and remained exceedingly weak and fractured during this period (Muradi 2014: 24–5). As we have already seen in Chapter 3, Sukarno's moves toward a more charismatic and overtly authoritarian politics were in many ways attempts to consolidate a more coherent legal order – one that would eventually evolve into a mobilizational legal regime by the late 1950s.

Criminal Law under New Order

As the tool of legitimate state coercion, once New Order was consolidated, criminal law replaced covert violence as the regime's preferred means for enforcing social order and preserving the position of enduring elites. Indeed, the adjudication of almost all types of cases was influenced strongly by the military and political elite (especially General Ali Murtopo and those who followed in his footsteps after 1980). Across the archipelago, the police remained weak and the military continued to play a disproportionate role in structuring the operation of criminal justice in the stages leading up to detention and trial (Muradi 2014: Chapter 2). As has been noted, politicized criminal cases "looked to target political groups that had to be eliminated by those in power in order simply to defend the permanence of their power" (*upaya mempertahankan kelanggengan kekuasaan semata*), including Islamists, students, and bastions of support for Nationalist or Christian politicians (Asrun 2004: 132). Thus, "the Suharto regime used the courts to repress opposition leaders who denounced certain policies of the government, student leaders involved in anti-government protests, and religious leaders (*kaum ulama*) who spoke out sharply against President Suharto's authoritarian politics" (Asrun 2004: 132). In fact, across the criminal arena, this was palpable in the adjudication of even the most mundane cases.

The late 1970s and early 1980s were a golden age for court gazetteers in Indonesia, although these tend to be far less detailed than their Chinese counterparts. Many provincial high courts (*pengadilan tinggi*) published one that included at least some basic data about all the first instance courts (*pengadilan negeri*) under its jurisdiction. From a sampling of these, we can distill a rough picture of what caseloads and court work looked like during New Order's most ascendant period, between about 1976 and 1982.

As Table 5.1 shows, in nine provinces across the archipelago a very large portion of courts' criminal cases were processed using summary or even more expedited processes (*Rol*), especially compared with what we saw in the post-*Reformasi* era discussed in Chapter 4. Moreover, the ratio of criminal trials to civil lawsuits is low, meaning that a relatively large number of civil suits were being processed, compared to criminal trials. Even if we discount provinces – such as North Sulawesi, East Nusa Tenggara, and Central Kalimantan – with high non-Muslim populations (for whom divorce and inheritance cases wind up in the civil court system, whereas for most Muslims these matters fall under the jurisdiction of religious courts – the *pengadilan agama*), there are still a large number of suits compared to prosecutions across much of the country. Many court buildings were built or renovated during the 1970s and judicial staffing and compensation improved markedly, while the regime clearly sought to deploy the formal legal apparatus as a means for settling disputes and enforcing social control in support of the newly ensconced elite. Still, the persistence of high numbers of civil suits relative to criminal trials, as well as the consistent dependence on expedited criminal procedures (*Sumir* and *Rol*) points to a lack of institutional capacity and the continuing influence of political and other powerful actors from outside the formal legal system.

Beyond the raw numbers, the gazetteers make clear that many courts were still having basic problems getting established and taking up their work as late as the early 1980s. For example, the president of the high court for Lampung Province (*Ketua Pengadilan Tinggi Tanjung Karang*) complained that his housing (and that of his deputy) was in a remote area and not connected to telephone networks (Lampung Gazetteer 1982: 11–13). Courts across much of Central Kalimantan pointed to a lack of boats, causing major problems for them in traveling to far-flung parts of their jurisdictions as well as in facilitating witnesses coming to appear in court when called (Central Kalimantan Gazetteer 1982: 28, 43–4, 94–5, 132). On the outskirts of Yogyakarta, the court in Sleman said its judges could not navigate the area of its jurisdiction very well, considering their 1953 Jeep Willys could not go too far and their 1951

Table 5.1 Criminal and civil cases at the height of New Order

Year	Province	Ordinary criminal (*Biasa*)	Summary criminal (*Sumir*)	Minor offenses (*Rol*)	Total criminal cases	Civil lawsuits (*Gugatan*)	Petitions (*Permohonan*)
1976[a]	West Java	760	3877	55,378	60,015	1042	1291
1976[b]	East Java	3048	12,942	78,285	94,275	2458	1928
1976[c]	North Sulawesi	241	967	6809	8017	1235	679
1979[d]	West Kalimantan	155	1018	6140	7313	147	2473
1981	Yogyakarta	171	855	9144	10,170	394	853
1981	Central Kalimantan	22	707	1855	2584	149	137
1981[e]	Lampung	1640	1458	7393	10,491	280	868
1981[f]	East Nusa Tenggara	618	810	4238	5666	833	1002
1982	West Nusa Tenggara	351	490	4649	5490	733	382

Source: Data drawn from: Central Kalimantan Gazetteer (1982); East Java Gazetteer (1980); East Nusa Tenggara Gazetteer (1982); Lampung Gazetteer (1982); North Sulawesi Gazetteer (1980); West Java Gazetteer (1978); West Kalimantan Gazetteer (1981); West Nusa Tenggara Gazetteer (1983); Yogyakarta Gazetteer (1982).

[a]Some local courts reported data for 1977 instead of 1976.

[b]Some courts reported data for 1975, 1977, or 1978, instead of 1976. Two local courts failed to report any data at all.

[c]Some local courts (mostly in remote areas) reported data for 1974, 1977, or 1978, instead of 1976.

[d]Two local courts reported data for 1976, instead of 1979.

[e]Some local courts reported data for 1982, instead of 1981.

[f]Some local courts reported data for 1980, instead of 1981.

Morris jeep had been totally inoperable for more than a year when the gazetteer was published (Yogyakarta Gazetteer 1982: 67).

Even in the West Javanese coastal city of Cirebon, the court complained of having only old jalopies and small-engine motorcycles to use for transportation. While, in the Jakarta suburb of Bogor, the court was short of office and hearing room space, because the prosecutor (*Jaksa*) and Military Court (*Pengadilan Militer*) were occupying much of its building (West Java Gazetteer 1978: 29, 83). Courts everywhere, even in downtown Surabaya (the second largest city in the country), spoke of insufficient staff and office space, as well as of such mundane problems as not having budgets to repair leaky roofs or replace broken typewriters (East Java Gazetteer 1980: 39–40).

Besides the gazetteers, one study of local criminal judges in East Java and their perceived role from the time period is illuminating. In 1981 Masyhur Effendi of Brawijaya University in Malang set out to explain the way criminal judges and the legal system influence the protection of citizens' human rights, interviewing forty-two judges from eleven different courts across urban and rural areas of the province, from Surabaya and Malang to Sampang and Banyuwangi (Effendi 1981: 8). More than half of these respondents said they did not have enough time (*tidak ada waktu cukup*) to think much or talk about problems of human rights, while more than a quarter of those who said they had thought about human rights admitted to holding views biased (*mewarnai*) against defendants (Effendi 1981: 15–16). Still, 70 percent of those who'd thought about the issue said they did consider human rights when deciding cases (Effendi 1981: 17).

Somewhat surprisingly, 65 percent of the judges also admitted that they privileged "social feelings of fairness" ("*rasa keadilan masyarakat*") above written law or regulations when making decisions (Effendi 1981: 24, 33), suggesting that political considerations (or at least informal social conventions) were explicitly crowding out the application of the law in criminal adjudication (especially to the extent that such considerations were less predictable or consistent than those of Chinese civil judges in the 2000s). In all, Effendi's report strikes a positive tone about judges' knowledge and respect for human rights, but his findings about their concrete attitudes and behavior belie a reality in which criminal adjudication remained largely subject to political directives and the overriding imperative to maintain social control and political order.

If we look at cases from the 1970s and 1980s, the political application of the criminal process to protect and enhance the position of elites is readily apparent. For example, three family members (a father and his two grown children) got into an argument with a young woman in their neighborhood in Tomohon – a town in the highlands of North Sulawesi – on the evening of August 4, 1986 (Case 49/Pid.B/1986/PN.TDO). The woman ended up being beaten and stabbed and the father was charged with assaulting and trying to kill her. Specifically, in the course of the argument, after his children had broken down the woman's door, beaten her, and ripped out much of her hair, the father (a retired military officer) drew his army-issued military knife and screamed, "if you try to run from here, I will kill you" (*keluar sini ngana pe lari kita mau bunuh*). He then stabbed her repeatedly with the military knife, causing serious injury and necessitating her hospitalization for four days. The local court in Tondano looked leniently upon the defendants, especially and explicitly because the father was a retired civil servant and military officer, absolving the two children of any criminal responsibility and sentencing the father only to three months in prison and nine months of probation. Though the man and his children went to their neighbor's house with the clear intent to harm her, and though he stabbed her repeatedly with his army-issued knife after threatening to kill her, the defendants' political and social status seems to have protected them from greater culpability.

This comes into sharp relief when we consider another case tried by the same court just a couple years later (Case 72/Pid.B/1989/PN.TDO). Three defendants were convicted of manslaughter and sentenced to between nine months and three years of prison time for their roles in killing another acquaintance, whose bike they were fixing in the motorcycle repair shop where they were at work on the night of January 24–5, 1987. The three defendants and the victim got into an argument at the shop that evening, which eventually developed into a fistfight, witnessed by the Chinese-Indonesian shopkeeper across the street (who called police and served as the main witness at trial). As the victim was being beaten badly, defendant 1 asked his friend defendant 2 for a knife, which he gave to him. Defendant 1 then stabbed the victim once in the right side of his chest, killing him. Defendant 3 had taken part in the fight, but did not supply the knife or stab the victim. He was given the lightest sentence, while defendant 1 received the heaviest. Although witnesses at trial testified to ongoing quarrels among the defendants and the victim, and the shopkeeper from across the street explained that the fight grew out of an argument and was not instigated specifically by the defendants, this did not seem to help their case. The defendants appealed, but the high court in Manado upheld their relatively harsh sentences. The three callow mechanics' apparent lack of social standing meant they were looked upon far more sternly by the court than the retired military man and his adult children had been when they attacked their young neighbor.

Looking at Surabaya, many New Order-era criminal cases were routine prosecutions of young men caught robbing people of cash and basic items like wristwatches at knifepoint on crowded streets in broad daylight (e.g. Cases 6/Pid.B/1979/PN.SBY, 9/Pid.B/1979/PN.SBY, 16/Pid.B/1979/PN.SBY, and 21/Pid.B/1979/PN.SBY). The most exciting such Case (7/Pid.B/1979/PN.SBY) included police and witnesses chasing down a robber foolish enough to flee the scene as a passenger in a bicycle taxi (*becak*) – clearly, he would have moved faster and been less conspicuous on foot. In another (Case 12/Pid.B/1979/PN.SBY), an indentured worker (*kuli*) was convicted of assault on the basis of testimony from two witnesses and sentenced to six months in prison for injuring another worker in a brawl.

In a somewhat jarring Case (10/Pid.B/1979/PN.SBY), a young mother left her slightly ill nine-month-old baby with her friend one morning, as she often did. The friend and her husband (both in their early twenties and quite poor) then took the baby and left Surabaya, going to a rural area in East Java. The mother called police once she realized what had happened, later that day, but they could not locate the couple or the baby. Twelve days later, the mother received an anonymous ransom note via post, demanding Rp.250,000 (or, if that proved to be too much, Rp.200,000) for the safe return of the baby. The couple was apprehended several days after that with the baby at the Surabaya bus terminal. The case file was missing formal decision and sentencing documents, but a summary of the trial's conclusion (handwritten in pencil on a plain piece of paper in the file) confirms that both defendants were convicted of kidnapping the baby and demanding ransom and were sentenced to one year in prison, even though the court could never establish precisely who had written or mailed the ransom note.

Later on, routine cases also showed a pattern of coming down hard on certain categories of defendants. In a 1984 arson Case (245/Pid.B/1984/PN.SBY), three workers in their mid-thirties were accused of burning down the company warehouses where they had been employed, causing nearly Rp.2 billion in damages but not injuring anyone. Twenty-three witnesses testified to their character (or lack thereof), as well as to the contents of the warehouses, and a great deal of physical evidence was presented to show that the fire was likely started intentionally, along with plans and photographs of the warehouses and some of their alleged contents. The defendants did not testify for themselves, however, and none of the witnesses seemed able to place them at the scene or fully explain what their motives may have been. Yet they were each convicted and sentenced – it appears from the faded hand-written documents in the file – to five years and seven months in prison for their crime. Had they not been lowly laborers, the court might likely have demanded better evidence to convict them, or at least sentenced them less harshly.

In two cases of robbery and burglary (Cases 240/Pid.B/1984/PN.SBY and 246/Pid.B/1984/PN.SBY, respectively), defendants were sentenced to four months and six months in prison respectively for stealing a boy scout uniform (*pakaian pramuka*) and for breaking into a house to steal a cassette recorder and other household goods. In the robbery, the young defendant from Lamongan was seen leaving the scene and apprehended with the stolen clothing. In the burglary, six witnesses testified and the stolen goods (which were recovered by police) were presented as evidence at trial, but no one actually saw the two young defendants enter or leave the residence.

Finally, we have two cases in which law enforcement seems to have targeted particular individuals and left others engaged in the same behaviors alone. In Case 241/Pid.B/1984/PN.SBY, a young man was arrested by several police officers (who testified at trial) after he had allegedly broken a beer bottle over another man's head during a street fight. There were at least a couple of others involved in the altercation, but they had not been arrested or charged. Meanwhile, the defendant was quickly convicted and sentenced to four months in prison. Similarly, in Case 247/Pid.B/1984/PN.SBY, three men in their mid-twenties were convicted and each sentenced to two months in prison and eight months of probation after being caught gambling by the police. The prosecutor called the officers to testify and presented sheets of gambling records at trial, which showed that the three defendants were neither the ringleaders nor the only ones involved in the activity – though they did appear to be the only ones arrested or prosecuted.

A case tried in Tangerang, West Java in 1996 exhibits similar patterns (Makamah Agung 1997b: Case 499.Pid.B/1996/PN.TNG). There, the court convicted seven young men from Sumatra, sentencing them to five months in prison for burglarizing two houses and stealing quite a lot of household goods and appliances. The main evidence was the testimony of the victims and an admission of guilt at trial by one of the defendants – at whose house the stolen goods had been recovered. The court imposed such light sentences for four reasons laid out in the decision: the defendants comported themselves decorously (*menujukkan sikap sopan*) and admitted to their crimes, they had never been in trouble with the law before, they did not get to the point of actually enjoying their ill-gotten gains, and they had been forgiven by their victims. These traditional attributes of repentance and forgiveness counted more in the calculation of the sentence, it seems, than the relatively high value of the goods stolen or the violent manner in which they'd broken into the two houses (by picking locks and breaking down doors).

If we look at a series of criminal cases in rural Kediri in East Java from 1982 (the first year the court for the rural *kabupaten*, site of Clifford Geertz's famous research on the religion of Java and an important base of support for the PKI in the 1960s, was separated from that of the urban *kotamadya*, famous for its concentration of *kretek* clove cigarette manufacturers), we can see similar attributes of neotraditionalism. Many of the cases were simply routine – a farmer who had stolen his neighbor's can of green paint (Case 253/Pid/B/1982/PN/KDI), a young man who had stolen a medicinal tree (Case 251/Pid.B/1982/PN.KDI), a farmer convicted of running a small gambling operation using roulette wheels made from the tops of cans and hubcaps (Case 231/Pid.B/1982/PN.KDI), a man who had stolen clove blossoms (*bunga cengkeh*) from a shop (Case 249/Pid.B/1982/PN.KDI), or a laborer put away for making off with his neighbor's radio/cassette recorder (Case 257/Pid.B/1982/PN.KDI), for example. In all these cases, defendants were easily convicted and sent to prison for between one-and-a-half and three months. There were a few more dramatic cases, such as the trial of a laborer who had tried to sell a stolen bicycle (Case 238/Pid.B/1982/PN.KDI), which involved testimony from an American doctor who claimed he had seen the bicycle stolen from in front of his clinic; or that of two fifteen-year olds who had broken into their village doctor's house to steal cash and valuables (Case 240/Pid.B/1982/PN.KDI). But most striking are four cases of violent crimes and how they were handled.

In Case 255/Pid/1982/PN.KDI, a twenty-three-year-old migrant laborer from Jombang was accused of breaking into a house with several of his friends at around 2:00 AM on July 1, 1982. He and his accomplices then allegedly threatened the house's occupants with physical violence, before making off with an eclectic mix of gold jewelry, two wristwatches, a radio and cassette recorder, ten pairs of trousers, a leather jacket, two bolts of cloth, and three lampshades. Because the total value of the stolen goods was relatively high (over Rp.1.6 million) and because he and his friends had threatened physical violence, the defendant's sentence as handed down by the court on December 8, 1982, was relatively harsh – ten months in prison. But this looks even harsher compared to that imposed in other violent criminal cases, and was perhaps due to the young defendant's status as a migrant laborer.

In another Case (259/Pid.B/1982/PN.KDI), a twenty-one-year-old driver struck and killed a passenger alighting from a small public bus (referred to here as a *Colt*, sometimes also known as a *bemo* or *mikrolet*). The driver failed to notice the bus stopping by the side of the road and did not even slow down or swerve (let alone stop) to avoid the passengers disembarking or crossing the road. He was convicted of manslaughter, but sentenced only to three months in prison (as opposed to the ten months the migrant laborer had received for robbery). In another vehicular Case (237/Pid.B/1982/PN.KDI), a student was driving along a main road when a dump truck passed him going the other direction. Several passengers were hanging off the sides of the dump truck and one of these was struck and killed by the defendant's truck. This defendant was sentenced to six months in prison, but this was suspended for one year (and if at the end of that time no further crimes had been committed, his record would be expunged). Both of these cases involved negligence on the part of drivers that led to the deaths of other people, but neither received a very severe punishment (and in one case, the defendant did not end up going to prison at all).

The most striking case, however, was that of a young woman who murdered her own newborn child (Case 239/Pid.B/1982/PN.KDI). The defendant was an eighteen-year-old student, who returned home from school in Surabaya pregnant, but did not want anyone to know. On the afternoon of July 9, 1982, she went down to the river's edge in her village and gave birth to a healthy baby boy, but killed the child and dumped his body in the river. When he was discovered a week later, some distance downstream, his brain was entirely missing from his skull (which had been split open) and many other internal organs were badly damaged. The defendant claimed that the pregnancy had resulted from a vicious sexual assault she'd suffered at the hands of four fellow-passengers on the train during another trip home the previous November. Horribly ashamed, she said she hid the pregnancy by wearing loose-fitting clothes and told no one of the attack. She admitted to killing the child and placing his body in the river. Upon conviction, however, she was sentenced only to five months in prison – less than the reckless driver had received for killing an illegal passenger hanging off the side of a speeding dump truck, just slightly more than the other driver had received for vehicular manslaughter, but only half that which a migrant laborer had received for stealing clothing and household goods.

Two rural Kediri cases from 1994 also show how the full force of criminal law could be brought against migrants and petty criminals, while those seemingly guilty of much worse transgressions could be spared, provided they were of sufficient social status. In one Case (71/Pid.B/1994/PN.KDI), a seventeen-year-old bicycle taxi driver (*tukang becak*) was convicted of pilfering a purple bicycle and sentenced to five months in prison. He and his friend had apparently asked to borrow the bicycle from a neighbor, who agreed to let them use it to ride home. But they rode instead to Jombang the next day, where they sold the bike and used the proceeds to buy sandals, a t-shirt, and some food. After the victim reported his bicycle stolen, the defendant's friend quickly turned on him and offered evidence to the police. The poor *tukang becak*'s outing in Jombang cost him dearly (indeed as dearly as a baby's murder had cost his young mother) because of his lack of social standing. Had he been better off, he may not have needed to steal the bicycle in the first place but could likely have found a way out of such severe punishment if he had.

This contrasts sharply with the case of a fifty-seven-year-old chicken wholesaler (Case 38/Pid.B/1994/PN.KDI) whose negligence was said to have caused the death of one of her employees. The defendant had wired a large electrical cable to run into her shop without using any sort of fuse, proper connection, or isolator (apparently she had just tapped the power line in the street). She did not even cover the copper wiring with rubber, encase it in a plastic pipe, or otherwise try to make sure no one came into contact with the live current. On August 17, 1994, one of her employees stumbled into the cable and became tangled in it, electrocuting herself in the process, and was pronounced dead at the nearby hospital a short time later. The court decided that there was no way to prove whether the current in the (apparently illegally-tapped) cable had been properly modulated by the state electric monopoly (PLN). Because of this and the fact that the employee could be deemed careless, the court acquitted the defendant of all criminal responsibility in the death of her employee. The prosecutor was incredulous and sought appeal as far as the Supreme Court in Jakarta, but to no avail. The chicken dealer was a sufficiently big fish in the small pond of rural Kediri to evade accountability for the worker's death, for which she was able to shift blame onto the power company or onto the worker herself. Had she been a migrant manual laborer, things may have unfolded differently.

There were also some very routine cases from the mid-1990s that nonetheless were appealed all the way to the Supreme Court (though without success in overturning the initial convictions). These included that of a teenager sentenced to two months in prison for shooting out his friend's eye with an air rifle while they were hunting birds (Case 82/Pid.B/1996/PN.KDI). Several other friends had been there, witnessed the incident, and testified to the fact that the shooting was an accident but did occur. Still, the defendant seemed to believe he should not face any criminal liability for blinding his friend. Such cases apparently were handled in sufficiently formally rational ways (or at least in a consistent manner intelligible to higher authorities remote from the immediate circumstances) as to withstand the scrutiny of multiple appeals.

Finally, there were cases in which defendants were convicted of serious crimes without extensive witness testimony and minimal other evidence, but that were also upheld on appeals to the Provincial and Supreme Courts. For example, a seventeen-year-old farm hand was convicted of sexually assaulting a fifty-year-old woman he had never met before, forcing her into a field after seeing her on a road (Case 63/Pid.B/1995/PN.KDI). No bystanders had seen the assault actually take place, though several witnesses could place the youth in the general vicinity that day. The victim testified that he had attacked her, and she was able to get to a hospital the same evening, where a doctor reported he found semen on her body and clothing and that she had bruises and other injuries consistent with being assaulted. But there was no direct evidence that the defendant had been her assailant other than her own testimony (and, of course, the defendant vehemently denied his guilt). He was convicted of rape and sentenced to two years in prison. Upon appeal, the High Court in Surabaya reduced the conviction from rape to "impugning moral respectability" (*menyerang kehormatan kesusilaan*), but left the sentence in place. Subsequently, the prosecution appealed to the Supreme Court, which reinstated the original conviction and upheld the sentence.

Looking beyond my sampled areas, Aryadi's scholarship suggests broadly similar patterns in the adjudication of theft cases in Yogyakarta during the late 1980s (Aryadi 1995: 91–108). Overall, the picture of a neotraditional legal regime in Indonesian criminal law under Suharto conforms strongly to our conventional wisdom regarding how a conservative military regime deploys state power to suppress real, potential, or imagined upstarts or opponents. The more counterintuitive place to find neotraditionalism under New Order is probably in the civil law arena, where we might expect Suharto's developmentalism to facilitate a rule by law order – a subject to which we now turn.

Civil Law under New Order

New Order's intervention in the adjudication process was not confined to criminal cases. Indeed, "this last mode of interference can be seen first of all in cases that pertain to the interests of the state, both in political criminal cases, as well as in civil and administrative cases" (*Model campur tangan terakhir ini dapat dilihat terutama pada kasus-kasus yang menyinggung kepentingan Negara baik pada kasus pidana politik maupun kasus perdata dan kasus administrasi*) (Asrun 2004: 129). Civil disputes can be more challenging to unpack, but actually show at least as strong a pattern of neotraditionalism as we have just seen in criminal cases.

Another issue in civil justice is the difficulty in enforcing court judgments. Skillful, negligent, or well-connected defendants could often delay enforcement for unreasonable lengths of time, if they ever complied at all. As one study of seven courts of the first instance in Bali noted, in 1984 and 1985, enforcement of civil judgments (which should have been immediate) often took upwards of several months, and sometimes nearly a year (and often required more than one request from the court) (Dermawan 1985). This was in part due to the lack of any legal provision specifically limiting the time between a court's judgment and actual execution or enforcement (Dermawan 1985: 34). This could lead some cases to be improperly criminalized (as will be discussed later). Or it could afford particular parties with another means to manipulate at least a small portion of the outcome of cases.

Some case files from the New Order period (especially the 1970s and 1980s) are fragmentary – for example, a real estate case from rural Kediri in 1984 (Case 54/Pdt.G/1984/PN.Kab.Kdr) – but the arguments and evidence presented at trial still show that a certain degree of politicization was in play. Both the defendant and the plaintiff (and later even the plaintiff's lawyer) had difficulty appearing in court for hearings. The plaintiff claimed that she had bought a house from the defendant for Rp.11 million, but the defendant responded that she had only received Rp.8 million and that the rest of the plaintiff's checks had bounced (something the plaintiff claimed was not relevant since she'd paid the remaining costs to the defendant in cash). Both sides agreed that the price to be paid was indeed Rp.11 million, but neither had written evidence either of cash payments or checks bouncing. There were eight hearings documented in the file, though the defendant failed to appear the first two times. The court agreed to hold hearings in other jurisdictions – Jombang and elsewhere – for the convenience of the parties, but after the first couple of hearings the plaintiff granted her lawyer power of attorney to appear on her behalf and did not come to court again. Her lawyer then had to write letters explaining his own repeated absences – including one on December 4 that he attributed to a bout of severe diarrhea – and gaps in the evidence. In the end, we cannot discern from the file how the case was ultimately concluded – despite the dispute being both routine and, at least on the surface, relatively easy to decide based on simple evidence.

In Manado, a naval officer sued an elderly housewife, who he said was illegally squatting on land he owned on the northern outskirts of the city (Case 112/Pdt.G/1975/PN.MDO). As the New Order regime had just coalesced into a powerful and coherent regime, this suit bears much resemblance to many filed in the late 1960s. The officer lacked clear documentation of his ownership claim, yet the defendant had some proof that she'd purchased the property in 1969 and had built the house that stood upon it with profits from her farming of cloves with her children. The court did not have an easy task in sorting through the complex documentation and conflicting testimony presented by both sides, who each also filed multiple motions and counterclaims, but it was able to rule conclusively in favor of the officer, ordering the old woman to vacate the house and leave the parcel of land at once. Just as when on trial for attacking neighbors in the criminal arena, military officers also enjoyed special positions of privilege in New Order's civil courts.

In another fraught land dispute (Case 122/Pdt.G/1975/PN.MDO), a farmer had legally occupied a parcel of vacant land near a main road heading out of town in 1961, according to his understanding of the

Agrarian Law. He petitioned to the land bureau of Manado City multiple times, and then to the North Sulawesi Provincial authorities when he did not get a response. He'd been occupying the land for over a decade and had built a shack on it where he lived with his family. He wanted the official and lawful right and express permission to rent or sell the land, but the provincial land bureau denied this in a letter sent to him in June, 1974, stating explicitly that the land had already been allocated for public use according to the city plan. The court ruled in favor of the government agencies, saying it did not have authority to overturn executive rulings on land. The farmer appealed to the Provincial High Court (recorded as Case 46/PT/1978 of the Manado High Court), but this court went even further, throwing out the original decision on the grounds that the court system did not even have authority to adjudicate disputes over public land, setting aside completely both the farmer's claims under the 1960 Agrarian Law and the local authorities' understandings of customary law (*adat* or, as known in Manado, *hukum tua*).

A very complicated 1975 dispute over inherited land, planted with valuable clove trees in the rural highlands of North Sulawesi (Case 211/Pdt.G/1975/PN.TDO), illustrates how courts under New Order felt confident in dismissing customary law claims and protecting or enhancing the rights and claims of the well-to-do. The plaintiff claimed that she'd inherited land that had belonged to her grandparents, and which her mother had divided with her uncle upon their mother's death. On her portion of the land, the plaintiff had planted thirty clove trees in 1950. Yet, in 1955, her cousin had begun to occupy part of the land she claimed as her own, taking control over seven of the trees and destroying five of these. He had then transferred the parcel he controlled (and the remaining two trees on it) to another person in 1966, who in turn sold or gave it to someone else in 1968, who held it for less than a year before turning it over to a fourth person still occupying it in 1975. The plaintiff sought the return of her land, compensation from her cousin for the trees he had destroyed, and compensation from the subsequent occupants for lost income from the remaining two trees. Her cousin argued that his father was also a rightful heir to at least a portion of the land, pointing to his grandparents' will of 1935. The defendants also called as witnesses two former chiefs with jurisdiction over customary law (*adat*, in the Minahasa region of North Sulawesi known as *Hukum Tua*), who testified that as of 1950 the land had been considered to belong to both the plaintiff and other heirs (including her uncle and cousin). There were also other witnesses, who spoke to the veracity of the will and of how the land was understood in the local village context.

The court set all this aside, however, awarding a full claim to the land to the plaintiff, though denying her requests for monetary damages. Clarifying land tenure rights and protecting the status of those deemed to hold them evidently trumped any concerns over traditional understandings and customary law. In marked contrast to earlier ways of thinking about rights to land and interpretations of important provisions of the 1960 Agrarian Law, actual occupancy or long-term use of the land in question appears not to have been factored into the court's decision.

Two rural Kediri cases from 1994 illustrate how civil litigation could often support existing elite privilege, especially in local courts. In the case of a man who sued the occupant of land he argued was rightfully his (Case 22/Pdt.G/1994/PN.Kab.KDI), the plaintiff argued that he had purchased a plot of land in 1956, but that the defendant had occupied it illegally from 1977–92, depriving him of his rightful income. In a 1987 suit (Case 67/Pdt.G/1987/PN.Kab.KDI), the same plaintiff had won rights to the land in a decision that was finally implemented (after all appeals were exhausted) when the defendant vacated the land in 1992. In 1994, the plaintiff thus wanted damages for fifteen years of lost income, from the time the defendant had first started occupying the land until he vacated it.

The defendant, despite his lower social status and previous record of loss to the plaintiff, did not give up easily. He filed a countersuit alleging that a different man had actually purchased the land in 1956 for the price of two cows, in a transaction recorded under the plaintiff's name because of the buyer's young age. That young buyer (who had worked the land for two decades) then sold it to the defendant in 1977, and he had worked on it without dispute from the plaintiff for ten years, prior to his 1987 suit. Thus, the defendant argued that under several provisions of the 1960 Agrarian Law, the land was lawfully his. The court threw out both suits in their entirety, ordering the parties to abide by the status quo in place after the 1992 implementation of the 1987 decision, without ever taking up consideration of how to interpret the Agrarian Law.

In a more complex case (Case 20/Pdt.G/1994/PN.Kab.KDI), a forty-five-year-old farmer sued a twenty-two-year-old truck driver (defendant 1) and his contract employer (defendant 2) for damages related to an accident in which he had suffered a broken leg and other injuries that required hospitalization, which had prevented him from working normally for two years. On a Saturday afternoon in July, 1993, the plaintiff had been riding his bicycle home after finishing work in his rice field when, as he was about to make a turn into his village, he was struck by defendant 1's pickup truck (which he said was traveling very fast), ruining his bicycle and landing him in hospital. Defendant 1 was on his own way home, with an empty truck, after delivering a load of fertilizer to a different village under contract from defendant 2 (owner of an agricultural supply shop). The plaintiff presented evidence of his medical costs, statements from hospital staff as to the extent of his injuries, and calculations of his lost income during his long convalescence. The defendants called legal experts as witnesses, who attacked the plaintiff's case on technicalities – e.g. by saying his allegations that the truck was traveling "at a high rate of speed" or that he was struck when he "was about to make a turn" were imprecise (i.e. How many km/h did he claim the truck was going? What did it mean that he was about to make a turn? Had he signaled his intention to turn? Was he pedaling across traffic in the middle of the road? Or was he just thinking about making a turn up ahead?). The basic-level court found for the defendants and dismissed the plaintiff's suit, ordering him also to absorb substantial court costs.

But the defendants – foolishly, it turns out, perhaps to try to clear themselves of any potential later liability – appealed to the High Court in Surabaya, which overturned the original decision and imposed new court costs on the defendants. The High Court reasoned that defendant 1 had already been found criminally liable for running down the plaintiff and that his actions also constituted "illegal behavior" (*perbuatan melawan hukum*), for which he could be held civilly liable. Since defendant 2 had hired defendant 1 to make the trip, he could also be held partially liable for the accident. The two defendants were ordered to pay the full medical costs (but no damages for lost income) to the plaintiff. Defendant 1 filed an appeal with the Supreme Court in Jakarta, but it was rejected *in toto*. It seems the local court was swayed by the defendants' technical arguments to outmaneuver the plaintiff, but the higher levels of the justice system reversed the initial ruling to uphold the spirit of the law and a principle of basic fairness – or at least of equity or protection for vulnerable social elements.

In one 1995 suburban Yogyakarta case, a plaintiff sued a lumber businessman for illegal behavior for defrauding him out of more than

Rp.2 million in 1988 (Makamah Agung 1997d: Case 12/Pdt.G/1995/PN.WT). The defendant had already been prosecuted in 1990 and convicted of criminal fraud in 1991, and this verdict was upheld on appeals all the way to the Supreme Court by August of 1993. The court awarded the plaintiff damages equal to the losses he could prove, but did not allow him to claim interest or other penalties, again acting apparently in the interests of social order while setting aside technical legal arguments.

In another suburban Yogyakarta case, with roots in an earlier era, a plaintiff sued a man who had sold him a parcel of land in 1971. He sought compensation equal to the price he'd bought it for, indexed to the price of gold (there had been severe inflation in Indonesia between 1971 and 1996), because the defendant had never changed the name on the official land registration (Makamah Agung 1997d: Case 13/PDT.G/1996/PN.WT). The defendant countersued, claiming the plaintiff had illegally occupied nearly 50 percent more land than he had actually purchased. To complicate matters even more, the plaintiff had built a house on the land and planted more than 200 coconut, jackfruit, and sengon trees on the very part of it the defendant said he had not legally purchased. After hearing from two witnesses, the court ruled that the plaintiff had a right to have his name put onto the land registration as owner, but was not entitled to compensation for the twenty-five-year delay. The defendant, in turn, had proven his argument that the plaintiff did not actually own the disputed portion of the parcel and ordered that it should be returned to him or else he would be entitled to compensation equal to the value of the land if vacant (i.e. not planted with fruit and fine wood-producing trees).

Decisions in two contract cases and two torts compiled from courts across Kalimantan in 1994–6 show similar patterns, even if they were selected for inclusion in an official compilation because of their adherence to proper procedures and norms (and thus should be less likely to show obvious markers of neotraditionalism). In the first contract case (Makamah Agung 1997a: Case 81/Pdt.G/1994/PN.Bpp), the district court in Balikpapan awarded the cost of his goods to a wholesaler, who had sold a variety of products on credit to a local shopkeeper who never paid him. The wholesaler was not awarded other damages or significant interest payments, which he also had originally sought. And the defendant was not penalized for having written three checks to the plaintiff that had bounced due to his lack of funds. But the court still supported the wholesaler in his claim. This despite the defendant's explanation that he was essentially bankrupt and insolvent, after two fires had wiped out most of his stock and destroyed one of his two shops completely. His claim to have worked out an alternative payment plan with the plaintiff (to pay for the goods in small monthly installments over several years) was similarly and summarily dismissed by the court.

In the second contract case, regarding a real estate sale in Samarinda (Makamah Agung 1997a: Case 56/Pdt.G/1996/PN.Smda), evidence of neotraditionalism is more difficult to see, as the defendant was a wealthy developer and the plaintiff (who won) was a homebuyer (who needed to pay for his house in small installments). The case turned on whether the defendant had refused or unduly delayed transferring the deed and legal ownership to the plaintiff after he'd paid off the house. The two parties had signed an agreement obligating the defendant to purchase the house back from the plaintiff if they could not resolve their differences and the court enforced this agreement – such that the defendant had to buy the house back at a significant markup. After much deliberation and conflicting testimony, the court focused on this agreement and its enforcement as the core of its decision.

Two torts (*ganti rugi*) from Kalimantan in the mid-1990s show similar patterns. In the first of these (Makamah Agung 1997a: Case 39/Pdt.G/1995/PN.PTK), a large bank in Pontianak sued a former employee and his friend who had perpetrated a scam. The ex-employee had been a telex operator in the bank's office, where he was able to falsify a very large telex transfer to a fictitious businessman – whose name and address then appeared on a fake ID his friend had produced, allowing him to claim the money. The two had been prosecuted, convicted in separate criminal cases, and sentenced to substantial time in prison. They had also been forced to disgorge all ill-gotten gains still in their possession, both large sums of cash, as well as motorcycles, televisions, electric ovens, video games, and even a house in Bogor (a Jakarta suburb), but the bulk of the money out of which they'd defrauded the bank had not been repaid. The suit asked the court to make them pay back the remaining amount with interest, which the court agreed to do, supporting the claim of the bank against the potential future solvency of the convicted fraudsters (even though the decision seems unlikely to have been enforceable).

In the second tort case (Makamah Agung 1997a: Case 03/Pdt.G/1996/PN.TG), a small businessman in Tanah Grogot sued the director of a corporation and a dump truck driver employed by that company. The driver had gotten into a traffic accident with the plaintiff's son, who had been riding his motorcycle with a friend as passenger. The son was killed and his motorcycle badly damaged. The driver had already been convicted of vehicular manslaughter in a criminal prosecution. The plaintiff sought damages for replacement of the motorcycle and a smaller amount as civil damages for the death of his son. The driver failed to appear in court, but the company director argued that he had no personal connection to the case (i.e. that the plaintiff should have, if anything, sued the company or only the driver himself). The court found for the plaintiff, but awarded damages only equal to the costs of replacing the damaged motorcycle (with no compensation for the loss of his son).

In one 1995 suit in Medan, capital of North Sumatra and third-largest city in Indonesia, a landlord sought return of his certificate of land title from his tenant, whom he said had been holding it unlawfully while occupying the house he'd rented (Makamah Agung 1997c: Case 79/Pdt.G/1995/PN.Mdn). The court summoned the defendant many times, but he failed to appear. After examining the documentation supplied by the plaintiff, the judges ruled that the tenant must indeed return the title certificate to the landlord and pay all court costs associated with the case. It's not clear, though, whether this decision could ever be enforced.

In a much more obviously contentious case involving eminent domain (Makamah Agung 1997c: Case 355/Pdt.G/1995/PN.Mdn), the City of Medan filed suit against a landholder for refusing to accept the payment it had offered for land he owned that was required for a public works project to elevate Medan's "southern arterial road." After much careful consideration of the letter of the law and of all of the evidence supplied by both sides, the court ruled in favor of the city and ordered the landholder to turn over his land and accept the buyout as originally offered. That courts protected the interests of landlords and local governments in cases against individuals and tenants is perhaps not surprising. That such cases were published as guiding examples is more telling – New Order's embrace of neotraditionalism was not something it was shy about.

Looking to West Java, in one confusing case from Sukabumi, a man from Bogor sued three partners (including one Japanese national) in a business called "Mr. Carbon," whom he claimed had defrauded him out of Rp.3 million in a scam to build a machine to produce activated carbon (*mesin pembuat karbon aktif*) (Makamah Agung 1997b: Case 02/Pdt/G/1990/PN.Smi). The plaintiff said he'd paid the defendants this money to purchase parts and build a prototype of the machine, for which they said they already had a patent (though it was later exposed that they had never applied for a patent and the machine had never been produced, even in prototype form). He also documented how they had formed a corporation, with assets and liabilities to be split 50–50 (50 percent for the plaintiff, 50 percent divided between the three others), in order to fabricate and market the machines and he sought his money back from other outlays he'd made for equipment and expenses. The defendants countered that they had never misrepresented their situation to the plaintiff and that they had actually put up all the money for equipment and expenses through the corporation (nearly Rp.35 million) and so should not have to pay anything in damages.

The court first reached a preliminary finding for the plaintiff, which would have the defendants refund the money he'd paid them and 100 percent of the total of all company expenses (which had all allegedly been incurred in bad faith). But it then also took up an incidental case, filed by another party who claimed he owned all the equipment and facilities the parties wanted to use, and that the defendants were his paid employees; thus he should have claim to all of the assets in question. The court dismissed this suit in its entirety and validated its preliminary ruling for the plaintiff. After this, the defendants appealed to the High Court in Bandung (Makamah Agung 1997b: Case 471/Pdt/1990/PT.Bdg), which also rejected the incidental case, but reduced the plaintiff's award in the main case to 50 percent of the company expenses (about Rp.16 million), citing the initial agreement between the parties that all assets and liabilities would be split 50–50. The courts at both levels wanted to protect the interests of legitimate business and punish fraudsters. But they also seem to have wanted to prevent the defendants from being bankrupted (all the more likely because the third defendant was in Japan and could not be located) and made sure to keep the possible overall owner out of the case. Blame was neatly assigned and business could continue.

In another case of misrepresentation from Sukabumi (Makamah Agung 1997b: Case 62/Pen.Pdt/G/1994/PN.Smi), two individuals (a man and his wife) sued several other individuals and a bank over title to a plot of land. The main plaintiff was a religious educator and founder of several schools (*madrasah*) in and around his village. He claimed to have been tricked out of title to the land where he established one such school and that he had no ties to the bank involved. After careful investigation, the court ruled that the bank actually owned the land and had granted use of it to a foundation (not the plaintiffs themselves) for the purpose of building a religious school (which the plaintiff had indeed established there). It thus rejected the suit in its entirety and ordered the plaintiffs to pay all court costs, privileging the interests of a large bank and local business elites over those of religious leaders in a case where the evidence and circumstances appeared frightfully murky and complex.

In a real estate case from Tangerang (Makamah Agung 1997b: Case 195/Pdt/1996/PN/TNG), just west of Jakarta, the court found that the plaintiff could claim ownership to a house on which the defendants' family had failed to pay a loan. The defendants were a mother and son, wife and adult child of the man who had taken out the loan but later died. After his death, they did not repay the funds and refused to vacate the property. So the creditor sued them to take possession. Though they filed a counterclaim, arguing that his suit was unreasonable and based on inaccurate facts, the mother left the area and could not be located and the son failed to appear in court when called. The court thus found for the plaintiff and awarded him the property, protecting the rights of creditors and landlords over any claims by less powerful actors (though the defendants' failure to appear certainly would not have helped their case either).

Finally, another land dispute from Bekasi (Makamah Agung 1997b: Case 52/Pdt.G/1996/PN.BKS), just east of Jakarta, erupted when a seller refused to vacate the property or transfer the land certificate after being paid by the buyer, who then filed suit to take possession. The argument revolved around whether the price agreed had actually been paid – or whether the buyer might still have some additional balance to pay before the transaction could be completed. The court ruled for the plaintiff, citing written sale agreements and receipts for funds paid as more reliable than oral testimony as to the real value of the land or price agreed. It did stop short, though, of awarding him any punitive damages (which he had sought), requiring the defendant only to turn over the land and pay some smaller fees and costs.

Overall, we can see clear patterns throughout the New Order period in civil adjudication. Courts sided persistently with the interests of those in positions of political, economic, or social power. Though the evidence I have been able to amass is less comprehensive or striking than in the case of criminal law for the same period, the contours of neotraditionalism are still visible. What is perhaps more surprising or counterintuitive is that this neotraditional legal regime persists through to the present day in the civil arena, perhaps still more starkly than under Suharto, even as it has been curtailed from operating in criminal law in the wake of *Reformasi* and democratization.

Civil Law since Reformasi

The situation of civil litigation since the fall of New Order in 1998 is more complex, but maintains a pattern of largely politicized adjudication protecting powerful vested interests. This is most glaringly apparent in the large number of civil disputes brought into the criminal justice system through the influence of one party or another, which I will examine shortly. But neotraditionalism remains pervasive throughout the civil system, even as it has been largely supplanted by a rule by law in the criminal arena.

Enforcement of civil judgments also remains a concern. A study of courts in one large, one medium-sized, and two small regencies (*kabupaten*) in the eastern part of East Java province in 2002 confirms this (Hariyani et al. 2002). Though all of the individual cases analyzed in detail were filed during the waning years of New Order, the researchers' interviews of court clerks and officials, judges, and others, as well as their examination of more recent aggregate data from the four courts, reveal great disparities between localities when it came to enforcement (with Banyuwangi faring better, Situbondo and Bondowoso doing worse, and Jember somewhere in the middle), as well as lingering issues over delays in compulsory enforcement actions (some of which were likely even exacerbated by new regulations enacted in the 1980s) (Hariyani et al. 2002: 26–9). This meant that incentives for criminalizing civil disputes persisted and enforcement of judgments was still an arena in which undue influence or intervention could be deployed.

The distribution of cases between civil suits and criminal prosecutions changed markedly between the New Order period and the mid-2000s. Though data are not widely or easily available, in those provinces that have published comprehensive reports, criminal cases outstripped civil suits by wide margins in nearly every case. As we can see in Table 5.2, even in Yogyakarta and Lampung – the two places where I could obtain data from both periods, the total number of civil suits increased only relatively slightly between 1981 and 2005 or 2006, while the number of criminal prosecutions soared (especially those in the category of full prosecutions, *biasa*, rather than summary judgments or minor offenses, *sumir* and *rol*). Indeed, only in the relatively remote

Table 5.2 Criminal and civil cases in the mid-2000s

Year	Province	Ordinary criminal (*Biasa*)	Summary criminal (*Sumir*)	Minor offenses (*Rol*)	Total criminal cases	Civil lawsuits (*Gugatan*)	Petitions (*Permohonan*)
2005[a]	Lampung	3377	53	24,238	27,668	199	126
2006	Yogakarta	1103	348	49,948	51,399	430	381
2003[b]	North Maluku	17	20	26	63	23	1
2004[c]	Jambi	1584	–	24,907	26,491	127	229
2004[d]	West Sumatra	1709	14	66,265	67,988	376	250

Source: Data drawn from: Jambi Gazetteer (2006); Lampung Gazetteer (2006); North Maluku Gazetteer (2005); West Sumatra Gazetteer (2006); Yogyakarta Gazetteer (2007).

[a]Some data from one court are from 2000, instead of 2005.

[b]Information only provided by one (Klas II) court.

[c]About half the courts reported data for 2001, instead of 2004.

[d]Some courts reported data for 2005 or 2002, instead of 2004.

and rural province of North Maluku were civil suits more numerous than criminal prosecutions by 2003.

That civil suits became relatively so much less numerous suggests that they may well have become less attractive as a vehicle for the redress of social issues and fallen into being more of a tool by which powerful vested interests could maintain their positions. Such a dynamic is revealed more clearly if we examine patterns and individual cases from specific basic-level courts in the current era. This is evident even if we begin with courts in largely Christian North Sulawesi, where civil dispute resolution is dominated by family law cases that likely would have ended up in religious courts in most other parts of the country.

For example, in Airmadidi, of the 432 suits between 2011 and late 2014, for which I managed to find records, 283 (66 percent) were divorce cases. But it is also notable that the next largest category (at 94 total suits) was disputes over land, while suits over "illegal behavior" (PMH) formed the third-largest category (with twenty-seven cases). As can be seen even cursorily from Table 5.3, divorce cases were numerous, but other types of economic and social cases were hardly absent.

Many of the cases in other categories in 2011 were actually disputes over land rights. All six Cases (27/Pdt.G/2011/PN.AMD; 35/ Pdt.G/2011/PN.AMD; 40/Pdt.G/2011/PN.AMD; 50/ Pdt.G/2011/ PN.AMD; 53/ Pdt.G/2011/PN.AMD; and 61/ Pdt.G/2011/PN.AMD) of illegal behavior that year were over land occupation or sales. Though the records I was able to see were not fully complete for all cases, in only one of these disputes (Case 35/Pdt.G/2011/PN.AMD, which involved the supposedly wrongful harvesting of coconuts by the defendant from trees growing on land over which the plaintiff, who eventually lost, claimed customary ownership, *tanah adat*, rights), did the court rule in favor of the party who seemed poorer or more disadvantaged. Instead, wealthier landowners usually managed to defeat tenants and lower-income farmers reasonably easily.

In 2012, a similar pattern was visible in many cases. In one Case (90/Pdt.G/2012/PN.AMD), a large mining company from Jakarta managed to convince a number of local defendants to settle a case over a disputed contract to explore potential deposits of metals. In a different dispute, between a liquefied natural gas company and several workers who accused it of not performing on contracts they'd signed, the court rejected the plaintiffs' suit in its entirety (Case 113/Pdt.G/2012/ PN.AMD). Even when poorer plaintiffs won, they sometimes had to pay costs or compensation that hurt them significantly. In Case

Table 5.3 Airmadidi civil cases (2011 to October 2014)

Year	Total suits	Divorce	Inheritance	Torts	Sales	PMH	Land	Contract	Other
2011	93	61	4	2	2	6	20	2	0
2012	114	74	3	1	1	9	23	1	2
2013	110	76	4	3	1	4	20	3	0
2014	115	72	0	2	2	8	31	2	1
TOTAL	432	283	8	8	6	27	94	8	3

Some rows will not sum to total because certain suits containing multiple elements are counted in more than one category.

47/Pdt.G/2012/PN.AMD, a farmer sued a planter for illegally occupying land he said he owned and planting it with coconut palm trees (likely part of a larger operation, though this was not explicitly revealed in the records I obtained). He had destroyed 100 of the defendant's trees before bringing the suit. The court ruled for the plaintiff, saying the land was legitimately his and should be vacated by the defendant. Still, the plaintiff was ordered to pay Rp.10 million to the defendant in damages for his illegal behavior in cutting down the trees and to pay a further Rp.966,000 to the court in administrative costs.

Similar trends persisted in 2013 and 2014. For instance, in one 2013 dispute (Case 63/Pdt.G/2013/PN.AMD), a plaintiff alleged that several defendants had sold him a parcel of land, only to reoccupy it later. Even after the local court found initially for the defendants and rejected the buyer's claim, the High Court in Manado reversed this decision on appeal and awarded the land and damages to the wealthy plaintiff. In a clearer example of neotraditionalism at work (Case 108/Pdt.G/2013/PN.AMD), a plaintiff tried in vain to sue a relative who had usurped his inheritance of a plantation (*kebun*) through his connections as a police officer and military veteran. After several months, the plaintiff was pressured into withdrawing his case entirely and ordered by the court to pay costs of Rp.241,000.

Tondano's local court, with jurisdiction over the Minahasa highlands, including the town of Tomohon, exhibited a generally similar pattern of case types and neotraditional adjudication during 2009–12, with the noticeable exception of 2012, when a spate of contract disputes overwhelmed everything else but divorce cases. Most of the suits from 2009 and 2010 share many aspects in common with those discussed from Airmadidi. In one Case (75/Pdt.G/2010/PN.TDO), a plantation owner brought suit against some less-than-wealthy neighbors who had allegedly harvested lumber from his land. Though the local court ruled for the defendants, protecting their access to forestland not clearly covered by the plaintiff's land title certificate, the High Court in Manado reversed this decision on appeal and awarded both land title and damages to the owner of the plantation, protecting and preserving his privileged social and economic position (Table 5.4).

Full records of recent cases and decisions in the civil section of the Manado court were more difficult to obtain, likely due to its much heavier caseload and problems of understaffing and lack of space. What immediately stands out, however, from the data I was able to collect, are the high numbers of land disputes in both 2005 and 2009, as well

Table 5.4 Tondano civil cases (2009, 2010, 2012)[a]

Year	Total suits	Divorce	Inheritance	Torts	Sales	PMH	Land	Contract	Other
2009	175	133	3	2	2	2	29	6	0
2010	203[a]	107	5	1	2	2	38	3	0
2012	330	178	10	0	0	10	20	110	3
TOTAL	708	418	18	3	4	14	87	119	3

Some rows will not sum to total because certain suits containing multiple elements are counted in more than one category.
[a]Data is missing for 47 of these 203 cases (one volume of the register was accidentally "sent to the warehouse" early).

as the relatively low numbers of cases related to nonperformance of contractual or other obligations (*wanprestasi*).

In the few cases for which I was able to access complete files, it was also notable that litigation in the provincial capital was often more complex than what appeared to be the norm in the hinterlands and highlands. One complicated case over a real estate deal gone bad in 2005 (Case 230/Pdt.G/2005/PN.MDO) provides a good example of what the court often confronted. A man purchased a house in the Malalayang district of Manado from another man in August 2004, with all deeds and transfers properly recorded in front of a qualified notary, as the law requires. Thirteen months later, however, he was still unable to gain access to the property, which continued to be occupied by an elderly woman who had sold it to the first man just a few days before the sale to the second man. The purchaser thus sued the woman, seeking to have her evicted and vacate the house immediately, and to pay him rent for thirteen months at a rate of Rp.1 million per month. The man he bought the property from was also named as a joint defendant (*turut tergugat*) in the suit. On the surface, the plaintiff's case appeared simple. But there was a substantial and troubled backstory (Table 5.5).

The original purchaser (who later became a joint defendant) appeared in 2004, introducing himself as the owner of a goldmine in Bitung, who lived in the Tikala district of Manado, and offering to buy the old woman's house for Rp.300 million. She agreed to sell him the house at that price and they drew up all the appropriate documents. Those filed with the notary, however, listed the purchase price as much lower than the price he'd agreed to pay, as he and a friend of his had convinced the woman to do this to reduce tax obligations and to simplify the process.

Later, the man arranged to meet with the woman at the KFC restaurant in what at the time was Manado's most fashionable oceanfront shopping mall (a lot of important or devious discussions across Indonesia in recent years seem to have occurred over food-court fried chicken). He explained that he could not pay right away, but promised to pay in short order. In the meantime, he sold the house and recorded a new deed and transfer to the man who became the plaintiff in the suit (in front of the same notary). After this, he absconded with the money he'd been paid (Rp.350 million) and could not be found at the time of the trial. The address on his ID card (KTP) was apparently false, since no one in Tikala knew who he was or could remember anyone by his

Table 5.5 Manado civil suits

Year	Total suits	Divorce	Inheritance	Torts	Contracts	Land	PMH	Administrative suits, sales, and others	Missing
2005	333	69	3	7	5	12	1	9	227
2009	327	144	5	5	11	35	8	10	109

name having lived there and he was not recorded as a resident by the local government.

Claiming to have been the victim of fraud (*penipuan*, which she'd reported to the police), the woman argued that she should not have to leave her house and she even countersued the plaintiff and the alleged fraudster, seeking to have all the transactions voided and all titles and deeds to be returned to her name. Eventually, after a process of investigation and adjudication that lasted more than eighteen months, the Manado court dismissed the plaintiff's suit and rejected the defendant's countersuit, also requiring the plaintiff to pay court costs of Rp.311,000. Among the critical findings from witness testimony and examination of documentary evidence were that the old woman had admonished the plaintiff not to buy the house because the original buyer had not paid her and had pressured her into recording fraudulent and incomplete information on the original documents pertaining the sale.

Presumably, if he had been located, the joint defendant would also have faced criminal liability. Somewhat surprising to me was that the notary involved did not seem, in the court's judgment, to bear any responsibility for the problem, even though under Indonesian law (as in other Civil Law systems and in contrast to many Common Law systems) she should bear some obligation to ensure the veracity of documents she is asked to authenticate, and not only the identities of the persons appearing to sign them (Pompe 1992: 174–5; Lev 2000c: 306).

In East Java's capital of Surabaya, I was not able to access recent full case files of civil disputes, but I was able to examine some of the registers available in early 2010. As can be seen in Table 5.6, Surabaya was marked by a very high rate of disputes related to alleged failure to perform on contractual or other obligations (*wanprestasi*), even though divorces are still prevalent. I was not able to gather aggregate data from registers on civil cases in Kediri, but overall it was clear, from my interviews with court leaders and clerical staff, that relatively few disputes were being filed either there or in Lamongan or Tuban. Indeed, in Kediri and Tuban, admittedly incomplete data from the court websites suggest that rural Kediri adjudicated roughly 435 civil suits between 2014 and early 2016 (Rural Kediri Court Website Data 2016), while Tuban's court heard 135 such cases between 2013 and early 2016 (Tuban Court Website Data 2016). In Kediri, I was also able to access full case files from several suits.

Table 5.6 Surabaya civil suits

Year	Total suits	Divorce	Inheritance	Contracts	Land	PMH	Adminis-trative suits, sales, and others	Missing
2005	760	331	16	116	32	56	2	207
2009	853	252	5	78	14	127	5	372

Case 37/Pdt.G/2001/PN.Kab.KDI was a suit filed by twenty-one suppliers against the owner of a company that managed a restaurant called French Village Chicken (*Ayam Kampung Prancis*). The plaintiffs claimed that the defendant had purchased thousands of chickens, but failed to pay for any of them. After examining sales records and questioning the defendant as to why he did not have any proof of payment (to which he could provide no clear answer), the court ruled for the plaintiffs, awarding them Rp.31,631,000 for the cost of the chickens, plus an additional 5 percent of that amount in damages for each month since they had filed their case until the defendant had paid them in full – a sort of mirror image of the Chinese chicken sale case discussed earlier in the Introduction.

In another 2001 suit (Case 40/Pdt.G/2001/PN.Kab.KDI), a man borrowed Rp.600,000 (then equivalent to 1200 grams of gold) from the owner of a gold shop in Pare on July 25, 1971. According to their written contract, the man promised to pay back Rp.750,000 or 1500 grams of gold by July 25, 1972. He also promised that the shop-owner could take his house if he did not pay. But he never did pay. And then he sold his house and land in 1981. The house was sold again in 1987, and a third time in 1990. But the shop-owner never received her money back or any gold from the man. After repeatedly reminding him of his debt to no avail, she eventually filed suit. But the first five or six hearings of the case could not proceed, as the defendant did not appear when called. After he showed up, the case finally went forward, with the plaintiff documenting the debt and the agreement and the defendant unable to refute any of her claims.

A pivotal point in this case – one that was also somewhat problematic – was that the original agreement said nothing about potential future inflation or repayment in cash being pegged to the price of gold. Yet, Indonesian inflation between 1971 and 2001 was severe, such that the court decided the man should pay the owner Rp.120 million (based on the 1500 grams of gold at the 2001 price of Rp.80,000 per gram) plus interest of 3 percent compounded annually from 1972 to 2001 (for a total of Rp.104 million). If he did not pay expeditiously after the decision was issued, he would face fines of Rp.50,000 per day.

In 2010, a land dispute also dragged on for many months because the defendants failed to appear (Case 46/Pdt.G/2010/PN.Kab.KDI). Five relatives sued for rights to land that had belonged to a member of their family. He had been married to a woman who had predeceased him and had no children. Just before he died, he allegedly gave an oral will, transferring his land to a relative of his late wife (rather than his brother or other immediate family). The court found no reason to doubt the veracity of this pre-death transfer, despite no written records existing, and dismissed the suit *in toto*.

In a higher-stakes land case from 2010 (Case 48/Pdt.G/2010/PN.Kab.KDI), a group of relatives sued their village and village chief, who had taken land, to which they believed they should have been entitled through inheritance, for use as a mine. Eventually, they agreed to settle, in an arrangement that essentially preserved the status quo, with the land directly in use for the mine being recognized as belonging to the village, and all other adjacent areas (where the plaintiffs still lived) being transferred formally to them. Specifically, small payments made in 1970 to the relative who'd owned the land at the time were to be deemed as payment for purchase of the parcel used for mining. The power and position of the village chief were preserved, even as the famer's family was granted some measure of longer-term livelihood security, and social stability rooted in a neotraditional legal regime was maintained.

In all, despite my less comprehensive evidence for this area of law and time period, we can be fairly confident in assessing a neotraditional legal regime as remaining in force in civil law after *Reformasi*, even as democratization helped push Indonesian criminal law toward a rule by law order. The prevalence of land and other types of disputes common during the New Order era, as well as the continuing tendencies of courts to adjudicate and decide cases in ways that helped systematically to protect the power of established elites and vested interests are clear. The declining use of civil litigation, especially in relative terms, also suggests that less empowered seekers of justice have been turning away from courts as they perceive the odds to be stacked against them.

Another feature of some varieties of neotraditionalism has persisted and even intensified, however, which is also of note – that of criminalization of civil disputes. After a vibrant history during the New Order period, we see frequent abuse and manipulation of the legal system in the current era by powerful actors to mobilize state coercive power against less powerful adversaries with whom they have some sort of economic or social dispute.

Criminalized Civil Disputes in the Present Day

As we saw in the case of the fertilizer salesman discussed at the start of the book, Indonesian civil disputants can find themselves facing criminal prosecution if their cases take a wrong turn (Supriyanto 2004). One lawyer I interviewed in Manado in February, 2010, claimed that the single biggest issue in Indonesian law was civil cases being mistaken for criminal ones because police lacked education and were easily manipulated (or corrupted). In fact, coopting the criminal justice apparatus for private advantage in civil dispute resolution is so pervasive that an official of the East Java Provincial Police published a scholarly treatise on the phenomenon (Yahman 2011) and another Manado lawyer told me plainly in June, 2010, that, "many people like to use the power of the police to resolve civil disputes."

Speaking specifically about the conversion of contract disputes (*wanprestasi*) into criminal fraud cases (*penggelapan*), Yahman explains that

> someone often seeks a shortcut, one of which is to be found by means of reporting (a criminal case) to the police authorities. The simple argumentation proposed by the seeker of justice for reporting to the police is to make the opposing party "fear" the imminent imposition of criminal sanctions, with the ultimate aim of getting his best possible performance (*seseorang sering mencari jalan pintas, salah satunya dengan cara melaporkan kepada pihak Kepolisian (perkara pidana). Argumentasi sederhana yang dikemukakan oleh pencari keadilan untuk melapor kepada pihak Kepolisian adalah agar pihak lawan "takut" akan pengenaan sanksi pidana dan akhirnya tujuan untuk medapatkan prestasi segera akan diperoleh*). (Yahman 2011: 4)

Such tactics extend beyond contract cases, as one Surabaya lawyer explained to me in 2014, to such areas as disputed sales and rental agreements being reported as thefts and torts or business deals gone bad being reported as fraud, assault, or criminal violations of myriad types of regulations.

One moldy file from the bowels of the Surabaya Court seemed when I examined it in 2010 not to have been opened since it had been archived in 1979. It was missing details of many court documents, had no information about any possible conviction or sentence, and suggested a type of criminalization in an earlier era. In this Case (5/Pid.B.1979/PN.SBY) of document falsification (*pemalsuan surat*), a forty-three-year-old man was accused of issuing a fake notarized document (*akte notaris*) related to the sale of a house (basically a form of contract to sell the house). Because of the defendant's fake document, the prosecution alleged, the seller of the house (a wealthy Chinese-Indonesian, though he used a Javanese name) had incurred losses equal to the Rp.20 million sale price of the home. As far as I could piece together from the incomplete file, the seller's wife had written a power of attorney (*surat kuasa*) giving the defendant the authority to draw up a contract for sale of the house she owned with her husband. The defendant's contract then apparently could not be enforced after the sellers had turned over their house to a buyer, who then was not able or willing to make payment in full.

It seems the case was appealed (as the city prosecutor turned it over at one point to the higher provincial-level prosecutor's office, *Kejaksaan Tinggi Jawa Timur*), but it is not clear how the dispute was resolved or what remedies were ultimately imposed. What is clearer, though, is that this had originated as a civil dispute over a real estate sale between a seller and a buyer. It would seem that the defendant fell victim to the machinations of an influential businessman, who sought to criminalize what at root was essentially a civil dispute with the buyer of his house.

In Case 249/Pid.B/1984/PN/SBY, a thirty-year-old man was convicted of criminal fraud (*penipuan*) for trying to claim that a gold necklace he had allegedly taken wrongfully from someone else was actually his. He was sentenced to four months in prison for his actions. In other cases, criminal responsibility was laid upon ordinary individuals by courts that were either unable to handle civil litigation (such as torts) or afraid to risk antagonizing powerful interests.

The 1979 prosecution, and conviction, of a bus driver in Surabaya (Case 15/Pid.B/1979/PN.SBY) is a case in point. The bus driver was charged with manslaughter (*kealpaan*) in the death of a young boy hit by his bus while in front of his house on one of the city's main six-lane thoroughfares. The driver was traveling at about 40 km/hr (25 mph) when his bus struck a pickup truck that was making a turn. The collision caused the bus to swerve up onto the curb, striking the boy. Although the pickup truck likely played a role in the accident and the bus driver was not speeding or otherwise obviously negligent, he was convicted of manslaughter and given a one-year suspended prison sentence. The bus company was not, as far as I can tell, sued or subject to other civil sanction.

Another case, tried in Bogor (just south of Jakarta) in 1996, shows similar attributes (Makamah Agung 1997b: Case 362/Pid.B/1996/PN.BGR). The defendant was convicted of fraud after bouncing a check he had written to purchase several parcels of land from an agent authorized by their owners to sell them. This agent later did give the defendant a receipt (*surat kwitansi*) for the funds and closed the sale. It is not clear whether or not the notary's final paperwork (*akte notaris jual-beli*) for the sale was ever completed, but several witnesses testified that it never was (one witness explicitly said that this was because payment was never completed). But the defendant went on to work with two others to sell the land he had acquired to a number of other buyers (in smaller lots). The court ruled that all these sales were invalid (because the defendant had never had any right to sell land he had not properly purchased) and sentenced the defendant to two years and ten months in prison. While this is a less clear-cut example of a civil dispute being criminalized, there is sufficient ambiguity surrounding the behavior of the agent who made the initial sale that it seems likely not to have been as one-sided as the decision makes it appear.

In theory, the transformation undertaken with *Reformasi* in 1998, which is still ongoing, ought to have brought an end to such cozy relationships between economic actors and judicial agencies and officials. Criminalizing civil disputes to serve the interests of the wealthy or powerful would seem to be a prime example of "collusion" (*kolusi*) – along with corruption (malfeasance or outright embezzlement) and nepotism, one of the alleged great evils of New Order that needed to be swept away. While many new institutions have been created and some old elites (at least at the lower levels) have given way to new faces, rules and processes have not substantially changed in many institutions, including basic-level courts. These had existed prior to New Order and their characters had been powerfully shaped by Suharto's regime – particularly regarding the capacity to criminalize civil disputes.

As recently as 2009, the owner of an oil paint manufacturing business was prosecuted and sentenced to three months in prison for operating his business without proper licenses (Case 36/Pid.B/2009/PN.SBY). The case seems to have stemmed from a dispute between the paint manufacturer and a steel pipe company, after which provincial police suddenly decided to check the defendant's permits and licenses. According to witness testimony from the pipe company's chief paint-purchasing agent, his employer had bought paint from the defendant at prices of up to Rp.11,500 per kg between 2002 and 2008.

Former employees of the defendant confirmed that his factory did indeed produce significant quantities of paint (one worker testified that the business had sold 2000 kg of paint to a company in Surabaya for Rp.23 million in August 2008, for example), while police officers confirmed that they had investigated and found permits lacking, and that they had confiscated most of the equipment on site, including several 200 kg barrels of oil and a can-sealing machine). An official of the municipal department of industry, trade, and agriculture said that the defendant had failed to register his business with that department despite having income, staff, and assets over the thresholds at which such registration is required (five or more employees, yearly income of over Rp.900 million, or machines such as those confiscated). The defendant maintained that he set up the factory with his own funds, did not employ more than five people or directly impact natural resources, and generally had tried to abide by the law and regulations. He produced a small business license, issued in 2004 by the municipal department of industry and trade, as well as a municipal company registration valid from 2003–11, along with tax documents and articles of incorporation dating back to his 1993 establishment of the business. He did concede, however, that he had never obtained an official record of exactly the type of registration now deemed necessary by the police and municipal agency, leading to his conviction.

Far away, in Manado, capital of North Sulawesi Province, a complex dispute in 2009–10, involving a soft drink bottling plant, distributors, and other contractors, became a criminal investigation that could have landed the bottling plant owner in prison (according to my interviews in February 2010 and November 2014 with three lawyers involved in the case). Here too, competing commercial interests threatened to derail the civil adjudication and dispute resolution process. When contracts and trade cannot be hashed out without illicit recourse to institutions of state coercion, society's interests are compromised, contributing to a perception, articulated by one lawyer I spoke with in June 2010, that, "in criminal cases, the police ask for bribes. In civil cases, the judges do. No one knows any shame about this anymore."

Perhaps most salient is a case I was able to observe from the margins in July 2010, and then follow up in February 2013. A small businessman, "Mr. T," in a village on the outskirts of a medium-sized city in East Java, found himself the defendant in a suit for illegal behavior (*perbuatan melawan hukum*, or PMH) over documents that had allegedly gone missing (and which the plaintiff claimed he had stolen or destroyed). Specifically, the plaintiff was related to another businessman, whom she said had invested in Mr. T's business, and she sought documentation of these investments to use against her relative in another matter. The police had already exonerated him and the plaintiff had no standing to file the civil suit. Yet, poor Mr. T found himself caught in an expensive, frustrating, and potentially dangerous legal limbo between a civil suit and a failed criminal prosecution.

The plaintiff had filed a criminal complaint of theft (*pencurian*) against Mr. T in 2009, alleging that he had stolen the documents. The local police (*Polres*) investigated Mr. T and found no evidence to warrant passing on to the prosecutor for criminal charges. Under Indonesian law, this should have been the end of it – as claimants are not permitted to file civil suits against defendants after unsuccessful criminal complaints (as Mr. T's lawyer explained, "she'd already exercised her rights" [*haknya sudah digunakan*] in the criminal complaint) – but the police bureaucracy had allowed this case to go forward through its failure to act in a forthright manner.

The police informed the plaintiff, who had filed the complaint, that their investigation had turned up insufficient evidence to merit charging Mr. T. But, of course, she did not give the letter they sent her to the court that had accepted her PMH suit against Mr. T. This left him in a difficult position. More than two years after the initial allegations, he had to try to block an unlawful civil suit from proceeding against him, but he needed the cooperation of the police to do so. When I interviewed Mr. T and his lawyer, in July 2010, they had already made several attempts to document the failed criminal complaint, but to no avail. I accompanied the lawyer to the police headquarters, where the chief of police (*kapolres*) demanded an explicit bribe (cash in an envelope) of Rp.1 million just to speak with him at all. When he emerged from the meeting (I waited outside), the lawyer explained that the police chief insisted he was only authorized to release any letter or documentation about Mr. T's case to the plaintiff as the complainant (*pelapor*).

Unable to obtain the records of his own criminal case crucial to his defense in the civil suit, Mr. T grew tired of sending his lawyer to bribe the police, only to be continually disappointed. By the next time I was able to follow up with him, in February 2013, he had settled the suit and agreed to pay the plaintiff some portion of the damages she had originally sought. Though not a case of criminalization of civil justice *per se*, the travails of the unfortunate Mr. T illustrate how the criminal law enforcement apparatus can still be mobilized (or immobilized) to the advantage of particular parties in civil disputes.

Concluding Thoughts

Once Suharto consolidated his New Order regime by about 1974, all law in Indonesia became a political vehicle for supporting an established hierarchy and entrenched elite. Both criminal *and* civil adjudication fell under the influence of kleptocratic bureaucrats and tycoons in collusion with each other and those in military uniform. The gangsterish cronyism of New Order's "*preman* state" (Lindsey 2001, 2006) exemplified rule by a conservative hierarchy bent on politicizing law and adjudication for its own preservation. In some ways, this was a continuation of patterns present during the first decade of Indonesia's independence, when old power-holders retained their social and political positions and the instruments and institutions of colonial politicization of justice had yet to be overturned or eroded. But such an order persisted, even after democratization, at least in some areas of law.

While Suharto's fall in 1998 and the *Reformasi* that followed effectively diminished the ability of elites to use the coercive power of criminal law explicitly to repress dissent and keep the populace in line, these changes did little to undermine the use of the civil dispute resolution process to protect the interests of the powerful. We see this in contract disputes and land cases, as well as in suits over illegal behavior and sales. We also see its manifestation in the widespread criminalization of civil disputes, which lawyers call the single worst problem in the legal system and about which police officials write dissertations. Indonesia's particular hybrid blend of neotraditionalism in civil law and a rule by law in the criminal arena appears likely to endure, even as the country's basic political and social institutions, alongside fundamental norms, show signs of increasing instability.

CHINA

In China, a different kind of hybrid regime has emerged since 1978, despite perceptions at the outset of reform that the CCP under Deng Xiaoping was committed to reducing political intervention in both civil and criminal adjudication. While a rule by law order developed and solidified in civil law, as discussed in Chapter 4, neotraditionalism has been the core of the criminal process almost since the very start of reform, since this type of regime facilitates CCP elites retaining power and position. From the early days of "strike hard" campaigning in the 1980s, to the crackdown against alleged anti-Party elements in the wake of June 4, 1989, to renewed campaigns in the 1990s and the ongoing influence of Party organs – both within courts and from the outside – on the adjudication process, the criminal system's neotraditional legal regime has taken multiple forms and utilized a variety of tactics. But it has remained a constant fixture of China's legal and political landscape (Clarke & Feinerman 1995) (indeed, on the routinization of "campaign-style policing" during the reform era, see Tanner 2005).

Strike Hard (*Yanda*): Neotraditional Criminal Law in the 1980s and Early 1990s

Criminal law in China has been characterized by a neotraditional legal regime since the constitution of the polity was settled in the late 1970s. During the 1980s, campaign politics – through strike hard (*yanda*, 严打) and other movements, such as those against bourgeois liberalization – were the norm. The crackdown against dissenters and a new generation of "counter-revolutionaries" following the 1989 protests was the apex of this wave of politicization and intervention by nonjudicial state actors into the adjudication process. After the restoration of more quotidian politics around 1992, one might be tempted to assume that the criminal justice system became less politicized, but this would be a mistake. Even as the criminal procedure law was revised – twice – ostensibly with the aim of protecting the rights of the accused and promoting transparency, and prosecutions for counterrevolutionary crimes have become a thing of the past, China's criminal apparatus remains subject to frequent and systemic intervention by nonjudicial state and Party actors in the adjudication of specific cases in order to maintain and bolster the existing hierarchical organization of the polity.

The *yanda* campaigns of the 1980s were a critical turning point in the politics of crime and punishment in the People's Republic. After many years of relying frequently on "mass justice" of one sort or another to facilitate social control – including widespread use of the people's militias (民兵), especially in rural areas (on urban militias, see Perry 2007) – a new emphasis was placed at the dawn of the reform era on public security, procuratorial, and judicial organs (the so-called 公检法 triumvirate). This was not coincidental, but rather part of a move to demobilize justice from its revolutionary agenda, reduce the role of Party committees, develop the roles and importance of state agencies, and lend greater stability to China's criminal law regime. It is thus not without irony that a primary method for effecting this change was through a set of mobilizational campaigns (on the persistence of such patterns of ideas and actions within the CCP more generally, see Sorace 2017).

The basic campaign was launched in early 1983 by Deng Xiaoping, ostensibly as part of his general agenda of promoting a "basically prosperous society" (小康社会). Spectacular cases, like that of "the two Wangs" (mass murderers from Shenyang on the lam in the Northeast for much of the year), were used to great effect in mobilizing mass opinion in support of a general crackdown on crime. Massive numbers of new personnel and previously unimagined resources flowed to police, procuratorial, and judicial organs (Dutton & Lee 1993). By July 1983, Deng went so far as to instruct the Ministry of Public Security, at a special conference held at the seaside resort town of Beidaihe, to strike hard against serious problems of crime, reportedly saying approvingly that, "striking hard strengthens the Party's dictatorial force, this is what dictatorship is" [严打就是加强党的专政力量，这就是专政] (刘 2015).

By August, the Politburo of the CCP had issued a policy statement on the campaign (关于严厉打击刑事犯罪活动的决定) and by September the Standing Committee of the National People's Congress had issued similar notices. Throughout the country, criminal law enforcement became much more intense, even as the apparatus backed away from any overtly revolutionary or socially transformative agenda. Rather, the motivation for the campaign was to strengthen the institutions of criminal law so as to preserve and protect a set of newly rigid hierarchical relations locked in place after the end of the Maoist era.

The general scholarly view of *yanda* is that it undermined any incipient attempts to build a rule by law order in post-Mao China. Encapsulated well by Murray Scot Tanner, by launching the campaign in 1983, "Deng reduced his own 1978 Third Plenum calls for 'rule by law' to an historical footnote, and swept aside four years of legislative efforts at strengthening criminal justice procedures" (Tanner 2000: 107). The politicization of criminal justice was unmistakable; as Harold Tanner nicely summarized, "the Communist Party made it clear that … crime was no longer regarded as a 'contradiction among the people' … Hooligans were not apolitical rowdies, but vehement haters of socialism" (Tanner 1999: 91). Important analyses in China also argued starkly that "rule by law is not rule by policy or something else," that *yanda* became a "classic case of the *campaignization* of the rule of law" (一种典型的法治运动化形式), and even that "though the times are different, as if a great change has taken place since the Cultural

Revolution compared with today, the basic system is still the same as before" (虽然时代不同，如今与文革相比已发生了很大的变化，但基本体制仍然依旧) (周 & 周 2002: 31). Political campaigning to preserve social order and political hierarchy trumped the development of a rule by law, as even many inside the system lauded the utility of such methods (e.g. 孟 2001).

The launch of *yanda* at such a critical moment in the development of an independent criminal justice system, reinserted the CCP – and specifically the Party's Political and Legal Affairs committees (政法委) – into all aspects of criminal justice work, from investigation and adjudication to sentencing and appeals, as these committees became coordinating leaders of the campaign on the ground (Tanner 1999: 86–7, 2000: 108–9; Trevaskes 2007: 124–6). Even more starkly, special "command posts" and "*yanda* offices" were also established at the grassroots to facilitate the cooperation of courts, procurators, and public security bureaus and, if necessary, to make institutional end runs around CCP committees to further expedite the implementation of the campaign (Tanner 1999: 87, 2000: 114). Susan Trevaskes, in her 2007 book, elucidates a number of ways in which *yanda*'s neotraditional politicization of criminal law in support of static hierarchies played out in Baotou, Inner Mongolia, and across many other provinces and localities around the country (Trevaskes 2007: chapters 5 and 6).

My own research uncovered just such a set of processes, with surging numbers of arrests and prosecutions and expedited investigation and adjudication based on explicit and ruthless campaign coordination. Across Hubei Province, for example, trials for murder increased by 90 percent year-on-year in 1983 (compared with 1982), while those for rape nearly tripled, and those for robbery increased almost fourfold. Meanwhile, nearly 6000 cases of "hooliganism" (流氓) were adjudicated in Hubei in 1983, a category of crime that had not even been tracked in 1982 (李其凡主编 1995: 215). Similar dynamics also played out at more local levels around the country.

For example, in Puning County, located in an out-of-the-way part of eastern Guangdong Province, the total number of criminal cases jumped from a relatively average 97 in 1982 to 181 in 1983, the highest since 1960, before climbing to 225 in 1984 (普宁县人民法院志编 1989: 61). The biggest jumps were specifically in prosecutions for fraud, hooliganism (流氓), theft, and robbery – all ordinary crimes for which we can assume a roughly constant rate of actual occurrence. More vigorous prosecution and draconian sentencing seem to have been the primary markers of the campaign, as we can see from the case of a Mr. Chen – a seventeen-year-old in Puning County who was given the death penalty (suspended for two years) for robbing neighbors of four wrist watches in 1983 (普宁县人民法院志编 1989: 53).

In Rui'an, a county-level city in coastal Zhejiang's Wenzhou, criminal prosecutions also spiked 48 percent to 227 in 1983 (going up further to 317 in 1984), the highest level since the end of the Cultural Revolution (though still lower than the record 1924 at the start of the Great Leap Forward in 1958) (瑞安市法院编 1995: 56). Trials for "hooliganism" (流氓) specifically showed a marked increase, with forty-five in 1983 and ninety-one in 1984, after never having exceeded fifteen in any prior year and there having been no trials at all on such charges from 1980–2 (瑞安市法院编 1995: 66–8). There were also more trials for a variety of other crimes related to sexual assault and general impropriety. Severe sentences were frequently imposed. For example, twelve death sentences were pronounced in 1983, matching the combined total for 1972–82, while sentences to more than five years in prison more than doubled year-on-year in 1982 and increased by another 40 percent in 1983, before dropping back toward their long-term average level in 1985 (瑞安市法院编 1995: 71–3).

In Jingjiang, a county-level city in southern Jiangsu Province, procuratorial officials met with public security and court leaders to work out a strategy for how to implement central *yanda* directives, agreeing in August 1983 to an explicit plan of collusion to expedite detentions, arrests, decisions on the admissibility of evidence, and criminal trials (靖江市人民检察院 2002: 116). Indeed, the procuratorate's gazetteer boasts of fifteen times more arrests in the last five months of 1983 than the previous year, and of a concomitant reduction in the time needed to approve a formal arrest (批捕) down to an average of two days (and often even less). The number of cases resulting in full prosecutions also saw a fivefold increase compared to 1982 (靖江市人民检察院 2002: 126).

The campaign worked so well that in January and June 1984, the Jingjiang procuratorate, court, and public security bureau held two more formal meetings, which led to even deeper collaboration – including officials sitting in on meetings in each other's organizations and cooperating to streamline procedures for evidence collection and investigation – and more increases in arrests and prosecutions (靖江市人民检察院 2002: 116–17). Even as late as 1986, while the procuratorate and public security bureau were cooperating on a campaign against theft, procurators were permitted to sit in during police interrogations and evidence-gathering against a suspect accused of stealing RMB10,000. The whole process, from first opening the case through to beginning prosecution in the intermediate court, took less than three days (靖江市人民检察院 2002: 127). It was also during the *yanda* years that Jingjiang procurators began appearing in court for every – or nearly every – criminal trial, ensuring more vigorous prosecution and higher conviction rates (靖江市人民检察院 2002: 147), though the only years during which Jingjiang procurators actually lost cases in the post-Mao era were 1982–6 (靖江市人民检察院 2002: 151).

Not every jurisdiction was able to keep pace with the demands of the *yanda* campaign. In southwestern Yunnan's Dali Bai Autonomous Prefecture, for example, procurators were unable to appear in court for many trials in 1983, simply because "there were many cases but few staff" (案多人少), even though the procuratorate had seen the advantages of appearing in court more regularly in 1982 (大理白族自治州人民检察院 1997: 90). There were more than 180 times that year when procurators failed to appear in court (大理白族自治州人民检察院 1997: 112). In that same year, although the number of investigations of economic crimes increased by more than 40 percent, the procuratorial staff available for these investigations was reduced by six people, creating tremendous pressure on those remaining on the job (大理白族自治州人民检察院 1997: 96). Finally, the Dali procurators made much more frequent use of the appellate process (抗诉), even as their conviction rates went up substantially during *yanda* (e.g. from 97 percent in 1982 to 99.2 percent in 1983), and despite the fact that their rates of success at winning reversals (改判) were less than 50 percent in many years (大理白族自治州人民检察院 1997: 113).

Even after the end of the first *yanda* campaign in 1986, the politicized mood in criminal adjudication did not abate substantially. Instead, a renewed focus on the prosecution of counterrevolutionary crimes took hold after the Tiananmen incident on June 4, 1989, and then new rounds of *yanda* followed in 1996 and 2001. These frequent waves of political mobilization of law and the legal process in support of entrenched hierarchies helped ensure a neotraditional legal regime remained in place in the criminal arena through the latter Deng years (c. 1987–92) and all of the Jiang Zemin era (1992–2002). Though the picture became more complex after 2002, the late 1980s and 1990s represent a surprising continuation of many trends from the initial *yanda* heyday.

In the wake of June 4, 1989, a national crackdown against counterrevolutionaries and "subversives" was initiated (Ren 1997: 102–3). After significant declines in criminal prosecutions between 1985 and 1988, numbers shot back up in 1989 – attributed by some, such as basic-level courts in districts of Shijiazhuang City in Hebei, to a "resurgence of anarchism" (石家庄市新华区人民法院编 1996: 47; 石家庄市桥西区人民法院编 1994: 39). In one of these districts, the number of prosecutions from 1989–93 increased by more than 60 percent, compared to the rate for the previous four years, to a level comparable with 1983 (石家庄市桥西区人民法院编 1994: 39).

In Guangzhou City, the number of detained suspects for whom the public security bureau sought approval from the procurator to arrest formally rose by 17 percent in 1989, compared to 1988, back up to a level not seen since 1983, before rising a further 15 percent the following year. What's more, five suspects were arrested for counterrevolutionary crimes in 1989, along with another twelve in 1990, nearly matching the eighteen arrested in 1983 for such offenses, and exceeding the sum total of five detained on similar charges between 1985 and 1988 (广州市检察院 1995: 93). Some slogans brought into use among Guangzhou procurators that year also resonated with familiar *yanda* themes: "first, be resolute, second, be prudent, make sure to handle things accurately" (一要坚决，二要慎重，务必搞准)（广州市检察院 1995: 103–4).

Actual prosecutions did not increase nearly so dramatically, and larger numbers of cases were remanded back to the public security bureau by the procurator in 1989 and 1990. For example, Mr. Chen, a restaurant worker, observed others fighting and blocking traffic near Haizhu Square in Central Guangzhou, late one night after he got off work at 2:00 AM in June 1989. Some in the crowd reported him to the public security bureau as one of the offenders, but upon the procurator's investigation, he was exonerated as a mere bystander (广州市检察院 1995: 104–5). Under pressure to act decisively against economic crime and corruption, the procurator also demurred to a remarkable degree, declining to prosecute (免予起诉) 80 of the 479 cases presented by the public security authorities in autumn of 1989 and exercising similar discretion in more than 5 percent of cases overall.

In Lingling Prefecture, now a district of Hunan's Yongzhou City on the Xiang River, there were six trials for counterrevolutionary crimes in the spring and summer of 1989, following the upheaval in Beijing, that involved eight defendants. Though his may not seem like that many, there had been only fifty-nine trials for counterrevolutionary crimes there between 1980 and 1992, so more than 10 percent of all such trials took place within a few months in 1989 (零陵地区中级人民法院 1995: 92). By the end of the year, there had been eleven trials, the most for counterrevolutionary crimes since *yanda* had ended several years before (零陵地区中级人民法院 1995: 108).

In response to central directives to combat economic crime and corruption, the Lingling district court established thirty-six reception centers for confession and informing in August of 1989, each with its own dedicated hotline where perpetrators could turn themselves in and informers could denounce those they believed guilty of misdeeds (零陵地区中级人民法院 1995: 100). Overall, the number of criminal trials in Lingling increased by 35 percent in 1989, so that there were more than in any year since 1984. Trials for murder were up by 67 percent, while those for robbery and theft were up by 93 percent, and those for rape nearly tripled, compared to 1988 (零陵地区中级人民法院 1995: 108).

Such trends persisted as the deep freeze of reform set in after the Tiananmen Incident, up until Deng Xiaoping's famed "Southern Tour" in 1992. What may be less intuitively obvious, however, is that politicization of criminal adjudication in support of established elites continued through the latter part of the 1990s, even as China was undergoing extremely rapid economic reform, enjoying breathtaking macroeconomic growth, and making substantial strides in regularizing and depoliticizing civil litigation and adjudication.

Neotraditionalism against the Backdrop of Rapid Economic Reform, 1992–2002

This period in Chinese criminal law is relatively harder to document, as most of the gazetteers and other written sources do not extend this far forward, while my own firsthand fieldwork began in 2006. Yet, many secondary sources outline the contours of a new round of *yanda* in 1996 and 1997. This began on April 20, 1996, with a renewed push to crack down against drug-related crime, violent crime, and sexual assault, as well as crime in general, emanating from central public security authorities. The new *yanda* consisted of three waves: the first from April through July, 1996, in which public security organs at every level coordinated a summer of intensified activity; the second, which continued from August through to the end of the year; and the third, during most of 1997 and focused especially on ensuring the "harmony" and security of the return of Hong Kong to Chinese sovereignty and the convening of the CCP's 15th Party Congress (谢 2013: 51). Then, once again, from April, 2001, through to the end of 2002, yet another *yanda* campaign swept across China, this one targeting organized crime (黑社会) and "evil forces" (恶势力) and leading to over five million prosecutions in roughly eighteen months (谢 2013: 52).

Looking again at Jingjiang Prefecture in Jiangsu, we can see that prosecutions more than doubled in 1996, before falling back to more reasonable trends in 1997 and 1998 (靖江市人民检察院 2002: 131). In a representative case of that town's campaign, a thirty-one-year-old small businesswoman from Anhui was sentenced to death (and executed) for stabbing a man who later died of complications to his wounds in April 1997. She had allegedly carried on an affair with the man previously and then one night, after he and his brother knocked at her door while inebriated, she and her husband tracked the two down in an alley where she stabbed her former lover twice in the back with a large knife she'd taken from her kitchen (靖江市人民检察院 2002: 141). The severity of the sentence stands out as befitting *yanda*, but was not normal for most ordinary times – though her failure to render aid (he was taken to hospital by his drunk younger brother) may have counted against her, even if there had been no campaign. The defendant had no prior criminal background, had a legitimate motive for confronting the victim, and did not obviously intend to murder him.

The second iteration of *yanda* had much the same spirit and effects as the first, even if it may have been slightly less intense. The third *yanda* campaign at the turn of the millennium brought back the mobilizational and politicized environment yet again. All in all, criminal adjudication, unlike civil litigation, experienced nearly constant political intervention and interference for more than two decades after 1978. This was true even as reforms that would seem superficially to make criminal justice less politicized were enacted, especially the 1996 Criminal Procedure Law (Jones 2005: 201).

Though reforms to laws on the books may indeed have been intended to strengthen the role of the judiciary, rein in the police and procurators, and expand the rights of the accused, they were not implemented in a sufficiently thorough or consistent way so as to guarantee those changes (Fu 1998). In fact, though some tactics and practices were curtailed, the overall strength and scope of police and procuratorial powers were enhanced by the 1996 reforms, making the systematic repression of any who might challenge established elites more expedient and comprehensive (McConville et al. 2011: 13–16).

For example, police in many localities employed creative tactics to extend pretrial (or even pre-arrest) detention far beyond the limits outlined in the Criminal Procedure Law – in fact, in one study based on a large national sample from the period, police made formal applications for arrest to the procurator within the time frame required by law in only 2 percent of cases (McConville et al. 2011: 48–9).

Many have also noted that defense lawyers and legal advice were not made accessible to suspects or defendants by the 1990s reforms. In fact, these problems with deep historical roots were, if anything, made more intense by specific rule changes in the 1990s (especially regarding potential criminal liability for defense lawyers), leaving those facing the imposition of state coercive power with little recourse (Michelson 2003; Liu & Halliday 2009, 2016; 田 & 陈 2013: 319–29).

Neotraditionalism in Criminal Law since 2002

Despite the liberal Minister of Justice Xiao Yang's rise to power as President of the Supreme People's Court in 1998, and his introduction of the first Five-Year Plan for reform and strengthening of the Chinese court system in 1999, neotraditionalism remained the order of the day in the criminal arena. Although we are well into the period of the SPC's fourth Five-Year Plan (2014–18) at the time of writing, and some important developments have occurred – for example regarding jurisdiction for trials of the first instance and appeals in cases involving capital offenses, as well as in a number of other aspects of criminal procedure after revisions to the law in 2012 – the underlying root dynamics of criminal adjudication have remained unchanged. Indeed, certain facets of political influence into criminal investigation and adjudication in support of entrenched hierarchies have become still more transparent in the current period (for additional details on how this has worked in the realm of criminal defense, see: Liu & Halliday 2016), as I uncovered in my field research.

A criminal judge in rural Jiangxi, whom I interviewed in 2007, emphasized the deep cynicism that permeated the legal system and the lack of mobilizational ideology. "Of course, on the surface, I am a Party member. When I wear the judge's robes, there is an emblem on them to signify that I serve the Party and believe in its thought (思想). But in my heart, I believe in nothing. Most people here stopped believing in the Party right after the Anti-Rightist Campaign (1957) and Great Leap Forward (1958–62)," he said. Perhaps more surprisingly, he maintained that the entire criminal process had become *less* transparent (透明) and *less* fair (公正) since the 1980s, when he became a judge. Access to defense counsel or legal advice was also much more restricted for those accused of crimes in the new millennium than it had been several decades earlier. The population of criminals had changed – with more offenders as young as fifteen turning up in adult courts after the mid-1990s – as had the relative rates of certain crimes in his county (murder and robbery had increased dramatically, while corruption and rape had become less frequent charges, for example).

There was also an overall understanding that for relatively simple cases in which the police had physical evidence or witness testimony, the best way to mitigate one's sentence was to confess. As the Jiangxi judge put it rather crudely, "if you are accused of rape and your sperm or DNA were found on the woman's body, you'd better confess if you want the lightest possible sentence." And, indeed, he claimed that 98 percent of defendants brought before his court in routine cases had, in fact, confessed. Benjamin Liebman's pathbreaking recent research has also found similar patterns based on more systematic analysis of many cases in Henan Province (Liebman 2015).

Though not necessarily representative and certainly not a comprehensive sampling, some of the relatively routine criminal trials I managed to attend in Sichuan and Jiangxi in 2006 and 2007 are instructive. For example, in the trial of a twenty-year-old from Chongqing who'd gotten into a serious altercation in a Chengdu disco (Case CD.Crim.2006.3), there was a people's assessor (人民陪审员, a middle-aged state-owned-factory worker, who said she had been selected and sent by the local People's Congress and expressed gratitude for the days off from her regular work), but she stayed quiet throughout, leaving the questioning to the two professional judges. The defendant had apparently become incensed when another young man had pushed or hit his girlfriend, so he hit him over the head with a beer bottle and then used the broken bottleneck to stab him in the shoulder, causing serious injury. The procurator was able to present photographs of the victim's injuries and doctors' reports about their treatment, written testimony from the victim, witnesses (including the bystander who had called the police), and the police officers who had responded to the scene and proceeded to detain and question the defendant, along with the defendant's confession. The defendant did not have a lawyer or other representative, but did present the bloodstained t-shirt that he said he had worn that night and described how the victim had allegedly attacked him first, hitting him in the face and causing significant injury and bleeding.

After the court adjourned, I was able to interview the judges and people's assessor briefly. All three said they were absolutely convinced of the defendant's guilt and that in their minds it did not matter if the victim had hit him first. An example had to be made of this "ruffian" to deter others and preserve social order. So the presiding judge said he was likely to be sentenced to four years or more in prison when the verdict and sentence were issued formally.

An otherwise routine case of violent crime in urban Jiangxi involved juvenile defendants (Case NC.Crim.2007.3). Such proceedings are normally closed in China, but, by happenstance, I was allowed to sit in on this one. Two judges and a people's assessor (a middle-aged man wearing a blue badge I never observed on anyone else in any court in China) oversaw a trial that combined civil with criminal elements. Two fifteen-year-old boys had assaulted another teenager during a brawl in an Internet café, where all three had been playing video games and using instant messaging services to communicate with girls. In the course of the fight, one of the defendants stabbed the victim in the eye with a small knife, while the other stabbed him with a larger blade in the chest. The victim spent months in hospital in Nanchang and also had to go for more specialized treatments to both Beijing and Shanghai – all at great cost to his family.

The court found both defendants guilty of deliberately causing injury (故意伤害) and sentenced them to three years and three months in a juvenile detention facility. On the civil side, the court was unable to award all of the damages sought by the victim, as some of these exceeded the statutory limits for punitive damages and in some other cases the receipts and documentation presented could not substantiate everything being claimed as expenses. Still, the defendants were ordered to pay RMB180,000 and 90,000, respectively. The victim's representative said after the verdict that he was basically satisfied with the outcome, but expressed formal displeasure for the record with the reduction in damages. The defendants were present, but not allowed to answer for themselves because they were juveniles. Their mothers were both in court, however, one of whom said she could accept the court's decisions, while the other said she would have to consult with other family members first. Though the outcome of the trial seemed never to have been in doubt, the juvenile defendants were treated considerably more leniently than they might have been had they been older (as for example in the case of the disco brawler in Chengdu, who had caused less severe injuries to his victim).

A nonviolent burglary Case (CD.Crim.2006.2) was very much open-and-shut. In fact, the whole trial was over less than twenty minutes after it started and was overseen by a single young judge. The defendant, a young man from Zigong, had climbed into the window of a college student's apartment in Chengdu and stolen his laptop computer. He had been observed climbing in by one witness, who presented written testimony against him. The victim's roommate had later seen the defendant trying to sell the stolen computer at a used computer store and also testified. Finally, the computer store owner confirmed that the defendant had indeed tried to sell the computer in question. When asked by the judge to explain his version of the facts, the defendant claimed that the victim actually had owed him money and had agreed that he could take the computer to pawn it, and that the two would then split the money. He could not explain, however, why he would have had to take the computer by climbing in through the window, and the judge was unconvinced, proclaiming him guilty and sentencing him to sixteen months in prison and a fine of RMB1000.

Though the defendant's claims seemed flimsy, the court seemed to downplay the seriousness of the case against this young migrant (despite the relatively severe sentence imposed). In fact, the judge explained to me afterwards that she was the most junior in her division and therefore frequently handled all cases deemed relatively uncomplicated or unimportant – such cases also could be assigned to just one judge rather than a three-judge panel (合议庭) to save resources and time.

Even some trials handled by full three-judge panels were conducted in fairly informal and rushed fashion. In Case NC.Crim.2007.1, four men between the ages of twenty-six and thirty-six were accused of cutting lengths of computer cable (150–70 m) out of equipment and storage in a chemical plant, which they apparently intended to sell on the black market for RMB1000–1500. The procurator was able to present confessions from all four defendants, testimony from a factory employee who said he'd seen them taking the cable, the wire cutter they'd allegedly used to cut the cable, and photos of the stolen cable that had been recovered from the defendants. The defendants also admitted to the charges when asked by the presiding judge in court.

Various aspects of the proceedings in this Nanchang trial were abnormally informal. The procurator and the judges were wearing t-shirts under simple blazers, rather than the normal robes or formal uniforms of their offices. The defendants also had little education, but the judges did not take much care to explain matters to them. In fact, one of them, who claimed to be totally illiterate, said he did not understand when the judge asked him what ethnicity (民族) he was. The judge said, "Han, I suppose" (汉族吧), but the defendant again protested that he did not understand and asked the judge to explain the term "ethnicity." At this, the presiding judge grew angry. He admonished the defendant for being obstinate and warned that his attitude could influence the severity of his sentence. After that, none of the defendants said anything for the rest of the trial, nodding their heads whenever the judges put any questions to them. The verdict and sentence were not expected until a later date, but after the defendants had been ushered out, the presiding judge called the procurator over to the bench and appeared to excoriate him for several minutes for problems with the paperwork in the case file (though I could not hear very clearly from the audience and the judge's sidebar tirade was mostly in a local dialect of northern Jiangxi that I had some difficulty understanding).

In another similar Case (NC.Crim.2007.2), two judges and a people's assessor presided over the trial of a twenty-two-year-old man accused of stealing an electric bicycle and a mobile phone (小灵通) from a housing complex in the middle of the night on April 4, 2007. The defendant had a prior conviction for theft in 2003 and had been released from prison only in late 2006 – something both the procurator and presiding judge mentioned repeatedly. In this case also no one wore uniforms or robes – only t-shirts under ill-fitting and stained blazers. Besides me, there was only one elderly man in the court audience, who fell asleep once during the trial (snoring audibly) and at one point left the room to answer his mobile phone. Only the presiding judge and the procurator spoke, but the assisting judge interrupted the proceedings every couple of minutes by loudly clearing his throat, coughing, and spitting on the courtroom floor. The procurator was able to offer a confession from the defendant, testimony from the teenage owner of the stolen goods, and pictures of the bicycle and phone (which the defendant assented to recognizing as what he had stolen).

After the conclusion of the procurator's presentation, the defendant admitted to everything and offered no defense, asking only for leniency from the court. The presiding judge said the court would reconvene for a verdict in seven to ten days and adjourned the proceedings. The assisting judge coughed and spat on the floor again, before everyone left the room.

Some relatively routine cases, however, were handled in a way that stressed scrupulous attention to every detail of procedure, even when the outcome was in little doubt. For instance, a case against a thirty-five-year-old Yi Minority woman and a fifty-year-old Han man, accused of picking pockets at a Chengdu shopping mall (Case CD.Crim.2006.4) was actually suspended and remanded back to the police for further investigation and clarification. The male defendant admitted to stealing money from a shopper's coat pocket and then passing it off to the woman, who admitted receiving it from him. The police recorded that they admitted to having stolen RMB2000, but the accused woman explained at trial that she already had RMB1100 in her pocket before her accomplice passed her the stolen cash. They thus only really stole RMB900. The single judge assigned to try the case then suspended the proceedings and ordered the file returned to the police.

After the others had left the room, the judge explained to me that this was necessary to comply with the letter of the law and procedure (and to avoid any possibility of problems with the court's supervision department or on appeal), even though the defendants' sentences would be little changed (at most the different amount of stolen money might reduce the time they needed to serve by a month). As it was, she would only have sentenced them each to two to three months in prison had they simply expressed contrition and remorse in court. Given what had just unfolded, they would need to remain in detention for at least several weeks while the police concluded the supplementary investigation, so their total time incarcerated might actually end up being longer than if they had not brought up the discrepancy at all.

Even in some relatively routine cases, in which trials were conducted with great attention to procedure, defendants sometimes could appear befuddled and overwhelmed by a process that perhaps seemed stacked against them or predetermined. In Case CD.Crim.2006.1, a young Yi Minority man stood accused of mugging a young woman in Chengdu, attacking her and throwing her off her bicycle to steal her purse, mobile phone, and a small amount of cash (RMB13), when she was riding home from work at about 1:00 AM. The defendant said when asked at the start of the trial that he did not know how old he was and had no ID card (身份证), but that he had been told in 1989 that he was around seven years old, so he guessed he was about twenty-four (at the time of the trial in 2006). Though not his native language, he said he was comfortable with his trial being conducted in Mandarin, but then asked for clarification of terms a number of times, saying he had not understood. The procurator presented testimony from the victim, photographs of her injuries, and documentation of what the stolen goods were worth, as well as a written confession from the defendant.

At every turn, the defendant denied attacking the victim. He admitted stealing her purse, containing the money and mobile phone, but claimed he had only run up alongside her bicycle as she was riding and snatched it from the front basket without touching her, much less pushing her to the ground. The procurator began to read details from the defendant's confession, attesting to the manner in which he'd attacked the victim. He interrupted, claiming he never said anything like that to the police. The presiding judge asked him if the fingerprints on each page of the confession were indeed his, and he agreed that they were. How could his confession not be genuine, then, the judge asked. When he was speaking to the police, they seemed to be writing down much more than he was actually saying, the defendant replied. When he told them he was barely literate in Chinese and asked for a non–police officer to read back to him what had been written down, they refused, told him that was not permitted, and said he was obliged to stamp his fingerprints on each page. In custody and afraid, he complied, but now he claimed the confession had been largely fabricated.

This made the procurator change tactics, saying that even if the defendant's story of police mistreatment were true, the photos of the victim's injuries and her testimony proved that he must have thrown her off the bicycle. Eventually, the defendant could do little more than to offer an apology and an explanation of his dire economic straits (including hunger and homelessness after he had left his village for the city to look for work), at the end of which he broke down in tears and had to be ushered out of the courtroom by bailiffs (法警). After a recess of about ten minutes, during which the judges also left the room, the defendant was brought back in and the presiding judge pronounced him guilty and sentenced him to four years in prison and a fine of RMB1000. She explained to him that he had thirty days to appeal his sentence to the intermediate court and he nodded his head in agreement when she asked him if he understood. But, as he was being led back out, he turned to one of the bailiffs holding him by the arms and asked audibly what the meaning of the word "appeal" (上诉) was. Clearly, the defendant never received comprehensive legal advice about how to respond to discrepancies in his confession, while his limited education and Chinese language abilities appeared seriously to hamper his comprehension of his own trial. But none of this seemed to matter to the court. The case was processed according to proper procedure, a violent criminal was off the streets, and another case was off the court's backlogged docket.

Though they do not occur very often, nonroutine or exceptional cases can also be elucidative. The rural Jiangxi criminal judge I interviewed in 2007 contrasted such cases with routine ones, in that suspects did not confess. In fact, as opposed to a 98-percent confession rate, more than 80 percent of those accused of corruption or bribery refused to confess. This made such cases frustratingly hard to adjudicate. Very seldom do those paying or receiving bribes keep receipts or written records, he pointed out, and they were much more likely to claim in court that any confession they might have made had been extracted from them under duress (or had been somehow altered or falsified after the fact by police or procurators), or to offer evidence of having been abused while in police custody (often describing how they had been beaten, denied sleep or proper food for days or longer, etc.).

The chief judge of the criminal division of a medium-sized city's intermediate court explained, when I interviewed him in 2009, that cases involving defendants with high levels of education or high social standing could almost never be investigated through normal procedures, because such suspects were too smart to confess. They would refuse to say anything or offer elaborate alibis and the police would be at a loss. Luckily, almost all such suspects were Party members. This, he emphasized, meant they could be investigated by the CCP Discipline and Inspection Commission (纪检委), an extralegal entity with sweeping powers to detain suspects, collect evidence, and make use of almost any means it might choose to achieve its objectives (for more on this Party agency, see Gong 2008; Guo 2014; Sapio 2008; Li 2016a). Nearly every official or other defendant of high social status or education to be tried recently in his court had indeed been first investigated by the Discipline and Inspection Commission, he said, before a near-complete file was turned over to the police so that the accused could be formally arrested and charged.

Similarly, this same judge explained that cases with a real or potential impact on social stability would be handled through special political processes. Such cases mainly consisted of three types: serious violent crime (e.g. murder), corruption on the part of high-ranking cadres or state officials, and criminal activity related to petitioning, protest, or "mass incidents" of any kind. In addition to a role for the Discipline and Inspection Commission in corruption cases, the Political and Legal Affairs Committee (政法委) of the prefectural CCP Committee would become involved in all these cases from the outset. In fact, the Committee would call the court president and vice president, as well as the head of the relevant court division, and representatives from the Public Security Bureau and Procuratorate, to meet with its leadership and agree on a strategy for handling the case and an intended outcome early in the investigation process. They would meet several more times throughout the process to ensure all matters were unfolding as agreed. This basic framework was confirmed by a mid-level cadre (处级干部 / 处长) of that prefecture's Political and Legal Affairs Committee, whom I was able to interview a few days later.

Additionally, in sensitive or socially impactful cases, the court's adjudication committee (审判委员会) would always handle the matter within the court from start to finish, according to the criminal division chief, as well as several court presidents I was able to interview in rural Sichuan in 2006 and urban Jiangxi in 2007. So involved would the committee be that it would meet each evening after the close of trial proceedings and would draft the decision document collectively. In such cases, the court's criminal division chief would almost always be assigned the role of presiding judge (审判长), to ensure there were no hiccups in terms of procedures or events in the courtroom, but the real role of principal judge (主审法官) – especially as it pertained to determining the reasoning for the decision – would be played by the committee. Such cases occur relatively rarely and they are especially difficult for researchers to observe or access. They also tend to last longer than routine trials and so are not easy to observe in one visit or even a series of visits to a court. But I was able to observe at least parts of two complicated and sensitive trials of this sort, as well as to interview some of the actors involved in each.

The first of these was the murder trial of an itinerant woodcutter in rural Sichuan (Case MS.Crim.2006.1), which I was able to observe in April 2006. The trial was held in the large main courtroom of the intermediate court, with seating for at least a couple of hundred spectators (though only about twenty-five were present besides myself, almost all of them apparently family members of either the victim or the defendant, seated in separate groups on opposite sides of the court). There were three seemingly unconnected observers sitting near the back of the audience section, whom I later learned were there to watch the proceedings on behalf of the Political and Legal Affairs Committee. This was the first and main day of the trial, and so the presiding judge (the court's criminal division chief, in his late forties) moved things along at a brisk pace, convening for about two hours and fifteen minutes in the morning before breaking for a ninety-minute lunch and then reconvening for another two-and-a-half hours in the afternoon. In addition to the presiding judge, the chief of the court's civil division (in his fifties) sat on the panel, and presided over the civil portion of the trial. Rounding out the panel was a younger judge (in his thirties), who all the others said repeatedly over lunch was a rapidly rising star.

All the parties agreed on some of the basic facts of the case. The thirty-six-year-old defendant (a villager from another county in the same prefecture) had been hired by the victim (a fifty-eight-year-old villager with a large tract of forest land near his house) to cut down trees on his land that would later be sold for lumber. During the day, while the workers were eating lunch, there was a disagreement between them and the victim over their consumption of some of his food and tea without permission. After working all day, the defendant went through the garden to the victim's house that evening and found him in his living room. There, he beat the victim with a wooden pole, striking him in the back of the head several times and causing severe bleeding. After this, he strangled the victim with a rubber hose. Leaving the victim unconscious (perhaps dead) on the floor, the defendant took a substantial sum of cash from a safe that had been left open in a cabinet in the living room and left the house. He then went to Chengdu (on the other side of the province) before making his way to rural Henan. Once in Henan, he called his sister-in-law on the telephone, before returning to a different county of his home prefecture (neither his home nor the site of his crime), where the police took him into custody.

Once the trial got underway, however, it quickly became obvious that there were issues with much of the evidence and sharp differences between the procurator's narrative of what had unfolded that evening at the victim's house and that told by the defense attorney (a lawyer in his mid-forties appointed by the court for the indigent defendant), and indeed the account offered by the defendant himself. According to the procurator, the defendant went to the victim's house that night to rob him, breaking in from the rooftop where he found and picked up a wooden pole normally used for hanging drying laundry, after learning that the victim's associate in the city had just paid him RMB10,000 to purchase the wood that had been cut that day. During the robbery, the victim resisted, but the defendant was determined, beating him savagely with the pole, eventually breaking it over his head. After the pole had been broken, the defendant took up the rubber hose (normally used for channeling water from the kitchen sink to the drain in the corner of the floor) and strangled the victim with it until he stopped struggling. Leaving his victim for dead on the floor with the hose tied round his neck, the defendant then went to the cabinet, where he had seen the victim put the money away but fail to lock the safe, removed RMB9600 in cash, and ran out of the back door, locking it behind him. He then made for Henan by bus. But when he learned from his sister-in-law that police were in pursuit, he returned to his home prefecture (but not his home county), where he thought he might hide himself better.

According to the defendant's lawyer, the altercation he'd had with the victim earlier in the day was more than an exchange of unkind words: the defendant was beaten badly in front of all the other workers by the victim (with the unreasonable excuse that he'd consumed too much food and tea while on his lunch break from chopping trees). He thus decided to go to the victim's house that night, looking to retaliate by beating him up. When he got there, the victim set upon him and the two struggled with each other for some time, with the eventual result that the defendant knocked the victim to the ground by hitting him with the pole (that was apparently part of a bed-frame in the room where they had been fighting), which broke over his head. He then did try to strangle the victim with the hose, but left him, still breathing, on the floor with the hose near his neck (not tied around his head), before taking the money and fleeing for Henan, leaving the door of the victim's house ajar. Evidently the victim then bled to death, expired from other causes, or someone else entered the house and finished him off after the defendant had left. His sister-in-law eventually convinced the defendant to turn himself in, which he did upon his return to his home prefecture's nearest long-distance bus station, located in a neighboring county. He thus set out to commit assault (故意伤害), but ended up killing the victim by accident before stealing from him (盗窃) in a panic. Once he realized the severity of the situation, however, he returned home to surrender to police and face justice.

The defendant interrupted his own lawyer several times to correct his recounting of the events in the case, and then was allowed to speak afterwards and offer his own version of the facts. He claimed to have gone to the victim's house neither to confront him nor to rob him, but to retrieve a key he'd lost during the day while cutting trees on his land. When he arrived at the house, therefore, he first went up to the rooftop to look for the key amid the laundry that was drying there. Specifically, he suspected it had been picked up by the victim and put in his pocket, so he looked first in the pockets of the pair of trousers the victim had been wearing earlier. He did not find the key, but he did find RMB200 in cash, which he put into his own pocket. He then went downstairs to ask for his key. When he got there, he and the victim got into a scuffle, which eventually escalated to the point that he hit the victim over the head with the wooden pole he had found close at hand and tried to strangle him with the hose, leaving him still breathing on the floor with the hose near his neck. In a panic, he ran out, leaving the door ajar, but did not take any money from the safe (he denied knowing even that there was a safe in the room), and fled to Henan. A few days later, he spoke with his sister-in-law and, fearing for his family, returned to try to sort things out, and was taken into custody soon after he got off the bus.

All three versions of the narrative had the victim being beaten badly by the defendant with a wooden pole – to the point of breaking the pole over his head and knocking him to the floor. All three versions also had the defendant strangling the victim with the same rubber hose, but only the procurator's had the victim actually expiring from this strangulation. Further complicating the matter was the confession the defendant had given upon his arrest, which mostly matched the procurator's story, but was more vague on key details – he admitted to stealing money from the victim, for example, but did not seem to specify how much he had taken or whether he'd gotten it from the safe or the trousers – and did not mention anything about the missing key or going to the victim's house to confront him about any altercation earlier in the day. Ultimately, the court would have to decide, based on witness testimony and physical evidence, which narrative to believe and whether to convict the defendant of murder, manslaughter (i.e. unintentional homicide), theft, assault, or some combination of these offenses. It would also need to discern whether the defendant had broken into the victim's house and whether he had returned from Henan in an effort to hide or to turn himself in to authorities. Combined with the criminal trial was also a civil suit, adjudicated during a special phase of the trial (presided over by the head of the civil division), in which the victim's family sought damages from the defendant to compensate for their emotional suffering and to provide for some of his lost income.

The procurator presented testimony from a number of witnesses. It should be noted that this fact alone made this case a rarity. As McConville and his coauthors observed, among the 1109 criminal trials they examined, only nineteen included live (versus written) witness testimony, and in eighteen of these only one witness testified (and in twelve cases this one witness was the victim) (McConville et al. 2011: 242). First, the victim's daughter said she had met with her father in the garden of his house not long before the murder and had discussed both his finding a key and him getting paid RMB10,000 in cash that day. A neighbor also testified that he was aware of the work being done, of the large cash payment made, and of the altercation over the food in the afternoon. Other workers who also cut trees for the victim that day testified to the general circumstances as well. The police officer first on the scene offered testimony describing the victim's injuries and the state of the living room, and presented photographs of the victim and scene. Finally, the police detectives who had investigated the physical evidence appeared in court with the wooden pole and the rubber hose used to kill the victim.

Their presentation of the physical evidence was flawed, however. The officers told the judges they'd found a lot of blood on the scene and tested some of it, which matched the blood type of the victim. When asked, they admitted they did not test it against the defendant's blood type. Nor did they check for fingerprints on the pole, and were handling it openly in court, without gloves, as they said they had done routinely since collecting it at the scene. Finally, they had cut the rubber hose into small segments (roughly 20 cm each in length), supposedly so they could fit it into their evidence bag, and it was thus no longer in a state similar to that in which it had been discovered. The judges were appalled at the police incompetence and the procurator's audacity in submitting such flawed evidence, and they were withering in their criticisms when I spoke with them both during the lunch recess and at the conclusion of the afternoon's proceedings.

As for the civil suit, this was easier for the court to decide. It was not in doubt that the defendant had caused serious injury – and almost certainly death – to the victim. His family was not suing to recover damages related to the stolen money or damaged property, only for their suffering from his death and for a portion of his lost income. The judges were able to rule rather quickly, therefore, in favor of the victim's family as plaintiffs, awarding them RMB40,000 in damages for emotional suffering and RMB50,000 as partial compensation for the victim's lost income, after a civil phase that lasted roughly forty-five minutes immediately following the lunch recess.

Regarding the criminal matter, the court was not yet ready to conclude the trial or issue an official verdict by the end of that day. The presiding judge and the court president explained, however, when I spoke with them that afternoon, that the defendant would definitely be found guilty and that the sentence would almost certainly be one of death, suspended for one or two years (after which time, if the defendant committed no further criminal acts while incarcerated, his sentence would be converted either to life imprisonment or fifteen years, at the discretion of the court upon review). When I interviewed the court president again later that same year, this time in Beijing (where he'd been transferred to the Supreme People's Court), he told me that the defendant in the murder case had indeed been convicted and sentenced to death suspended for two years. He explained that this had already been worked out by the Adjudication Committee and agreed upon with the Political and Legal Affairs Committee before the trial had begun. The problems with the evidence and the conflicting testimony thus made the trial harder to stage-manage, but the basic contours and ultimate outcome were never in doubt.

In another fraught case (Case NC.Crim.2007.4), the factory director of a state-owned underwear manufacturer (technically an urban collective, 集体企业) in urban Jiangxi was accused of taking bribes and also of misappropriating (essentially embezzling) factory funds. This case was quite complex and, as was explained to me later by the court president, had also been investigated by the Discipline and Inspection Commission, discussed and debated by the Political and Legal Affairs Committee, and essentially decided in advance by the adjudication committee, even though it was being tried in a basic-level court and was a relatively small-scale affair. Still, it seemed the state and court system were leery of airing too much dirty laundry and sought to keep the case as controlled as possible.

The defendant was fifty years old and dressed in street clothes without a jail vest. In fact, he seemed to have been transferred directly into the courtroom by the bailiffs upon his arrival, as just prior to the start of his trial, the court's small holding cell had been occupied only by two young men awaiting their own trial for assault. He was accompanied by a defense attorney he had retained privately – who was also well-dressed and roughly forty-five years old. The procurator was the same officer I had seen appear in court for other less sensitive cases earlier in the day. There were three judges – the presiding judge was the deputy chief of the court's criminal division (刑事庭副庭长) – including one female judge who did not speak, alongside the presiding judge and another slightly younger judge who asked most of the questions and seemed to be the principal adjudicating judge (主审法官). The trial began at around 10:30 AM, recessed for lunch from 11:50 until 12:30, and then continued until it ended at about 2:00 PM. No verdict or sentence was delivered that day – the judges said afterwards that the decision would need to be prepared in consultation with the adjudication committee and would be ready in about seven to fourteen days. Any sentence might come then or might need to be decided after the decision had been issued.

According to the procurator, the defendant had sought a personal loan of RMB100,000 from a businessman in town in late 2004. The defendant then invested this money in a real estate development in another city that had never been finished and became a "broken tail project" (Sorace & Hurst 2016). Unable to pay back the loan, he approached the businessman to work out a solution to his debt. The businessman then brought up the matter of two storefronts in the middle of the city that the factory owned, but over which the defendant, as manager, had *de facto* personal control. As the factory was undergoing structural reforms that would enhance the personal powers of its manager even further, the businessman agreed to forgive the loan if he could be guaranteed access to occupy one of these storefronts, even saying directly that he would consider the funds a gift if the reforms could successfully get him into the retail space ("改制成功的话，这一笔钱就送给你的了"). After this discussion, the defendant returned twice to ask the businessman for additional loans of RMB50,000 at the end of 2004 and RMB20,000 in January 2005. All three loans, whose repayment could apparently be foregone in exchange for access to the state factory-owned storefront, constituted bribes paid by the businessman and accepted by the defendant.

Ultimately, however, the defendant was not able to secure access for the businessman to the storefront in question. So he tried to extort money from the current tenant (the shopkeeper he couldn't evict) to pay off the loans and cover his debts from the real estate boondoggle. The shopkeeper was not so easily bullied, though, and offered a loan of RMB250,000, but only with an official factory stamp on the lending agreement and a guarantee that the loan would be repaid via a deduction of RMB2000 per month in his rent each month for the next two years. This would both assure repayment (and at a high rate of return for the creditor) and preclude the factory director from evicting the shopkeeper for at least two years. The defendant agreed, taking a personal loan of RMB250,000 from the shopkeeper and issuing him with a formal letter with a factory stamp saying the funds would be repaid via a deduction in his rent. This, the procurator charged, amounted to misappropriation of the factory's funds (in the form of lost rent) for his personal use (in repaying the loan to the tenant).

The procurator first presented as evidence written testimony from the businessman, who confirmed the loan amounts, timing, and the agreement about the storefront, saying he had demanded repayment by Chinese New Year 2005 when it became clear he would not get access to the storefront. He followed up with written testimony from the shopkeeper, who also confirmed the main points and said he had agreed explicitly to make a loan to the factory (not a personal loan to the defendant), to be repaid through rent-discounting over two years. After that, a statement from a mutual acquaintance was presented, saying he had arranged the first meeting between the businessman and the defendant after being approached by the former about gaining access to the factory's storefront. Finally, the underwear factory accountant testified that she had noticed that rent had not been collected in full from the shopkeeper for several months in late 2005. After she had raised this point with the director, since she knew of no records of payments or details of any arrangement to discount or credit payments, she was surprised when he allegedly replied that, "you do not need to worry about this rent, nor do you have to go collect it; rather, I'll collect it myself" (这一个房租不要你管，也不用你去收，而我自己来收吧). Yet, the accountant said, the defendant never did collect the missing rent – at least in any way that was recorded or traceable for the firm. Upon the procurator's questioning in court, the defendant admitted to all the main points, arguing only that he was actually trying to repay the factory for the lost rental income from the shopkeeper with his own personal funds.

The defense lawyer did not present new evidence, seeking instead to call into question two key points in the prosecution's case. First, the go-between mentioned in his testimony that when he had approached the businessman to seek the second loan (of RMB50,000) for the defendant, the businessman had become "somewhat angry" (有点生气). If the loans were really bribe payments, the defense attorney asked, why would the businessman be indignant at paying for the storefront he was after? Besides, the loan amounts were trivial compared to what the storefront would be worth to him in business gained. The lawyer and his client both interrupted the procurator several times during his presentation of the case to debate this point – at one point even engaging in a spirited argument lasting more than fifteen minutes. So it was no surprise that he returned to it in his own presentation. The second point was that the shopkeeper's testimony was unclear as to the details of the agreement and that, in fact, the loan was only meant to have been guaranteed by the factory and would be repaid through rent deductions only if the director did not pay himself. This may still have been an improper arrangement, but it did not amount to misappropriation of factory funds. It was also not clear from any of the evidence that the unpaid rent was related to any agreement between the defendant and the shopkeeper, rather than simply a result of the latter's negligence or dishonesty.

At the end of the trial, the defendant was led out of the room – this time to the holding cell, which had been vacated by the two young marauders, whose trial had by then begun in another courtroom. Almost as soon as he was out of the room, his lawyer began bantering and joking with the procurator. He then tossed him a cigarette across the aisle of the courtroom and the two walked out the back entrance, presumably to smoke together and discuss the case. One of the judges and the court clerk both confirmed that the defense attorney had formerly worked for the procuratorate and even then had appeared to be friends with the officer sent to prosecute this case. The other fifteen or so people in the audience then filed out. After a few minutes of talking to the clerk, I also left the room to wait for the judges, who had agreed to be interviewed but needed a few minutes first. When I left the room, I noticed several of the people who had been in the audience clustered around the small holding cell, speaking animatedly with the defendant who was locked inside, as the bailiffs stood near the open exterior door, awaiting the arrival of his transport back to jail.

Criminalized Civil Disputes in Contemporary China

Overall, the problem of criminalized civil disputes is less pervasive and severe in China than in Indonesia, but it is still a significant issue (Hurst 2015). China's civil law reforms since the 1980s have opened the door for a myriad of disputes involving contracts, torts, and product liability. But they have not succeeded in preventing all misuse of the criminal process. Glaring examples abound of cases that ought to be treated as civil contract disputes being taken up as criminal prosecutions of contract fraud due to the malfeasance or incompetence of procuratorial and judicial officials (唐 2011: 37). This problem became sufficiently widespread and severe to warrant the convention of a conference in Beijing in April 2010 on the conflict between the criminalization of civil disputes and the ideal of an "harmonious society" (中国网 2010; 唐 2011: 37), even as the very role of civil litigation in promoting the harmonious society goal had long been questioned (正义网 2008).

Prior to the enactment in the 1980s of key statutes on civil procedure and right of recourse to courts in civil disputes, the issue of criminalization was not especially important (since the civil justice system was so scanty to begin with). Once a more complete civil judicial apparatus was constructed, however, the potential for its abuse surfaced. As laws and regulations governing commercial activity have become more complex and comprehensive, opportunities for improper criminalization have become narrower but more numerous, provoking increasingly frequent and vituperative public outcries.

In one particularly famous instance, a Shanghai business leader named Yan Liyan (南方周末 2010) was charged with contract fraud (合同诈骗) in a case many took to have been improperly criminalized from an essentially civil dispute. Based on the allegations of the procurator, the defendant improperly manipulated the terms of a business loan in 2000 and 2001 to gain unlawful advantage. This, however, would not be a sound basis for a charge of contract fraud, but instead could be for a charge of deceptive lending (骗取贷款). The problem, though, is that the statute defining deceptive lending as a crime only took effect in 2006 and could not be applied retroactively (唐 2011: 37). Thus, even if the alleged activities rose to the level of criminal behavior, Yan could not have been legitimately charged on the basis of the laws in effect at the time he had brokered the loans in question.

Despite clear prohibitions on criminalizing cases such as Yan's, this happens repeatedly in the Chinese legal system. Indeed, such cases abound. Many Chinese analysts allege that procurators and police are often motivated by crude self-interest in pursuing such cases (that is, they accept illicit payments or otherwise cultivate improper advantageous relations with economic actors who are parties to the cases) (唐 2011: 38). Continuing to prosecute such cases carries risks for procurators (such as being tarred with "incorrect cases" on their records), increases the social and political costs for settling economic disputes, and undermines social stability (唐 2011: 38). Yet, without tighter controls on their behavior, procurators and police will likely continue to be so lured.

Indeed, even if the prosecution of economic disputants on dubious charges could be stamped out, there are other means through which procurators could still improperly intervene in civil justice. Another issue, which does not strictly speaking rise to the level of criminalization of civil disputes, is the pursuit of procuratorial appeals (抗诉) in civil cases. Procurators frequently deploy their legal authority to intervene and seek reversal of outcomes in a very wide variety of cases (最高人民检察院民事行政厅 2004). Unlike most other systems, Chinese law affords procurators, whose primary responsibility is criminal investigation and prosecution, the power to "supervise" (监督) procedures and outcomes (judgments) in civil cases. There has long been concern about how this power is exercised, as well as whether and how procurators might overstep their mandate to interfere in civil cases for corrupt or self-serving reasons (袁& 倪 2006; 杨 2010). Since procurators have both illicit self-interest and legitimate broadly framed legal-supervision authority as potential bases for their intervention in civil disputes, China's justice system will continue to be plagued by excessive criminalization for some time.

Concluding Thoughts

The overall forty-year trend in Chinese criminal law is clear and is broadly in line with an emerging conventional wisdom based on prior research (e.g. Belkin 2000; Biddulph 2007; Liebman 2007, 2015; Sapio 2010; McConville et al. 2011). After reform had begun in earnest and a new criminal code was adopted in 1979, the Chinese state and CCP moved quickly to preclude the development of any capability for courts or other institutions to engage in criminal adjudication free from substantial intervention by the Party, public security organs, and other politically important actors. Through *yanda* campaigns, repression of 1989 protesters and other dissenters, renewed campaigns in the 1990s, and the push for more control in courts and through other institutions since the mid-2000s, a neotraditional regime has been cemented that is not likely to be dislodged at any point soon. We can see, in fact, further development of such a regime over the past several years through the rollout of increasingly strict and encompassing frameworks for repression and social control. As the "grid system" (网格) brings more and more of Chinese society under its surveillance and "stability maintenance" purview, there will be less and less space for proscribed activities to occur that will not be subject to repression through a fully instrumentalized criminal apparatus.

Finally, as extralegal institutions continue to take on larger roles in China's criminal system, any potential for transitioning to a rule by law regime is reduced. We can observe at the upper echelons of the polity how the CCP's Discipline and Inspection Commissions have assumed many roles that could well be seen as properly belonging to police, procurators, and courts. In politically or socially sensitive cases, we can also observe how political and legal affairs committees and adjudication committees can take power away from judges and even courts in determining how trials will proceed and what verdicts will be reached. In lower-level more routinized cases, institutions like the *cheng'guan* (城管) continue to exert social control without legal accountability (课题研发组 2006), augmenting the work of police and courts without opening these parts of the legal system to citizens at all.

CONCLUSION

Neotraditional regimes are in many respects the most stable of any type I have discussed. They are also among the most flexible. So long as elites remain stable and continue to desire intervention in adjudication to protect their position, there are few factors that can undermine such regimes. This stands in sharp contrast to mobilizational regimes that are inherently unstable. It is also an important point of difference from rule by law regimes, which require not only stable elites but a continual commitment by those elites to refrain from intervening in the adjudication process and to prevent such intervention by others. Likely because of this greater stability, we can observe neotraditional regimes in many contexts and time periods.

In addition, the great flexibility of neotraditional regimes means that they can easily be incorporated into various hybrids, usually alongside rule by law regimes. This can be observed in both Chinese and Indonesian contexts today. In Indonesia, democracy precludes the unabashed use of criminal prosecution for repression in support of elite protection. But, at the same time, economic, social, and political elites have few qualms about using the civil adjudication system to preserve their power or promote their interests. Democratic political liberalization without transparency or leveling of economic or social relations facilitates Indonesia's hybrid order, which is in turn protected and nurtured by the persistence of that particular mix of legal regimes.

The CCP's ongoing commitment to retaining authoritarian control at all costs, alongside China's continuing and deepening embrace of the market and developmentalism, has enabled a different hybrid of regimes. Market transactions and economic development are eased and hastened by a rule by law order in the civil arena, even as political control is retained through a neotraditional regime in criminal law. Both hybrids are self-reinforcing to the degree that legal regime change in Indonesia could occur only if there were to be very significant economic and social change (or an unflinching reimposition of authoritarianism), while in China no change is likely unless and until some truly watershed political shift were to happen (or if market-oriented reform were to be completely abandoned).

In fact, hybrid regimes may be important equilibrium outcomes for legal orders incorporating neotraditionalism. Indonesia's experience during the New Order period suggests that fully neotraditional regimes across all areas of law may be less stable, though such arrangements seem perhaps more common than others in developing and newly independent countries. The roots of instability lie in the weakness of legal institutions subjected to pervasive and continual intervention in all aspects of their adjudication by sclerotic political and social elites. Should a crisis ensue, it could create strong pressure for the powerful to stop intervening in either criminal or civil adjudication, or force open the polity to meaningful political participation by previously excluded actors, facilitating competition and contestation, and likely precipitating a transition toward a mobilizational regime.

Finally, neotraditional regimes are likely to turn up in at least some areas of law, even when rule by law orders seem fully ensconced. This is because refraining from all intervention in adjudication is threatening to powerful actors. If elites stay out of the civil law arena, they are liable to lose economic or social influence or advantage. Staying out of the criminal system means that, without important tools of repression at their disposal, elites can be challenged politically. Hybrid regimes like China's or Indonesia's are thus not mere aberrations, but likely relatively common occurrences to which we should pay more careful attention.

CONCLUSION: CHINESE AND INDONESIAN POLITICS BEYOND LAW; LAW AND POLITICS BEYOND INDONESIA AND CHINA

> *Block's just cunning. He's gathered a lot of experience . . . But his ignorance is greater than his cunning. What do you think he'd say if he were to learn that his trial hasn't even begun, if he were to be told that the bell for the start of his trial hasn't even been rung yet?*
>
> (Kafka 2005: 140–1).

INTRODUCTION

Through a study of the legal systems of the largest and fourth-largest countries in the world, the preceding chapters have offered a comprehensive and detailed microlevel analysis of the politics of law and legal institutions in Indonesia and China over the past seventy-five years. This book is also the first side-by-side comparison of these two countries. While conditions and events in both countries continue to evolve, even as I have been engaged in writing this book (for example, with China's "Fourth Plenum on the Rule of Law" in October 2014 or Indonesia's flagrantly political prosecution of Jakarta Governor Basuki "Ahok" Tjahaja Purnama for alleged blasphemy in 2016–17 mentioned in Chapter 4), the underlying general patterns and dynamics have provided fertile ground for taking important first steps toward building a theory of legal regimes that I hope future research might continue to refine in light of ongoing changes and developments.

Based on my empirical research, I have offered a typology of legal regimes that extends the possibility for systematic analysis of law and politics in action well beyond the established Western democratic core. But this typology is only the first step of a longer journey.

It is inductively derived, based on a close reading of history, law, and politics in two important countries over a recent critical period. But it carries implications for other systems, countries, regions, and time periods. In order to understand these implications, we first have to step back to consider legal regimes as legal systems, the full extent and limitations of the leverage gained by comparing China and Indonesia, and the aspects of legal regimes that transcend law and venture deeper into other realms of political and social life.

LEGAL REGIMES AS LEGAL SYSTEMS

Legal regimes cannot be arranged along a single axis or continuum. Even less are they stages in a linear or teleological process. Rather, they are broad categories of sets of relationships and influences that structure and govern the way in which legal institutions function in particular contexts. These frameworks of relationships and rules, and the institutions that inhabit them in specific countries, can also be viewed as legal systems. Doing so extends their theoretical compass to include literatures and schools of thought beyond those of legal realism and critical legal studies that I discussed in the Introduction and Chapter 1.

H. L. A. Hart tells us that in any legal system, "those rules of behaviour which are valid according to the system's ultimate criteria of validity must be generally obeyed, and, on the other hand, its rules of recognition specifying the criteria of legal validity and its rules of change and adjudication must be effectively accepted as common public standards of behaviour by its officials" (Hart 1994: 116). Joseph Raz extends and expands upon this general idea, but also points out that "Legal systems are not 'autarkic' social organizations. They are an aspect or dimension of some *political* system" (Raz 1980: 201, italics added).[1] Political structures and power dynamics shape the rules of behavior that constitute *both* what Hart would call the "primary rules" that govern behavior *and* the "secondary rules" that determine who is empowered to make, change, or recognize primary rules and specify how disputes or transgressions of primary rules are to be adjudicated. The manner in which

[1] Hans Kelsen developed a somewhat different version of this under his framework of a "theory of pure law" (Kelsen 1992), which was criticized in blistering terms by none other than Carl Schmitt. For an excellent critique of Raz from a friendlier tradition, see Martin 2014.

primary and secondary rules actually operate in concert within a legal system, in turn, has significant effects on social relationships and political power dynamics (indeed, this general line of inquiry is also explored to some extent in Summers 2006). As I explained in Chapter 1, political decisions and power relations structure the way legal institutions behave, but the outcomes of their behavior have second-order influences on social and political relationships and decisions.

Even mobilizational legal regimes are still legal systems. Their primary and secondary rules can change rapidly, as polities are contested and reconstituted. But they always have such rules. Their rules governing behavior often emphasize the promotion of specific agendas of social change or redistribution of political power. Likewise, their rules governing the making and adjudication of law frequently allow, even demand, intervention by nonlegal actors into the judicial process in ways that can seem alien to observers or students of some older or more established systems. But this does not make them, by definition, lawless or utterly disorderly, though we may rightly look upon many of them as normatively problematic or morally compromised. Rather than turning a blind eye, studying such regimes as legal systems lets us assess their political roots and implications with greater acuity.

Rule by law regimes are also legal systems, but with primary rules less subject to frequent change and secondary rules more familiar to scholars operating with a "classical rule of law" template in mind. Seeing these regimes in this light allows us to get beyond the crude image of cynical autocrats tying their own hands to promote efficiency and legitimacy, and to examine more nuanced aspects of many influential closed or authoritarian legal orders. In particular, treating rule by law regimes as legal systems can push us past puzzling over sometimes uncomfortable combinations of superficially incompatible attributes of democracy, oligarchy, development, and law.

Neotraditional regimes have primary rules that emphasize the maintenance of hierarchy, just as rule by law regimes do, but their secondary rules bear greater resemblance to their mobilizational cousins, in that they permit or even require a type of politicization of the adjudication process. Recognizing this lets us see how these regimes form a distinct subtype, not just conceptually but also in terms of actual systems operating on the ground. This, in turn, facilitates the systematic analysis of what are perhaps the most common systems of law throughout history and around the world today; systems that all too often have escaped scholarly notice.

Looking at instances of legal regimes as legal systems in a manner compatible with this sort of legal positivism has distinct advantages, even if it may do little to satisfy critics determined to ground legal practice and adjudication in *a priori* abstract covering-law moral principles (e.g. Dworkin 1986). Among the most obvious strengths of bringing legal regimes under the legal systems tent is the increased ability to analyze a much wider range of legal orders on their own terms, alongside more traditional comparators. We can examine elements or outcomes of legal politics in England or France alongside those in China or Indonesia, provided we take into account key dimensions of difference in their basic legal regimes. This is an advance on earlier scholarship that has frequently tended to write off important countries and cases as incomparable *in toto* (when bothering to consider them at all).

Once we admit that Indonesia or China has a legal system and define the contours of that system within a legal regime, we can make clearer and more powerful statements about law and politics there. Rather than dismissing the legal system of the Maoist period as simply hopelessly politicized, or that of New Order as similarly hopelessly corrupt, we can assess how specific factions in China or established military and commercial elites in Indonesia influenced the adjudication process in either the civil or criminal arena (or both) and what sorts of effects this had on two key aspects of politics: how judicial and legal institutions developed or atrophied at the ground level, and how the outcomes of adjudication influenced the dynamics of political or social relationships.

LEGAL REGIMES AND POLITICS

Legal regimes are products of political processes and power relations. As such, they embody the political realities from which they spring, even as they shape the contours of important areas of political and social life. By recognizing this causal duality, we can incorporate important insights of scholars who rightly point out that all law and adjudication are inherently political and bound up with power relations, while at the same time steering clear of any reductionist tendencies to assume – as some Marxians might – that all law is merely a superstructural reflection of the underlying relations of production, or – as some others might – that law exists only as an output of fundamentally undiscoverable internal intellectual or psychological processes in the minds of empowered actors.

Yet, deploying a new conceptual framework necessarily provokes several questions, the first among them: do Legal Regimes provide analytic leverage beyond a "law and politics" perspective? If they do, what sort of other outcomes, beyond those directly associated with politics, can be analyzed fruitfully through the lens of legal regimes? Finally, what are the limits of a legal regimes perspective?

There is no obvious reason to stop with narrowly political outcomes or phenomena in the application of legal regimes to social research. Broader social, economic, and relational outcomes can certainly be studied from similar angles. I deliberately excluded family law from this study because it does not fit easily with much of the rest of civil law and because it was not feasible to gather comparable data from Indonesia and China (due to the prevalence of religious courts as dispute-resolution venues in the former and of sealed family law records in the latter). But family law stands out as a ripe area for analysis from a legal regimes perspective. In fact, some work has already taken steps in this direction for the cases of China (e.g. Diamant 2001; Michelson 2003, 2007a) and Indonesia (e.g. O'Shaughnessy 2009). There are also obvious implications for reversing the gaze (or at least the roles of independent and dependent variables) of prior research (e.g. Michelson 2006, 2007a, 2007b; Liebman 2015), as it were, and examining the impacts of legal regimes back onto the social norms and relationships that underpin them. This would help supplement the field of law and society more generally, as most prior research in that tradition has tended to treat social norms and relations more as independent or causal factors (rather than outcomes), while looking at formal rules and institutions purely as outcomes of underlying social processes.

Still, there are limits. Studying legal regimes cannot get us inside the heads of individuals (or collectively of social groups) to let us see what they think about the law or how they perceive their relations to or within the legal system. Many questions that are central to much of the law and society literature may remain out of reach, even as legal regimes can open new, sometimes adjacent, topics and fields to more rigorous or holistic study.

On balance, legal regimes can bridge several important gaps between law and society, legal positivism, legal realism, critical legal studies, and political science research on law and legal institutions. Measured progress toward a more unified field of inquiry is possible, provided that concepts are specified clearly and their contours, complementary strengths, and corresponding limitations are kept in mind.

A FURTHER NOTE ON COMPARISON AND COMPARATIVE LEVERAGE

Comparing subnationally within China and Indonesia, across rural and urban areas, as well as between civil and criminal law and over different time periods, supplements my cross-national comparative analysis across the two countries by holding constant aspects of history, political ideology, and social structure. The within-country comparisons are "most-similar systems" or "method of difference" designs, while the between-country comparison is a "most-different systems" or "method of agreement" design. As discussed in Introduction and in Chapters 1 and 2, an important advantage of this two-step method is that it allows *both* for the control of variation on causal or independent variables *within* countries *and* for the control of variation in outcomes *across* countries. Holding variation constant across specific causal factors makes plain which ones are actually driving the processes or outcomes of interest. Looking subsequently at disparate national contexts in which similar outcomes obtain provides a test of the generalizability or idiosyncrasy of those revealed relationships.

Beyond the present study, the sort of two-step comparative method I have employed can be used to study multiple countries while examining more than simply national-level differences on some outcome or set of outcomes. It could also be applied to the study of regionally bounded phenomena that spring up in numerous and disparate national contexts, like ethnic conflict and separatism. Finally, this sort of approach could help facilitate more systematic cross-national comparative analysis of large countries scholars usually study in isolation – such as the United States, India, Russia, or China.

No method is without weaknesses, however. The two-step approach outlined here is substantially more challenging than most other cross-national or subnational comparative methods. Multiple countries must be engaged in equally sophisticated and nuanced ways, requiring greater efforts on the part of researchers in both data collection and interpretation than other methods. There are also many things the method cannot do and caution is required not to overextend claims of generalizability or universality based on it. Still, careful application of

Millian two-steps holds great potential for future research in comparative politics and beyond.

LAW AND POLITICS BEYOND INDONESIA AND CHINA

The concepts and arguments developed from this study of China and Indonesia can be extended into general frameworks and hypotheses, testable in contexts further afield. For instance, we might reimagine the Jim Crow South in the United States, from roughly 1880–1960, as a neotraditional order. Landowning whites occupied an entrenched position atop a hierarchy that included white sharecroppers, African-American landowners and sharecroppers, and shorter-term contingent agricultural laborers. This rigid hierarchy exerted exceptions over norms in all aspects of criminal and civil adjudication. Aside from widespread extralegal "mob justice" – in many cases involving lethal violence – formal legal dispute resolution and criminal punishment were imbued deeply with the power relations and influence of a closed polity and a set of legal institutions subject to constant intervention from other powerful actors. Understanding the American South during this critical era as a neotraditional legal regime, rather than some imperfect rule of law, helps us get past simplistic characterizations and to unpack its more fundamental dynamics.

Similarly, we can examine post-Soviet Russia with an eye to teasing out how various parts of its legal system have transformed from a mobilizational legal regime to some hybrid of neotraditionalism and rule by law, beginning even in the final decades of the USSR's existence (complete with widespread criminalization of civil disputes: Solomon 2013). This would offer greater analytical mileage than simply assessing its progress toward some ideal-typical rule of law or trying to fit its complex legal transformations into another Procrustean conceptual bed, such as that furnished by ideas of transitional justice. Russia in the time of Putin may be converging on what this book allows us to see as an equilibrium position in terms of its legal institutions and politics. But that equilibrium, of course, looks nothing like what a rule of law template would predispose us to see.

Even in a region as diverse and rapidly changing as Latin America, many countries likely resemble Indonesia, with hybrid legal regimes, neotraditional in the civil arena and rule by law in the criminal arena. This is because most Latin American countries are formal democracies, which at the same time are dominated by entrenched social and economic elites that seek actively to protect their advantaged positions in venues of legalized dispute-resolution – i.e. civil law. By conceiving of such Latin American legal regimes this way, researchers could analyze the politics of law and legal institutions in the region with greater acuity and in sharper comparative perspective, moving beyond a narrow focus on constitutions or elite judicial behavior.

Finally, there are some countries about which expert views are divided or unclear when it comes to characterizing the functioning of their legal systems. Japan is a prominent example, with a rigid and detailed constitution, at least nominally pluralistic democratic political system, seemingly conflicting patterns of legal activism (including on consumer advocacy, environmental and public health issues, taxpayer lawsuits, etc.), and general non-litigiousness. In criminal law, many have remarked on the widespread and persistent reliance on confessions, aspects of the penal system, and other idiosyncrasies of Japanese crime and punishment. While I do not have a ready hypothesis for how Japan might best be characterized using legal regimes, the basic framework could well prove useful in nailing down just how Japan's legal order works, the political and social roots of why it works that way, and what some of the broader implications might be.

By adopting legal regimes in place of less precise or more narrowly focused conceptual tools like transitional justice, law and economics, law and democratization, or law and development, researchers could place their work in sharper relief against the study of other places and times, and also articulate their arguments in crisper theoretical and conceptual terms. Legal regimes are not the only way to study law and politics, and they are not always the best way. But they do offer a window into how legal institutions operate, the politics of how they come to operate in such a way, and the broader social and political implications of their operation that is unclouded by teleological assumptions and that facilitates the comparison of law and legal systems across a wider range of national and temporal contexts than has been the norm to date. By taking some ideas from the study of China and Indonesia to places like Latin America, Russia, Japan, the United States, or beyond, scholars could advance this general project.

CONCLUSION

Indonesia is the world's largest and most important new democracy, yet little attention has been paid to the systematic study of its legal system. China is the largest country in the world by population and the most globally influential authoritarian state, but few researchers have focused on the dynamics of how its legal institutions work (choosing instead to confine their research to more specialized individual areas like commercial dispute resolution or reform through labor). This book is the first to approach the study of these two large and important countries' legal politics systematically *and* comparatively for the period from 1949 to the present day. It is also the first to make extensive use of the analysis of individual case materials from basic-level courts across multiple regions and time periods in both countries. As such, it illuminates numerous aspects of the Chinese and Indonesian legal systems that previously had been occluded and which thus are inherently valuable as subjects of study. But I hope it does more than that.

This book also puts forward a new theoretical and conceptual framework with broader implications. It sets the Indonesian and Chinese cases more sharply in a comparative context and also facilitates the comparative analysis of a wider universe of cases. In this, its utility should extend to a community of scholars beyond the relatively small circles of expertise on China or Indonesia.

Law may have inherent tendencies toward conservatism and stagnation, as well as (in at least some contexts) toward fierce contestation over fundamentally normative principles and claims. The study of law and legal institutions need not suffer from the same pathologies. Closely engaged, informed, and nuanced scholarship on a larger world of law than just the traditional Common Law or European core promises new theoretical insights as well as new knowledge about the nuts and bolts of prosecution or dispute resolution in different contexts. Like poor Mr. Block, the beleaguered corn merchant awaiting trial for some unknown crime (and fellow client of Joseph K's imperious lawyer, who mocks his ignorance) in Kafka's story, we have toiled much and come a long way in our study of law and politics, but we have hardly yet begun.

Han Fei and Grotius were both right. All rulers or governments need law to substantiate and systematize their rule. But private actors also always have recourse to legal activism and even manipulation. This is as true for Indonesian businessmen and police officers, or for Chinese farmers and Party cadres, as it is for American district attorneys or German environmentalists. Legal regimes shape the politics of legal institutions, even where many might assume law to be impotent or nonexistent. Their influence may certainly not always be normatively positive or consistent, but it demands to be understood on its own terms and in specific national and historical contexts. If nothing else, future scholarship may refine and reassess what I have argued here to extend the boundaries of inquiry, while also more accurately describing the politics of legal institutions around the world. And that would indeed be "an unqualified human good."

REFERENCES

Agamben, Giorgio (1998). *Homo Sacer: Sovereign Power and Bare Life* [Translated by Daniel Heller-Roazen]. Stanford, CA: Stanford University Press.

Alford, William P. (1995). "Tasselled Loafers for Barefoot Lawyers: Transformations and Tensions in the World of Chinese Lawyers." *The China Quarterly* 141: 22–38.

(ed.) (2007). *Raising the Bar: The Emerging Legal Profession in East Asia.* Cambridge, MA: Harvard University Press.

Alisjahbana, S. Takdir (1966). *Indonesia: Social and Cultural Revolution.* Kuala Lumpur: Oxford University Press.

Allen, Franklin, Jun Qian, & Meijun Qian (2005). "Law, Finance, and Economic Growth in China." *Journal of Financial Economics* 77(1): 57–116.

Andreas, Joel (2007). "The Structure of Charismatic Mobilization: A Case Study of Rebellion during the Chinese Cultural Revolution." *American Sociological Review* 72(3): 434–58.

Ang, Yuen Yuen & Nan Jia (2014). "Perverse Complementarity: Political Connections and the Use of Courts among Private Firms in China." *The Journal of Politics* 76(2): 318–32.

Aristotle (1984). *The Politics* [Translated, with Introduction, Notes, and Glossary by Carnes Lord]. Chicago, IL: University of Chicago Press.

Aryadi, Gregorius (1995). *Putusan Hakim dalam Perkara Pidana: Studi Kasus Tentang Pencurian dan Korupsi di Daerah Istimewa Yogyakarta [Judges' Decisions in Criminal Cases: A Study of Cases about Theft and Corruption in the Yogyakarta Special Region].* Yogyakarta: Universitas Atma Jaya.

Asrun, A. Muhammad (2004). *Krisis Peradilan: Makamah Agung di Bawah Soeharto [Crisis of Justice: The Supreme Court under Suharto].* Jakarta: ELSAM.

Ball, John (1982). *Indonesian Legal History, 1602–1848.* Sydney: Oughtershaw Press.

Balme, Stéphanie (2010). "Local Courts in Western China: The Quest for Independence and Dignity," in Randall Peerenboom (ed.) *Judicial Independence in China: Lessons for Global Rule of Law Promotion.* Cambridge: Cambridge University Press, pp. 154–79.

Barry, Donald D., George Ginsburgs, & Peter B. Maggs (eds.) (1979). *Soviet Law after Stalin*. Leyden: A.W. Sijthoff.

Baumgartner, Frank R. & Bryan D. Jones (1993). *Agendas and Instability in American Politics*. Chicago, IL: University of Chicago Press.

Bedner, Adriaan (2001). *Administrative Courts in Indonesia: A Socio-Legal Study*. The Hague: Kluwer Law International.

Belkin, Ira (2000). "China's Criminal Justice System: A Work in Progress." *Washington Journal of Modern China* 6(2): 61–84.

Bennett, Gordon (1976). *Yundong: Mass Campaigns in Chinese Communist Leadership*. Berkeley, CA: Center for Chinese Studies, China Research Monographs.

Benton, Lauren (2002). *Law and Colonial Cultures: Legal Regimes in World History, 1400–1900*. Cambridge: Cambridge University Press.

Berman, Harold J. (1963). *Justice in the U.S.S.R.: An Interpretation of Soviet Law*. Cambridge, MA: Harvard University Press.

(1970). "Soviet Perspectives on Chinese Law," in J. A. Cohen (ed.) *Contemporary Chinese Law: Research Problems and Perspectives*. Cambridge, MA: Cambridge University Press, pp. 313–27.

(1983). *Law and Revolution: The Formation of the Western Legal Tradition*. Cambridge, MA: Harvard University Press.

Bertrand, Jacques (1995). *Compliance, Resistance, and Trust: Peasants and the State in Indonesia*, PhD Dissertation in Politics, Princeton University

Biddulph, Sarah (2007). *Legal Reform and Administrative Detention Powers in China*. Cambridge: Cambridge University Press.

Blasek, Katrin (2015). *Rule of Law in China: A Comparative Approach*. Heidelberg: Springer.

Boone, Catherine (2014). *Property and Political Order in Africa: Land Rights and the Structure of Politics*. Cambridge: Cambridge University Press.

Borschberg, Peter (2011). *Hugo Grotius, the Portuguese, and Free Trade in the East Indies*. Singapore: NUS Press.

Bosma, Ulbe (2007). "The Cultivation System (1830–1870) and its Private Entrepreneurs on Colonial Java." *Journal of Southeast Asian Studies* 38(2): 275–91.

(2013). *The Sugar Plantation in India and Indonesia, 1770–2010*. Cambridge: Cambridge University Press.

Bowen, John R. (2003). *Islam, Law and Equality in Indonesia: An Anthropology of Public Reasoning*. Cambridge: Cambridge University Press

Breman, Jan (2010). *Kolonial Profijt van Onvrije Arbeid: Het Praenger Stelsel van Gedwongen Koffieteelt op Java, 1720–1870 [Colonial Profit from Unfree Labor: the Praenger System of Forced Coffee Cultivation on Java, 1720–1870]*. Amsterdam: Amsterdam University Press.

Brondgeest, J. P. T. J. (1897). *Het Burgerlijk Wetboek voor Nederlandsch-Indië [The Civil Code for the Netherlands' Indies]*. Batavia & 's Gravenhage: G. Kolff & Co.

Brown, Nathan J. (1997). *The Rule of Law in the Arab World: Courts in Egypt and the Gulf*. Cambridge: Cambridge University Press.

Buehler, Michael (2008). "Shari'a By-Laws in Indonesian Districts: an Indication for Changing Patterns of Power Accumulation and Political Corruption." *Southeast Asia Research* 16(2): 165–95.

(2016). *The Politics of Shari'a Law: Islamist Activists and the State in Democratizing Indonesia*. Cambridge: Cambridge University Press.

Buehler, Michael & Paige Johnson Tan (2007). "Party–Candidate Relationships in Indonesian Local Politics: A Case Study of the 2005 Regional Elections in Gowa, South Sulawesi Province." *Indonesia* 84: 41–69.

Burbank, Jane (1995). "Lenin and Law in Revolutionary Russia." *Slavic Review* 54(1): 23–44.

Burns, Peter (2004). *The Leiden Legacy: Concepts of Law in Indonesia*. Leiden: KITLV Press.

Butt, Simon (2008). "Surat Sakti: the Decline of Judicial Decisions in Indonesia," in Tim Lindsey (ed.) *Indonesia: Law and Society* (2nd Edition). Annendale: The Federation Press, pp. 346–62.

Carlson, Allen, Mary E. Gallagher, & Melanie Manion (2010). "Introduction" in Allen Carlson, Mary E. Gallagher, Kenneth Lieberthal, and Melanie Manion (eds.) *Contemporary Chinese Politics: New Sources, Methods, and Field Strategies*. Cambridge: Cambridge University Press, pp. 1–14.

Carlson, Allen, Mary Gallagher, Kenneth Lieberthal, & Melanie Manion (eds.) (2010). *Contemporary Chinese Politics: New Sources, Methods, and Field Strategies*. Cambridge: Cambridge University Press.

Cheesman, Nick (2015). *Opposing the Rule of Law: How Myanmar's Courts Make Law and Order*. Cambridge: Cambridge University Press.

Chen, Jianfu (1995). *From Administrative Authorisation to Private Law; A Comparative Perspective of the Developing Civil Law in the People's Republic of China*. Dordrecht: Martinus Nijhoff Publishers.

(2013). *Criminal Law and Procedure in the People's Republic of China: Commentary and Legislation*. Leiden: Brill.

Ch'ü, T'ung-tsu (1961). *Law and Society in Traditional China*. Paris: Mouton.

Cicero, Marcus Tullius (1928). *De Re Publica & De Legibus* [with English Translation by Clinton Walker Keyes]. London: William Heinemann.

Cioffi, John W. (2009). "Legal Regimes and Political Particularlism: An Assessment of the 'Legal Families' Theory from the Perspectives of Comparative Law and Political Economy." *Brigham Young University Law Review* 2009(6): 1501–52.

Clarke, Donald C. (1996a). "Power and the Politics of the Chinese Court System: the Execution of Civil Judgments." *Columbia Journal of Asian Law* 10(1): 1–92.

(1996b). "The Creation of a Legal Structure for Market Institutions in China," in John McMillan & Barry Naughton (eds.) *Reforming Asian*

Socialism: the Growth of Market Institutions. Ann Arbor, MI: University of Michigan Press, pp. 39–59.

(1998–1999). "Alternative Approaches to Chinese Law: Beyond the 'Rule of Law' Paradigm." *Waseda Proceedings of Comparative Law* 2: 49–62.

(2003). "Economic Development and the Rights Hypotheses: The China Problem." *American Journal of Comparative Law* 51(1): 89–111.

Clarke, Donald C. & James V. Feinerman (1995). "Antagonistic Contradictions: Criminal Law and Human Rights in China." *The China Quarterly* 141: 135–54.

Cohen, Jerome Alan (1968). *The Criminal Process in the People's Republic of China, 1949–1963; An Introduction*. Cambridge: Harvard University Press.

Collier, Ruth Berins & David Collier (1991). *Shaping the Political Arena: Critical Junctures, the Labor Movement, and Regime Dynamics in Latin America*. Princeton, NJ: Princeton University Press.

Cover, Robert M. (1986). "Violence and the Word." *The Yale Law Journal* 95(8): 1601–29.

Crouch, Melissa (2013). *Law and Religion in Indonesia: Conflict and the Courts in West Java*. Abingdon: Routledge.

Dahl, Robert A. (1972). *Polyarchy: Participation and Opposition*. New Haven, CT: Yale University Press.

Damaska, Mirjan R. (1991). *The Faces of Justice and State Authority: A Comparative Approach to the Legal Process*. New Haven, CT: Yale University Press.

David, René & John E. C. Brierley (1985). *Major Legal Systems in the World Today* (3rd Edition). London: Stevens & Sons.

Davidson, Jamie S. & David Henley (eds.) (2007). *The Revival of Tradition in Indonesian Politics: The Deployment of Adat from Colonialism to Indigenism*. London: Routledge.

De Bussy, J. H. (1918). *Geschiedenis van Het Wetboek van Strafrecht voor Nederlandsch-Indië [History of the Criminal Code for the Netherlands' Indies]*. Amsterdam: J.H. de Bussy.

De Greiff, Pablo & Roger Duthie (eds.) (2009). *Transitional Justice and Development: Making Connections*. New York: Social Science Research Council.

Dermawan, I. Gede (1985). *Eksekusi Perkara Perdata dalam Praktek [The Execution of Civil Cases in Practice]*. Denpasar: Laporan Penelitian Fakultas Hukum Universitas Udayana.

Diamant, Neil J. (2001). "Making Love Legible in China: Politics and Society during the Enforcement of Civil Marriage Registration, 1950–1966." *Politics and Society* 29(3): 447–80.

Diamant, Neil J., Stanley B. Lubman, & Kevin J. O'Brien (eds.) (2005). *Engaging the Law in China: State, Society, and Possibilities for Justice*. Stanford, CA: Stanford University Press.

Dicey, Albert Venn (1889). *Introduction to the Study of the Law of the Constitution*. London: MacMillan.
Dressel, Bjoern (2015). "Courts and Judicialization in Southeast Asia," in William Case (ed.) *Routledge Handbook of Southeast Asian Democratization*. Abingdon: Routledge, pp. 268–81.
Durkheim, Émile (1978). *The Division of Labor in Society* [Translated by George Simpson] Glencoe: Free Press.
Dutton, Michael (1992). *Policing and Punishment in China*. Cambridge: Cambridge University Press.
(2005). *Policing Chinese Politics, A History*. Durham: Duke University Press.
Dutton, Michael & Tianfu Lee (1993). "Missing the Target? Policing Strategies in the Period of Economic Reform," *Crime and Delinquency* 39(3): 316–36.
Dworkin, Ronald (1986). *Law's Empire*. Cambridge, MA: Harvard University Press.
Effendi, Masyhur (1981). *Laporan Hasil Penelitian: Persepsi Hakim Pidana didalam Menjatuhkan Keputusan (Penghayatan dan Pengalaman Hak Asasi Manusia) pada Beberapa Pengadilan Negeri Jawa Timur [Report of Research Results: Perceptions of Criminal Judges in Handing Down Decisions (Appreciation and Experience of Human Rights) in Several Local Courts of East Java]*. Malang: Universitas Brawijaya.
Epp, Charles R. (1998). *The Rights Revolution: Lawyers, Activists, and the Supreme Court in Comparative Perspective*. Chicago, IL: University of Chicago Press.
Erb, Maribeth, Carole Faucher, & Priyambudi Sulistianto (eds.) (2009). *Regionalism in Post-Suharto Indonesia*. New York: Routledge.
Estlund, Cynthia L. (2002). "The Ossification of American Labor Law." *Columbia Law Review* 102(6): 1527–612.
Evans, Peter B. (1979). *Dependent Development: The Alliance of Multinational, State, and Local Capital in Brazil*. Princeton, NJ: Princeton University Press.
Ewick, Patricia & Susan S. Sibley (1998). *The Common Place of Law*. Chicago, IL: University of Chicago Press.
Fasseur, Cornelis (1992). *The Politics of Colonial Exploitation: Java, The Dutch, and the Cultivation System* [trans. R. E. Elson & Ary Kraal; (ed.) R. E. Elson]. Ithaca, NY: Cornell Southeast Asia Program.
Feener, R. Michael (2013). *Shari'a and Social Engineering: The Implementation of Islamic Law in Contemporary Aceh, Indonesia*. Oxford: Oxford University Press.
Feith, Herbert (1962). *The Decline of Constitutional Democracy in Indonesia*. Ithaca, NY: Cornell University Press.
Finch, Susan & Daniel S. Lev (eds.) (1965). *Republic of Indonesia Cabinets, 1945–1965*. Ithaca, NY: Cornell University Modern Indonesia Project.

Frazier, Mark W. (2010). *Socialist Insecurity: Pensions and the Politics of Uneven Development in China*. Ithaca, NY: Cornell University Press.

Fu, Hualing (1998). "Criminal Defence in China: The Possible Impact of the Criminal Procedural Law Reform." *The China Quarterly* 153: 31–48.

Fu, Hualing & Richard Cullen (2011). "From Mediatory to Adjudicatory Justice: The Limits of Civil Justice Reform in China," in Margaret Y.K. Woo & Mary E. Gallagher (eds.) *Chinese Justice: Civil Dispute Resolution in Contemporary China*. Cambridge: Cambridge University Press, pp. 15–57.

Fuller, Douglas B. (2010). "How Law, Politics, and Transnational Networks Affect Technology Entrepreneurship: Explaining Divergent Venture Capital Investing Strategies in China." *Asia Pacific Journal of Management* 27(3): 445–59.

Furnivall, J. S. (1956). *Colonial Policy and Practice: A Comparative Study of Burma and Netherlands India*. New York: New York University Press.

Gaastra, Femme S. (1989). *Bewind en Beleid bij de VOC: De Financiële en Commerciële Politiek van de Bewindhebbers, 1672–1702 [Government and Policy in the VOC: The Financial and Commercial Politics of the Directors, 1672–1702]*. Zutphen: Walburg Pers.

(2003). *The Dutch East India Company: Expansion and Decline* [Translated by Peter Daniels]. Zutphen: Walburg Pers.

Gallagher, Mary E. (2006). "Mobilizing the Law in China: 'Informed Disenchantment' and the Development of Legal Consciousness." *Law and Society Review* 40(4): 783–816.

(2017). *Authoritarian Legality in China: Law, Workers, and the State*. Cambridge: Cambridge University Press.

Gans-Morse, Jordan (2017). *Property Rights in Post-Soviet Russia: Violence, Corruption, and the Demand for Law*. Cambridge: Cambridge University Press.

Garlan, Edward N. (1941). *Legal Realism and Justice*. New York: Columbia University Press.

Geertz, Clifford (1963). *Agricultural Involution: The Processes of Economical Change in Indonesia*. Berkeley, CA: University of California Press.

Gibson, Edward L. (2013). *Boundary Control: Subnational Authoritarianism in Federal Democracies*. Cambridge: Cambridge University Press.

Ginsburg, Tom (2000). "Does Law Matter for Economic Development? Evidence from East Asia." *Law and Society Review* 34(3): 829–56.

(2003). *Judicial Review in New Democracies: Constitutional Courts in Asian Cases*. Cambridge: Cambridge University Press.

(2010). "The Politics of Courts in Democratization," in James J. Heckman, Robert L. Nelson, & Lee Cabatingan (eds.) *Global Perspectives on the Rule of Law*. Abingdon: Routledge, pp. 175–91.

(2011). "Pitfalls of Measuring the Rule of Law." *Hague Journal on the Rule of Law* 3(2): 269–80.

Ginsburg, Tom & Tamir Moustafa (eds.) (2008). *Rule By Law: The Politics of Courts in Authoritarian Regimes*. Cambridge: Cambridge University Press.

Ginsburg, Tom, Zachary Elkins, & James Melton (2009). *The Endurance of National Constitutions*. Cambridge: Cambridge University Press.

Givens, John Wagner (2013). *Suing Dragons? Taking the Chinese State to Court*, DPhil Dissertation in Politics and International Relations, University of Oxford.

Gong, Ting (2008). "The Party Discipline Inspection in China: Its Evolving Trajectory and Embedded Dilemmas." *Crime, Law and Social Change* 49(2): 139–52.

Goodpaster, Gary (2007). "Law Reform in Developing Countries," in Tim Lindsey (ed.) *Law Reform in Developing and Transitional States*. London: Routledge, pp. 106–39.

Government Printing (1914). *Atoeran Pengadilan Landgerecht di Tanah Djawa dan Madoera [Regulations on Courts of the First Instance in Java and Madura]*. Batavia: Landsdrukkerij.

Grotius, Hugo (1950). *De Iure Praedae Commentarius: Commentary on the Law of Prize and Booty* [Translated by Gwladys L. Williams & Walter H. Zeydel] Oxford: The Clarendon Press.

Gudoshnikov, Leonid Moiseevich (1959). *Legal Organs of the People's Republic of China* [JPRS Translation of Book Originally Published in 1957]. New York: United States Joint Publication Research Service.

Guo, Xuezhi (2014). "Controlling Corruption in the Party: China's Central Discipline Inspection Commission." *The China Quarterly* 219: 597–624.

Han, Bing Siong (1961). *An Outline of the Recent History of Indonesian Criminal Law*. 's Gravenhage: Martinus Nijhoff.

(1998). "The Japanese Occupation of Indonesia and the Administration of Justice Today: Myths and Realities." *Bijdragen tot de Taal-, Land- en Volkenkunde* 154(3): 416–56.

Han, Fei (1939). *The Complete Works of Han Fei Tzu (韓非子): A Classic of Chinese Legalism, Volume I* [Translated with Introduction, Notes, Glossary, and Index by W.K. Liao]. London: Arthur Probsthain.

Hariyani, Iswi, I. Wayan Yasa & M. Khoidin (2002). *Kepastian Hukum Eksekusi Putusan Pengadilan dalam Perkara Perdata [The Legal Certitude of Execution of Court Decisions in Civil Cases]*. Jember: Laporan Penelitian Fakultas Hukum Universitas Jember.

Hart, Herbert Lionel Adolphus (1994). *The Concept of Law* (2nd Edition). Oxford: Clarendon Press.

Hayek, Friedrich August (1944). *The Road to Serfdom*. London: Routledge.

(1982). *Law, Legislation and Liberty: A New Statement on the Liberal Principles of Justice and Political Economy*. London: Routledge & Kegan Paul.

Hayner, Priscilla B. (2010). *Unspeakable Truths: Transitional Justice and the Challenge of Truth Commissions*. London: Routledge.

Hazard, John N. (1960). *Settling Disputes in Soviet Society: The Formative Years of Legal Institutions*. New York: Columbia University Press.

(1965). "Unity and Diversity in Socialist Law." *Law and Contemporary Problems* 30: 270–90.

He, Ni (2014). *Chinese Criminal Trials: A Comprehensive Empirical Inquiry*. New York: Springer.

He, Xin (2009). "Enforcing Commercial Judgments in the Pearl River Delta of China." *American Journal of Comparative Law* 59(2): 41956.

(2011). "Debt-Collection in the Less Developed Regions of China: An Empirical Study from a Basic-Level Court in Shaanxi Province." *The China Quarterly* 206: 253–75.

(2012). "Black Hole of Responsibility: The Adjudication Committee's Role in a Chinese Court." *Law and Society Review* 46(4): 681–712.

He, Xin & Yang Su (2013). "Do the 'Haves' Come Out Ahead in Shanghai Courts?" *Journal of Empirical Legal Studies* 10(1): 120–45.

Helmke, Gretchen (2004). *Courts under Constraints: Judges, Generals, and Presidents in Argentina*. Cambridge: Cambridge University Press.

Hendley, Kathryn (1996). *Trying to Make Law Matter: Legal Reform and Labor Law in the Soviet Union*. Ann Arbor, MI: University of Michigan Press.

(1997). "Legal Development in Post-Soviet Russia." *Post-Soviet Affairs* 13(3): 228–51.

(2017). *Everyday Law in Russia*. Ithaca, NY: Cornell University Press.

Hilbink, Lisa (2007). *Judges beyond Politics in Democracy and Dictatorship: Lessons from Chile*. Cambridge: Cambridge University Press.

Hinton, Alexander Laban (ed.) (2011). *Transitional Justice: Global Mechanisms and Local Realities after Genocide and Mass Violence*. New Brunswick: Rutgers University Press.

Hirschl, Ran (2004). *Towards Juristocracy: The Origins and Consequences of the New Constitutionalism*. Cambridge MA: Harvard University Press.

Hobbes, Thomas (1985). *Leviathan* [Edited with an Introduction by C. B. MacPherson]. New York: Penguin Books.

Hooker, Michael Barry (1978). *A Concise Legal History of South-East Asia*. Oxford: Clarendon Press.

Hosen, Nadirsyah (2003). "Indonesian Political Laws in Habibie Era: Between Political Struggle and Law Reform." *Nordic Journal of International Law* 72: 481–518.

Howson, Nicholas Calcina (2010). "Judicial Independence and the Company Law in the Shanghai Courts," in Randall Peerenboom (ed.) *Judicial Independence in China: Lessons for Global rule of Law Promotion*. Cambridge: Cambridge University Press, pp. 134–53.

Huang, Philip C. C. (2001). *Code, Custom, and Legal Practice in China: The Qing and the Republic Compared*. Stanford, CA: Stanford University Press.

Huntington, Samuel P. (1968). *Political Order in Changing Societies*. New Haven, CT: Yale University Press.

Hurst, William (2009). *The Chinese Worker after Socialism*. Cambridge: Cambridge University Press.

(2010). "Cases, Questions, and Comparison in Research on Contemporary Chinese Politics," in Allen Carlson, Mary Gallagher, Kenneth Lieberthal, & Melanie Manion (eds.) *Contemporary Chinese Politics: New Sources, Methods, and Field Strategies*. Cambridge: Cambridge University Press, pp. 162–77.

(2011). "Politics, Society, and the Legal System in Contemporary China," in John Garrick (ed.) *Law, Wealth, and Power in China: Commercial Law Reforms in Context*. London: Routledge, pp. 72–88.

(2015). "Criminalizing Civil Justice in China and Indonesia." Paper presented at the Midwest Political Science Association Annual Meeting, Chicago, IL.

(2016). "Chinese Law and Governance: Moving Beyond Responsive Authoritarianism and the Rule of Law." *Journal of Chinese Governance* 1(3): 457–69.

Hurst, William & Kevin J. O'Brien (2002). "China's Contentious Pensioners." *The China Quarterly* 170: 345–60.

Ikatan Hakim Indonesia (1965). *Ajo Berkonggres! [Come Let Us Congress!]*. Surakarta: Bagian Publikasi Ikatan Hakim Indonesia Ranting Surakarta.

Jacob, Herbert, Erhard Blankenburg, Herbert M. Kritzer, Doris Marie Provine, & Joseph Sanders (1996). *Courts, Law, and Politics in Comparative Perspective*. New Haven, CT: Yale University Press.

Jacobsohn, Gary Jeffrey (2003). *The Wheel of Law: India's Secularism in Comparative Constitutional Context*. Princeton, NJ: Princeton University Press.

Ji, Weidong (2009). "'To Take the Law as the Public': The Diversification of Society and Legal Discourse in Contemporary China," in Stéphanie Balme & Michael W. Dowdle (eds.) *Building Constitutionalism in China*. New York & Basingstoke: Palgrave-MacMillan, pp. 125–40.

Jones, Carol (2005). "Crime and Criminal Justice in China, 1949–1999," in James Sheptycki & Ali Wardak (eds.) *Transnational and Comparative Criminology*. London: GlassHouse Press, pp. 179–207.

Jowitt, Ken (1974). "An Organizational Approach to the Study of Political Culture in Marxist-Leninist Systems." *American Political Science Review* 68(3): 1171–91.

(1975). "Inclusion and Mobilization in European Leninist Regimes." *World Politics* 28(1): 69–97.

(1987). "Moscow 'Center'." *East European Politics & Societies* 1(3): 296–348.

Joyner, Christopher C. (1999). *Governing the Frozen Commons; The Antarctic Regime and Environmental Protection*. Columbia, SC: University of South Carolina Press.

Kafka, Franz (2005). *The Trial, with an Epilogue by Max Brod* (Translated by Edwin Muir). London: Vintage.
Kahin, George McTurnan (2003). *Nationalism and Revolution in Indonesia.* Ithaca, NY: Cornell Southeast Asia Program (originally published in 1952 by Cornell University Press).
Kang, David C. (2002). *Crony Capitalism: Corruption and Development in South Korea and the Philippines.* Cambridge: Cambridge University Press.
Kelsen, Hans (1992). *Introduction to the Problems of Legal Theory* [Translated from the original German by: Bonnie Litschewski Paulson & Stanley L. Paulson]. Oxford: Oxford University Press.
Kennedy, Duncan (1987). "Toward a Critical Phenomenology of Judging," in A. C. Huchinson & P. Monahan (eds.) *The Rule of Law: Ideal or Ideology.* Toronto: Carswell, pp. 141–67.
Kingsbury, Damien & Harry Aveling (eds.) (2003). *Autonomy and Disintegration in Indonesia.* London: Routledge.
Kinkel, Jonathan J. (2015). "High-End Demand: The Legal Profession as a Source of Judicial Selection Reform in Urban China." *Law and Social Inquiry* 40(4): 969–1000.
Kinkel, Jonathan J. & William Hurst (2015). "The Judicial Cadre Evaluation System in China: From Quantification to Intra-State Legibility." *The China Quarterly* 224: 933–54.
Klug, Heinz & Sally Engle Merry (2016). "Introduction," in Heinz Klug & Sally Engle Merry (eds.) *The New Legal Realism, Volume II: Studying Law Globally.* Cambridge: Cambridge University Press, pp. 1–9.
Krasner, Stephen D. (ed.) (1983). *International Regimes.* Ithaca: Cornell University Press.
Landry, Pierre (2008). "The Institutional Diffusion of Courts in China: Evidence from Survey Data," in Tom Ginsburg & Tamir Moustafa (eds.) *Rule by Law: The Politics of Courts in Authoritarian Regimes.* Cambridge: Cambridge University Press, pp. 207–34.
Lev, Daniel S. (1966). *The Transition to Guided Democracy: Indonesian Politics, 1957–1959.* Ithaca, NY: Cornell Southeast Asia Program.
(1972). "Judicial Institutions and Legal Culture in Indonesia," in Claire Holt et al. (eds.) *Culture and Politics in Indonesia.* Ithaca, NY: Cornell University Press, pp. 247–318.
(1973a). "Bush-Lawyers in Indonesia: Stratification, Representation, and Brokerage." University of California, Berkeley, Working Paper Number 1 from the Program in Law and Society.
(1973b). *Islamic Courts in Indonesia: A Study in the Political Bases of Legal Institutions.* Berkeley, CA: University of California Press.
(2000). *Legal Evolution and Political Authority in Indonesia, Selected Essays.* The Hague: Kluwer Law International.

(2000a). "Judicial Unification in Post-Colonial Indonesia," in Daniel S. Lev (ed.) *Legal Evolution and Political Authority in Indonesia: Selected Essays*. Cambridge, MA: Kluwer Law International, pp. 33–70.

(2000b). "The Lady and the Banyan Tree: Civil Law Change in Indonesia," in Daniel S. Lev (ed.) *Legal Evolution and Political Authority in Indonesia: Selected Essays*. Cambridge, MA: Kluwer Law International, pp. 119–42.

(2000c). "Between State and Society: Professional Lawyers and Reform in Indonesia," in Daniel S. Lev (ed.) *Legal Evolution and Political Authority in Indonesia: Selected Essays*. Cambridge, MA: Kluwer Law International, pp. 305–36.

Li, Ling (2016a). "The Rise of the Discipline and Inspection Commission, 1927–2012: Anticorruption Investigation and Decision-Making in the Chinese Communist Party." *Modern China* 42(5): 447–82.

(2016b). "The Chinese Communist Party and People's Courts." *American Journal of Comparative Law* 64(1): 37–74.

Li, Tania (2001). "Masyarakat Adat, Difference, and the Limits of Recognition in Indonesia's Forest Zone." *Modern Asian Studies* 35(3): 645–76.

Li, Yuwen (2014). *The Judicial System and Reform in Post-Mao China: Stumbling Towards Justice*. Farnham: Ashgate.

Liang, Bin (2008). *The Changing Chinese Legal System, 1978–Present: Centralization of Power and Rationalization of the Legal System*. New York: Routledge.

Liebman, Benjamin L. (2007). "China's Courts: Restricted Reform." *The China Quarterly* 191: 620–38.

(2015). "Leniency in Chinese Criminal Law? Everyday Justice in Henan." *Berkeley Journal of International Law* 33(1): 153–222.

Lin, Ye (1989). "The Tort System in China" [Translated by Li Xiaoming & Henry Pitney]. *Law and Contemporary Problems* 52(3): 143–67.

Lindsey, Tim (2001). "The Criminal State: Premanisme and the New Indonesia," in Grayson J. Lloyd & Shannon L. Smith (eds.) *Indonesia Today: Challenges of History*. Lantham: Rowman & Littlefield, pp. 283–97.

(2006). "From Soepomo to Prabowo: Law, Violence, and Corruption in the *Preman State*," in Charles A. Choppel (ed.) *Violent Conflicts in Indonesia: Analysis, Representation, Resolution*. Abingdon: Routledge, pp. 19–36.

(ed.) (2008). *Indonesia: Law and Society*. Sydney: The Federation Press.

Lindsey, Tim & Mas Achmad Santosa (2008). "The Trajectory of Law Reform in Indonesia: A Short Overview of Legal Systems and Change in Indonesia," in Tim Lindsey (ed.) *Indonesia: Law and Society* (2nd Edition). Sydney: The Federation Press, pp. 2–22.

Liu, Sida (2006a). "Beyond Global Convergence: Conflicts of Legitimacy in a Chinese Lower Court." *Law and Social Inquiry* 31(1): 75–106.

(2006b). "Client Influence and the Contingency of Professionalism: The Work of Elite Corporate Lawyers in China." *Law and Society Review* 40(4): 751–82.

Liu, Sida & Terence C. Halliday (2009). "Recursivity in Legal Change: Lawyers and Reforms of China's Criminal Procedure Law." *Law & Social Inquiry* 34(4): 911–50.

(2016). *Criminal Defense in China: The Politics of Lawyers at Work*. Cambridge: Cambridge University Press.

Locke, John (1690). *Two Treatises of Government*. London: A. Churchill.

Lötveit, Trygve (1973). *Chinese Communism, 1931–1934: Experience in Civil Government*. Lund: Studentlitt.

Lubman, Stanley B. (1970). "Methodological Problems in Studying Chinese Communist 'Civil Law'," in J. A. Cohen (ed.) *Contemporary Chinese Law: Research Problems and Perspectives*. Cambridge, MA: Cambridge University Press, pp. 230–60.

(1999). *Bird in a Cage: Legal Reform in China after Mao*. Stanford, CA: Stanford University Press.

Lutiko, Ratno (2013). *Legal Pluralism in Indonesia: Bridging the Unbridgeable*. Abingdon: Routledge.

Ma, Zhao (2015). *Runaway Wives, Urban Crimes, and Survival Tactics in Wartime Beijing, 1937–1949*. Cambridge, MA: Harvard University Press.

Mahfud MD, Moh. (1998). *Politik Hukum di Indonesia [Legal Politics in Indonesia]*. Jakarta: LP3ES.

(2009). *Politik Hukum di Indonesia (edisi revisi) [Legal Politics in Indonesia (revised edition)]*. Jakarta: Rajawali Pers.

Makamah Agung (1997a). *Beberapa Putusan Berkuatan Hukum tetap pada Pengadilan Negeri dan Pengadilan Tinggi di Wilayah Hukum Pengadilan Tinggi Balikpapan [Several Decisions Enforced Legally in the District Courts and the High Court in the Area of Jurisdiction of the High Court of Balikpapan]*. Jakarta: Makamah Agung.

(1997b). *Beberapa Putusan Berkuatan Hukum tetap pada Pengadilan Negeri dan Pengadilan Tinggi di Wilayah Hukum Pengadilan Tinggi Jawa Barat [Several Decisions Enforced Legally in the District Courts and the High Court in the Area of Jurisdiction of the High Court of West Java]*. Jakarta: Makamah Agung.

(1997c). *Beberapa Putusan Berkuatan Hukum tetap pada Pengadilan Negeri dan Pengadilan Tinggi di Wilayah Hukum Pengadilan Tinggi Medan dan Riau [Several Decisions Enforced Legally in the District Courts and the High Court in the Area of Jurisdiction of the High Court of Medan and Riau]*. Jakarta: Makamah Agung.

(1997d). *Beberapa Putusan Berkuatan Hukum tetap pada Pengadilan Negeri dan Pengadilan Tinggi di Wilayah Hukum Pengadilan Tinggi Yogyakarta [Several Decisions Enforced Legally in the District Courts and the High Court in the Area of Jurisdiction of the High Court of Yogyakarta]*. Jakarta: Makamah Agung.

Martin, Brian G. (1996). *The Shanghai Green Gang: Politics and Organized Crime, 1919–1937*. Berkeley, CA: University of California Press.

Martin, Margaret (2014). *Judging Positivism*. Oxford & Portland OR: Hart Publishing.

Massier, Ab (2008). *The Voice of the Law in Transition: Indonesian Jurists and their Languages, 1915–2000*. Leiden: KITLV Press.

Massoud, Mark Fathi (2013). *Law's Fragile State: Colonial, Authoritarian, and Humanitarian Legacies in Sudan*. Cambridge: Cambridge University Press.

Mattei, Ugo & Laura Nader (2008). *Plunder: When the Rule of Law is Illegal*. Oxford: Blackwell.

McCann, Michael W. (1994). *Rights at Work: Pay Equity Reform and the Politics of Legal Mobilization*. Chicago, IL: University of Chicago Press.

(2016). "Preface to The New Legal Realism, Volumes I and II," in Heinz Klug & Sally Engle Merry (eds.) *The New Legal Realism, Volume II: Studying Law Globally*. Cambridge: Cambridge University Press, pp. xv–xxiii.

McConville, Mike et al. (2011). *Criminal Justice in China: An Empirical Inquiry*. London: Edward Elgar.

McMillan, Richard (2005). *The British Occupation of Indonesia, 1945–1946: Britain, the Netherlands and the Indonesian Revolution*. London: Routledge.

McVey, Ruth T. (1982). "The Beamtenstaat in Indonesia," in Benedict O'G Anderson & Audrey Kahin (eds.) *Interpreting Indonesian Politics: Thirteen Contributions to the Debate*. Ithaca, NY: Cornell Southeast Asia Program, pp. 84–91.

(1994). "The Case of the Disappearing Decade," in David Bourchier & John Legge (eds.) *Democracy in Indonesia: 1950s and 1990s*. Clayton: Monash University, pp. 3–15.

Meierhenrich, Jens (2008). *The Legacies of Law: Long-Run Consequences of Legal Development in South Africa, 1652–2000*. Cambridge: Cambridge University Press.

Meijer, Marinus Johan (1967). *The Introduction of Modern Criminal Law in China*. Hong Kong: Lung Men Bookstore [Re-print of the 1949 Edition, Batavia: Koninklijke Drukkerij De Unie].

Merryman, John Henry & Rogelio Pérez-Perdomo (2007). *The Civil Law Tradition: An Introduction to the Legal Systems of Europe and Latin America* (3rd Edition). Stanford, CA: Stanford University Press.

Mertha, Andrew C. (2005). *The Politics of Piracy: Intellectual Property in Contemporary China*. Ithaca, NY: Cornell University Press.

Mertz, Elizabeth (2016). "Introduction, New Legal Realism: Law and Social Science in the New Millennium," in Elizabeth Mertz, Stewart MacAulay, & Thomas W. Mitchell (eds.) *The New Legal Realism, Volume I: Translating Law-and-Society for Today's Legal Practice*. Cambridge: Cambridge University Press, pp. 1–25.

Michelson, Ethan (2003). *Unhooking from the State: Chinese Lawyers in Transition*, PhD Dissertation in Sociology, The University of Chicago.

(2006). "The Practice of Law as an Obstacle to Justice: Chinese Lawyers at Work." *Law and Society Review* 40(1): 1–38.

(2007a). "Climbing the Dispute Pagoda: Grievances and Appeals to the Official Justice System in Rural China." *American Sociological Review* 72(3): 459–85.

(2007b). "Lawyers, Political Embeddedness, and Institutional Continuity in China's Transition from Socialism." *American Journal of Sociology* 113(2): 352–414.

Migdal, Joel S. (1988). *Strong Societies and Weak States: State-Society Relations and State Capabilities in the Third World.* Princeton, NJ: Princeton University Press.

Mill, John Stuart (1843). *A System of Logic: Ratiocinative and Inductive [Volume I].* London: John W. Parker.

Minzner, Carl F. (2011). "China's Turn Against Law." *American Journal of Comparative Law* 59(4): 935–84.

Montesquieu, Charles de Secondat Baron de (1778). *The Spirit of Laws* [Translation of *De l'esprit des loix*]. Edinburgh: Alexander Donaldson.

Moore, Barrington Jr. (1967). *Social Origins of Dictatorship and Democracy: Lord and Peasant in the Making of the Modern World.* Boston, MA: Beacon Press.

Moustafa, Tamir (2007). *The Struggle for Constitutional Power: Law, Politics, and Economic Development in Egypt.* Cambridge: Cambridge University Press.

Moustafa, Tamir & Tom Ginsburg (2008). "Introduction: The Functions of Courts in Authoritarian Politics," in Tom Ginsburg & Tamir Moustada (eds.) *Rule By Law: The Politics of Courts in Authoritarian Regimes.* Cambridge: Cambridge University Press, pp. 1–22.

Mühlhahn, Klaus (2009). *Criminal Justice in China, A History.* Cambridge, MA: Harvard University Press.

Muradi (2014). *Politics and Governance in Indonesia: The Police in the Era of Reformasi.* Abingdon: Routledge.

Naseemullah, Adnan (2017). *Development after Statism: Industrial Firms and the Political Economy of South Asia.* Cambridge: Cambridge University Press.

Neumann, Franz L. (1942). *Behemoth: The Structure and Practice of National Socialism.* Oxford: Oxford University Press.

(1986). *The Rule of Law: Political Theory and the Legal System in Modern Society.* Leamington Spa, Heidelberg, & Dover NH: Berg.

North, Douglass C. (1961). *The Economic Growth of the United States, 1790–1860.* Upper Saddle River, NJ: Prentice Hall.

(1982). *Structure and Change in Economic History.* New York: W.W. Norton.

(1990). *Institutions, Institutional Change, and Economic Performance.* Cambridge: Cambridge University Press.

O'Shaughnessy, Kate (2009). *Gender, State, and Social Power in Contemporary Indonesia: Divorce and Marriage Law*. Abingdon: Routledge.

Oda, Hiroshi (2009). *Japanese Law* (3rd Edition). Oxford: Oxford University Press.

Olsen, Tricia D., Leigh A. Payne, & Andrew G. Reiter (2010). *Transitional Justice in Balance: Comparing Processes, Weighing Efficacy*. Washington, DC: United States Institute for Peace.

Olson, Mancur (1993). "Dictatorship, Democracy, and Development." *American Political Science Review* 87(3): 567–76.

Peerenboom, Randall (2001). "Seek Truth from Facts: An Empirical Study of the Enforcement of Arbitral Awards in the People's Republic of China." *American Journal of Comparative Law* 49(1): 249–327.

(2002). *China's Long March toward the Rule of Law*. Cambridge: Cambridge University Press.

(2006). "Judicial Independence and Judicial Accountability: An Empirical Study of Individual Case Supervision." *The China Journal* 55: 67–92.

(2010). "Judicial Independence in China: Common Myths and Unfounded Assumptions," in Randall Peerenboom (ed.) *Judicial Independence in China: Lessons for Global Rule of Law Promotion*. Cambridge: Cambridge University Press, pp. 69–94.

Pei, Minxin, Zhang Guo'an, Pei Fei & Chen Lixin (2010). "A Survey of Commercial Litigation in Shanghai Courts," in Randall Peerenboom (ed.) *Judicial Independence in China: Lessons for Global Rule of Law Promotion*. Cambridge: Cambridge University Press, pp. 221–33.

Perry, Elizabeth J. (2007). *Patrolling the Revolution: Worker Militias, Citizenship, and the Modern Chinese State*. Lanham, MD: Rowman & Littlefield.

Plato (1991). *The Republic of Plato* (2nd Edition) [Translated by Allan Bloom]. New York: Basic Books.

Polanyi, Karl (1957). *The Great Transformation: The Political and Economic Origins of Our Time*. Boston, MA: Beacon Press.

Pompe, Sebastian (1992). *Indonesian Law, 1949–1989: A Bibliography of Foreign-Language Materials with Brief Commentaries on the Law*. Leiden & Boston: Brill.

(2005). *The Indonesian Supreme Court: a Study in Institutional Collapse*. Ithaca, NY: Cornell University Press.

Posner, Richard A. (1981). *The Economics of Justice*. Cambridge, MA: Harvard University Press.

(2014). *Economic Analysis of Law* (9th Edition). New York: Wolters Kluwer.

Potter, Pittman B. (1999). "The Chinese Legal System: Continuing Commitment to the Primacy of State Power." *The China Quarterly* 159: 673–83.

(2001). *The Chinese Legal System: Globalization and Local Legal Culture*. New York: Routledge.

Pound, Roscoe (1942). *Social Control through Law*. New Haven, CT: Yale University Press.
(1948). *Some Problems of the Administration of Justice in China*. Nanjing: National Chengchi University.
Przeworski, Adam & Henry Teune (1970). *The Logic of Comparative Social Inquiry*. New York: Wiley.
Rajah, Jothie (2012). *Authoritarian Rule of Law: Legislation, Discourse, and Legitimacy in Singapore*. Cambridge: Cambridge University Press.
Raz, Joseph (1980). *The Concept of a Legal System: An Introduction to the Theory of Legal System*. Oxford: Clarendon Press.
Read, Benjamin (2012). *Roots of the State: Neighborhood Organization and Social Networks in Beijing and Taipei*. Stanford, CA: Stanford University Press.
Ren, Xin (1997). *Tradition of the Law and the Law of Tradition: Law, State, and Social Control in China*. Westport, CT: Greenwood Press.
Repnikova, Maria (2014). *Limited Political Liberalisation in Authoritarian Regimes: Critical Journalists and the State in China*, DPhil Dissertation in Politics, University of Oxford.
Robespierre, Maximilien (1794). *Report upon the Principles of Political Morality* (Committee of Public Safety) [English translation of French original]. Philadelphia, PA: The Convention.
Rosadi, Otong & Andi Desmon (2012). *Studi Politik Hukum: Suatu Optik Ilmu Hukum [Research on Legal Politics: A Perspective on Jurisprudence]*. Yogyakarta: Thafa Media.
Rousseau, Jean Jacques (1986). *Political Writings* [Translated and Edited by Fredrick Watkins]. Madison, WI: The University of Wisconsin Press.
Rudolph, Lloyd I. & Susanne Hoeber Rudolph (1967). *The Modernity of Tradition: Political Development and Change in India*. Chicago, IL: University of Chicago Press.
Sapio, Flora (2008). "Shuanggui and Extralegal Detention in China." *China Information* 22(1): 7–37.
(2010). *Sovereign Power and the Law in China*. Leiden & Boston: Brill.
Saragih, Bintan Regen (2006). *Politik Hukum [Legal Politics]*. Bandung: CV Utomo.
Schmitt, Carl (2005). *Political Theology: Four Chapters on the Concept of Sovereignty* [Translated by George Schwab, Foreword by Tracy B. Strong]. Chicago, IL: The University of Chicago Press.
(2007). *The Concept of the Political, Expanded Edition* [Translated and with an Introduction by George Schwab, with a Forward by Tracy B. Strong and Notes by Leo Strauss]. Chicago, IL: The University of Chicago Press.
Schulte Nordholt, Henke & Gerry van Klinken (eds.) (2007). *Renegotiating Boundaries: Local Politics in Post-Suharto Indonesia*. Leiden: KITLV Press.
Scott, James C. (1976). *The Moral Economy of the Peasant: Rebellion and Subsistence in Southeast Asia*. New Haven, CT: Yale University Press.

Serban, Mihaela (2015). "Rule of Law Indicators as a Technology of Power in Romania," in Sally Engle Merry, Kevin E. Davis, & Benedict Kingsbury (eds.) *The Quiet Power of Indicators: Measuring Governance, Corruption, and Rule of Law*. New York: Cambridge University Press, pp. 199–221.

Seymour, James D. & Richard Anderson (1999). *Old Ghosts New Ghosts: Prisons and Labor Reform Camps in China*. Armonk, NY: M.E. Sharpe.

Shapiro, Martin (1981). *Courts: A Comparative and Political Analysis*. Chicago, IL: University of Chicago Press.

(1989). "Political Jurisprudence, Public Law, and Post-Consequentialist Ethics: Comment on Professors Barber and Smith." *Studies in American Political Development* 3: 88–102.

(2008). "Courts in Authoritarian Regimes," in Tom Ginsburg & Tamir Moustafa (eds.) *Rule by Law: The Politics of Courts in Authoritarian Regimes*. Cambridge: Cambridge University Press, pp. 326–35.

Shapiro, Martin & Alec Stone Sweet (2002). *On Law, Politics, and Judicialization*. New York: Oxford University Press.

Singh, Vishal (1959). "The Political Situation in Indonesia," in B. H. M. Vleeke (ed.) *Indonesia's Struggle, 1957–1959*. The Hague: Netherlands Institute of International Affairs, pp. 5–21.

Sinha, Aseema (2015). "Scaling Up: Beyond the Subnational Comparative Method for India." *Studies in Indian Politics* 3(1): 128–33.

Slater, Dan (2010). *Ordering Power: Contentious Politics and Authoritarian Leviathans in Southeast Asia*. Cambridge: Cambridge University Press.

Slater, Dan & Daniel Ziblatt (2013). "The Enduring Indispensability of the Controlled Comparison." *Comparative Political Studies* 46(10): 1301–27.

Snyder, Richard (2001). "Scaling Down: The Subnational Comparative Method." *Studies in Comparative International Development* 36(1): 93–110.

Solinger, Dorothy J. (2009). *States' Gains, Labor's Losses: China, France, and Mexico Choose Global Liaisons, 1980–2000*. Ithaca, NY: Cornell University Press.

Solomon, Peter H. (1996). *Soviet Criminal Justice under Stalin*. Cambridge: Cambridge University Press.

(ed.) (1997). *Reforming Justice in Russia, 1864–1996: Power, Culture, and the Limits of Legal Order*. Armonk, NY: M.E. Sharpe.

(2013). "Criminalization, Decriminalization and Post-Communist Transition: the Case of the Russian Federation," in Kay Goodall, Margaret Malloch & Bill Munro (eds.) *Building Justice in Post-Transition Europe? Processes of Criminalization within Central and Eastern European Societies*. London: Routledge – pp. 95–114.

Sorace, Christian P. (2017). *Shaken Authority: China's Communist Party and the 2008 Sichuan Earthquake*. Ithaca, NY: Cornell University Press.

Sorace, Christian P. & William Hurst (2016). "China's Phantom Urbanisation and the Pathology of Ghost Cities." *Journal of Contemporary Asia* 46(2): 304–22.

Stern, Rachel E. (2010). "On the Frontlines: Making Decisions in Chinese Civil Environmental Suits." *Law & Policy* 32(1): 79–103.

(2011). "From Dispute to Decision: Suing Polluters in China." *The China Quarterly* 206: 294–312.

(2013). *Environmental Litigation in China: A Study in Political Ambivalence*. Cambridge: Cambridge University Press.

Stewart, Potter (1964). United States Supreme Court Concurring Opinion, Jacobellis v. Ohio, 378 U.S. 197.

Stone Sweet, Alec (1999). "Judicialization and the Construction of Governance." *Comparative Political Studies* 32(2): 147–84.

(2000). *Governing with Judges: Constitutional Politics in Europe*. New York; Oxford University Press.

Strayer, Joseph R. (ed.) (1986). *Dictionary of the Middle Ages, Volume 7*. New York: Charles Scribner's Sons.

Summers, Robert S. (2006). *Form and Function in a Legal System: A General Study*. Cambridge: Cambridge University Press.

Sundhaussen, Ulf (1982). *The Road to Power: Indonesian Military Politics, 1945–1967*. Kuala Lumpur: Oxford University Press.

Supriyanto, Hari (2004). *Perubahan Hukum Privat ke Hukum Publik [Transformation of Private Law into Public Law]*. Yogyakarta: Universitas Atma Jaya Yogyakarta.

Susanti, Bivitri (2008). "The Implementation of the Rights to Health Care and Education in Indonesia," in Varun Gauri & Daniel Brinks (eds.) *Courting Social Justice: Judicial Enforcement of Social and Economic Rights in the Developing World*. Cambridge: Cambridge University Press, pp. 224–67.

Tamanaha, Brian Z. (2004). *On the Rule of Law: History, Politics, Theory*. Cambridge: Cambridge University Press.

Tanner, Harold M. (1999). *Strike Hard! Anti-Crime Campaigns and Chinese Criminal Justice, 1979–1985*. Ithaca, NY: Cornell East Asia Series.

Tanner, Murray Scot (2000). "State Coercion and the Balance of Awe: The 1983–1986 'Stern Blows' Anti-Crime Campaign." *The China Journal* 44: 93–125.

(2005). "Campaign-Style Policing and Its Critics," in Børge Bakken (ed.) *Crime, Punishment, and Policing in China*. Lanham: Rowman & Littlefield, pp. 171–88.

Teitel, Ruti G. (2000). *Transitional Justice*. Oxford: Oxford University Press.

Thompson, E. P. (1975). *Whigs and Hunters: The Origin of the Black Act*. London: Allen Lane.

Tiffert, Glenn D. (2009). "Epistrophy: Chinese Constitutionalism and the 1950s," in Stéphanie Balme & Michael W. Dowdle (eds.) *Building*

Constitutionalism in China. New York & Basingstoke: Palgrave-MacMillan, pp. 59–76.

Trevaskes, Susan (2007). *Courts and Criminal Justice in Contemporary China*. Lanham: Lexington Books.

Tsai, Kellee S. (2002). *Back-Alley Banking: Private Entrepreneurs in China*. Ithaca, NY: Cornell University Press.

Tsou, Tang (1976). "Prolegomenon to the Study of Informal Groups in CCP Politics." *The China Quarterly* 65: 98–114.

van Ittersum, Martine Julia (2003). "Hugo Grotius in Context: van Heemskerck's Capture of the 'Santa Catarina' and its Justification in 'De Jure Praedae' (1604–1606)." *Asian Journal of Social Science* 31(3): 511–48.

(2006). *Profit and Principle: Hugo Grotius, Natural Rights Theories and the Rise of Dutch Power in the East Indies, 1595–1615*. Leiden: Brill.

von Benda-Beckmann, Franz & Keebet von Benda-Beckmann (2013). *Political and Legal Transformations of an Indonesian Polity: the Nagari from Colonization to Decentralization*. Cambridge: Cambridge University Press.

von Benda-Beckmann, Keebet (1984). *The Broken Stairways to Consensus: Village Justice and State Courts in Minangkabau*. Dordrecht: Foris.

Vu, Tuong (2010). *Paths to Development in Asia: South Korea, Vietnam, China, and Indonesia*. Cambridge: Cambridge University Press.

Wang, Yuhua (2015). *Tying the Autocrat's Hands: The Rise of the Rule of Law in China*. Cambridge: Cambridge University Press.

Weber, Max (1978). *Economy and Society: An Outline of Interpretive Sociology* [Edited by Günther Roth & Claus Wittich, Translated by Ephraim Fischoff et al.]. Berkeley, CA: University of California Press.

(1995). *General Economic History* [Translated by Frank H. Knight, with a New Introduction by Ira J. Cohen]. New Brunswick: Transaction Publishers.

Wedeman, Andrew H. (2003). *From Mao to Market: Rent Seeking, Local Protectionism, and Marketization in China*. Cambridge: Cambridge University Press.

Weinrib, Ernest J. (1987). "The Intelligibility of the Rule of Law," in A. C. Huchinson & P. Monahan (eds.) *The Rule of Law: Ideal or Ideology*. Toronto: Carswell, pp. 59–84.

(2012a). *Corrective Justice*. Oxford: Oxford University Press.

(2012b). *The Idea of Private Law* (Revised Edition). Oxford: Oxford University Press.

Whiting, Susan H. (2000). *Power and Wealth in Rural China: The Political Economy of Institutional Change*. Cambridge: Cambridge University Press.

Wignjosoebroto, Soetandyo (1994). *Dari Hukum Kolonial ke Hukum Nasional: Suatu Kajian tentang Dinamika Sosial-Politik dalam Perkembangan Hukum*

Selama Satu Setengah Abad di Indonesia (1840–1990) [From Colonial Law to National Law: A Study of Social-Political Dynamics in the Evolution of Law over the Course of One and a Half Centuries in Indonesia (1840–1990)]. Jakarta: PT RajaGrafindo Persada.

Williamson, Oliver E. (1985). *The Economic Institutions of Capitalism*. New York: The Free Press.

Winters, Jeffrey A. (2011). *Oligarchy*. Cambridge: Cambridge University Press.

Woo, Margaret Y. K. & Yaxin Wang (2005). "Civil Justice in China: an Empirical Study of Courts in Three Provinces." *The American Journal of Comparative Law* 53(4): 911–40.

Woo, Margaret Y. K. & Mary E. Gallagher (eds.) (2011). *Chinese Justice: Civil Dispute Resolution in Contemporary China*. Cambridge: Cambridge University Press.

Xiao-Planes, Xiaohong (2009). "Of Constitutions and Constitutionalism: Trying to Build a New Political Order in China, 1908–1949," in Stéphanie Balme & Michael W. Dowdle (eds.) *Building Constitutionalism in China*. New York & Basingstoke: Palgrave-MacMillan, pp. 37–57.

Xu, Xiaoqun (2008). *Trial of Modernity: Judicial Reform in Early Twentieth Century China, 1901–1937*. Stanford, CA: Stanford University Press.

Yahman (2011). *Karakteristik Wanprestasi dan Tindak Pidana Penipuan yang Lahir dari Hubungan Kontrakual [Characteristics of Default and the Criminal Offense of Fraud Related to Contractual Relations]*. Jakarta: Prestasi Pustaka.

Zhu, Suli (2010). "The Party and the Courts," in Randall Peerenboom (ed.) *Judicial Independence in China: Lessons for Global Rule of Law Promotion*. Cambridge: Cambridge University Press, pp. 52–68.

Zorab, Arratoon Albert (1954). *De Japanse Bezetting van Indonesië en haar Volkenrechtelijke Zijde [The Japanese Occupation of Indonesia and its International Law Aspect]*. Leiden: Universitaire Pers Leiden.

Zou, Keyuan (2006). *China's Legal Reform: Towards the Rule of Law*. Leiden: Brill-Martinus Nijhoff Publishers.

陈甦 (ed.) (2009). 当代中国法学研究 *[Research on Contemporary Chinese Legal Studies]*. 北京: 中国社会科学出版社.

韩延龙 (ed.) (1995). 中华人民共和国法制通史, *1949–1995 [Comprehensive History of the Legal System of the People's Republic of China, 1949–1995]*. 北京: 中央党校出版社 (2 volumes).

江西省人民法院 (1951). 人民法庭资料 *[Information on the People's Tribunals]* 南昌: 江西省人民法院 (internal circular distributed to prefecture and county-level political and legal institutions).

蒋秋明 (2011). 南京国民政府审判制度研究 *[Trial System During the Period of Nanjing Nationalist Government]* 北京: 光明日报出版社.

课题研发组 (2006). 城管执法操作实务 *[Operational Practice of Chengguan Law Enforcement]*. 北京: 国家行政学院出版社.

刘复之 (2015). "'严打'就是专政" ["Strike Hard" is Dictatorship] Published on the Chinese Ministry of Public Security Website, December 6, 2012, www.mps.gov.cn/n16/n1327/n4834/n1452675/1469707.html [accessed September 16, 2015].

孟富强 (2001). "公安思想政治工作是夺取严打整治斗争全胜的法宝" [Public Security Thought and Political Work is the Magic Weapon for Capturing Total Victory in the Strike Hard Corrective Punishment Struggle] 山东公安专科学校学报 2001(5): 8–11.

南方周末 (2010). "颜立燕往事" [Yan Liyan's Background] 南方周末 July 8, 2010, www.infzm.com/content/47339 [accessed June 3, 2012].

人民司法社论 (1962). "一定把复查案件工作做好" [Be Certain to Complete the Work of Re-Examining Cases Well]. 人民司法 1962(1): 3–4.

唐晓梅 (2011). "论民事案件刑事化的危害及对策" [Considering the Criminalization of Civil Cases, Harm, and Countermeasures]. 凯里学院学报 29(1): 37–9.

田文昌 & 陈瑞华 (2013). 刑事辩护的中国经验: 田文昌，陈瑞华对话纪录 *[China's Experience of Criminal Defense: Record of a Dialogue between Tian Wenchang and Chen Ruihua]*. 北京: 北京大学出版社.

谢岳 (2013). 维稳的政治逻辑 *[The Political Logic of Stability Maintenance]*. Hong Kong: 清华书局.

杨彦军 (2010). "民事行政诉讼活动违法行为调查机制研究" [Research into the Investigation Mechanisms of Illegal Behavior in the Administrative Procedure Activities of Civil Law]. 法学杂志 2010(1): 1058.

杨永华 & 方克勤 (1987). 陕甘宁边区法制史稿 *[Treatise on the Legal System History of the Shaan-Gan-Ning Border Region]*. 北京: 法律出版社.

姚院 (2011). 上海公共租界特区法院研究 *[Research on Courts in the Special District of the Shanghai International Settlement]*. 上海: 上海人民出版社.

应新龙课题组 (2011). "'售后服务'的质与量: 新民事审判监督程序在上海法院的运作情况分析" [The Character and Quality of "After-Sales Service": Analysis of the Operational Situation of the New Civil Adjudication Supervision Procedures in the Shanghai Courts], in 张斌 (ed.) 法官的思考与探索: 上海市金山区人民法院调研成果竞选 上海: 上海大学出版社, pp. 178–204.

袁金彪 & 倪培兴 (2006). "论民事审判监督正当程序之建构" [On the Construction of Fair Procedures for the Supervision of Civil Judgments]. 人民检察 2006(1): 37–40.

张斌 (ed.) (2011). 法官的思考与探索: 上海市金山区人民法院调研成果竞选 *[Judges' Reflections and Explorations: Selected Results of Research on Shanghai City's Jinshan District Court]*. 上海: 上海大学出版社.

张友南 & 孙伟 (2011). "中央苏区时期劳动法问题研究" [Research on Problems in Labor Law during the Period of the Central Soviet]. 江西社会科学 2011(3): 132–7.

周一平 & 周郴保 (2002). "'严打'的法理学探析" [Legal-Scientific Exploration and Analysis of "Strike Hard"]. 甘肃政法成人教育学院学报 2002(3): 30–6.

朱苏力 (2000). 送法下乡: 中国基层司法制度研究 *[Sending Law Down to the Countryside: Research on China's Basic-Level Justice System]*. 北京: 中国政法大学出版社 [Authored under the name 苏力].

最高人民法院 (1962). "最高人民法院关于当前人民法院刑事审判工作的若干意见" [Assorted Opinions of The Supreme People's Court on the People's Courts' Present Handling of Criminal Trials]. 人民司法 1962(2): 1–2.

最高人民检察院民事行政厅 (2004). 人民检察院民事行政抗诉案例选 *[Selected Cases of People's Procuratorate Civil and Administrative Appeals]*. 北京: 法律出版社.

WEBSITES

Rural Kediri Court Website Data (2016). www.sipp.pn-kedirikab.go.id/list_perkara/page/1 [accessed March 8, 2016].

Tuban Court Website Data (2016). www.sipp.pn-tuban.go.id/#page-1 [accessed March 8, 2016].

正义网 (2008). "民事冲突与和谐社会" [Civil Law Conflict and the Harmonious Society], www.review.jcrb.com/200805/ca715291.htm [accessed May 30, 2012].

中国网 (2010). "民事纠纷刑事化与和谐社会之冲突研究会在北京举行" [Research Conference Held in Beijing on the Conflict between the Criminalization of Civil Disputes and the Harmonious Society], www.china.com.cn/news/law/2010-04/22/content_19886226.htm [accessed May 30, 2012].

GAZETTEERS

China

包头法院志编纂委员会 (1990). 包头法院志 [Baotou Court Gazetteer]. 呼和浩特: 内蒙古人民出版社.

成都市锦江区法院志 (1999). [Chengdu City, Jinjiang District Court Gazetteer]. 成都: 四川辞书出版社.

大理白族自治州人民检察院 (1997). 大理白族自治州检察志 [Dali Bai Nationality Autonomous Prefecture Procuratorial Gazetteer]. 昆明: 云南民族出版社.

冯开方主编 (1993). 三明法院志，1941–1992 [Sanming Court Gazetteer, 1941–1992].

佛山市中级法院 (1991). 佛山法院志 [Foshan Court Gazetteer].

广州市检察院 (1995). 广州检察志 [Guangzhou Procuratorial Gazetteer]. 广州: 广东人民出版社.

河北省秦皇岛市中级人民法院 (1993). 秦皇岛法院志 [Qinhuangdao Court Gazetteer].

吉安法院志 (2002). [Ji'an Court Gazetteer].

江西省志 (江西省法院志) (1996). [Jiangxi Province Gazetteer (Jiangxi Province Courts Gazetteer)].

靖江市人民检察院 (2002). 靖江检察志 [Jingjiang Procuratorial Gazetteer]. 南京: 江苏人民出版社.

李其凡主编 (1995). 湖北法院志 [Hubei Court Gazetteer]. 北京: 人民法院出版社.

零陵地区中级人民法院 (1995). 零陵地区志: 法院志 [Lingling Prefecture Gazetteer: Court Gazetteer]. 零陵地区文化局新闻出版社.

萍乡市中级法院 (1995). 萍乡市法院志 [Pingxiang County-Level City Court Gazetteer].

普宁县人民法院志编 (1989). 普宁县人民法 [Puning County Court Gazetteer].

青川县人民法院法院志编写组 (1988). 青川县法院志，1942–1985 [Qingchuan County Court Gazetteer, 1942–1985].

瑞安市法院编 (1995). 瑞安法院志 [Rui'an Court Gazetteer].

三台县法院志编纂领导小组编 (1999). 三台县法院志 [Santai County Court Gazetteer].

石家庄市长安区人民法院编 (1994). 长安区人民法院志 (1958.4–1994.6) [Chang'an District People's Court Gazetteer, April 1958–June 1994].

石家庄市桥西区人民法院编 (1994). 石家庄市桥西区人民法院志 [Shijiazhuang City Qiaoxi District People's Court Gazetteer].

石家庄市新华区人民法院编 (1996). 石家庄市新华区人民法院志，1962–1995 [Shijiazhuang City Xinhua District People's Court Gazetteer, 1962–1995].

天水市秦城区人民法院编(1993).秦城区法院志， 1949年9月-1990年12月 [Qincheng District Court Gazetteer, September 1949–December 1990].

厦门政法志编纂委员会 (1996). 厦门政法志, 1906–1990 [Xiamen Political and Legal Gazetteer, 1906–1990]. 厦门: 厦门大学出版社.

万年县法院志 (2003). [Wannian County Court Gazetteer]. 北京: 万志出版社.

王玉琴主编 (1996). 鞍山法院志 [Anshan Court Gazetteer]. 辽宁鞍山市: 鞍山中级法院.

玉山县法院志编纂委员会 (1999). 玉山县法院志 [Yushan County Court Gazetteer]. 江西省地方志.

岳普湖县史志办公室 (2004). 岳普湖县政法志 [Yuepuhu County Political and Legal Gazetteer]. 乌鲁木齐: 新疆人民出版社.

云南省昆明市中级人民法院编 (1994). 昆明法院志 [Kunming Court Gazetteer].

Indonesia

Central Kalimantan Gazetteer (1982). *Dokumentasi Situasi Wilayah Hukum Pengadilan Tinggi dan Daerah Hukum Pengadilan Negeri: Pengadilan Tinggi Palangka Raya dan Pengadilan Negeri dalam Wilayah Hukumnya [Documentation of the Situation within the Jurisdiction of the High Courts and of the Local Courts: The High Court of Palangka Raya and Local Courts within its Jurisdiction]*. Jakarta: Departamen Kehakiman.

East Java Gazetteer (1980). *Dokumentasi Situasi Wilayah Hukum Pengadilan Tinggi dan Daerah Hukum Pengadilan Negeri: Pengadilan Tinggi Surabaya dan Pengadilan Negeri dalam Wilayah Hukumnya [Documentation of the Situation within the Jurisdiction of the High Courts and of the Local Courts: The High Court of Surabaya and Local Courts within its Jurisdiction]*. Jakarta: Departamen Kehakiman.

East Nusa Tenggara Gazetteer (1982). *Dokumentasi Situasi Wilayah Hukum Pengadilan Tinggi dan Daerah Hukum Pengadilan Negeri: Pengadilan Tinggi Kupang dan Pengadilan Negeri dalam Wilayah Hukumnya [Documentation of the Situation within the Jurisdiction of the High Courts and of the Local Courts: The High Court of Kupang and Local Courts within its Jurisdiction]*. Jakarta: Departamen Kehakiman.

Jambi Gazetteer (2006). *Dokumentasi Situasi Daerah Hukum Pengadilan Tinggi dan Pengadilan Negeri dalam Wilayah Propinsi Jambi [Documentation of the Situation of the High Court and Local Courts within the Jurisdiction of the Province of Jambi]*. Jakarta: Makamah Agung Republik Indonesia.

Lampung Gazetteer (1982). *Dokumentasi Situasi Wilayah Hukum Pengadilan Tinggi dan Daerah Hukum Pengadilan Negeri: Pengadilan Tinggi Tanjung Karang dan Pengadilan Negeri dalam Wilayah Hukumnya [Documentation of the Situation within the Jurisdiction of the High Courts and of the Local Courts: The High Court of Tanjung Karang and Local Courts within its Jurisdiction]*. Jakarta: Departamen Kehakiman.

(2006). *Dokumentasi Situasi Daerah Hukum Pengadilan Tinggi dan Pengadilan Negeri dalam Wilayah Propinsi Lampung [Documentation of the Situation in The High Court and Local Courts within the Jurisdiction of the Province of Lampung]*. Jakarta: Makamah Agung Republik Indonesia.

North Maluku Gazetteer (2005). *Dokumentasi Situasi Daerah Hukum Pengadilan Tinggi dan Pengadilan Negeri dalam Wilayah Propinsi Maluku Utara [Documentation of the Situation in The High Court and Local Courts within the Jurisdiction of the Province of North Maluku]*. Jakarta: Makamah Agung Republik Indonesia.

North Sulawesi Gazetteer (1980). *Dokumentasi Situasi Wilayah Hukum Pengadilan Tinggi dan Daerah Hukum Pengadilan Negeri: Pengadilan Tinggi Manado dan Pengadilan Negeri dalam Wilayah Hukumnya [Documentation of the Situation within the Jurisdiction of the High Courts and of the Local*

Courts: The High Court of Manado and Local Courts within its Jurisdiction]. Jakarta: Departamen Kehakiman.

West Java Gazetteer (1978). *Dokumentasi Situasi Wilayah Hukum Pengadilan Tinggi dan Daerah Hukum Pengadilan Negeri: Pengadilan Tinggi Bandung dan Pengadilan Negeri dalam Wilayah Hukumnya [Documentation of the Situation within the Jurisdiction of the High Courts and of the Local Courts: The High Court of Bandung and Local Courts within its Jurisdiction]*. Jakarta: Departamen Kehakiman.

West Kalimantan Gazetteer (1981). *Dokumentasi Situasi Wilayah Hukum Pengadilan Tinggi dan Daerah Hukum Pengadilan Negeri: Pengadilan Pontianak dan Pengadilan Negeri dalam Wilayah Hukumnya [Documentation of the Situation within the Jurisdiction of the High Courts and of the Local Courts: The High Court of Pontianak and Local Courts within its Jurisdiction]*. Jakarta: Departamen Kehakiman.

West Nusa Tenggara Gazetteer (1983). *Dokumentasi Situasi Wilayah Hukum Pengadilan Tinggi dan Daerah Hukum Pengadilan Negeri: Pengadilan Tinggi Mataram dan Pengadilan Negeri dalam Wilayah Hukumnya [Documentation of the Situation within the Jurisdiction of the High Courts and of the Local Courts: The High Court of Mataram and Local Courts within its Jurisdiction]*. Jakarta: Departamen Kehakiman.

West Sumatra Gazetteer (2006). *Dokumentasi Situasi Daerah Hukum Pengadilan Tinggi dan Pengadilan Negeri dalam Wilayah Propinsi Sumatera Barat [Documentation of the Situation in The High Court and Local Courts within the Jurisdiction of the Province of West Sumatra]*. Jakarta: Makamah Agung Republik Indonesia.

Yogyakarta Gazetteer (1982). *Dokumentasi Situasi Wilayah Hukum Pengadilan Tinggi dan Daerah Hukum Pengadilan Negeri: Pengadilan Tinggi Daerah Istimewa Yogyakarta dan Pengadilan Negeri dalam Wilayah Hukumnya [Documentation of the Situation within the Jurisdiction of the High Courts and of the Local Courts: The High Court of Yogyakarta Special Region and Local Courts within its Jurisdiction]*. Jakarta: Departamen Kehakiman.

(2007). *Dokumentasi Situasi Daerah Hukum Pengadilan Tinggi dan Pengadilan Negeri dalam Wilayah Propinsi Yogyakarta [Documentation of the Situation in The High Court and Local Courts within the Jurisdiction of the Province of Yogyakarta]*. Jakarta: Makamah Agung Republik Indonesia.

LEGAL CASES

Indonesia

Airmadidi Cases

34/Pid.B/2011/PN.AMD

80/Pid.B/2011/PN.AMD

27/Pdt.G/2011/PN.AMD
35/Pdt.G/2011/PN.AMD
40/Pdt.G/2011/PN.AMD
50/Pdt.G/2011/PN.AMD
53/Pdt.G/2011/PN.AMD
61/Pdt.G/2011/PN.AMD
47/Pdt.G/2012/PN.AMD
139/Pid.B./2012/PN.AMD
146/Pid.B/2012/PN.AMD
90/Pdt.G/2012/PN.AMD
113/Pdt.G/2012/PN.AMD
63/Pdt.G/2013/PN/AMD
108/Pdt.G/2013/PN.AMD

Kediri Cases
231/Pid.B/1982/PN.KDI
237/Pid.B/1982/PN.KDI
238/Pid.B/1982/PN.KDI
239/Pid.B/1982/PN.KDI
240/Pid.B/1982/PN.KDI
249/Pid.B/1982/PN.KDI
251/Pid.B/1982/PN/KDI
253/Pid.B/1982/PN.KDI
255/Pid.B/1982/PN.KDI
257/Pid.B/1982/PN.KDI
259/Pid.B/1982/PN.KDI
38/Pid.B/1994/PN.KDI
71/Pid.B/1994/PN.KDI
63/Pid.B/1995/PN.KDI
82/Pid.B/1996/PN.KDI
52/Pdt.G/1984/PN.Kab.KDI
54/Pdt.G/1984/PN.Kab.Kdr
20/Pdt.G/1994/PN.Kab.KDI
22/Pdt.G/1994/PN.Kab.KDI
37/Pdt.G/2001/PN.Kab.KDI
39/Pdt.G/2001/PN.Kab.KDI
40/Pdt.G/2001/PN.Kab.KDI
46/Pdt.G/2010/PN.Kab.KDI
48/Pdt.G/2010/PN.Kab.KDI
357/Pid.B/2013/PN.Kab.KDI
358/Pid.B/2013/PN.Kab.KDI
379/Pid.B/2013/PN.Kab.KDI

Manado Cases
394/Pid/1955/PN.MDO
112/Pdt/1975/PN.MDO
122/Pdt/1975/PN.MDO
230/Pdt.G/2005/PN.MDO
375/Pid.B/2005/PN.MDO
414/Pid.B/2005/PN.MDO
14/Pid.B/2009/PN.MDO
17/Pid.B/2009/PN.MDO
35/Pid.B/2009/PN.MDO
149/Pid.B/2009/PN.MDO
158/Pid.B/2009/PN.MDO
164/Pid.B/2009/PN.MDO
236/Pid.B/2009/PN.MDO
238/Pid.B/2009/PN.MDO
240/Pid.B/2009/PN.MDO
242/Pid.B/2009/PN.MDO
243/Pid.B/2009/PN.MDO
244/Pid.B/2009/PN.MDO
245/Pid.B/2009/PN.MDO
254/Pid.B/2009.PN.MDO
313/Pid.B/2009/PN.MDO
330/Pid.B/2009/PN.MDO

Pamekesan Cases
01/Pdt/1959/PN.PMK
09/Pdt/1959/PN.PMK
54/Pdt/1959/PN.PMK
105/Pdt/1959/PN.PMK
177/Pdt/1959/PN.PMK
200/Pdt/1959/PN.PMK
236/Pdt/1959/PN.PMK
38/Pdt/1962/PN.PMK
03/Pdt/1962/PN.PMK
60/Pid/1962/PN.PMK
102/Pid/1962/PN.PMK
103/Pid/1962/PN.PMK
06/Pdt/1964/PN.PMK
42/Pdt/1964/PN.PMK
94/Pdt/1964/PN.PMK
92/Pdt.G/1966/PN.PMK
98/Pdt.G/1966/PN.PMK

61/Pdt.G/1968/PN.PMK
02/Pdt.G/1971/PN.PMK

Surabaya Cases
05/Pid.B/1979/PN.SBY
06/Pid/B/1979/PN.SBY
07/Pid.B/1979/PN.SBY
09/Pid.B/1979/PN.SBY
10/Pid.B/1979/PN.SBY
12/Pid.B/1979/PN.SBY
13/Pid.B/1979/PN.SBY
15/Pid.B/1979/PN.SBY
16/Pid.B/1979/PN.SBY
21/Pid.B/1979/PN.SBY
241/Pid.B/1984/PN.SBY
245/Pid.B/1984/PN.SBY
246/Pid.B/1984/PN.SBY
247/Pid.B/1984/PN.SBY
249/Pid.B/1984/PN.SBY
36/Pid.B/2009/PN.SBY
157/Pid.B/2009/PN.SBY
464/Pid.B/2009/PN.SBY
497/Pid.B/2009/PN.SBY
664/Pid.B/2009/PN.SBY
738/Pid.B/2009/PN.SBY
1509/Pid.B/2009/PN.SBY
2299/Pid.B/2009/PN.SBY
2855/Pid.B/2009/PN.SBY

Tondano Cases
49/Pid.B/1986/PN.TDO
72/Pid.B/1989/PN.TDO
04/Pdt.G/1968/PN.TDO
87/Pdt.G/1968.PN.TDO
151/Pdt.G/1968/PN.TDO
184/Pdt.G/1968/PN.TDO
45/Pdt.G/1975/PN.TDO
211/Pdt.G/1975/PN.TDO
65/Pdt.G/1988/PN.TDO
71/Pdt.G/1988/PN.TDO
108/Pdt.G/1992/PN.TDO
110/Pdt.G/1992/PN.TDO
114/Pdt.G/1992/PN.TDO
12/Pid.B/2001/PN.TDO

23/Pid.B/2001/PN/TDO
145/Pid.B/2001/PN.TDO
75/Pdt.G/2010/PN.TDO
03/Pid.B/2012/PN.TDO
15/Pid.B/2012/PN.TDO
34/Pid.B/2012/PN.TDO
35/Pid.B/2012/PN.TDO
64/Pid.B/2012/PN.TDO
113/Pid.B/2012/PN.TDO
114/Pid.B/2012/PN.TDO
199/Pid.B/2012/PN.TDO

China

Cases Observed at Trial during Fieldwork

Urban Jiangxi:

NC.Crim.2007.1: Theft & Sale of Stolen Goods
NC.Crim.2007.2: Theft
NC.Crim.2007.3: Assault
NC.Crim.2007.4: Embezzlement, Corruption, & Fraud

Urban Sichuan:

CD.Civ.2006.1: Contract dispute over unpaid pension benefits to laid-off SOE worker
LZ.Civ.2006.3: Dispute of traffic accident
CD.Crim.2006.1: Assault and Robbery
CD.Crim.2006.2: Theft/Burglary
CD.Crim.2006.3: Assault
CD.Crim.2006.4: Theft/Pickpocketing

Rural Sichuan:

LZ.Civ.2006.1: Contract dispute over failure to pay lawyer
LZ.Civ.2006.2: Dispute over loan repayment
LZ.Civ.2006.4: Dispute over construction supplies and contracting
LZ.Civ.2006.5: Dispute over SOE pension obligations
MS.Civ.2006.1: Tort stemming from a serious traffic accident
MS.Crim.2006.1: Murder

1949 Cases from the Sichuan Provincial Archives

SC.1947.1: Theft Trial of Wang Liumin (王刘民) (Archive Record Number 9-45155)
SC.1949.1: Luo Huangmin (罗黄民) Pursues Justice (Archive Record Number 9-44992)

SC.1949.2: Murder Trial of Liu Guoyu (刘国玉) (Archive Record Number 9-45124)
SC.1949.3: Murder Case of Han Zhangmin (韩张民) (Archive Record Number 9-44978)
SC.1949.4: Murder Trial of Zai Gejin (再革金) (Archive Record Number 9-45070)

Cases from the County P Public Security Bureau Archive
(Number: type of case, archive record number):
P 1950.1: Banditry (土匪), Z1-1-117
P 1950.2: Unlawful Landlord (不法地主), Z1-1-118
P 1950.3: Special Matters/Spying (特务)/Counter-Revolutionary Crimes (反革命), Z1-1-69
P 1950.4: Banditry, Z1-1-76
P 1951.1: Political Banditry (政治土匪), Z1-2-83
P 1952.1: Rape, Z1-3-100
P 1952.2: Unlawful Landlord, Z1-3-101
P 1952.3: Leadership of a Reactionary Organization (反动会道门头子), Z1-3-487
P 1952.4: Special Matters, Z1-3-539
P 1952.5: Theft, Z1-3-568
P 1952.6: Rape, Z1-3-569
P 1953.1: Manslaughter, Z1-4-176
P 1953.2: Wrecking (破坏), Z1-4-247
P 1954.1: Wrecking, Z1-5-3
P 1954.2: Theft, Z1-5-4
P 1954.3: Theft, Z1-5-15
P 1955.1: Counter-Revolutionary Crimes, Z1-6-34
P 1955.2: Fraud (作骗), Z1-6-40
P 1955.3: Escape from Labor Reform (劳改脱逃跑), Z1-6-48
P 1955.4: Bad Elements (坏分子), Z1-6-188
P 1955.5: Theft of Public Grain (盗窃公粮), Z1-6-193
P 1956.1: Counter-Revolutionary Crimes, Z1-7-178
P 1956.2: Theft, Z1-7-181
P 1957.1: Wrecking, Z1-8-11
P 1957.2: Theft, Z1-8-66
P 1957.3: Murder, Z1-8-70
P 1957.4: Intentional Injury (故意伤害), Z1-8-104
P 1957.5: Theft, Z1-8-115
P 1957.6: Reactionary Speech at Labor Reform (劳改中反动标语), Z1-8-122
P 1958.1: Murderous Banditry (土匪杀人), Z1-9-253
P 1958.2: Intentional Injury, Z1-9-272
P 1958.3: Bad Elements, Z1-9-790

P 1958.4: Organized Escape from Labor Reform (劳改组织脱逃跑), Z1-9-310
P 1958.5: Theft at Labor Reform, Z1-9-342
P 1958.6: Counter-Revolutionary Crimes, Z1-9-343
P 1958.7: Theft, Z1-9-344
P 1958.8: Escape from Labor Reform and Theft, Z1-9-345
P 1958.9: Counter-Offensive Fraudulent Calculation (反攻倒算), Z1-9-363
P 1959.1: Theft, Z3-1-370
P 1959.2: Wrecking, Z3-1-372
P 1959.3: Banditry, Z3-1-382
P 1959.4: Counter-Revolutionary Crimes, Z3-1-391
P 1959.5: Theft, Z3-1-396
P 1959.6: Banditry, Z1-10-4
P 1959.7: Counter-Revolutionary Crimes, Z1-10-18
P 1959.8: Wrecking, Z1-10-65
P 1959.9: Theft, Z1-10-123
P 1959.10: Counter-Revolutionary Crimes, Z3-1-366
P 1960.1: Theft, Z3-1-420
P 1960.2: Hooliganism (流氓), Z3-1-423
P 1960.3: Hooliganism, Z3-1-427
P 1960.4: Theft, Z3-1-446
P 1960.5: Reactionary Speech, Z3-1-453
P 1960.6: Rightists (右派), Z3-1-462
P 1961.1: Theft, Z3-1-465
P 1961.2: Unlawful Landlord, Z1-10-628
P 1961.2: Wrecking, Z3-1-478
P 1962.1: Wrecking of Food Policy (破坏粮食政策), Z1-10-329
P 1963.1: Theft, Z1-10-498
P 1963.2: Counter-Revolutionary Elements (反革命分子), Z3-1-526
P 1963.3: Theft, Z3-1-529
P 1963.4: Murder, Z1-10-428
P 1963.5: Rape, Z1-10-454
P 1964.1: Wrecking Elements (破坏分子), Z3-1-534
P 1964.2: Arson (纵火), Z3-1-539
P 1965.1: Class Reprisals (阶级报复), Z1-10-568
P 1965.2: Wrecking Elements, Z3-1-556
P 1965.3: Forgery of an Official Seal (伪造公章), Z3-1-561
P 1965.4: Wide Communication of Political History (伟达政历), Z3-1-566
P 1966.1: Counter-Revolutionary Elements, Z3-1-569
P 1966.2: Murder, Z3-1-570
P 1966.3: Theft, Z1-10-624
P 1966.4: Medical Accident (医疗事故), Z1-10-627
P 1966.5: Unlawful Landlord, Z3-1-575

P 1966.6: Dereliction of Duty during Supervision by a Semi-Landlord Rich Peasant (半地主式富农分子退职管制), Z3-1-578
P 1967.1: Theft, Z3-1-579
P 1967.2: Special Matters, Z3-1-580
P 1967.3: Theft of a Cow (盗牛), Z1-10-637
P 1967.4: Rape, Z1-10-635
P 1968.1: Wrecking the Socialist Economy (破坏社会主义经济), Z1-10-653
P 1968.2: Rape, Z1-10-671
P 1968.3: Reactionary Expression (反动言论), Z3-1-600
P 1969.1: Counter-Revolutionary Crimes, Z1-10-697
P 1969.2: Counter-Revolutionary Crimes, Z1-10-680
P 1970.1: Corruption (贪污), Z1-10-742
P 1970.2: Theft, Z1-10-745
P 1971.1: Theft, Z1-10-767
P 1972.1: Rape of a Female Rusticated Youth (强奸女知青), Z1-10-776
P 1972.2: Theft, Z1-10-780

INDEX

CAMBRIDGE STUDIES IN LAW AND SOCIETY

Books in the Series

Diseases of the Will
Mariana Valverde

The Politics of Truth and Reconciliation in South Africa: Legitimizing the Post-Apartheid State
Richard A. Wilson

Modernism and the Grounds of Law
Peter Fitzpatrick

Unemployment and Government: Genealogies of the Social
William Walters

Autonomy and Ethnicity: Negotiating Competing Claims in Multi-Ethnic States
Yash Ghai

Constituting Democracy: Law, Globalism and South Africa's Political Reconstruction
Heinz Klug

The Ritual of Rights in Japan: Law, Society, and Health Policy
Eric A. Feldman

The Invention of the Passport: Surveillance, Citizenship and the State
John Torpey

Governing Morals: A Social History of Moral Regulation
Alan Hunt

The Colonies of Law: Colonialism, Zionism and Law in Early Mandate Palestine
Ronen Shamir

Law and Nature
David Delaney

Social Citizenship and Workfare in the United States and Western Europe:
The Paradox of Inclusion
Joel F. Handler

Law, Anthropology and the Constitution of the Social: Making Persons and Things
Edited by Alain Pottage and Martha Mundy

Judicial Review and Bureaucratic Impact: International and Interdisciplinary Perspectives
Edited by Marc Hertogh and Simon Halliday

Immigrants at the Margins: Law, Race, and Exclusion in Southern Europe
Kitty Calavita

Lawyers and Regulation: The Politics of the Administrative Process
Patrick Schmidt

Law and Globalization from Below: Toward a Cosmopolitan Legality
Edited by Boaventura de Sousa Santos and Cesar A. Rodriguez-Garavito

Public Accountability: Designs, Dilemmas and Experiences
Edited by Michael W. Dowdle

Law, Violence and Sovereignty among West Bank Palestinians
Tobias Kelly

Legal Reform and Administrative Detention Powers in China
Sarah Biddulph

The Practice of Human Rights: Tracking Law Between the Global and the Local
Edited by Mark Goodale and Sally Engle Merry

Judges Beyond Politics in Democracy and Dictatorship: Lessons from Chile
Lisa Hilbink

Paths to International Justice: Social and Legal Perspectives
Edited by Marie-Bénédicte Dembour and Tobias Kelly

Law and Society in Vietnam: The Transition from Socialism in Comparative Perspective
Mark Sidel

Constitutionalizing Economic Globalization: Investment Rules and Democracy's Promise
David Schneiderman

The New World Trade Organization KnowledgeAgreements: 2nd Edition
Christopher Arup

Justice and Reconciliation in Post-Apartheid South Africa
Edited by François du Bois and Antje du Bois-Pedain

Militarization and Violence against Women in Conflict Zones in the Middle East: A Palestinian Case-Study
Nadera Shalhoub-Kevorkian

Child Pornography and Sexual Grooming: Legal and Societal Responses
Suzanne Ost

Darfur and the Crime of Genocide
John Hagan and Wenona Rymond-Richmond

Fictions of Justice: The International Criminal Court and the Challenge of Legal Pluralism in Sub-Saharan Africa
Kamari Maxine Clarke

Conducting Law and Society Research: Reflections on Methods and Practices
Simon Halliday and Patrick Schmidt

Planted Flags: Trees, Land, and Law in Israel/Palestine
Irus Braverman

Culture under Cross-Examination: International Justice and the Special Court for Sierra Leone
Tim Kelsall

Cultures of Legality: Judicialization and Political Activism in Latin America
Javier Couso, Alexandra Huneeus, Rachel Sieder

Courting Democracy in Bosnia and Herzegovina: The Hague Tribunal's Impact in a Postwar State
Lara J. Nettelfield

The Gacaca Courts and Post-Genocide Justice and Reconciliation in Rwanda:Justice without Lawyers
Phil Clark

Law, Society, and History: Themes in the Legal Sociology and Legal History of Lawrence M. Friedman
Robert W. Gordon and Morton J. Horwitz

After Abu Ghraib: Exploring Human Rights in America and the Middle East
Shadi Mokhtari

Adjudication in Religious Family Laws: Cultural Accommodation: Legal Pluralism, and Gender Equality in India
Gopika Solanki

Water On Tap: Rights and Regulation in the Transnational Governance of Urban Water Services
Bronwen Morgan

Elements of Moral Cognition: Rawls' Linguistic Analogy and the Cognitive Science of Moral and Legal Judgment
John Mikhail

A Sociology of Transnational Constitutions: Social Foundations of the Post-National Legal Structure
Chris Thornhill

Mitigation and Aggravation at Sentencing
Edited by Julian Roberts

Institutional Inequality and the Mobilization of the Family and Medical Leave Act: Rights on Leave
Catherine R. Albiston

Authoritarian Rule of Law: Legislation, Discourse and Legitimacy in Singapore
Jothie Rajah

Law and Development and the Global Discourses of Legal Transfers
Edited by John Gillespie and Pip Nicholson

Law against the State: Ethnographic Forays into Law's Transformations
Edited by Julia Eckert, Brian Donahoe, Christian Strümpell and Zerrin Özlem Biner

Transnational Legal Process and State Change
Edited by Gregory C. Shaffer

Legal Mobilization under Authoritarianism: The Case of Post-Colonial Hong Kong
Edited by Waikeung Tam

Complementarity in the Line of Fire: The Catalysing Effect of the International Criminal Court in Uganda and Sudan
Sarah M. H. Nouwen

Political and Legal Transformations of an Indonesian Polity: The Nagari from Colonisation to Decentralisation
Franz von Benda-Beckmann and Keebet von Benda-Beckmann

Pakistan's Experience with Formal Law: An Alien Justice
Osama Siddique

Human Rights under State-Enforced Religious Family Laws in Israel, Egypt, and India
Yüksel Sezgin

Why Prison?
Edited by David Scott

Law's Fragile State: Colonial, Authoritarian, and Humanitarian Legacies in Sudan
Mark Fathi Massoud

Rights for Others: The Slow Home-Coming of Human Rights in the Netherlands
Barbara Oomen

European States and their Muslim Citizens: The Impact of Institutions on Perceptions and Boundaries
Edited by John R. Bowen, Christophe Bertossi, Jan Willem Duyvendak and Mona Lena Krook

Environmental Litigation in China
Rachel E. Stern

Indigeneity and Legal Pluralism in India: Claims, Histories, Meanings
Pooja Parmar

Paper Tiger: Law, Bureaucracy and the Developmental State in Himalayan India
Nayanika Mathur

Religion, Law and Society
Russell Sandberg

The Experiences of Face Veil Wearers in Europe and the Law
Edited by Eva Brems

The Contentious History of the International Bill of Human Rights
Christopher N. J. Roberts

Transnational Legal Orders
Edited by Terence C. Halliday and Gregory Shaffer

Lost in China?, Law, Culture and Society in Post-1997 Hong Kong
Carol A. G. Jones

Security Theology, Surveillance and the Politics of Fear
Nadera Shalhoub-Kevorkian

Opposing the Rule of Law: How Myanmar's Courts Make Law and Order
Nick Cheesman

The Ironies of Colonial Governance: Law, Custom and Justice in Colonial India
James Jaffe

The Clinic and the Court: Law, Medicine and Anthropology
Edited by Tobias Kelly, Ian Harper and Akshay Khanna

A World of Indicators: The Making of Government Knowledge Through Quantification
Edited by Richard Rottenburg, Sally E. Merry, Sung-Joon Park and Johanna Mugler

Contesting Immigration Policy in Court: Legal Activism and its Radiating Effects in the United States and France
Leila Kawar

The Quiet Power of Indicators: Measuring Governance, Corruption, and Rule of Law
Edited by Sally Engle Merry, Kevin Davis, and Benedict Kingsbury

Investing in Authoritarian Rule: Punishment and Patronage in Rwanda's Gacaca Courts for Genocide Crimes
Anuradha Chakravarty

Contractual Knowledge: One Hundred Years of Legal Experimentation in Global Markets
Edited by Grégoire Mallard and Jérôme Sgard

Iraq and the Crimes of Aggressive War: The Legal Cynicism of Criminal Militarism
John Hagan, Joshua Kaiser, and Anna Hanson

Culture in the Domains of Law
Edited by René Provost

China and Islam: The Prophet, the Party, and Law
Matthew S. Erie

Diversity in Practice: Race, Gender, and Class in Legal and Professional Careers
Edited by Spencer Headworth and Robert Nelson

A Sociology of Transnational Constitutions: Social Foundations of the Post-National Legal Structure
Chris Thornhill

Shifting Legal Visions: Judicial Change and Human Rights Trials in Latin America
Ezequiel A. González Ocantos

The Demographic Transformations of Citizenship
Heli Askola

Criminal Defense in China: The Politics of Lawyers at Work
Sida Liu and Terence C. Halliday

Contesting Economic and Social Rights in Ireland: Constitution, State and Society, 1848–2016
Thomas Murray

Buried in the Heart: Women, Complex Victimhood and the War in Northern Uganda
Erin Baines

Palaces of Hope: The Anthropology of Global Organizations
Edited by Ronald Niezen and Maria Sapignoli

The Politics of Bureaucratic Corruption in Post-Transitional Eastern Europe
Marina Zaloznaya

Revisiting the Law and Governance of Trafficking, Forced Labor and Modern Slavery
Prabha Kotiswaran

Incitement on Trial: Prosecuting International Speech Crimes
Richard Ashby Wilson

Criminalizing Children: A History of Welfare and the State in Australia
David McCallum

Global Legislators: How International Organizations Make Trade Law for the World
Susan Block-Lieb and Terence C. Halliday

Duties to Care: Dementia, Relationality and Law
Rosie Harding

Insiders, Outsiders, Injuries, and Law: Revisiting "The Oven Bird's Song"
Mary Nell Trautner

Hunting Justice: Development, Law, and Activism in the Kalahari
Maria Sapignoli

Injury and Injustice: The Cultural Politics of Harm and Redress
Edited by Anne Bloom, David M. Engel and Michael McCann

Ruling Before the Law: The Politics of Legal Regimes in China and Indonesia
William Hurst